Glenda Bendure
& Ned Friary

Snorkel - Nanili Ba...
Ho...
Kap...
Dive - Lan... Divers.

MAUI

INCLUDES MOLOKA'I AND LANA'I

CONTENTS

Our authors are independent,
dedicated travelers. They don't
research using just the internet
or phone, and they don't take
freebies, so you can rely on their
advice being well researched and
impartial. They travel widely,
visiting thousands of places, and
take great pride in getting all the
details right and telling it like it is.

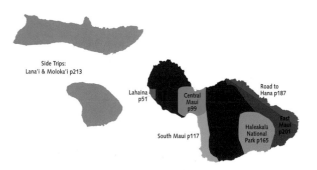

Side Trips:
Lana'i & Moloka'i p213

Lahaina
p51

Central
Maui
p99

Road to
Hana p187

East
Maui
p201

South Maui p117

Haleakalā
National
Park p165

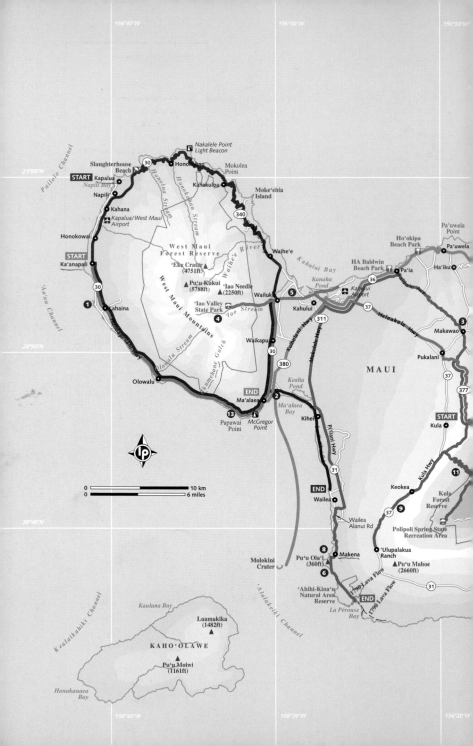

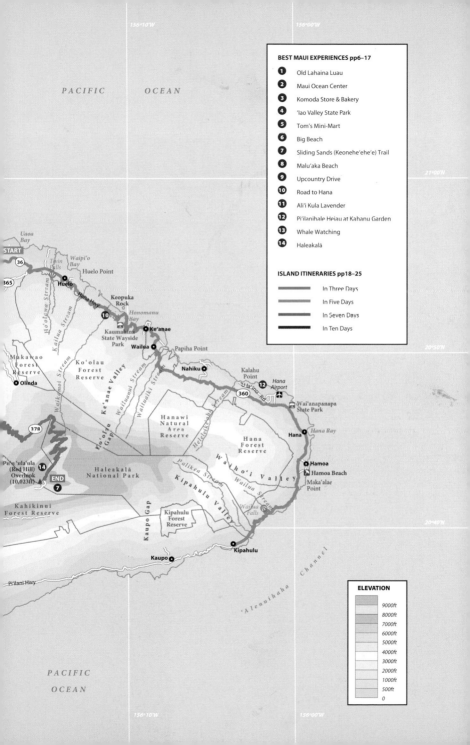

BEST MAUI EXPERIENCES pp6–17

1. Old Lahaina Luau
2. Maui Ocean Center
3. Komoda Store & Bakery
4. 'Iao Valley State Park
5. Tom's Mini-Mart
6. Big Beach
7. Sliding Sands (Keonehe'ehe'e) Trail
8. Malu'aka Beach
9. Upcountry Drive
10. Road to Hana
11. Ali'i Kula Lavender
12. Pi'ilanihale Heiau at Kahanu Garden
13. Whale Watching
14. Haleakalā

ISLAND ITINERARIES pp18–25

In Three Days
In Five Days
In Seven Days
In Ten Days

PACIFIC OCEAN

156°10'W
156°00'W
21°00'N
20°50'N
20°40'N

Uaoa Bay

START

36
365

Twin Falls
Waipi'o Bay
Huelo Point

Huelo

Hana Hwy

Keopuka Rock

10

Honomanu Bay

Kaumahina State Wayside Park

Ke'anae

Wailua

Papiha Point

Makawao Forest Reserve

Olinda

Ko'olau Forest Reserve

Ke'anae Valley

Nahiku

Kalahu Point

Hana Airport

12

360
'Ula'ino Rd

Wai'anapanapa State Park

Hana

Hana Bay

378

Hanawi Natural Area Reserve

Pi'iholo Gap

Wailuaiki Stream
Waikamoi Stream
Waikani Stream

Heleleikeaha Stream

Hana Forest Reserve

Pu'u 'ula'ula (Red Hill) Overlook (10,023ft)

14
END
7

Haleakalā National Park

Palikea Stream

Wailua Stream

Wai'ho'i Valley

Hamoa
Hamoa Beach
Maka'alae Point

Kipahulu Valley

Waimoku Falls

Kahikinui Forest Reserve

Kaupo Gap

Kipahulu Forest Reserve

Kaupo

Kipahulu

Pi'ilani Hwy

'Alenuihaha Channel

PACIFIC OCEAN

156°10'W
156°00'W

ELEVATION

9000ft
8000ft
7000ft
6000ft
5000ft
4000ft
3000ft
2000ft
1000ft
500ft
0

BEST MAUI EXPERIENCES

You can't stop grinning, can you?

Admit it – you're smiling now, even before you step on the plane. It starts with the *idea* of Maui…the anticipation. Maybe you can already hear the twang of a steel guitar, feel balmy breezes. Once you arrive, the real thrill begins. Maui's amazing landscapes and adventures tumble one after another: drop-dead-gorgeous beaches, breathtaking hikes, spectacular road trips. 'Maui *no ka 'oi*' (Maui is the best) is an apt mantra heard around the island. Honeymoon-ers favor Maui. So do surfers, snorkelers and spiritual seekers, to name just a few. Even humpback whales make a beeline for Maui each winter. There's splendor everywhere, from soulful sunrises to sunset swims. The following pages contain our recommendations for an unforgettable Maui experience.

❶ BEST PLACE TO LUAU:
Old Lahaina Luau (p68)

Maybe you've always dreamed of going to a luau. Or maybe you're a skeptic, wary of ending up at a cheesy tourist cliché. Well, no worries, this one's the real deal – the most authentic luau on Maui, if not in all Hawaii. The minute you walk in you're greeted with a cool mai tai and a sweet-smelling lei, setting the tone right. Get there early, before the seating takes place, to stroll the grounds and get a lesson in traditional poi pounding and hula dancing. Then, as the sun lowers on the horizon, watch as an entire pig is ceremoniously lifted from the *imu,* the traditional earthen oven where it's been slow roasting all day. The sound of the surf lapping in the background and the seaside setting add a romantic touch. When you get up to the buffet table it's a cornucopia of island fruits, fish and scrumptious Hawaiian dishes. Nothing is watered down, including the mai tais they keep bringing round. The hula troupe and the musicians are terrific, and the addition of Hawaiian chants and storytelling adds another layer of authenticity.

OLD LAHAINA LUAU

1

MAUI OCEAN CENTER

❷ BEST RAINY-DAY RETREAT: Maui Ocean Center (p115)

Stormy weather might spoil a day at the beach but it's a perfect time for getting up close and personal with Hawaii's wild ocean dwellers. Actually, this tropical aquarium is so awesome that even if the sun breaks through you won't be able to tear yourself away. Pulsating jellyfish, curious sea turtles and tank after tank of all the dazzling creatures you've seen while snorkeling (though these fish come with labels, so you can finally identify them, thank you very much). But that's just the primer: wait till you reach the deep-water tank. And we're talking deep – you actually walk through the center of this baby inside a glass tunnel as sharks, eagle rays and Portuguese man-o-war circle around you. Admit it, you've always wanted to come eye to eye (or is it tooth to tooth?) with some of the biggest, baddest beasts of the sea. If it's got you revved up, take the next step: three days a week, four daring people get to dive into this shark-filled tank to swim with the fishes.

ERIC LIN

❸ BEST SWEET SHOP:
Komoda Store & Bakery (p153)

This landmark bakery was started by a Japanese plantation worker, Takezo Komoda, in 1916 and is still a family-run operation. The aging store hails back to those early days, as do the recipes that have made this unassuming place the most famous bakery on Maui. Get in line – and there will be a line – in front of the old glass counter. Eye the coconut turnovers and the guava-filled *malasadas,* but when it's your turn, tell Mrs Komoda you'll start with the cream puffs. Then wander over to the side of the store, where there's a couple of small tables, a pot of hot coffee and a scene that has barely changed one delicious wink in generations.

❹ BEST GREEN SPOT: 'Iao Valley State Park (p113)

Nowhere is Maui's verdant, moody beauty better captured than at 'Iao Valley, where a phallic-shaped, emerald-green pinnacle shoots straight up from the valley floor. 'Iao Needle, as the pinnacle is called, is the centerpiece of this mystical state park. Snuggled sensuously into deep folds of lush rainforested mountains, 'Iao is such a sumptuous sight it's easy to understand why Hawaiian kings placed a *kapu* (taboo) on the valley, forbidding commoners from laying eyes on it. Lucky you, the *kapu* has been lifted. You brought your camera, right? You'll find lots of scenic angles. Start by walking across the bouncy footbridge, where local kids take turns jumping into the stream below. Then meander past fragrant ginger and over to the taro patches. Stop here for a photo that takes in the footbridge with cloud-shrouded 'Iao Needle in the background. Perfect. 'Iao, by the way, means 'cloud supreme' – three guesses why. Then walk along the stream till you find the ideal swimming hole. Try not to shiver as you dip into brisk mountain-fed water in this historic place where battles were fought, chiefs were buried and serenity now reigns.

KARL LEHMANN

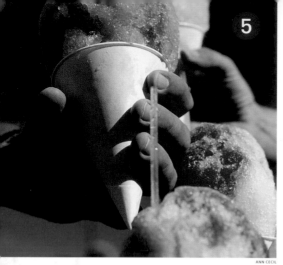

ANN CECIL

❺ BEST SHAVE ICE:
Tom's Mini-Mart (p110)

You'll reach this little neighborhood shop and think: this can't be the place. But then the woman behind the counter starts up the old-fashioned ice shaving machine and you notice it's taking a bit longer than usual, coming out a bit slower. And that's the secret. This is Maui's finest shave ice, soft and fluffy. The syrups are no slackers either. Mango not only looks the right color, but it bursts with such flavor you can almost feel fresh mango juice dripping down your chin. It's definitely worth the detour – we can't leave all the best secrets to the locals, can we?

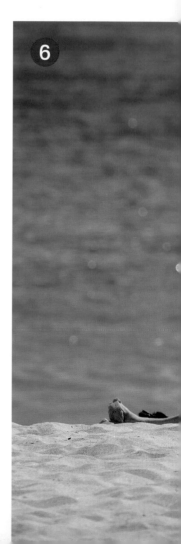

This is where Mauians come to celebrate Maui the way it used to be.

❻ BEST BEACH: Big Beach (p138)

Close your eyes and conjure up the idyllic Hawaiian beach. An endless expanse of gleaming sands, no development in sight, unbelievably blue water, a surfer waiting with a board as a wave crashes at his feet. Open your eyes – you're at Big Beach, the heart of Makena State Park. If one beach captures the spirit of Maui, this is it: wild, vast and in a completely natural state. But unvisited, no. This is where Mauians come to celebrate Maui the way it used to be. Go join them. Worship the waves. Applaud the sunsets. Big Beach is big enough for everyone.

GREG ELMS

NED FRIARY

❼ BEST HIKE: Sliding Sands (Keonehe'ehe'e) Trail (p177)

Winding down this trail from the crater lookout, the first thing you notice is how eerily quiet everything is. The only sound is the crunching of loose volcanic cinders beneath your hiking boots. The path descends gently into an unearthly world, a lunar landscape of stark lava sights and ever-changing clouds. Fellow hikers look like thinly spaced pairs of ants as they move in the distance along the lightly defined trail. You proceed deep into the belly of the world's largest dormant volcano: the floor of this vast place is immense enough to swallow a city. A string of russet and gray cinder cones rises from the crater floor. Looking back toward the summit, eyes focused on the steep crater walls, it's impossible not to be awed by the raw beauty. Just when you think everything is barren, into view comes the Ka Lu'u o ka O'o cinder cone, where native plants have taken root. These are tough little fellows with thick-skinned leaves, including the exquisite silversword that grows solely in volcanic cinders and takes 50 years just to bloom. It's a timeless place.

SIMON FOALE

❽ BEST SNORKELING:
Malu'aka Beach (p138)

As you step onto this beach it's easy to see where the action's centered. And it's definitely not on the sand. The catamarans anchored offshore reveal that this is the whispered 'secret Turtle Town' the tour boats promise to snorkelers. Boat, schmoat, why not just float? Don your mask and snorkel right here on the shore, and start swimming in the direction of the tour boats. Before you get halfway out you'll likely spot a magnificent green sea turtle feeding on the ocean floor. Gazing down on one of these 200lb creatures swimming beneath you is nothing short of mesmerizing.

❾ BEST DRIVE THAT ENDS AT A WINERY: Upcountry (p158)

You know those time-lapse nature documentaries that show plants shooting straight up out of the ground, unfolding their leaves and bursting into full flower in a matter of seconds? Perhaps with the *Hallelujah* chorus in the background? That's how it feels driving through the Upcountry. It bursts to the brim with lush green pastures, brilliant gardens and fruiting trees. Depending on the season, purple blossoms drop from jacaranda trees lining the roadside, or showy golden oaks flutter bright yellow buds. The places to pause are pastoral: a cup of Maui grown coffee at Grandma's, or a hillside picnic with spectacular ocean views. Ramble the roads as they catch your fancy, but get to Tedeschi Vineyards in time for a winery tour. Then step up to the bar to sample island-grown grape and pineapple wines. You're hardly the first to make a toast here. The old stone cottage that serves as the tasting room was originally built as a guest cottage for King Kalakaua, Hawaii's 'Merrie Monarch,' who enjoyed coming to the Upcountry for a little R&R. Maybe it was all those bucolic vistas that made him so merry.

MITCHELL SILVER

❿ BEST ROAD TRIP: Road to Hana (p187)

Slip on a bathing suit and grab your hiking boots on your way out the door. Then get ready for an adventure. Of all the heart-stoppingly dramatic drives in Hawaii, this is the Big Kahuna. A roller-coaster of a ride, the Hana Hwy winds down into jungly valleys and back up towering razor-edge cliffs, curling around some 600 twists and turns along the way. Oh, and don't be fooled by the term 'highway' – in places the road gets so narrow you'll be pulling over just to let oncoming traffic pass. Some 54 one-lane bridges cross nearly as many waterfalls, some eye-popping torrents and others so gentle they beg a dip. The scent of wild ginger sweetens the air, and even the trees burst into flower, adding splashes of orange to the green scene. But the thrill ride's only half the fun. Get your sweaty palms off the wheel and take a swim beneath a waterfall, stroll into the forest and explore the historic wonders along the way. Get on the road early and you'll have plenty of time to make your own adventure.

KARL LEHMANN

10

⓫ BEST PLACE TO INHALE:
Ali'i Kula Lavender (p159)

Up for a little aromatherapy? Start by strolling the fragrant gardens at this hillside lavender farm perched on the edge of a cloud forest. Take your time, breathe deeply and let the rejuvenating perfume soothe your soul. Maybe you'll catch one of those radiant rainbows as the mist wafts through and a heavenly ocean view when it drifts back out – a scene that plays back and forth throughout the day. Feeling relaxed? Good. Now meander over to the little shop, order a cup of lavender herb tea, sit on the deck with its sweeping views and relish the moment.

ABBOT LOW MOFFAT III

11

GREG ELMS

⑫ BEST ANCIENT HAWAIIAN SITE:
Pi'ilanihale Heiau at Kahanu Garden (p198)

If Polynesia had its own seven wonders of the world, this ancient stone temple would be Maui's entry. Standing in front of Hawaii's largest heiau – five stories high, big enough to hold nearly 10 football fields – it's impossible not to feel dwarfed by the scale of it all. The remote setting on a windswept coast adds to the sense of being in a sacred place. It's a step back in time without any glimpse of the modern to blemish the scene. Be still and you can almost hear the footsteps of the ancients, and summon up images of a high priest walking up the terraced stone steps to offer sacrifices to the gods. The bountiful Polynesian gardens surrounding the temple – swaying coconut palms and sturdy breadfruit trees – add even more depth to the vision of how it must have looked hundreds of years ago when this was a thriving village and home to Pi'ilani, the 16th-century chief who ruled Maui. Gazing upon this engineering wonder, it's easy to understand why so many of Maui's roads bear Pi'ilani's name today.

KARL LEHMANN

⓭ BEST WILDLIFE VIEWING: Whale Watching (p32)

Seems humpback whales find Maui romantic, too. Every winter, thousands of them frolic off Maui's western coast, courting, mating, calving and breaching in what can be seen only as pure joy. If you're in Maui at the same time as the whales, treat yourself to a whale-watching cruise. But whales are also readily spotted from cliffside lookouts, west-facing beaches, the lanai of your oceanfront condo – just about any place will do. Lucky snorkelers and divers who stick their heads in the water at the right time can even hear them singing – love songs, we imagine!

⓮ BEST SUNRISE SPOT: Haleakalā (p166)

Huddled at predawn, blanket wrapped around you, shivering in the frozen air beside a hundred other people buzzing like bees trying to keep warm. The frozen cinder earth beneath your feet crunches as you walk on it. Everything seems surreal and there's a sense that something unworldly is about to unfold. Then the darkness begins to lift. A soft orange glow appears on the summit first. Everyone lets out a gasp – followed by cheers. The rich tones of amber and ocher light up on the crater floor below. The sunrise warms more than the crater walls. As it has for hundreds of years, the mana of the ancients, some primordial spirit, warms the very soul. Little wonder that the intrepid traveler Mark Twain, who in 1866 spent two days trekking up the mountain just to watch the day's awakening, described the event as 'the sublimest spectacle I ever witnessed.' And all you have to do is roll out of bed in the middle of the night, drive 10,000ft up a switchback mountain in the pitch dark and huddle with the fortunate ones awaiting their turn.

KARL LEHMANN

ISLAND
ITINERARIES

See the itineraries at the beginning of each regional chapter for more detailed routes.

IN THREE DAYS *This leg: 70 miles*

❶ KA'ANAPALI (p80) Plunge into Maui with a plunge into the sea. Head straight to **Kahekili Beach Park (p81)** if you're seeking peace and quiet, or to **'Dig-Me Beach' (p80)** if a buzz of resort action fits the bill. Snorkel out to the tip of **Pu'u Keka'a (Black Rock; p80)** for an eye-popping underwater scene.

❷ LAHAINA (p51) Harbor and island views go down smoothly with a seafood lunch at one of Lahaina's fine waterfront restaurants. Walk it off with a stroll around this captivating old whaling town. Later, loll under the USA's largest banyan tree in **Banyan Tree Square (p56)**, pop into some shops and then feast your stomach and your eyes on the **Old Lahaina Luau (p68)**.

❸ 'IAO VALLEY STATE PARK (p113) A blast of green starts day two at this oh-so-pretty park with cool streams, misty mountains

and Maui's emerald jewel, the 'Iao Needle. Follow those tasty views with a tasty lunch in time-honored **Wailuku (p109)**.

❹ KANAHA BEACH PARK (p103) When the wind picks up in the afternoon, it's show time! A circus parade of rainbow sails whips back and forth across the bay as windsurfers and kitesurfers strut their stuff. It's mind-blowing to watch, and there are instructors waiting right on the beach if *you're* ready to fly.

❺ HALEAKALĀ NATIONAL PARK (p165) Grab a parka and picnic lunch, and head out early (3am!) to catch the breathtaking sunrise atop this magnificent volcano. Spend the rest of day three hiking into the belly of the beast and climbing around the cool cinder cones.

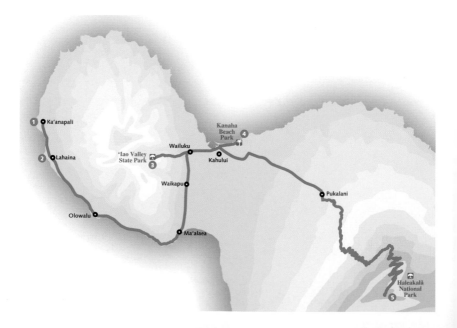

IN FIVE DAYS *This leg: 90 miles*

⑥ ROAD TO HANA (p187) If you have five days, plan your first three as above. Day four is another early one, but sooo worth it. Grab a cup of jolting java at **Anthony's (p148)** in Pa'ia while they pack your picnic lunch. Now you're ready for the most magical drive in all Hawaii: waterfalls, hiking trails and lush scenery galore. Snack on delish banana bread at **Ke'anae Peninsula (p194)**and be humbled by Hawaii's largest temple at **Kahanu Garden (p198)**. At **Wai'anapanapa State Park (p198)**, break out that picnic on the prettiest black-sand beach you've ever seen.

⑦ HANA (p206) This wide spot in the road is well worth a poke around. Enjoy some local flavor with shave ice at the beach park and a visit to Hana's homegrown museum. Then keep moving – there's still lots to see!

⑧ WAILUA FALLS (p211) Think that stunning road to Hana packed all the gushing thrills? Just wait till you reach these roadside falls, a top contender for Maui's most gorgeous waterfall. Better bring extra camera batteries!

⑨ HALEAKALĀ NATIONAL PARK (KIPA-HULU AREA) (p184) The road continues to 'Ohe'o Gulch (p184) with its 24 – count 'em – irresistible pools to choose from, each backed by its own little waterfall. Speaking of waterfalls, you may have just enough time to hike to the 200ft bridal-veil cascade of **Makahiku Falls (p186)**.

⑩ KIPAHULU (p211) Got a little explorer left in you? Seek out the grave of aviator Charles Lindbergh before heading back up the Hana Hwy. If you prefer to take it a bit slower, stop and spend the night in Hana (p206).

⑪ MOLOKINI CRATER (p29) You've seen the best of Maui from land – on day five, see it from the sea. Clear waters and gazillions of fish make this submerged volcanic crater a guaranteed thrill, whether you're a veteran diver or newbie snorkeler.

⑫ MAUI OCEAN CENTER (p115) How convenient. Right where the Molokini boat docks sits one of the finest tropical aquariums on the planet. Now go identify all those brilliant fish you've just seen.

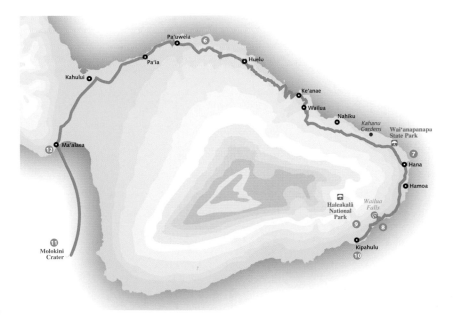

IN SEVEN DAYS *This leg: 80 miles*

⓭ KULA (p158) If you have a full week on Maui, plan your first five days as above. Start day six off right with a leisurely drive through pastoral Upcountry. See how many varieties of riotous protea flowers you can count at **Sunrise Market & Protea Farm (p161)**. Then wind over to **Ali'i Kula Lavender (p159)** and immerse yourself in a sea of heaven-scented purple. Oh, if only *all* gardens could smell this good.

⓮ POLIPOLI SPRING STATE RECREATION AREA (p162) Feel the refreshing mist on a trek among tall redwoods in this fairy-tale-like cloud forest that climbs the slopes of Haleakalā.

⓯ TEDESCHI VINEYARDS (p164) Let the heady scent of fermenting grapes fill your head on a winery tour at 'Ulupalakua Ranch. Then swagger over to the tasting room to swig the final products.

⓰ MAKAWAO (p152) On the way back, swing east and browse the *paniolo*-meets-Picasso shops in this artsy ranch town.

⓱ PA'IA (p145) There's still time to jet over to **Ho'okipa Beach Park (p145)** to watch windsurfers rip on wicked waves. Then it's back to Baldwin Ave to cruise Pa'ia's eclectic cafés and funky shops. Revel in that once-in-a-lifetime meal at **Mama's Fish House (p149)**, but be sure to get seated before sunset.

⓲ MALU'AKA BEACH (p138) On day seven, slip on a snorkel and swim the coral gardens to discover why this one's dubbed Turtle Beach. Honkin' big green sea turtles munch away on the bottom as you swim past – wow!

⓳ BIG BEACH (p138) Pack a picnic – once you get here you won't want to leave. Ever. But it's OK: you can swing back by to catch one of the best sunsets Maui has to offer after you finish driving south.

⓴ LA PÉROUSE BAY (p140) The day's sightseeing ends here at the road's end. Breathe in the wild windswept scenery. Clamber over twisted lava flows, reminders of how Maui began. Cool. Now go back for that glorious Big Beach sunset.

IN TEN DAYS *This leg: 50 miles*

㉑ KAPALUA (p92) If you've got 10 wondrous days in Maui (lucky you!), plan your first seven as above. On the morning of day eight, golfers get to chase that little white ball around Maui's greenest **greens (p94)**, while thrill seekers wing it on the island's longest **zipline (p94)**. In the afternoon, snorkel with dolphins at **Slaughterhouse Beach (p93)**. Then walk out to the aptly named **Dragon's Teeth (p92)** and roar at the sea. Top the day off with a sizzling sunset dinner at the **Pineapple Grill (p94)**.

㉒ KAHEKILI HIGHWAY (p95) It's time to hit the road again for day nine. The adventure that awaits around the raw northern tip of Maui is like no other. If you thought the Hana Hwy was narrow, just wait till you see this one! Seek out **Nakalele Blowhole (p97)**, ooh and aah at the scenery, and don't miss **Ohai Viewpoint (p97)**.

㉓ WAIHE'E RIDGE TRAIL (p98) In the afternoon get out of the car and lace up your hiking boots. Misty mountain views and jungly waterfalls are just starters on this soulful ridge trail that goes deep into the luxuriant West Maui Mountains.

㉔ HALEKI'I-PIHANA HEIAU (p109) Celebrate the end of your day by gazing upon Central Maui from the ancient hilltop temple where Maui's last king reigned.

㉕ WHALE-WATCHING CRUISE (p32) On day 10, it's back to the water. If it's winter you can't leave Maui without hopping aboard a whale-watching boat. No excuses. If it's not humpback season, give **Trilogy Excursions (p63)** a call and sign up for their wet and wild sail to Lana'i instead.

㉖ KEALIA POND NATIONAL WILDLIFE REFUGE (p115) Take a walk on the wild side, getting up close and intimate with rare waterbirds along a new boardwalk that leads nearly a half-mile across marsh and dunes.

㉗ KEAWAKAPU BEACH (p120) Tired of that sunset yet? Naaah, we didn't think so. End your trip with a sunset swim at Kihei's finest.

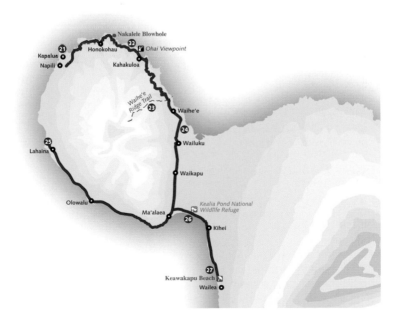

KEIKI EXPRESS

❶ KA'ANAPALI (p80) *Keiki* (children) love a day at the beach, and Ka'anapali's generous sands invite all sorts of splashy fun. Stay at family-friendly **Ka'anapali Beach Hotel (p86)**, where ukulele sing-alongs and hula lessons add Hawaiian flair to the action.

❷ LAHAINA (p51) Head to America's largest **banyan tree (p56)**, whose dangling aerial roots invite at least one Tarzan-style swing. Little tots will want to ride the **Sugar Cane Train (p63)**. The rest of the clan can take the plunge with a **surfing lesson (p61)** on Lahaina's gentle waves.

❸ MAUI OCEAN CENTER (p115) Everyone loves aquariums, and parents have a tough time dragging their kids out of the shark tunnel. Want to really impress them? Let Mom go into the tank and feed the sharks while Dad watches in horror!

❹ MOLOKINI CRUISE (p29) OK, now it's time to turn the ocean into your own aquarium by donning a mask and snorkeling

Maui's top underwater sight. If it's winter, whales are an awesome bonus.

❺ HALEAKALĀ NATIONAL PARK (p165) Hiking isn't for all kiddies – luckily there's **Pony Express (p160)**, where horses do the hiking for you. Moonscape scenery will wow kids of all ages.

SUSTAINABLE MAUI

❶ BIO-BEETLE (p108) Go green by renting an environmentally friendly car for this tour.

❷ SURFING GOAT DAIRY (p158) Check out the inner workings – literally – of this farm that produces all that delicious Maui goat cheese. While you're there, let your kids play with their kids on a farm tour.

❸ O'O FARM (p161) Harvest your own organic lunch. Then watch a top chef whip it together on this delicious Kula farm outing.

❹ ALI'I KULA LAVENDER (p159) Smell the crisp air as you munch on lavender scones.

❺ TEDESCHI VINEYARDS (p164) Tip a glass of Maui's own pineapple wine at this Upcountry vineyard.

❻ ALEXANDER & BALDWIN SUGAR MUSEUM (p114) See how it's done, from green cane stalks to sugar crystals.

❼ MAUIGROWN COFFEE (p69) Sample a cup of Maui Mokka grown on the slopes

above Lahaina. Then check out the fruiting coffee trees out back.

❽ MAUI PINEAPPLE COMPANY (p94) Pick your own Maui Gold – pineapple, that is – on a tour of this working plantation.

❾ KIPAHULU 'OHANA (p186) Soak up traditional culture on a hike to an ancient taro farm led by Native Hawaiian guides.

WATER ADVENTURES

❶ **MOLOKINI CRATER (p29)** Dive into crystal-clear waters teeming with all manner of sea creatures.

❷ **KIHEI WHARF (p124)** Join the welcoming locals in an outrigger canoe paddle along the Kihei coast.

❸ **ULUA BEACH (p133)** Snorkel out to the rocks for an eye-candy mix of brilliant coral and tropical fish – and keep an ear open for the songs of passing whales.

❹ **WAILEA BEACH (p133)** Sail, swim and body board gentle waves at Maui's ultimate resort beach.

❺ **MAKENA LANDING (p137)** Launch a kayak to paddle south through Turtle Town or gear up for a shore dive to explore lava caves with white-tipped reef sharks.

❻ **KANAHA BEACH PARK (p103)** Go fly a kiteboard or try windsurfing – this wind-whipped beach is tops for both.

❼ **HO'OKIPA BEACH PARK (p145)** If you're on the pro windsurfing or surfing circuit,

meet your buddies here. The rest of us can grab a voyeur's seat on the adjacent hillside and watch the death-defying action.

❽ **LAHAINA BREAKWALL (p61)** Grab a surfboard and hone your skills on these gentle waves.

❾ **DT FLEMING BEACH PARK (p92)** Ride the pounding waves for awesome bodysurfing at this ironwood-backed beauty.

OFFSHORE EXPLORATION

❶ **LANA'I CITY (p217)** Book a room at the plantation-era **Hotel Lana'i (p220)**. Wander the mom-and-pop shops, talk story with locals over dinner at **Blue Ginger Café (p219)** and relish the small-town charm.

❷ **HULOPO'E BEACH (p221)** See for yourself why this beach has become so famous that day-trippers from Maui sail all the way over here just to snorkel its pristine waters.

❸ **MUNRO TRAIL (p224)** If you have a third day in Lana'i take to the hills, hiking the island's rugged spine.

❹ **KALAUPAPA (p237)** Trust your life to a mule as you descend 1600 switchbacking feet down a precipitous cliff to America's most unusual national historical park. Prefer to use your own two feet? You can...but hit the trail before the mules do, or you'll be knee-deep in you know what.

❺ **PAPOHAKU BEACH (p240)** Go put a set of footprints on the longest and least-crowded beach in Hawaii.

❻ **EAST MOLOKA'I (p232)** Spend your last day leisurely making your way the 28 scenic miles from **Kaunakakai (p229)** to the spectacular **Halawa Valley (p233)**. Along the way stop to see the Father Damien–built **St Joseph's Church (p232)** and the ancient **'Ualapu'e Fishpond (p232)**.

OUTDOOR ACTIVITIES & ADVENTURES

This is where the real adventure begins! Take to the ocean, and no place else on the planet measures up to Maui. Waveriders, rejoice: Maui has the hottest windsurfing, the highest surfable waves and the most happening kitesurfing scene anywhere. Prefer your thrills beneath the surface? Hawaii's premier snorkel destination – Molokini – awaits just offshore, and myriad snorkel and dive spots are dotted around the island. Best whale watching? No competition. OK, but what about staying dry? Maui hiking is nothing short of extraordinary. Haleakalā National Park boasts crater trails so unearthly that astronauts trained for their moonwalk there. Kapalua's golf course is such a beaut the PGA Tour opens there each January. Airborne? Can do. Ziplines will rip you above the treetops at eagle speed. Now there's a bird's-eye view of paradise you won't soon forget.

Also see individual listings in the destination chapters for more details about activities on Maui.

AT SEA

Ah, the Pacific Ocean. You probably noticed it on your flight over. Here are all the ways you can frolic in Maui's ultimate playground.

BODYSURFING & BOOGIE BOARDING

If you want to take your waves lying down, bodysurfing and boogie boarding are suitable water activities for anybody.

Good beginner to intermediate shorebreaks can be found at the Kama'ole Beach Parks (p121) and Charley Young Beach (p122) in Kihei, and at Ulua Beach (p133) and Wailea Beach (p133) in Wailea. For really hot stuff, experienced bodysurfers head to DT Fleming Beach Park (p92) and Slaughterhouse Beach (p93) in Kapalua; Big Beach (p138) in Makena; and HA Baldwin Beach Park (p147) near Pa'ia.

The sport of surfing
was **born on Hawaii.**

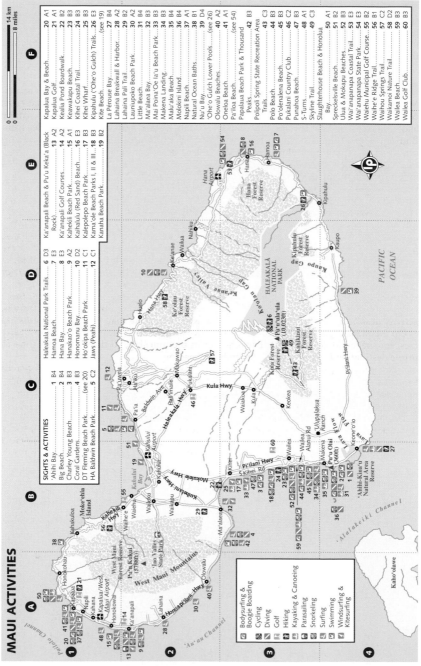

MAUI ACTIVITIES

SIGHTS & ACTIVITIES

Ahihi Bay	1	B4
Big Beach	2	B4
Charley Young Beach	3	B3
Coral Gardens	4	B3
DT Fleming Beach Park	(see 20)	
HA Baldwin Beach Park	5	C2
Haleakala National Park Trails	6	D3
Hamoa Beach	7	E3
Hana Bay	8	E3
Hanakao'o Beach Park	9	A2
Honomanu Bay	10	D2
Ho'okipa Beach Park	11	C1
Jaws (Peahi)	12	C1
Ka'anapali Beach & Pu'u Keka'a (Black Rock)	13	A2
Ka'anapali Golf Courses	14	A2
Kahekili Beach Park	15	A1
Kaihalulu (Red Sand) Beach	16	E3
Kalepolepo Beach Park	17	B3
Kama'ole Beach Parks I, II & III	18	B3
Kanaha Beach Park	19	B2
Kapalua Bay & Beach	20	A1
Kapalua Golf	21	A1
Kealia Pond Boardwalk	22	B3
Keawakapu Beach	23	B3
Kihei Coastal Trail	24	B3
Kihei Wharf	25	B3
Kipahulu ('Ohe'o Gulch) Trails	26	E3
Kite Beach	(see 19)	
La Perouse Bay	27	B4
Lahaina Breakwall & Harbor	28	A2
Lahaina Pali Trail	29	B2
Launiupoko Beach Park	30	A2
Little Beach	31	B4
Ma'alaea Bay	32	B3
Mai Poina'Oe Ia'u Beach Park	33	B3
Makena Landing	34	B4
Malu'aka Beach	35	B4
Molokini Island	36	B4
Napili Beach	37	A1
Natural Ocean Baths	38	B1
Nu'u Bay	39	D4
'Ohe'o Gulch Lower Pools	(see 26)	
Olowalu Beaches	40	A2
Oneloa Beach	41	A1
Pa'iloa Beach	(see 54)	
Papalaua Beach Park & Thousand Peaks	42	B3
Polipoli Spring State Recreation Area Trails	43	C3
Polo Beach	44	B3
Po'olenalena Beach	45	B3
Pukalani Country Club	46	C2
Punahoa Beach	47	B3
S-Turns	48	A1
Skyline Trail	49	C3
Slaughterhouse Beach & Honolua Bay	50	A1
Spreckelsville Beach	51	B2
Ulua & Mokapu Beaches	52	B3
Wai'anapanapa Coastal Trail	53	E3
Wai'anapanapa State Park	54	E3
Waiehu Municipal Golf Course	55	B2
Waihe'e Ridge Trail	56	B1
Wahou Springs Trail	57	C2
Wakamoi Nature Trail	58	D2
Wailea Beach	59	B3
Wailea Golf Club	60	B3

Bodysurfing & Boogie Boarding
Cycling
Diving
Golf
Hiking
Kayaking & Canoeing
Parasailing
Snorkeling
Surfing
Swimming
Windsurfing & Kitesurfing

Special bodysurfing flippers, which are smaller than snorkel fins, will help you paddle out. Boogie boards can be rented for around $10 per day at locations around the island.

DIVING

Maui is a mecca for divers thanks to its excellent visibility, warm water temperatures and hundreds of fish species that you'll find nowhere else in the world. Here you can often see spinner dolphins, green sea turtles, manta rays and moray eels. With a little luck you might even hear humpback whales singing underwater – you'll never forget it.

Most dive operations on Maui offer a full range of dives as well as refresher and advanced certification courses. If you've never tried it before, introductory dives for beginners get you beneath the surface in just a couple of hours. Experienced divers needn't bring anything other than a swimsuit and certification card. Book directly, and don't monkey around with the activity desks.

On Maui, the granddaddy of dives is crescent-shaped Molokini (p29). The other prime destination is untouched Cathedrals on the south side of Lana'i, which takes its name from the array of amazing underwater caverns, arches and connecting passageways.

For more information on dive spots, pick up Lonely Planet's *Diving & Snorkeling Hawaii*, which includes color photos illustrating sites and fish.

FISHING

Deep-sea sportfishing charters set out from Maui for such legendary game as 'ahi (yellowfin tuna) and, most famous of all, Pacific blue marlin, which can reach 1000lb. Licenses aren't required, and charter boats are available right on the pier in Lahaina Harbor and Ma'alaea. Sharing a boat costs around $135 to $200 per person. Many boats let you keep only a small fillet from your catch; see **Maui Fishing** (www.mauifishing.com) for reasons why…and more.

KAYAKING

On Maui, kayakers really get an adventure. The top spot is Makena (p137), an area rich with marine life, including sea turtles, dolphins and wintering humpback whales. In the calmer summer months, another excellent destination is Honolua–Mokule'ia Bay Marine Life Conservation District (p93), at Slaughterhouse Beach and Honolua Bay north of Kapalua, where there are turtles aplenty and dolphin sightings. Keep in mind that water conditions on Maui are usually clearest and calmest early in the morning, so that's an ideal time to head out.

The top island outfitter for kayak rentals and tours is South Pacific Kayaks (p124).

KITESURFING

Also called kiteboarding, this latest entry into the pantheon of wave sports is, if you'll pardon the expression, really taking off.

DIVING & SNORKELING OUTFITTERS

Company	Page	Tours	Price	Departs	Dive/snorkel spots
Lahaina Divers (☎ 667-7496)	p61	Boat dives, snorkel tours	$120-140 (2 tanks), $70 (snorkel tours)	Lahaina	Molokini, Lana'i
Maui Dive Shop (☎ 879-3388)	p124	Boat dives, snorkel tours	$90 (1 tank), $130-140 (2 tanks), $40-50 (snorkel trips)	Lahaina, Ma'alaea	Molokini, Lana'i
Maui Dreams Dive Company (☎ 874-5332)	p124	Shore dives	$60-90 (1 tank), $90-120 (2 tanks)	Kihei	Wailea, Makena
Pacific Dive (☎ 667-5331)	p61	Boat dives, shore dives	$60 (shore dive), $90 (scooter dive)	Lahaina	West Maui, Molokini
Pacific Whale Foundation (☎ 249-8811)	p116	Snorkel tours	$55	Lahaina, Ma'alaea	Molokini

RESPONSIBLE DIVING

The popularity of diving is placing immense pressure on many sites. Please consider the following tips to help preserve the ecology and beauty of reefs.

- Avoid touching living marine organisms with your body or dragging equipment across the reef. Polyps can be damaged by even the gentlest contact. Never stand on coral. If you must hold on to the reef, touch only exposed rock or dead coral.
- Be conscious of your fins. Even without contact, the surge from heavy fin strokes near the reef can damage delicate organisms. When treading water in shallow reef areas, take care not to kick up clouds of sand. Settling sand can easily smother the delicate organisms of the reef.
- Do not use reef anchors, and take care not to ground boats on coral.
- Minimize your disturbance of marine animals. It is illegal to approach endangered marine species too closely; these include whales, dolphins, sea turtles and the Hawaiian monk seal. In particular, do not ride on the backs of turtles!
- Practice and maintain proper buoyancy control. Major damage can be done by divers descending too fast and colliding with the reef. Make sure you are correctly weighted and that your weight belt is positioned so that you stay horizontal.
- Resist the temptation to feed marine animals. You may disturb their normal eating habits, encourage aggressive behavior or feed them food that is detrimental to their health.
- Spend as little time in underwater caves as possible, as your air bubbles may be caught within the roof and leave previously submerged organisms high and dry.
- Don't leave any rubbish, and remove any litter you find. Plastics in particular are a serious threat to marine life. Turtles can mistake plastic for jellyfish and eat it.
- Don't collect (or buy) coral or shells. Aside from the ecological damage, taking home marine souvenirs depletes the beauty of a site and spoils the enjoyment of others.

Divers Alert Network (DAN; ☎ 919-684-8111, 800-446-2671; www.diversalertnetwork.org) gives advice on diving emergencies, insurance, decompression services, illness and injury.

Kitesurfing is a bit like strapping on a snowboard, grabbing a huge kite and riding with the wind across the water. It looks damn hard and certainly takes stamina, but if you already know how to ride a board, there's a good chance you'll master it quickly. According to surf legend Robby Naish (see the boxed text on p107), who pioneered kitesurfing, it's the most accessible of all extreme sports.

There's no better place to learn than on Maui's Kite Beach (p103), at the western end of Kanaha Beach Park. Visiting kitesurfers need to check with locals to clarify the no-fly zones. You can get the lowdown on everything to do with kitesurfing from the **Maui Kiteboarding Association** (www.mauikiteboardingassociation.com) and **Maui Kitesurfing Community** (www.mauikitesurfing.org).

OUTRIGGER CANOEING

Hawaii was settled by Polynesians who paddled outrigger canoes across 2000 miles of open ocean, so you could say canoeing was Hawaii's earliest sport. The first Europeans to arrive were awestruck at the skill Hawaiians displayed, timing launches and landings perfectly, and paddling among the waves like dolphins.

Today canoe clubs keep the outrigger tradition alive. A few, like the Kihei Canoe Club (p124), invite visitors to dip a paddle with them – a great way to experience the sport if you're going to be on Maui awhile. Another option is to take a guided outrigger canoe ride with Maui Nui O Kama Canoe Club Cultural Tour in Kihei (p124) or Hawaiian Sailing Canoe Adventures in Wailea

Top Picks

BEACHES FOR KEIKI

- **Kalepolepo Beach Park** (p122)
- **Spreckelsville Beach** (p147)
- **Launiupoko Beach Park** (p77)
- **Kapalua Beach** (p92)
- **Wailea Beach** (p133)

MOLOKINI CRATER

No underwater site draws more visitors than Molokini, the fascinating volcanic crater that lies midway between the islands of Maui and Kaho'olawe. Half of the crater rim has eroded away, leaving a crescent-moon shape that rises 160ft above the ocean surface, with a mere 18 acres of rocky land high and dry. But it's what's beneath the surface that draws the crowds. Snorkelers and divers will be thrilled by steep walls, ledges, white-tipped reef sharks, manta rays, turtles and abundant fish.

The legends about Molokini are myriad. One says Molokini was a beautiful woman who was turned to stone by jealous Pele, goddess of fire and volcanoes. Another claims one of Pele's lovers angered her by secretly marrying a *mo'o* (shape-shifting water lizard). Pele chopped the sacred lizard in half, leaving Molokini as its tail and Pu'u 'Olai in Makena as its head. Yet another tale alleges that Molokini, which means 'many ties' in Hawaiian, is the umbilical cord left over from the birth of Kaho'olawe.

The coral reef that extends outward from Molokini is awesome, though it's lost some of its variety over the years. Most of the black coral that was once prolific in Molokini's deeper waters made its way into Lahaina jewelry stores before the island was declared a marine conservation district in 1977. During WWII the US Navy shelled Molokini for target practice, and live bombs are still occasionally spotted on the crater floor.

There are a few things to consider when planning your excursion to Molokini. The water is calmest and clearest in the morning, so don't fall for discounted afternoon tours – go out early for the smoothest sailing and best conditions. For snorkelers, there's simply not much to see when the water's choppy. The main departure points for outings to Molokini are Ma'alaea (p116) and Lahaina (p60) harbors. You'll get out there quicker if you hop a boat from Ma'alaea, which is closer to Molokini. Going from Lahaina adds on more sail time, but if it's winter it'll also increase the possibilities for spotting whales along the way, so it's sometimes worth an extra hour out of your day.

See the table on p27 for recommended diving and snorkeling outfitters.

(p134), both of which offer cultural insights as you paddle along the coast.

PARASAILING

Because parasailing upsets humpback whales, the activity is banned in Maui during the winter season. But from mid-May to mid-December, soaring 200ft above the ocean tethered to a speedboat towline is a quick seven-minute thrill, available from the beach huts at Ka'anapali Beach. Expect to pay around $65 per rush.

SAILING

Breezy Lahaina (p51) is the jump-off point for most sails. If you're in the mood to just unwind, hop on a sunset sail. For an exciting daylong journey consider a sail to Lana'i.

SNORKELING

Some of Maui's most amazing sights lie just beneath the ocean surface. Don a mask and fins and a whole other world opens up. The waters around Maui are a kaleidoscope of colorful fish, coral and honkin' big sea turtles. Best of all you don't need special skills. If you can float, you can snorkel – it's a cinch to learn. If you're

Molokini Crater   CASEY & ASTRID MAHANEY

THE ORIGINAL BOARDRIDERS

The sport of surfing was born on Hawaii. Because ancient Hawaiians had no written language, the exact date of surfing's inception is unknown, but researchers have traced chants mentioning *he'e nalu* (surfing) and petroglyphs depicting surfers back to at least 1500 AD.

One thing that they are sure of is that wave riding was an integral part of the old Hawaiian *kapu* (taboo) system of governing. The *ali'i* (ruling class) were the only ones allowed to ride the prized *olo* (long surfboard), which reached up to 16ft in length. The finest craftsmen scoured the jungles for just the perfect wiliwili tree, the lightweight wood used for these royal surfboards. Commoners made do with 6ft boards made of heavy breadfruit or koa wood.

Religious ceremonies enveloped every aspect of ancient surfing. Before chopping down a tree to make a surfboard, an elaborate prayer ritual took place. After the board was roughly carved with an adze, it was planed with coral, then blackened with *ti* leaf or root and polished with *kukui* (candlenut tree) nut oil. A high priest then blessed the board before it was finally ridden.

When the first missionaries arrived in Hawaii in the 1820s they promptly started stamping out the 'hedonistic' act of surfing and, save a few holdouts, by 1890 surfing was all but extinct.

Then in the early 1900s modern surfing's first icon, Duke Kahanamoku, stepped off the beach and into history. Kahanamoku grew up on the sands of Waikiki, where, with a handful of friends, he rode the reefs on traditional *olo*-style boards. In 1911 Duke and the Waikiki beachboys caught the attention of author Jack London, whose detailed accounts in *Cruise of the Snark* captured the imagination of the Western world. After winning Olympic gold in swimming at Stockholm in 1912, Duke began to spread the gospel of surfing far and wide, traveling the world demonstrating the Hawaiian 'Sport of Kings.'

Duke rode the waves for the rest of his life, and when he died in 1968 thousands of devotees attended the beachboy funeral procession to Waikiki Beach, where his ashes were taken by canoe and cast into the sea. One of his regal surfboards, which weighs a hefty 150lb, still hangs outside the Bailey House Museum (p110) in Wailuku.

a newbie, just fess up at the dive shop or beach hut where you rent your snorkel gear and they'll eagerly show you everything you need to know. And it's cheap: snorkel sets rent for under $10.

From the Shore

For phenomenal snorkeling right from the beach, prime spots are Malu'aka Beach (p138), dubbed 'Turtle Beach,' in Makena; 'Ahihi-Kina'u Natural Area Reserve (p140), south of Makena; Ulua Beach (p133) in Wailea; Pu'u Keka'a (p80), aka Black Rock, in Ka'anapali; Kapalua Beach (p92); and, in summer, Slaughterhouse Beach and Honolua Bay (p93), north of Kapalua.

Snorkelers should get an early start, as not only does the first half of the morning offer the calmest water conditions, but at some of the more popular places crowds begin to show by 10am.

Top Picks

SNORKEL SPOTS
- **Malu'aka Beach** (p138)
- **Ulua Beach** (p133)
- **'Ahihi-Kina'u Natural Area Reserve** (p140)
- **Molokini Crater** (p29)
- **Pu'u Keka'a (Black Rock)** (p80)
- **Honolua Bay** (p93)

Snorkel Trips

The hottest spots for snorkeling cruises are the largely submerged volcanic crater of Molokini (p29), off Maui's southwest coast, and Lana'i's Hulopo'e Beach (p221). Both brim with untouched coral and an amazing variety of sealife. See the table on p27 for recommended snorkel-trip outfitters.

Launiopoko Beach, Lahaina

SURFING

On Maui, which lies smack in the path of all the major swells that race across the Pacific, surfing reaches legendary peaks. The island's north shore sees the biggest waves, which roll in from November to March, though some places, like famed Ho'okipa Beach (p145), have good wave action year-round.

If you're new to the sport, head to Lahaina, which has beginner-friendly waves and instructors that can get you up on a board in just one lesson. You won't be tearing across mammoth curls, but riding a board is easier than it looks and there's no better place to get started. Two primo owner-operated surf schools that have the perfect blend of patience and persistence

MAUI SURF BEACHES & BREAKS *Jake Howard*

While there are hippie holdouts from the 1960s who believe the spirit of Jimi Hendrix roams the Valley Isle's mountains, today Maui's beaches are where most of the island's action is found. On the north shore, near the town of Ha'iku (p156), is the infamous big-wave spot known as Pe'ahi, or Jaws. Determined pro surfers, such as Laird Hamilton, Dave Kalama and Derrick Doerner, have helped put the planet's largest, most perfect wave on the international map, appearing in everything from American Express commercials to mutual fund ads. Jaws' waves are so high that surfers must be towed into them by wave runners.

Not into risking your life on your vacation? No worries, there are plenty of other waves to ride. Maui's west side, especially around Lahaina (p51), offers a wider variety of surf. The Lahaina Breakwall and Harbor's fun reef breaks cater to both beginner and intermediate surfers. To the south is Ma'alaea Pipeline, a fickle right-hand reef break that is often considered one of the fastest waves in the world. On the island's northwest corner is majestic Honolua Bay. This right point break works best on winter swells and is considered one of the premier points, not just in Hawaii, but around the world.

Gentler shorebreaks good for bodysurfing can be found around Pa'ia (p145), Kapalua (p92) and the beaches between Kihei (p120) and Makena (p136).

Jake Howard is a senior writer at Surfer *magazine and lives in San Clemente, CA*

Clothing-optional Little Beach, Makena State Park, South Maui GREG ELMS

are Goofy Foot Surf School (p61) and Nancy Emerson's School of Surfing (p61). A great place to rent quality surfboards is Hana Hwy Surf (p147), which also maintains a surf report hotline (☎ 871-6258) that's updated daily. You can also get a surf report online at OMaui (www.omaui.com). Hawaii Surfing News (www.holoholo.org/surfnews) lists everything from surf conditions to upcoming events. See the Maui Surf Beaches & Breaks box (p31) for the lowdown on surf locales.

SWIMMING

Whoever coined the phrase 'Maui *no ka 'oi*' (Maui is the best) was surely thinking of Maui's beaches, which are arguably the best in the Hawaiian Islands.

The northwest coast from Ka'anapali to Kapalua and the southwest coast from Kihei to Makena harbor scores of sandy beaches with good year-round swimming conditions. The windward northern and eastern coasts are generally rough for swimming in winter but quiet down in summer, when they can become as calm as a swimming pool. For the skinny on beach picks, see the Maui's Best Beaches box on the facing page.

WHALE WATCHING

Each winter about two-thirds of the entire North Pacific humpback whale population – roughly 10,000 whales – comes to the shallow coastal waters off the Hawaiian Islands to breed and give birth. And like other discerning visitors to Hawaii, these intelligent creatures favor Maui. The western coastline of the island is their chief birthing and nursing ground. Luckily for whale watchers, humpbacks are coast-huggers, preferring shallow waters to protect their newborn calves.

Much of Hawaii's ocean waters are protected as the Hawaiian Islands Humpback Whale National Marine Sanctuary (www.hawaiihumpback whale.noaa.gov), whose Kihei headquarters (p123) is abuzz with all sorts of cool whale happenings. You'll find great whale watching right from the shore at many places, including Papawai Point (p78), and along

MAUI'S BEST BEACHES

These beaches are in geographical order, circling the island.
- **Honolua Bay** (p93) Surfing in winter, snorkeling in summer.
- **Kapalua Beach** (p92) Pretty sands, calm snorkeling and swimming year-round.
- **DT Fleming Beach** (p92) A beaut that'll make you wonder if you've reached the South Pacific.
- **Kahekili Beach** (p81) Ka'anapali's least-crowded snorkeling and swimming spot.
- **Ka'anapali Beach** (p80) A happening resort beach with all the expected facilities.
- **Charley Young Beach** (p122) A hidden gem right in the heart of bustling Kihei.
- **Keawakapu Beach** (p120) The perfect beach for a sunset swim.
- **Ulua Beach** (p133) For morning snorkeling and afternoon bodysurfing.
- **Wailea Beach** (p133) Golden sands galore at South Maui's top resort beach.
- **Malu'aka Beach** (p138) The best place to snorkel with turtles.
- **Big Beach** (p138) For long beach strolls, boogie boarding and bodysurfing.
- **Little Beach** (p139) Haunt of the clothing-optional crowd.
- **Kanaha Beach** (p103) For kickin' kitesurfing and windsurfing.
- **Ho'okipa Beach** (p145) Where experts head for primo surfing and windsurfing.
- **Pa'iloa Beach** (p198) Maui's most stunning black-sand beach.
- **Kaihalulu (Red Sand) Beach** (p207) A secluded red jewel at the end of a trail.

beach walks in Kihei (p121) and Wailea (p133).

Of course, to really get within splashing distance of 40-ton leviathans acrobatically jumping out of the water, take a whale-watching cruise. And no one does them better than Pacific Whale Foundation (www.pacificwhale.org), a conservation group that takes pride in its green, naturalist-led whale watch trips. Maui's peak whale-watching season is from January through March, although whales are usually around for a month or so on either side of those dates.

WINDSURFING

This sport reaches its peak on Maui. Ho'okipa Beach (p145), near Pa'ia, hosts top international windsurfing competitions. The wind and waves combine at Ho'okipa in such a way that makes gravity seem arbitrary. Ho'okipa is for experts only, though, as hazards include razor-sharp coral and dangerous shorebreaks. For kick-ass wind without taking your life in your hands, the place to launch is Kanaha Beach (p103) in Kahului, but avoid the busy weekends when the water becomes a sea of sails.

Dolphins are frequent visitors to the West Maui coast   GREG ELMS

Overall, Maui is known for its consistent winds. Windsurfers can find action in any month, but as a general rule the best wind is from June to September and the flattest spells are from December to February.

At Ma'alaea (p115), where the winds are usually strong and blow offshore toward Kaho'olawe, conditions are ripe for advanced speed sailing. In winter, on those rare occasions when *kona* (leeward) winds

blow, the Ma'alaea-Kihei area can be the only place windy enough to sail. Get the inside scoop on the windsurfing scene at **Maui Windsurfing** (www.mauiwindsurfing.net).

Most windsurfing shops are based in Kahului and handle rentals, give lessons, sell windsurfing gear and even book package tours that include gear, accommodations and car. For a list of recommendable outfitters, see p105.

ISLAND VOICES

NAME: EMILY CARLSON
OCCUPATION: VOLUNTEER & OUTREACH FACILITATOR, HAWAIIAN ISLANDS HUMPBACK WHALE NATIONAL MARINE SANCTUARY
RESIDENCE: KIHEI

How can snorkelers and divers get involved in marine conservation? One way is to join the reef survey I do on the first Saturday of every month. We all meet at 9am at Malu'aka Beach (p138). I give a brief orientation, go over the method. I have slates and pencils that can be taken underwater. If it's your first time you could just try to identify what you're seeing with the help of underwater picture cards, or if you know your fish a bit, you could be both identifying and counting. When you return to the beach and fill out the scan chart, you can mark species only, or species and abundance.

How does this help the environment? It's actually very valuable because it goes into an online database. Go to www.reef.org to see it. The benefit is that you can start to get a look at the health of the ecosystem by determining the types and numbers of species you're finding. You can say, well, you've got a lot of herbivores, or a lot of carnivores here. This is a healthy reef because you're seeing different types of fish. Or you look and see there are certain kinds of fish that come in when the reef is really in decline.

Isn't that what scientists do? Recreational divers and snorkelers, they're the ones out there all the time seeing what's going on. They're getting a very accurate report. Researchers can't be out at all the reefs all the time. So management agencies can use this as a tool. For visitors, it gives a deeper look into what this special place is all about.

Can people do it on their own? Reef surveys can be done anytime and by anyone. It doesn't have to be an organized thing. You can even come by the office and get a slate. But it's more fun in a group. You get out of the water and everyone will be saying, 'What did you see?' and 'Oh my god, did you see that!?' Or someone will say, 'I saw a fish that looked like a wrasse but not like one I've seen before,' and they'll describe it, and someone else will say, 'Oh that was a cleaner wrasse, they hide in the crevices.' Not only is it a great way to learn your fish, but you get to share it with everybody.

Are there other volunteer options? Yes! It's easy to fit in some volunteering while on vacation. Visitors looking to get involved can call me at ☎ 879-2818.

ON LAND

When your waterlogged body has had enough, there's a plethora of things to do on land. Maui's hiking and horse trails lead you into some of the most unique ecosystems on earth. And if knocking around a little white ball is your thing, would-be Tigers can stalk the very greens where the real Tiger plays.

ATV

They tear across the woods like hyped-up lawnmowers and aren't going to win any sustainability awards, but if ATVs are your thing we ain't going to lie to you – you can let it ride on Maui. The place to go is Haleakala ATV Tours (p161) on the lower slopes of Haleakalā.

CYCLING

Cyclists on Maui face a number of challenges: narrow roads, heavy traffic, an abundance of hills and mountains, and the same persistent winds that so delight windsurfers. On the plus side, many of Maui's roads, including the Pi'ilani Hwy in South Maui, have bike lanes. Rent your bike from a reliable shop such as South Maui Bicycles (p131) in Kihei or Island Biker (p108) in Kahului.

The full-color *Maui County Bicycle Map* ($6), available from bicycle shops, shows all the roads on Maui that have cycle lanes and gives other nitty-gritty details. Consider it essential if you intend to do your exploring by pedal power.

GOLF

With scenic ocean vistas and emerald mountain slopes, golfing just doesn't get much better. The most prestigious of all of Maui's courses is the Plantation Course (see Kapalua Golf, p94), which kicks off the annual PGA tour. Only slightly less elite are the championship greens at Wailea (p134) and Ka'anapali (p83).

At the other end of the spectrum, you can enjoy a fun round at the friendly Waiehu Municipal Golf Course (p98) and at lesser-known country clubs elsewhere around the island. Pick up the free tourist magazine *Maui Golf Review* for in-depth course profiles and tips on playing specific holes. Another good resource is Maui Golf (www .golf-maui.com).

HELICOPTER TOURS

Helicopters go into some amazing places that you might otherwise not experience. When you book ask about seat guarantees, and let it be known that you want a seat with a window, not a middle seat. On Maui winds pick up by midday and carry clouds up the mountains with them. For the clearest skies and calmest ride, book a morning flight. There are four main tours:

West Maui tour (20 to 30 minutes) Takes in jungly rain forest, remote waterfalls and 'Iao Valley – this is Maui's prettiest face.

East Maui tour (45 minutes) Highlights Hana, Haleakalā Crater and 'Ohe'o Gulch. Keep in mind this is the rainiest side of Maui. The good news: waterfalls galore stream down the mountain sides if you hit clear weather after a rainstorm. The bad news: it can be socked in with clouds.

Circle Island tour (one hour) Combines the West Maui and East Maui tours.

West Maui and Moloka'i tour (one hour) Includes the drama of West Maui as well as a zip along the spectacular coastal cliffs of Moloka'i. Definitely the Big Kahuna of knockout photo ops!

Heading off to the beach   GREG ELMS

HELICOPTER TOUR OPERATORS

Company	Phone	Tours	List prices
AlexAir	☎ 871-0792	West Maui	$90-145
		East Maui	$200
		Circle Island	$235-270
		West Maui & Moloka'i	$200
Blue Hawaiian	☎ 871-8844	West Maui	$150-175
		East Maui	$225-240
		Circle Island	$275-305
		West Maui & Moloka'i	$275-305
Mauiscape	☎ 877-7272	East Maui	$210
		Circle Island	$270
		West Maui & Moloka'i	$265
Sunshine	☎ 871-5600	West Maui	$150-175
		East Maui	$225-240
		Circle Island	$230-345
		West Maui & Moloka'i	$230-345

See the Helicopter Tour Operators table, above, for recommendable helicopter companies. All operate out of the Kahului Heliport, at the southeast side of Kahului Airport. Discounts off the list prices are common; ask when you book or look for coupons in the free tourist magazines.

HIKING

Hikers on Maui get to pick from an amazing diversity of trails that traverse coastal deserts, bamboo forests and lush green jungles. Hands down the most extraordinary trails are in Haleakalā National Park (p176), where hikes ranging from half-day walks to quad-busting multiday treks meander across the moonscape of Haleakalā Crater. In the Kipahulu ('Ohe'o Gulch; p184) section of the park, a trail leads up past terraced pools ideal for a dip and on to the towering waterfalls that feed them.

In Maui's Upcountry, Polipoli Spring State Recreation Area (p162) has an extensive trail system in cloud forest, including the breathtaking Skyline Trail (p163) that connects with Haleakalā summit.

North of Wailuku is the lofty Waihe'e Ridge Trail (p98), which penetrates deep into the misty West Maui Mountains. Near Ma'alaea Bay, the Lahaina Pali Trail (p116) follows an old footpath on the drier western slope of the same mountain mass.

Several pull-offs along the road to Hana (p187) offer short nature walks that lead to hidden waterfalls and unspoiled coastal views, including the Waikamoi Nature Trail (p190). A longer coastal trail between Wai'anapanapa State Park (p198) and Hana Bay follows an ancient Hawaiian footpath past several historic sights, as does the Hoapili (King's Hwy) Trail from La Pérouse Bay (p140) on the other side of the island.

Not-to-be-missed short nature walks

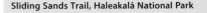

Sliding Sands Trail, Haleakalā National Park

that combine bird- and whale watching include the Kealia Pond boardwalk (p115) in Maʻalaea and the Kihei Coastal Trail (p121).

One of Maui's top environmental shakers, the **Sierra Club** (☎ 573-4147; www.hi.sierraclub .org/maui), sponsors guided hikes led by naturalists to various places around the island, mostly on Saturdays. Nonmembers are asked to pay $5 each; carpooling to trailheads may be available. Not only will you be sharing the trails with other eco-minded hikers, but the Sierra Club also sometimes hikes into fascinating places that are otherwise closed to the public.

Hiking Considerations

Maui has no snakes, no poison ivy and few wild animals that will fuss with hikers. There's only the slimmest chance of meeting up with a large boar in the backwoods, but they're unlikely to be a problem unless cornered.

Hikers do need to have their wits about them, however. Be careful on the edge of steep cliffs since cliffside rock in Maui tends to be crumbly. Flash floods are a potential threat in many of the steep, narrow val-

NA ALA HELE

Of special interest to hikers and naturalists is the work of **Na Ala Hele** ('Trails to Go On'; www.hawaiitrails.org), a group affiliated with Hawaii's Division of Forestry and Wildlife.

Na Ala Hele was established in 1988 with the task of coordinating public access to hiking trails and also maintaining and preserving historical trails. On Maui, the group has negotiated with private landowners and the military to gain access to previously restricted areas and re-establish abandoned trails.

The Na Ala Hele logo signpost – a brown sign that features a yellow hiking petroglyph figure – is marking an increasing number of trailheads as the organization's work continues. On Maui, Na Ala Hele works out of a small office in the **Division of Forestry and Wildlife** (DOFAW; ☎ 873-3508; www.dofaw.net) in Wailuku. It does an amazing job in spite of being woefully underfunded. So, if Maui's trails really inspire you, consider contacting Na Ala Hele and volunteering to help them keep things going.

GREG ELMS

Horseback riding near Kipahulu in East Maui

leys on Maui that require stream crossings. Warning signs include a distant rumbling, the smell of fresh earth and a sudden increase in the stream's current. If the water begins to rise, get to higher ground immediately. A walking stick is good for bracing yourself on slippery approaches, gaining leverage and testing the depth of streams.

Darkness falls fast once the sun sets and ridgetop trails are no place to be caught unprepared in the dark. Always carry a flashlight just in case. Long pants offer protection from overgrown parts of the trail, and sturdy footwear with good traction is a must. Pack 2L of water per person for a day hike, carry a whistle to alert rescue workers should the need arise, wear sunscreen and start out early.

HORSEBACK RIDING

Got a hankering to saddle up? With its abundant ranch land and a living cowboy culture, Maui offers some of Hawaii's best riding experiences. Choose a ride based on the landscape you'd like to see, since all are friendly, reputable outfitters.

The most unusual ride, offered by Pony Express (p160), meanders down into the barren hollows of Haleakalā Crater via Sliding Sands Trail. Maui Stables (p212), near Kipahulu, offers rides up the slopes past waterfalls. Makena Stables (p140) takes riders along the volcanic slopes that overlook pris-

tine La Pérouse Bay, while Mendes Ranch (p98) rides high atop the cliffs of the Kahekili Hwy. Families will like the easy rides at Thompson Ranch (p164) in Keokea.

MOUNTAIN BIKING

If you want to take off into the wilderness on a mountain bike head to the Upcountry. Experienced downhill riders will find adrenaline-stoked thrills on the Skyline Trail (p180), which follows the mountain's spine from Haleakalā National Park into Polipoli Spring State Recreation Area.

SPAS

Spa tourism is hot – hot as in 'ili'ili therapy (with hot lava stones), that is. Hawaiian spa treatments may sound a bit whimsical, but they're based on herbal traditions. Popular body wraps use seaweed to detoxify or wild ginger to remedy colds and jet lag. Other tropical treatments sound good enough to eat: coconut-milk baths and Kona-coffee scrubs….mmm.

Most spas are in the large resort hotels, such as the Hotel Hana-Maui (see Honua Spa, p208) and Grand Wailea Resort Hotel & Spa (p136), but if you prefer a more traditional setting consider the Luana Spa Retreat (p208), which offers treatments under a thatched hut in Hana.

TENNIS

Those looking to hone their game will find world-class facilities at Wailea Tennis Club (p134), Royal Lahaina Tennis Ranch in Ka'anapali (p83) and Kapalua Tennis (p94). If you just want to knock a ball around, many hotels and condos have tennis courts for their guests and the county maintains free tennis courts at many public parks.

YOGA

Maui has much to entice the alternatively inclined. Serious yoga students will find the dance of yoga in all its forms at Studio Maui (p156) in Ha'iku. If you're into Bikram yoga, Bikram Yoga Lahaina (p61) is your place. Just want to stretch near the beach? Head to Maui Yoga Path (p125) in Kihei.

ZIPLINING

Maybe gliding across the water isn't your thing. How about gliding above the treetops hanging from a zipline? Maui's ziplines let you soar freestyle along cables over gulches, woods and waterfalls while strapped into a harness. The hardest part is stepping off the platform for the first zip – the rest is pure exhilaration!

Everyone's favorite is Skyline Eco-Adventures' (p160) Haleakalā Skyline Tour, but it often books out months in advance. The same company has zipped up to Ka'anapali (p83) and opened a second zipline in the hills above the resort, this one pricier but easier to book. The newest zipline, by Kapulua Adventure Center (p94), in the West Maui Mountains up the slopes from Kapalua, differs from the others by having a dual track, allowing riders to zip side by side with a friend.

GREEN MAUI

Maui breathes green. From the top of Haleakalā volcano to the verdant rain forests along the famed road to Hana to the ocean depths where great whales gather, the natural beauty swallows you up. Green is also a way of thinking and living on this island, where people spend most of their waking hours outdoors, communing with each other and with nature. On any given weekend you'll find half of Maui at the beach picnicking, fishing or enjoying the water. Whether it's a surfer fighting to protect the shoreline or weekend volunteers restoring a cultural site, nearly everyone on Maui feels a close connection to the land and the sea. It won't take long for you to feel the *aloha 'aina* (love for the land), too. With scores of environmental groups plugging away, there's always something to get involved in, and visitors are invited to lend a hand – even for just a day.

MAUI GOES GREEN

Maui has a long history of protecting its environment. Islanders of all backgrounds are activists – from Native Hawaiians volunteering to restore an ancient fishpond to scientists fighting to keep invasive plants at bay. The island has no polluting heavy industry and not a single roadside billboard to blight natural vistas.

You'll be struck by just how lushly green Maui is. The total of all the land that's been set aside as parks, forest reserve and watershed covers nearly half of the island.

The crowning glory of it all is Haleakalā National Park (p165), which, thanks to the collaborative work of environmental groups, now extends from its original perch in the center of Maui clear down to the south coast. The rain-forested Kipahulu ('Ohe'o Gulch) section of the park, acquired by private conservation groups, was given to the park in 1969. In 2008 another private-public partnership of conservation-minded islanders purchased an

❀ SUSTAINABLE ICON

It seems like everyone's going 'green' these days, but how can you know which Maui businesses are genuinely eco-friendly and which are simply jumping on the sustainable bandwagon? Throughout the book, this Sustainable icon indicates listings that we are highlighting because they demonstrate an active sustainable-tourism policy. Some are involved in conservation or environmental education, while others maintain and preserve Hawaiian identity and culture, and many are owned and operated by local and indigenous operators. For quick reference, these listings are compiled in the GreenDex (p303).

additional 4340 acres near Kipahulu to add to Haleakalā National Park's boundaries.

When it comes to renewable energy, Maui is head and shoulders above the rest of Hawaii. Some 20% of Maui's electricity comes from wind power and from the burning of bagasse, the byproduct of sugar production (see p115). Since June 2006, 20 wind turbines climbing the slopes above wind-whipped Ma'alaea have been tied to the island power grid, producing enough emission-free energy to light 10% of the homes on Maui. A planned expansion of the wind farm could soon double the number of turbines. Meanwhile, a second commercial wind farm is in the planning stages for development on 'Ulupalakua Ranch property in the Upcountry.

As it goes with conservation, one green turn often leads to another. The state leases the hillside the Ma'alaea wind turbines occupy to Kaheawa Wind Power, the operator of the turbines. That lease money is set aside for funding conservation programs, including operating a hatchery for Maui's endangered nene and several native plant restoration projects.

Wind power is not all big biz either – a homegrown Maui company (see www .cowboybuilt.com) is beginning to build backyard windmills for rural folks living off the grid.

The next move may be harnessing the awesome surf along Maui's North Shore. Oceanlinx, an Australian renewable energy company, is performing preliminary environmental assessments in the hopes of installing three wave turbines that would have the capacity to power 1600 homes.

Governments and task forces get into the mix with the Hawai'i 2050 (www.hawaii2050.org) sustainability plan, a still-evolving program that combines public, private and community input to formulate policy on the future of the state's economy, society and environment. Focus Maui Nui (www.focusmauinui.com) is a similar county effort that aims to define Maui's vision for its future.

SUSTAINABLE MAUI

As you plan your trip, consider your impact on the island. You already know many of the things you can do to help the environment – use less fuel, conserve water, buy local.

Transportation

We're not going to pretend you don't need to rent a car to thoroughly explore the island, but there are ways to minimize your carbon footprint. Rent a smaller, less gas-guzzling vehicle. Not only will that be gentler on Maui's environment, but the island's notoriously narrow roads will be easier to negotiate. Consider renting a Bio-Beetle (p108), which runs on recycled cooking oil. Avoid unnecessary trips – enjoy beaches, activities and restaurants near your hotel. Look for ways to keep your vehicle full – if you've become friendly with the couple staying next door, suggest joining up for that Upcountry drive rather than using two cars. Or ditch the car and rent a bike (p288) or hop on the Maui Bus (p289) – at least some of the time.

For interisland travel to Lana'i and Moloka'i, consider taking a ferry, which is easier on the ozone than air travel. And boat travel is a great way to get close to Hawaii's spectacular marine life – whales and dolphins aren't visible from the plane!

Treading Lightly

Before arriving on Maui, clean your shoes and wipe off your luggage so you don't inadvertently bring seeds or insects, introducing yet another invasive species. When

Rental cars don't have to run on gas!

hiking, stay on trails; when snorkeling, stay off the coral. Don't disturb cultural sites.

Respect the 'Kapu – No Trespassing' signs that you'll see around the island. Although you may be tempted to push on through a closed gate, just to see what's beyond it, don't – unless a trustworthy local tells you it's actually OK. Respect the privacy of residents, whose quality of life is constantly being encroached upon.

You'll find green-friendly businesses listed with the Hawaii Ecotourism Association (www.hawaiiecotourism.org), which recommends outfitters, tours and other activities committed to ecotourism and sustainable travel. We've also indicated sustainable establishments throughout this book with a special icon (see the boxed text on p42).

Eating Locally

Every food product not grown or raised on Maui has to be shipped to the island by boat or plane. Considering the great distances and the amount of fuel used, that makes the 'locavore' or 'eat local' movement particularly relevant on Maui.

But there's no reason to be eating out of a box anyway. Maui is a virtual garden. Its rich soil produces everything from tropical bananas, mangoes and pineapples to cool-weather crops like lettuce, Maui onions and sweet Kula strawberries. Maui cattle have free range of green pastures, island goats produce creamy cheeses and, of course, there's an ocean full of fish.

Recycling

Just about every beach park has a bin for recycling aluminum cans, and you can often find eco-friendly businesses with bins for plastic and glass as well. Ask at your hotel how they recycle and if you should keep your cans and bottles separate…if they're not already committed recyclers, asking helps raise the consciousness level.

Bottled water may be convenient when you're sightseeing, but the tap water on Maui is perfectly fine for drinking, so resist the temptation to rely on those California spring-water imports. Or at the very least, take your plastic bottle home at the end of the day to refill from the tap for tomorrow's outing.

ON THE GROUND

The greener you go, the more up close and personal things get. Hike into a hidden valley, such as on the Waihe'e Ridge Trail (p98), rather than helicoptering over it and you'll hear birds instead of a propeller. Donning a mask to snorkel or paddling

SUPERFERRY

One of the most talked-about issues on the island has been the launching of the Hawaii Superferry, a high-speed ferry – the first car ferry between the Hawaiian Islands – operating between O'ahu and Maui.

Many Maui residents feel the ferry was rushed through without the proper environmental impact studies, and consideration for people and businesses near the dock. The concerns were myriad, from the possible impact of introducing invasive plant seeds caught in vehicles' tire treads to increased traffic on the already congested roads near Kahului Harbor. Surfers went on a tear when one of their prime surf locales was closed off to provide a security zone. The coalition of opponents included county officials, residents and nearly every major environmental group on Maui.

After months of legal challenges and delays, the Hawaii Superferry began carrying passengers to Maui in December 2007. But in March 2009, in a suit brought by the Sierra Club, the Hawaii Supreme Court ruled the state acted unconstitutionally by allowing the ferry to begin without an environmental study. The ferry immediately and indefinitely ceased operations.

along in a kayak lets you glide along silently with fish and turtles.

There are environmentally friendly organizations across the island that offer less impactful ways to be active and adventurous. Instead of a boat dive, perhaps try a shore dive (no diesel fuel, no dropped anchors) with a company that specializes in them, such as Maui Dreams Dive Company (p124) in Kihei or Pacific Dive (p61) in Lahaina. Opt for a sailboat cruise over a motorboat cruise. Not only is riding with the wind more eco-friendly, but sailboats get closer to whales and dolphins, which are repelled by the noise from motorboats. When booking, look at companies like Trilogy Excursions (p63) that fly a green flag, indicating the boats adhere to strict environmental practices and don't discharge waste into the ocean.

And there are heaps of opportunities to go local. Taking an outrigger canoe sail with Maui Nui O Kama Canoe Club (p124) or Hawaiian Sailing Canoe Adventures (p134) combines an earth-friendly adventure with a cultural experience – and a workout!

Local farms yield luscious fruits and vegetables for sale at farmers markets in Kihei (p125), Honokowai (p88) and Kapalua (p94), and at the Maui Swap Meet (p105) in Kahului. More and more restaurants are boasting locally caught seafood, Maui-raised beef and Maui-grown produce. Luckily the range is wide, from the deli at Mana Foods (p148) in Pa'ia to the gourmet food at I'O (p66) in Lahaina. One buy-local restaurant, Flatbread (p149) in Pa'ia,

takes it to the next step by giving a cut of the night's profits to local environmental groups that show up to rap with customers every Tuesday night.

Buying Maui-made products supports the local economy and often helps sustain the environment as well. Ali'i Kula Lavender (p159), for instance, produces organic lavender blossoms, which are then used by two dozen home-based businesses to make lavender jams, vinegars and salad dressings sold at the farm. For your picnics, buy a hunk of cheese from Surfing Goat Dairy (p158) and a bottle of wine from Tedeschi Vineyards (p164). All these make good gifts to bring home, as do the abundance of Maui-made artworks sold in cooperatives and galleries around the island. See www.madeinmaui.com for a list of products and shops.

HELPFUL ORGANIZATIONS

Notable groups committed to a green and sustainable Maui include:

Hawaii Ecotourism Association (www.hawaiiecotourism.org) Recommends outfitters and activities committed to sustainable travel.

Kahea (www.kahea.org) Activist organization tackling Hawaiian cultural rights and environmental issues.

Kauahea (www.kauahea.org) Connected to the Maui Arts & Cultural Center (p107), it promotes Hawaiian culture.

Malama Hawai'i (www.malamahawaii.org) Coordinates over 70 cultural and environmental organizations.

Maui Coastal Land Trust (www.mauicoastallandtrust.org) Protects Maui's shorelines.

Maui Tomorrow (www.maui-tomorrow.org) Promotes sustainable development policies and preservation of open space.

Na Ala Hele (www.hawaiitrails.org) Maintains and preserves hiking trails.

Sierra Club, Maui Chapter (www.hi.sierraclub.org /maui) Everything from political activism to weekend outings eradicating invasive plants from forests.

Surfrider Foundation, Maui Chapter (www.surfrider .org/maui) Surfer organization protecting Maui's ocean and beaches.

ENVIRONMENTAL ISSUES

Because it's one of the most geographically isolated places on earth, 2500 miles from the nearest continental land mass, Hawaii's environment constitutes a rare living textbook of Darwinian evolution – one so fragile that some of it is vanishing before our eyes. The havoc began the moment humans stepped into this unique landscape of plants and wildlife that had evolved without people, land mammals or agricultural crops. Today Hawaii accounts for approximately 75% of all documented plant and animal extinctions in the USA, and it is the undisputed 'endangered species capital of the world.'

That said, there have been some notable turn-arounds. Haleakalā National Park recently completed a decade-long project to fence in the park and eradicate wild cats and pigs. Thanks to that effort, both the endangered native silversword (see the boxed text on p174) and the nene (see the boxed text on p180) have come back from the brink of extinction.

The waters around Maui and the other Hawaiian Islands are home to more than half of all the coral found in the USA. The most significant threats to these reefs are also created by people – from overfishing and from land-based pollution from agriculture and golf courses. You can help by eating sustainable fish (see www.seafood watch.org). On the golf front, some courses are cleaning up their act and going truly green. Maui's most famous golf courses, at Kapalua (p94), have become certified by Audubon International as 'cooperative sanctuaries,' meaning they meet strict standards for restricted water and pesticide use, and maintain a landscape that provides habitat for wildlife.

The effects of global warming are another concern on Maui. Some scientists believe droughts that have hit the island in recent years are at least in part the consequence of climate change.

Many of Maui's environmental issues revolve around development, especially in water-thirsty south Maui, which relies upon precious water from Upcountry farms and central Maui to run its taps and turn desert into lawns.

On a grassroots level, a wide coalition of environmentalists, activists and other residents has made island conservation efforts a slow, but steady, success. They help fight invasive weeds, pulling up one plant at a time; monitor migrating whale and nesting turtle populations; advocate for the protection of coral reefs; and work to restore cultural sites. The rebuilding of the Kalepolepo Fishpond (p126) in Kihei and the restoration of Kahoʻolawe (p226) are activists' success stories. Those who want to volunteer, including short-term visitors, will find all sorts of opportunities to help keep Maui green; see p284 for a list of recommendations.

ENVIRONMENT

Breaching whales, an explosion of flowery tropical blooms and fascinating underwater sights that exist nowhere else on the planet – Maui's environmental wonders are in a class by themselves.

THE LAND

Maui, the second-largest Hawaiian island, has a land area of 728 sq miles. Set atop a 'hot spot' on the Pacific Plate, Maui arose from the ocean floor as two separate volcanoes. Lava flows and soil erosion eventually built up a valleylike isthmus between the volcanic masses, linking them in their present form. This flat region provides a fertile setting for fields of sugarcane and is home to Maui's largest urban center, the twin towns of Kahului and Wailuku.

The eastern side of Maui, the larger and younger of the two volcanic masses, is dominated by the lofty 10,023ft Haleakalā. This dormant volcano, whose crater-like floor is dotted with cinder cones, last erupted in 1790…which on the geological clock means it could be just snoozing. The second, more ancient volcano formed the craggy West Maui Mountains, which top out at the 5778ft Puʻu Kukui. Both mountains are high enough to trap the

January through March is prime time for whale watching off the West Maui coast

moisture-laden clouds carried by the northeast tradewinds, bringing abundant rain to their windward eastern sides. Consequently, the lushest jungles and gushiest waterfalls are found along the Hana Hwy, which runs along Haleakalā's eastern slopes, while the driest, sunniest beaches are on the western coasts.

WILDLIFE

All living things that reached Maui's shores were carried across the ocean on wing, wind or wave – seeds clinging to a bird's feather, or insects in a piece of driftwood. Scientists estimate that successful species arrived once every 70,000 years – and they included no amphibians and only two mammals: a bat and a seal.

However, the flora and fauna that made it to Maui occupied an unusually rich and diverse land. In a prime example of 'adaptive radiation,' the 250 flowering plants that arrived evolved into 1800 native species. Lacking predators, new species dropped defensive protections – thorns, poisons and strong odors disappeared, which explains why they fare so poorly against modern invaders.

When Polynesians arrived, they brought pigs, chickens, coconuts and about two dozen other species, not to mention people. The pace of change exploded after Western contact in the late 18th century. Cattle and goats were introduced and set wild, with devastating consequences. Even today, sitting on a Kihei beach looking out at Kahoʻolawe in the late afternoon, you'll

GREG ELMS

notice a red tinge from the dust whipping off the island, a consequence of defoliation by wild goats released there a century ago.

But there is progress. On Kahoʻolawe the goats are gone and native reforestation has begun; Haleakalā National Park has made great strides in reintroducing and protecting native species; and the first public garden totally dedicated to endemic Hawaiian species, Maui Nui Botanical Gardens (p104), has opened at the site of a former exotic zoo. Now that's an impressive change in attitude.

Animals

Most of Maui's wildlife attractions are found in the water or on the wing. Hawaii has no native land mammals.

SEALIFE

Of the almost 700 fish species living in Hawaiian waters, nearly one third are found nowhere else in the world. Maui's nearshore waters are a true rainbow of color: turquoise parrotfish, bright yellow tangs and polka-dotted pufferfish, just to name a few.

Green sea turtles *(honu)* abound in Maui's waters. To the thrill of snorkelers and divers, *honu* can often be seen feeding in shallow coves and bays. Adults can grow to more than 3ft in length – an awesome sight when one swims past you in the water. Much less common is the hawksbill turtle, which occasionally nests on Maui's western shores.

The sheltered waters between Maui, Lanaʻi and Molokaʻi are the wintering destination for thousands of North Pacific humpback whales. Of all the whales that frequent Hawaiian waters, it is the humpback, which entertains with acrobatic breaches

ANIMAL 911

Don't touch, approach or disturb marine mammals; most are protected, making it illegal to do so. Watch dolphins, whales, seals and sea turtles from a respectful distance. If you see a wild animal in distress, report it to the state **Division of Conservation & Resource Enforcement** (DOCARE; ☎ 984-8110).

and tail flips, that everyone wants to see. Humpbacks, the fifth-largest of the great whales, reach lengths of 45ft and weigh up to 45 tons. Humpback whales are coasthuggers and you can see them right from the beach in winter along Maui's west and southwest coasts.

Maui is also home to a number of dolphins. The one you're most likely to see is the spinner dolphin (so named for its acrobatic leaps from the water), which comes into calm bays during the day to rest.

With a little luck you might also see the Hawaiian monk seal, which lives primarily in the remote Northwestern Hawaiian Islands, but occasionally hauls out on Maui beaches. It was nearly wiped out last century, but conservation efforts have edged the species back from the brink of extinction.

BIRDS

Many of Hawaii's birds have evolved from a single species in a spectacular display of adaptive radiation. For example, all 57 species of Hawaiian honeycreepers likely evolved from a single finch ancestor. Left vulnerable to new predatory species and infectious avian diseases after Europeans arrived, half of Hawaii's native bird species are already extinct, and more than 30 of those remaining are still under threat.

The endangered nene, Hawaii's state bird, is a long-lost cousin of the Canada goose. Nene nest in high cliffs on the slopes of Haleakalā and their feet have adapted to the rugged volcanic environment by losing most of their webbing. Nene have black heads, light-yellow cheeks, a white underbelly and dark gray feathers.

At least six birds native to Maui are found nowhere else in the world and all are endangered, including the Maui parrotbill, which exists solely in the Kipahulu section of Haleakalā National Park, and the cinnamon-colored po'ouli, which was last seen in 2004 and may already be extinct. Alas, it's unlikely you'll see any of those birds. But other native forest birds, including the 'apapane, a vivid red honeycreeper, can be sighted on a walk through Hosmer Grove (p172) in the main section of Haleakalā National Park.

Maui's two waterbird preserves not only attract rare native species but also sit along major roadways, inviting passersby to take a look. Both the Kanaha Pond Bird Sanctuary (p103) and Kealia Pond National Wildlife Refuge (p115) are nesting sites for the ae'o (Hawaiian stilt), a black-necked wading bird with a white underbelly and long orange legs. Even though the total stilt population in all Hawaii is just 1500, on any given day you can expect to see them feeding along the marshy edges of these preserve ponds.

Plants

Maui seems to have a suitable niche for just about anything with roots. On a milefor-mile basis Hawaii has the highest concentration of climatic and ecological zones anywhere on earth. They vary from lowland deserts along the coast to lush tropical rain forests in the mountains. And the diversity within a small region can be amazing. In the Upcountry there are so many microclimate zones that hillside farms, such as Enchanting Floral Gardens (p159) in Kula, can grow tropical fruit trees just a few sloping acres from where temperate roses thrive. Go another mile up the slopes and don't bother looking for tropical fruit trees as you're now in the zone where cool-weather crops grow.

Many native species have adapted to very narrow geographic ecosystems, such as Maui's endangered silversword (p174), which grows at the summit of Haleakalā.

FLOWERING PLANTS & FERNS

For travelers, the flower most closely identified with Hawaii is the hibiscus, whose generous blossoms are worn by women tucked behind their ears. Thousands of varieties of hibiscus bushes grow in Hawaii; on most, the flowers bloom early in the day and drop

Maui blooms with native and exotic flowers, such as protea

SABRINA DALBESIO

before sunset. The variety most frequently seen is the introduced red *Hibiscus rosa-sinensis*, which is used as a landscape hedge throughout Maui. Much rarer is the *koki'o ke'oke'o*, a native white hibiscus tree that grows up to 40ft high; it can be seen at Maui Nui Botanical Gardens (p104) in Kahului.

Two native plants you'll see at the beach are pohuehue, a beach morning glory with pink flowers that's found just above the wrack line; and beach naupaka, a shrub with oval leaves and a small white five-petal flower that looks as if it's been torn in half.

PLANTS AS MEDICINE

Hawaii's traditional medicine utilizes native plants. Waxy green leaves from *ki* (ti) plants are placed upon the forehead to cure headaches. *'Ulu* (breadfruit), a green, spiky football-sized fruit, is a treatment for skin diseases, cuts and scratches. But unparalleled among traditional restoratives is *noni* (Indian mulberry), a knobby yellow-green fruit said to be effective against almost anything – and it tastes bad enough to prove it!

For an in-depth look at traditional Hawaiian medicine and native species, read Beatrice Krauss' *Plants in Hawaiian Medicine*.

Throughout the Upcountry you'll find gardens filled with protea, a flashy flower originally from South Africa that takes many forms. Named after the Greek god Proteus (who could change shape at will), blossoms range from small pincushiony heads to tall stalklike flowers with petals that look like feathers. You'll also see plenty of other showy exotic flowers throughout Maui, including the brilliantly orange-and-blue bird-of-paradise and various heliconias with bright orange and red bracts.

There are about 200 varieties of Hawaiian ferns and fern allies (such as mosses) found in rain forests and colonizing lava flows.

TREES & SHRUBS

The most revered of the native Hawaiian forest trees is koa, found at higher elevations on Maui. Growing up to 100ft high, this rich hardwood is traditionally used to make canoes, surfboards and even ukuleles.

Brought by early Polynesian settlers, the *kukui* tree has chestnutlike oily nuts the Hawaiians used for candles, hence its common name, candlenut tree. It's recognizable in the forest by its light silver-tinged foliage.

Two coastal trees that were well utilized in old Hawaii are *hala,* also called pandanus or screw pine, whose spiny leaves were used

PLACES TO HONOR THE SUN

On Maui, the sun rises up out of the ocean and sets there, too. So observing these luminous moments is, shall we say, popular. You can't go wrong at the following vantage points:

- Haleakalā Crater – sunrise (p171)
- Wai'anapanapa State Park - sunrise (p198)
- Big Beach or any other beach in South Maui – sunset (p136)
- Papawai Point – sunset (p78)
- Lahaina – sunset (p56)

for thatching and weaving; and the coconut palm *(niu)*, which loves coral sands and yields about 75 coconuts a year.

Kiawe, a non-native tree, thrives in dry coastal areas. A member of the mesquite family, kiawe is useful for making charcoal but is a nuisance for beachgoers, as its sharp thorns easily pierce soft sandals. Also plentiful along the beach are stands of ironwood, a conifer with drooping needles that act as natural windbreaks and prevent beach erosion.

Other trees that will catch your eye include the African tulip tree, a rain-forest tree abloom with brilliant orange flowers that grows profusely along the road to Hana; plumeria, a favored landscaping tree whose fragrant pink-and-white blossoms are used in lei making; and majestic banyan trees, which have a canopy of hanging aerial roots with trunks large enough to swallow small children.

NATIONAL, STATE & COUNTY PARKS

Haleakalā National Park (p165) accounts for nearly 10% of Maui's land area. The park not only offers superb hiking and other recreational activities but also protects Hawaiian cultural sites and the habitat of several endangered species. Maui's numerous state and county parks also play an important role in preserving undeveloped forest areas and much of Maui's coastline. The parks are well used by Maui residents – from surfers to pig hunters – as well as by tourists.

The state's Department of Land & Natural Resources (DLNR; Map p109; ☎ 984-8100; www.state.hi.us /dlnr; 54 S High St, Wailuku) has useful online information about hiking, conservation and aquatic safety. The DLNR oversees the Division of State Parks (☎ 984-8109; www.hawaii.gov /dlnr/dsp), which issues camping permits on Maui; and Na Ala Hele (p37), which coordinates public access to hiking trails.

MAUI'S TOP 10 PROTECTED AREAS

Natural Area	Features	Activities	Page
'Ahihi-Kina'u Natural Area Reserve	Pristine bay, lava flows, ancient sites	Hiking, snorkeling	p140
Haleakalā National Park (Kipahulu Section)	Towering waterfalls, cascading pools, ancient sites	Hiking, swimming, camping	p184
Haleakalā National Park (Summit Section)	Large dormant volcano	Hiking, camping, horseback riding	p169
'Iao Valley State Park	Streams, cliffs, swimming holes	Hiking, photography	p113
Kahanu Garden & Pi'ilanihale Heiau	National Tropical Botanical Garden, ancient site	Garden walk	p198
Kealia Pond National Wildlife Refuge	Bird sanctuary	Bird watching	p115
Makena State Park	Glorious unspoiled beaches	Swimming, surfing	p138
Molokini Crater	Submerged volcanic crater	Snorkeling, diving	p29
Polipoli Spring State Recreation Area	Cloud forest, uncrowded trails	Hiking, camping, mountain biking	p162
Wai'anapanapa State Park	Lava tubes, trail over rugged sea cliffs to Hana	Hiking, camping	p198

LAHAINA

Take a stunning seaside setting, add pleated mountains to the backdrop and sprinkle in some historical sights. Next, pepper the town with some of the hottest chef-driven restaurants in Hawaii and spike it with a sizzling entertainment scene. It's no wonder when people have something to celebrate they come to Lahaina. It's been that way since the first rambunctious whalers washed ashore and gave the town the frontier facade it still wears today. The old wooden storefronts that once housed saloons, dance halls and brothels are now crammed with art galleries, souvenir shops and, well, still plenty of watering holes. And the harbor where the whalers once docked? It's full of whale-*watching* boats.

LAHAINA
ITINERARIES

IN TWO DAYS *3 miles*

❶ HARBORFRONT (p56) Start your day in the heart of Lahaina at the bustling harbor, where catamarans jostle for attention, the **Pioneer Inn (p67)** hums with period ambience and the USA's largest banyan tree spreads its wings clear across **Banyan Tree Square (p56)**.

❷ WALKING TOUR (p62) Grab your walking shoes and go for a morning stroll around this charming old town, which has more whaling-era scenes than a Herman Melville novel.

❸ WHALE-WATCH CRUISE (p63) Back at the harbor, hop aboard a boat with **Pacific Whale Foundation (p63)** to see 40-ton leviathans up close and personal.

❹ FRONT STREET (p69) Top off the day with a little gallery browsing, pop into some shops and enjoy a **sunset dinner (p64)** at one of the oceanfront restaurants.

❺ SURFING LESSON (p61) On day two it's time to jump into the water. There's no better place to learn the Hawaiian art of surfing than on the gentle waves at the Lahaina Breakwall. Kids will enjoy the lessons at **Goofy Foot (p61)**; bigger folk can get pro tips from former champ **Nancy Emerson (p61)**.

❻ OLD LAHAINA LUAU (p68) Feast your stomach and your eyes at the island's most authentic luau, the perfect ending to any stay in Lahaina.

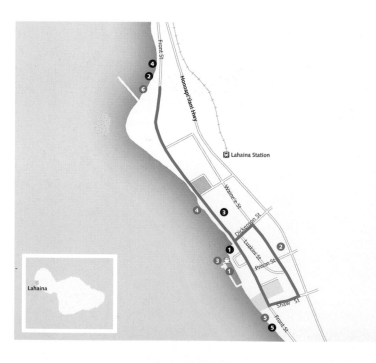

FOR FOODIES

❶ SUNRISE CAFÉ (p65) Early risers in the know start their day at this little gem, just a wave away from the harbor. Decadent chocolate waffles topped with strawberries and whipped cream perhaps? Or get serious with smoked salmon and poached eggs.

❷ ALOHA MIXED PLATE (p65) Dig your toes into the sand as you enjoy island grinds at this cheery beach shack with a million-dollar view. No place else even comes close for atmosphere.

❸ LAHAINA STORE GRILLE & OYSTER BAR (p66) If you love sushi but haven't yet tried *poke,* it's time to get acquainted. The fresh raw *'ahi* (tuna) tossed with sesame oil, shoyu and spicy secrets melts in your mouth. You'll leave a convert.

❹ MALA (p66) Time for tapas? Head to the oceanfront deck in the late afternoon to watch the surfing turtles, then linger while the sun drops behind Lana'i. Munch crunchy calamari. Inhale the garlic flat-bread. Or fly with the chicken wings saucy with pomegranate, ginger and chili.

❺ FEAST AT LELE (p68) The ultimate gourmet event in Lahaina, this themed multi-course beachside dinner paired with a Polynesian show takes your taste buds on an unforgettable voyage. The feast is the handiwork of Lahaina's celebrated chef James McDonald, who also operates the adjacent **I'O (p66)** restaurant.

Indulge your inner foodie at Lahaina's fine and fun eateries

GREG ELMS

LAHAINA

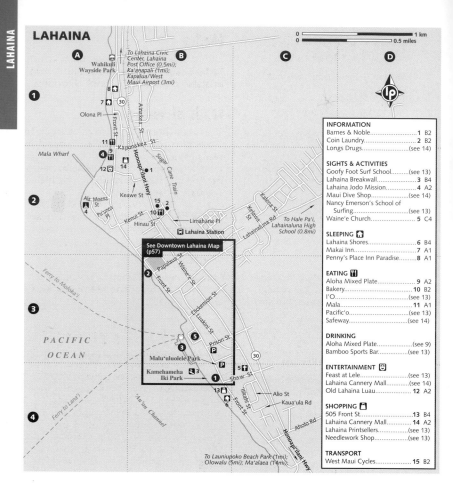

HISTORY

pop 18,000

In ancient times Lahaina housed a royal court for high chiefs and it was the bread-basket (or, more accurately, the breadfruit basket) of West Maui. After Kamehameha the Great unified the islands, he chose Lahaina as his base, and the capital remained there until 1845. The first Christian missionaries arrived in the 1820s and within a decade Hawaii's first stone church, missionary school and printing press were all in place in Lahaina.

In time Lahaina became the dominant port for whalers, not only in Hawaii but for the entire Pacific. The whaling years reached their peak in Lahaina in the 1840s, with hundreds of ships pulling into port each year. When the whaling industry fizzled in the 1860s, Lahaina became all but a ghost town. In the 1870s sugarcane came to Lahaina and it remained the backbone of the economy until tourism took over in the 1960s.

ORIENTATION

The focal point of Lahaina is its bustling small-boat harbor, backed by the old Pioneer Inn and Banyan Tree Sq. The main drag and tourist strip is Front St, which runs along the shoreline.

HIGHLIGHTS

❶ **BEST BEACH:** Kamehameha Iki Park (p62)
❷ **BEST VIEW:** Seaside Front St (p56)
❸ **BEST ACTIVITY:** Whale-watching cruise (p63)
❹ **BEST HAWAIIAN-STYLE EATERY:** Aloha Mixed Plate (p65)
❺ **BEST GREEN SPACE:** Banyan Tree Sq (p56)

Highlights are numbered on the map on p54.

INFORMATION
Bookstores

Barnes & Noble (Map p54; ☎ 661-8672; Lahaina Gateway, cnr Keawe St & Honoapi'ilani Hwy) The island's newest and largest bookstore.
Old Lahaina Book Emporium (Map p57; ☎ 661-1399; 834 Front St; ☽ 10am-7pm) Bookworms, you're in for a feast at Maui's top independent bookstore; new and used volumes, plus vintage Hawaiiana.

Emergency

Police (☎ 244-6400) For nonemergencies.
Police, fire and ambulance (☎ 911)

Internet Access

Buns of Maui (Map p57; ☎ 661-5407; Old Lahaina Center, 880 Front St; per min 8c; ☽ 7:30am-8:30pm Mon-Sat, 7:30am-6pm Sun) Only six computers, but it's seldom crowded and you can't beat the price at this little café named for its yummy cinnamon rolls.
Livewire Café (Map p57; ☎ 661-4213; 612 Front St; per 20min $3; ☽ 6am-9pm) Convenient location, good karma and coffee.

Laundry

Coin laundry (Map p54; Limahana Pl; ☽ 24hr) Opposite the bakery.

Libraries

Lahaina Public Library (Map p57; ☎ 662-3950; 680 Wharf St; ☽ noon-8pm Tue, 9am-5pm Wed & Thu, 10:30am-4:30pm Fri & Sat) Internet access.

Media

Lahaina News (☎ 667-7866; www.lahainanews.com) This free weekly, easily found around town, has the scoop on Lahaina's entertainment scene as well as local issues.

Medical Services

The Maui Memorial Medical Center in Wailuku (p103) is the nearest hospital in case of emergencies.
Longs Drugs (Map p54; ☎ 667-4384; Lahaina Cannery Mall, 1221 Honoapi'ilani Hwy; ☽ 7am-midnight) Lahaina's largest pharmacy.
Maui Medical Group (Map p57; ☎ 249-8080; 130 Prison St; ☽ 7:30am-9pm Mon-Fri, 8am-noon Sat & Sun) This clinic handles nonemergencies.

Money

Both banks have 24-hour ATMs.
Bank of Hawaii (Map p57; ☎ 661-8781; Old Lahaina Center, 880 Front St)

RIGHTEOUS & ROWDY

Lahaina owes much of its period appearance to two diametrically opposed groups of New Englanders who landed in the 1820s.

In 1823 William Richards, Lahaina's first missionary, converted Maui's native governor, Hoapili, to Christianity and persuaded him to pass laws against 'drunkenness and debauchery.' However, after months at sea, sailors weren't looking for a prayer service when they pulled into port – to them there was 'no God west of the Horn.' Missionaries and whalers almost came to battle in 1827 when Governor Hoapili arrested a whaler captain for allowing women to board his ship. The crew retaliated by shooting cannonballs at Richards' house. The captain was released, but laws forbidding liaisons between seamen and Hawaiian women remained in force.

It wasn't until Governor Hoapili's death in 1840 that laws prohibiting liquor and prostitution were no longer enforced and whalers began to flock to Lahaina. Among the sailors who roamed Lahaina's streets was Herman Melville, who later penned *Moby Dick*.

LAHAINA

First Hawaiian Bank (Map p57; ☎ 661-3655; 215 Papalaua St)

Post

Downtown post office station (Map p57; Old Lahaina Center, 32 Papalaua St; ☻ 8:15am-4:15pm Mon-Fri) Central if you're in town, but longer lines and fewer parking spaces than the Lahaina post office.

Lahaina post office (off Map p54; ☎ 661-0904; 1760 Honoapi'ilani Hwy, Lahaina, HI 96761; ☻ 8:30am-5pm Mon-Fri, 9am-1pm Sat) You'll have to go a couple of miles north of town, near the Lahaina Civic Center, to pick up general-delivery mail (held 30 days) sent to Lahaina.

Tourist Information

Lahaina Visitor Center (Map p57; ☎ 667-9193; www.visitlahaina.com; 648 Wharf St; ☻ 9am-5pm) The cashier desk at the gift shop in the Old Lahaina Courthouse doubles as the visitor information center and distributes a handy Lahaina pocket guide.

SIGHTS

Many of Lahaina's top sights are clustered around the harbor, and most of the rest are either on Front St or within a couple of blocks of it. This makes Lahaina an ideal town to explore on foot. See p62 for a recommended walking tour.

OLD LAHAINA COURTHOUSE
Map p57; 648 Wharf St

Lahaina's old courthouse, built in 1859, is a treasure trove of history and art. The location overlooking the bustling harbor was no coincidence. Smuggling was so rampant during the whaling era that officials deemed this the ideal spot to house the customs operations, the courthouse and the jail – all neatly wrapped into a single building. It also held the governor's office, and in 1898 the US annexation of Hawaii was formally concluded here.

The old jail in the basement has been turned into a gallery by the **Lahaina Arts Society** (☎ 661-0111; ☻ 9am-5pm) and the cells that once held drunken sailors now display artwork. It's a fun place to walk through. The paintings, jewelry and woodwork on sale here are creations of island artists who operate the gallery as a cooperative.

Lahaina Heritage Museum (☎ 667-1959; admission free; ☻ 9am-5pm) celebrates the town's culture

---

Don't Miss

- Art-filled basement jail cells in Old Lahaina Courthouse (p56)
- Thomas Edison's 1898 movies of Maui at Wo Hing Museum (p58)
- Fruiting coffee trees adjacent to Maui-Grown Coffee (p69)
- Period buildings on Front St viewed from the wave-splashed seawall opposite Dickenson St

---

and history. Changing exhibits might focus on anything from ancient Hawaiian society to 19th-century whaling, but whatever it is, it's well worth the climb to the 2nd floor to check it out. Also, take a look at the period photos of Lahaina scenes displayed in the 2nd-floor hall, including a c 1908 photo of the adjacent banyan tree.

🌳 BANYAN TREE SQUARE
Map p57; cnr Front & Hotel Sts

You know a tree has stature when throngs of townsfolk gather each year to celebrate its birthday! Marking the center of Lahaina, this awesome banyan tree sprawls across the entire square and ranks as the largest banyan tree in the USA. Planted as a seedling on April 24, 1873 to commemorate the 50th anniversary of missionaries in Lahaina, the tree has become a virtual forest unto itself, with 16 major trunks and scores of horizontal branches reaching across the better part of an acre. It attracts playful kids, who swing Tarzan-like on the aerial roots, and meditative types seeking a break from the crowds on Front St. On weekends artists and craft sellers set up booths beneath the tree.

FORT RUINS
Map p57; cnr Wharf & Canal Sts

Opposite the harbor stands a partial coral-block wall – all that remains from a fort built in 1832 to keep rowdy whalers in line. Each day at dusk a Hawaiian sentinel beat a drum to alert sailors to return to their ships. Stragglers who didn't make it back in time ended up imprisoned here. At the height of its use the fort had some 47 cannons, most salvaged from foreign ships that sank in Lahaina's tricky waters.

DOWNTOWN LAHAINA

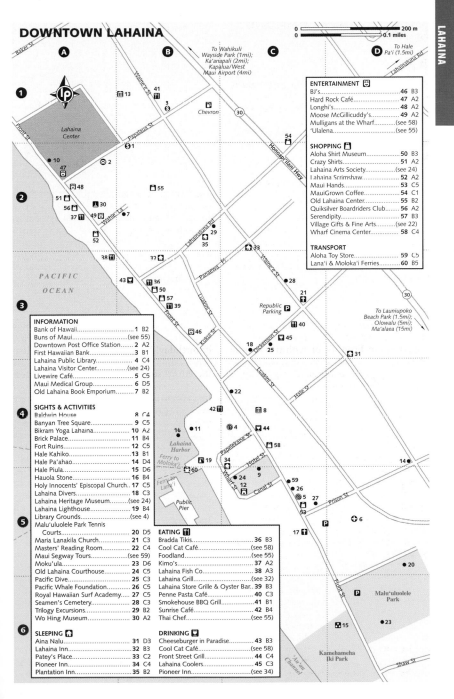

0   200 m
0   0.1 miles

To Wahikuli
Wayside Park (1mi);
Ka'anapali (2mi);
Kapalua/West
Maui Airport (4mi)

To Hale
Pa'i (1.5mi)

ENTERTAINMENT 📻
BJ's..**46** B3
Hard Rock Café.......................**47** A2
Longhi's.....................................**48** A2
Moose McGillicuddy's.........**49** A2
Mulligans at the Wharf...........(see 58)
'Ulalena.......................................(see 55)

SHOPPING 🛍
Aloha Shirt Museum................**50** B3
Crazy Shirts.............................**51** A2
Lahaina Arts Society............(see 24)
Lahaina Scrimshaw................**52** A2
Maui Hands.............................**53** C5
MauiGrown Coffee................**54** C1
Old Lahaina Center................**55** B2
Quiksilver Boardriders Club..**56** A2
Serendipity.............................**57** B3
Village Gifts & Fine Arts..........(see 22)
Wharf Cinema Center.............**58** C4

TRANSPORT
Aloha Toy Store.......................**59** C5
Lana'i & Moloka'i Ferries...........**60** B5

PACIFIC
OCEAN

Republic
Parking

To Launiupoko
Beach Park (1.5mi);
Olowalu (5mi);
Ma'alaea (15mi)

INFORMATION
Bank of Hawaii............................... 1 B2
Buns of Maui...............................(see 55)
Downtown Post Office Station...... 2 A2
First Hawaiian Bank........................3 B1
Lahaina Public Library.................... 4 C4
Lahaina Visitor Center................(see 24)
Livewire Café................................... 5 C5
Maui Medical Group...................... 6 D5
Old Lahaina Book Emporium.........7 B2

SIGHTS & ACTIVITIES
Baldwin House................................ 8 C4
Banyan Tree Square........................ 9 C5
Bikram Yoga Lahaina.................... 10 A2
Brick Palace................................... 11 B4
Fort Ruins...................................... 12 C5
Hale Kahiko...................................13 B1
Hale Pa'ahao.................................. 14 D4
Hale Piula...................................... 15 D6
Hauola Stone................................. 16 B4
Holy Innocents' Episcopal Church..17 C5
Lahaina Divers............................... 18 C3
Lahaina Heritage Museum.......(see 24)
Lahaina Lighthouse...................... 19 B4
Library Grounds...........................(see 4)
Malu'uluolele Park Tennis
  Courts...................................... 20 D5
Maria Lanakila Church.................. 21 C3
Masters' Reading Room................ 22 C4
Maui Segway Tours...................(see 59)
Moku'ula...................................... 23 D6
Old Lahaina Courthouse.............. 24 C5
Pacific Dive................................... 25 C3
Pacific Whale Foundation............ 26 C5
Royal Hawaiian Surf Academy.... 27 C5
Seamen's Cemetery...................... 28 B2
Trilogy Excursions........................ 29 B2
Wo Hing Museum......................... 30 A2

SLEEPING 🛏
Aina Nalu..................................... 31 D3
Lahaina Inn.................................. 32 B3
Patey's Place................................. 33 C2
Pioneer Inn................................... 34 C4
Plantation Inn............................... 35 B2

EATING 🍽
Bradda Tikis.................................. 36 B3
Cool Cat Café...............................(see 58)
Foodland......................................(see 55)
Kimo's.. 37 A2
Lahaina Fish Co............................ 38 A3
Lahaina Grill................................(see 32)
Lahaina Store Grille & Oyster Bar.. 39 B3
Penne Pasta Café.......................... 40 C3
Smokehouse BBQ Grill.................41 B1
Sunrise Café................................. 42 B4
Thai Chef.....................................(see 55)

DRINKING 🍷
Cheeseburger in Paradise.............. 43 B3
Cool Cat Café...............................(see 58)
Front Street Grill.......................... 44 C4
Lahaina Coolers............................ 45 C3
Pioneer Inn..................................(see 34)

Chevron

Lahaina
Center

Lahaina
Harbor

Ferry to
Moloka'i

Ferry to
Lana'i

Public
Pier

Malu'uluolele
Park

Kamehameha
Iki Park

Kama Channel

Shaw St

Top Picks

LAHAINA FOR KIDS

- **Whale-watching cruise** (p63)
- **Banyan tree** (p56)
- **Goofy Foot Surf School** (p61)
- **Sugar Cane Train** (p63)
- **Atlantis Submarine** (p63)

When it came to stones, Hawaiians were the ultimate recyclers. When the fort was dismantled in the 1850s, its stone blocks were used to build Hale Pa'ahao (p58), the new prison.

WO HING MUSEUM

ourpick Map p57; ☎ 661-5553; 858 Front St; admission $1; ☉ 10am-4pm

Built in 1912 as a meeting hall for the benevolent society Chee Kung Tong, this two-story temple provided Chinese immigrants with a place to preserve their cultural identity, celebrate festivities and socialize in their native tongue. After WWII Lahaina's ethnic Chinese population spread far and wide and the temple fell into decline. Now restored and turned into a cultural museum, it houses period photos, a ceremonial dancing-lion costume and a Taoist shrine.

Whatever you do, don't miss the tin-roof cookhouse out back, which holds a little theater showing fascinating films of Hawaii shot by Thomas Edison in 1898 and 1906, soon after he invented the motion-picture camera. These grainy B&W shots capture poignant images of old Hawaii, with *paniolo* (Hawaiian cowboys) herding cattle, cane workers in the fields and everyday street scenes. Take a look at the wall behind the screen to find a collection of opium bottles unearthed during an excavation of the grounds.

HALE PA'AHAO

Map p57; ☎ 667-1985; cnr Prison & Waine'e Sts; admission free; ☉ 10am-4pm Mon-Sat

A curious remnant of the whaling era, this stone-walled prison was built in 1852. Hale Pa'ahao (Stuck-in-Irons House) looks much like it did 150 years ago. Inside one of the whitewashed cells, an 'old seadog' mannequin spouts an entertaining recorded description of 'life in this here calaboose.' Another cell displays a list of arrests for the year 1855. The top three offenses were drunkenness (330 arrests), adultery and fornication (111), and 'furious riding' (89). There's no record of how much of that furious riding might have been done in a drunken state! Other wayward transgressions of the day included profanity, lascivious conduct, aiding deserting sailors and drinking 'awa (kava).

BALDWIN HOUSE

Map p57; ☎ 661-3262; 696 Front St; adult/family $3/5; ☉ 10am-4pm

The oldest Western-style building in Lahaina, the Baldwin House was erected in

Wo Hing Museum

GREG ELMS

1834 by Reverend Dwight Baldwin, a missionary doctor. It served as both his home and Lahaina's first medical clinic. The coral and rock walls are a hefty 24in thick, which keeps the house cool year-round. The exterior walls are now plastered over, but you can get a sense of how they originally appeared by looking at the Masters' Reading Room next door.

Think your flight to Hawaii was long? It took the Baldwins 161 days to get here from their native Connecticut. These early missionaries traveled neither fast nor light, and the house still holds the collection of china and furniture they brought with them around the Horn. Also on display are some fine Hawaiian quilts and period clothing. The admission fee includes a tour by well-versed docents.

WAINE'E (WAIOLA) CHURCH
Map p54; 535 Waine'e St

The first stone church in Hawaii, Waine'e Church was built in 1832 and cursed with a run of bad luck. In 1858 the belfry collapsed. In 1894 royalists, enraged that the minister supported Hawaii's annexation, torched the church to the ground. A second church, built to replace the original, burned in 1947, and the third was blown away in a storm a few years later. One might get the impression that the old Hawaiian gods didn't take kindly to the house of this foreign deity! The fourth version, now renamed Waiola Church, has been standing its ground since 1953 and still holds regular Sunday services.

The adjacent cemetery holds as much intrigue as the church. Here lie several notables, including Governor Hoapili, who ordered the original church built; Reverend William Richards, Lahaina's first missionary; and Queen Ke'opuolani, wife of Kamehameha the Great and the mother of kings Kamehameha II and III.

LIBRARY GROUNDS
Map p57; 680 Wharf St

History doesn't exist just in books at the Lahaina Public Library (p55). Although they don't reveal themselves at first glance, the grounds here hold a cluster of historic sites. The library yard was once a royal taro field, where Kamehameha III toiled in the mud to instill in his subjects the dignity of labor.

On the ocean side of the library sat the first Western-style building in Hawaii, the **Brick Palace**, erected by Kamehameha I around 1800 so he could keep watch on arriving ships. Despite the name, this 'palace' was a simple two-story structure built by a pair of ex-convicts from Botany Bay. All that remains today is the excavated foundation.

Walk to the nearby shoreline to see the **Hauola Stone**, a chair-shaped rock that the ancient Hawaiians believed emitted healing powers to those who sat upon it. To spot this water-worn stone, look to the right as you face the ocean – it's just above the water's surface, the middle of three lava stones. In the 14th and 15th centuries royal women sat on the stone while giving birth to the next generation of chiefs and royalty.

About 100ft to the south stands the **Lahaina Lighthouse**, the site of the first lighthouse in the Pacific. Commissioned in 1840 to aid whaling ships pulling into the harbor, the lighthouse cast a beam fueled by sperm-whale oil. The current structure dates from 1916.

HALE KAHIKO
Map p57; Lahaina Center, 900 Front St; admission free; 🕑 9am-6pm

Hale Kahiko authentically replicates part of an ancient Hawaiian village. The location at the back of a shopping center isn't without its irony, but the site nonetheless offers an insightful glimpse of Hawaiian life before Western development swept the landscape.

The three thatched *hale* (houses) here were hand-constructed true to the period using ohia-wood posts, native pili grass and coconut-fiber lashings. The grounds are planted in native plants that Hawaiians relied upon for food and medicine. Each

---

Top Picks

HISTORICAL HIGHLIGHTS
- Old Lahaina Courthouse (p56)
- Baldwin House (p58)
- Hale Pa'ahao (p58)
- Wo Hing Museum (p58)
- Hale Kahiko (p59)

LAHAINA

Island Insights

hale had a different function: one served as family sleeping quarters, one as a men's eating house and the third as a workshop where women made tapa (a coarse cloth made from pounded bark). Inside you'll find gourd containers, woven baskets and other essentials of Hawaiian life.

HALE PA'I
Off Map p54; ☎ 667-7040; 980 Lahainaluna Rd; admission by donation; ◷ 10am-4pm Mon-Fri

This cottage, known as Hale Pa'i, housed Hawaii's first printing press. Although its primary mission was making the Bible available to Hawaiians, the press also produced other works, including the first Hawaiian botany book and, in 1834, Hawaii's first newspaper. So heavily used was the original Ramage press that it wore out in the 1850s, but several of the items printed from it are still on display.

Should you want to try your hand as a 19th-century pressman, a replica of the original equipment can be used to hand-press your own copy of a page from the first Hawaiian primer. Reprints of amusing 'Temperance Maps' ($5), drawn by an early missionary to illustrate the perils of drunkenness, make unusual souvenirs.

Hale Pa'i is at the side of Lahainaluna High School, 1.5 miles east of Honoapi'ilani Hwy at the end of Lahainaluna Rd. It's wise to call in advance: the press is staffed by volunteers, so the hours can be a bit iffy.

LAHAINA JODO MISSION
Map p54; 12 Ala Moana St; admission free

Take time for a meditative moment at this Buddhist mission, where a 12ft-high bronze Buddha sits serenely in the courtyard looking across the Pacific toward its Japanese homeland. Cast in Kyoto, the Buddha is the largest of its kind outside Japan and was installed here in 1968 to celebrate the centennial of Japanese immigration to Hawaii. The grounds also hold a 90ft pagoda and a whopping 3-ton temple bell, which is rung 11 times each evening at 8pm. Inside the temple are priceless Buddhist paintings by Haijin Iwasaki.

Across the road is the long **Mala Wharf**, constructed in the 1920s to allow inter-island ferries to land passengers directly ashore. It never made the grade. Rough seas prevented the ferries from pulling up alongside the pier, forcing them to continue shuttling passengers across the shallows of Lahaina Harbor in small boats. The crumbling wharf is now closed, although Mala does have a launch ramp for small boats nearby.

ACTIVITIES

Lahaina is not known for its beaches, which are generally shallow and rocky. For swimming and snorkeling, head up the coast to neighboring Ka'anapali (p80). For boat tours, whale watching and other cruises, see p63.

Diving & Snorkeling

Dive boats leave from Lahaina Harbor, offering dives geared for all levels.

Lahaina's waves are tops for learning to surf

Home-grown **Lahaina Divers** (Map p57; ☎ 667-7496, 800-998-3483; www.lahainadivers.com; 143 Dickenson St; 2-tank dives from $120; ⏰ 8am-8pm), Maui's first PADI five-star center, offers a full range of dives, from advanced night dives to 'discover scuba' dives for newbies. The latter goes out to a reef thick with green sea turtles and makes a great intro to diving.

Maui Dive Shop (Map p54; ☎ 661-5388, 800-542-3483; www.mauidiveshop.com; Lahaina Cannery Mall, 1221 Honoapi'ilani Hwy; 2-tank dives from $130; ⏰ 8am-9pm) is another reliable full-service operation with a dive geared for everyone.

If you prefer a shore dive to a ship dive, gear up with **Pacific Dive** (Map p57; ☎ 667-5331; www.pacificdive.com; 150 Dickenson St; shore dives from $60; ⏰ 8am-5pm). Pacific Dive also rents snorkel gear for just $5 a day.

Surfing

Never surfed before? Lahaina is a great place to learn, with first-class instructors, gentle waves and ideal conditions for beginners. The section of shoreline known as **Lahaina Breakwall** (Map p54), north of Kamehameha Iki Park, is a favorite spot for novices. Surfers also take to the waters just offshore from Launiupoko Beach Park (p77).

Several places in Lahaina offer surfing lessons. Most guarantee you'll be able to ride a wave after a two-hour lesson or the class is free. Rates vary depending upon the number of people in the class and the length of the lesson, but for a two-hour

lesson expect to pay about $65 in a small group or $150 for a private lesson.

our pick **Goofy Foot Surf School** (Map p54; ☎ 244-9283; www.goofyfootsurfschool.com; 505 Front St; ⏰ 7am-9pm Mon-Sat) does a fine job of combining fundamentals with fun. In addition to lessons, it runs daylong surf camps and rents boards to experienced surfers.

Also highly recommended is Nancy Emerson, who was winning international surfing contests by the time she was 14. **Nancy Emerson's School of Surfing** (Map p54; ☎ 244-7873; www.mauisurfclinics.com; 505 Front St; ⏰ 8am-5pm) is the oldest surfing school on the island.

Besides honing a fine reputation for its instruction, **Royal Hawaiian Surf Academy** (Map p57; ☎ 276-7873; 117 Prison St; ⏰ 7:30am-5pm) has the coolest T-shirts.

Yoga

If it's time to stretch and breathe deeply, bring your mat to **Bikram Yoga Lahaina** (Map p57; ☎ 661-6828; www.bikramyoga.com; Lahaina Center, 900 Front St; class $16; ⏰ schedule varies). Classes include a daily morning session at 8am (9am Sunday).

Tennis

Public tennis courts are found at **Lahaina Civic Center** (off Map p54) and **Malu'uluolele Park** (Map p57). Both have lights to enable night playing.

GREG ELMS

WALKING TOUR

Chockablock with historic sites, Lahaina just begs a stroll.

❶ **BANYAN TREE SQUARE (p56)** Check out Hawaii's coolest tree, investigate the **Old Lahaina Courthouse (p56)** and **Fort Ruins (p56)**, and browse the harbor sights. Quirkiest are the four waterfront cannons raised from an 1816 shipwreck that in a comical twist now point at Lahaina's small-boat harbor, which is jam-packed with sunset sailboats and windjammers.

❷ **HOLY INNOCENTS' EPISCOPAL CHURCH** (561 Front St) This site was once a summer home of Queen Lili'uokalani, Hawaii's last monarch, so it's only fitting the church interior reflects a Hawaiian motif. The altar is made of native koa and paintings depict a Hawaiian Madonna, an outrigger canoe and Hawaiian farmers harvesting taro.

❸ **HALE PIULA** (Front St) This foundation is all that remains of Lahaina's attempt at a royal palace, which was abandoned in mid-construction because Kamehameha III preferred sleeping in a Hawaiian-style thatched house. The site, fronted by **Kamehameha Iki Park**, is used by local woodcarvers to build traditional outrigger canoes.

❹ **MALU'ULUOLELE PARK** (Front St) In ancient times this site held a pond-encircled island, Moku'ula, that was home to kings and the site of an ornate burial chamber. In 1918 it was landfilled to make a county park containing ball fields, tennis courts and barely a hint of its fascinating past.

❺ **WAINE'E CHURCH (p59)** Stroll the church's old cemetery, where several of the most important figures of 19th-century Maui are buried. Evocative inscriptions and photo cameos adorn many of the old tombstones.

❻ **HALE PA'AHAO (p60)** You'll find one of Lahaina's more notorious sights on the corner of – guess where – Prison St. Take a peek into old prison cells where drunken whalers once served time for debauchery.

WALK FACTS

Start Banyan Tree Sq
End Pioneer Inn
Distance 1.5 miles
Duration Two to three hours

LAHAINA WALKING TOUR

❼ **MARIA LANAKILA CHURCH & SEAMEN'S CEMETERY** (712 Waine'e St) Maui's first Catholic church dates from 1846 and contains an impressive tile-work portrait of Father Damien. The adjacent cemetery, despite its name, has only one seaman's tombstone identified. However, records from ship logs indicate many whaling-era sailors were buried here.

❽ **MASTERS' READING ROOM (p59)** This was an officers' club during the whaling heyday, providing captains with a watch on potential rabble-rousing in the nearby harbor. This coral-block building and the adjacent **Baldwin House (p58)** now belong to the Lahaina Restoration Foundation, which oversees Lahaina's historical sites.

❾ **LIBRARY GROUNDS (p59)** Cross the road to return to the harbor, stopping to view the **Brick Palace (p59)** and the **Haeula Stone (p59)**, waterfront sights at the rear of the library.

❿ **PIONEER INN (p67)** Cap off your tour with a cold drink at this bustling harbor-front landmark. For half a century the veranda-wrapped building was Lahaina's only hotel; Jack London slept here. Despite the whaling-era atmosphere, it was built in 1901 after the whaling days passed, but nobody seems to notice or care.

TOURS
At Sea
OCEAN TOURS

Lahaina Harbor is chock full of catamarans and other vessels catering to the tourist trade. You'll find scores of day cruises, from whale-watchers and glass-bottomed boats to daylong sails to Lana'i.

Atlantis Submarine (☎ 667-2224, 800-548-6262; www.atlantisadventures.com; adult/child under 12 $90/45) Visit a world usually reserved for divers aboard this 65ft sub that dives to a depth of 130ft to see coral, tropical fish and the sunken *Carthaginian*, a sailing brig that played a leading role in the 1965 movie *Hawaii*. Tours depart from 9am to 2pm from Lahaina Harbor.

our pick Pacific Whale Foundation (Map p57; ☎ 879-8811, 800-942-5311; www.pacificwhale.org; 612 Front St; adult/child 7-12 from $32/16; ⏱ 7am-6pm) The well-versed naturalists on this nonprofit foundation's cruises are the island's best. Several types of trips, all focusing on Maui's spectacular marine environment, leave from Lahaina Harbor. Immensely popular are the whale-watching cruises, which depart several times a day in winter. In the unlikely event you don't spot whales, your next trip is free – and kids under six years are always free.

Reefdancer (☎ 667-2133; Lahaina Harbor; adult/child 6-12 per 1hr $33/20, 1½hr $45/25; ⏱ departures 10am-2:15pm) This glass-bottomed boat has a submerged lower deck lined with viewing windows. The views aren't as varied as on a submarine but the underwater scenes are still eye candy and you won't feel claustrophobic.

our pick Trilogy Excursions (Map p57; ☎ 661-4743, 888-225-6284; www.sailtrilogy.com; 180 Lahainaluna Rd; adult/child 3-15 $190/95) This family-run operation specializes in personable eco-friendly catamaran tours that let you get your feet wet. The early (6am to 4pm) trip from Lahaina to Lana'i's Hulopo'e Beach includes a barbecue lunch and snorkeling time. Or catch the 10am boat that adds on dinner and sails back to Lahaina at sunset. In winter there's whale watching along the way and you can spot spinner dolphins year-round. Save 10% by booking online.

COCKTAIL & DINNER CRUISES

The distinction between a cocktail cruise and a whale-watching boat is a fluid one. Pacific Whale Foundation (at left), for instance, offers a sunset cocktail whale-watch cruise. And the following boats also book seasonal whale-watching excursions. Departure times depend on the season.

America II (☎ 667-2195; www.sailingonmaui.com; Slip 5, Lahaina Harbor; sunset sail adult/child under 12 $40/20) No cocktails and only token snacks, but this slick racing yacht sailed in the famed America's Cup. If the wind is blowing, your cruise really feels like an adventure. In winter cruises are timed to include whale watching.

Lahaina Cruise Company (☎ 667-6165; www.the lahainacruisecompany.com; Slip 3, Lahaina Harbor; cocktail cruise $50) If you tend to get seasick, consider this one. The company's 70ft-long *Kaulana* is the largest and most stable catamaran in the harbor. The sunset cocktail cruise features a spread of appetizers, live music and dancing.

Scotch Mist II (☎ 661-0386; www.scotchmistsailing charters.com; Slip 2, Lahaina Harbor; adult/child under 12 $50/30) They only serve champagne and Maui potato chips on this sunset cruise, but you're really here for the beautiful boat. She's a 50ft sailing yacht that's fast and seductive. Book in advance as the boat carries just two dozen passengers per sail. Snorkel cruises are also available seasonally.

Spirit of Lahaina (☎ 662-4477; www.spiritoflahaina .com; Slip 4, Lahaina Harbor; dinner cruise adult/child $76/45, cocktail cruise adult/child $55/33) Unlike some other dinner cruises, this power catamaran doesn't skimp on the buffet. The cocktail cruise includes a hula show, appetizers and drinks.

On Land

Maui Segway Tours (Map p57; ☎ 662-0888; www. mauisegwaytours.com; 640 Front St; 2hr tour $79; ⏱ 8am-5pm) Geek alert: sightseeing tours via a Segway scooter leave opposite Banyan Tree Sq, go as far as Mala Wharf and take in Lahaina's historical sights. Ah, c'mon, you know you've always wanted to try one...

Sugar Cane Train (Map p57; ☎ 667-6851, 800-499-2307; www.mauisteamtrain.com; 975 Limahana Pl; adult/child 3-12 $22/15; ⏱ 10am-5pm) The restored century-old steam train that once carried cane from the fields to Lahaina's sugar mill now carries tourists on a 30-minute ride between Lahaina and Ka'anapali, departing from Lahaina Station. The ride's a bit pokey and there's not really much to see, but kids will love it and steam-train buffs will no doubt want to hop aboard, too.

FESTIVALS & EVENTS

Lahaina's top festivals draw huge crowds, with Front St closed to traffic during these events. For updated details on Lahaina festivities, contact the **LahainaTown Action Committee** (☎ 667-9194; www.visitlahaina.com).

Chinese New Year On a weekend between mid-January and mid-February, Lahaina welcomes the lunar new year with a street festival on Front St, complete with colorful lion dances, martial-arts demos and an explosion of firecrackers.

Ocean Arts Festival The humpback whale migration is the theme of these festivities celebrated on a weekend in mid-March at Banyan Tree Sq with Hawaiian music, hula and games.

Banyan Tree Birthday Party Branch out a bit! Lahaina's favorite tree gets a two-day birthday party, complete with a frosted cake and a serenade by island musicians, plus piñatas for the *keiki* (children). It's held on the weekend closest to April 24.

🕮 **ourpick** **International Festival of Canoes** (www .mauifestivalofcanoes.com) Maui's premier cultural event draws master carvers from around the Pacific to carve outrigger canoes. The whole log-to-launch process takes place right in the town center over two weeks in May, culminating with the Parade of Canoes down Front St and ceremonial launchings from Kamehameha Iki Park. Festivities include Hawaiian music and island grinds. Don't miss it.

King Kamehameha Celebration Traditionally dressed Hawaiian riders on horseback, marching bands and floral floats take to Front St to honor Kamehameha the Great on this public holiday in mid-June. A ceremony and arts festival follows at Banyan Tree Sq.

HALLOWEEN, LAHAINA STYLE

Lahaina is party central. So it's no surprise that by the 1990s its modest kiddie-oriented Halloween parade had boomed into an all-out blast. The event was rechristened 'Mardi Gras of the Pacific,' spiced up with elaborate floats and outrageous costumes, and promoted far and wide. It grew into Maui's biggest bash, attracting upwards of 30,000 revelers to the jam-packed Front St for the October 31 celebration. After island families complained that risqué attire and heavy drinking had made the festival unsuitable for children, organizers dropped the Mardi Gras title and ratcheted it back down a notch. Consider it a fine-tuning of sorts. It seems to have struck a happy medium – these days about 20,000 partygoers come out for 'Halloween in Lahaina,' a street festival of music, dance and costume contests.

ART NIGHT

Art aficionados, this one's for you. Every Friday night is 'Art Night' in Lahaina. Dozens of galleries have openings, some with entertainment, wine and hors d'oeuvres. It's an unbeatable time to stroll the Front St art scene, meet artists and nibble a little cheese. The action's from 7pm to 10pm and it's all free – that is, unless you see a treasure that catches your fancy.

Fourth of July Bands perform tunes on the lawn of the public library from 5pm and fireworks light up the sky over the harbor at 8pm.

A Taste of Lahaina & Best of Island Music Festival At Maui's biggest culinary blast, held on a weekend in mid-September, the island's top chefs strut their stuff, offering tastings of their signature dishes. In addition to food booths, there are cooking demonstrations and wine tastings. And it's not just a foodies' fest. Music has come into its own in this annual event, attracting the island's best musicians and turning it into an upbeat party scene.

Halloween in Lahaina (p64) Front St morphs into a costumed street festival on Halloween night. Forget parking; take a bus or taxi to this one.

Holiday Lighting of the Banyan Tree Lahaina lights Hawaii's biggest tree on the first weekend in December with thousands of colorful lights, accompanied by music, carolers and a craft show. And, of course, Santa shows up for the *keiki*.

EATING

Rev up the taste buds. This is the finest dining scene on Maui. Whether you're looking for local grinds or five-toque nouvelle cuisine, it's all here. One thing to keep in mind: so many folks staying in Ka'anapali pour into Lahaina at dinnertime that the traffic jams up, so give yourself extra time and call ahead to make reservations.

THE BAKERY   Bakery $
Map p54; ☎ 667-9062; 991 Limahana Pl; snacks $1.50-5.50; ☼ 5:30am-1pm Mon-Fri, to noon Sat
It may be in a nondescript industrial park but once you walk through the rickety screen door this is one sweet place. Here you'll find sinful pecan sticky buns, flaky pastries and heaped sandwiches made to order. Don't bother with the lackluster salads – veggies aren't a specialty here.

The chef's table at Lahaina Store Grille & Oyster Bar
KENT HWANG

ALOHA MIXED PLATE
Hawaiian $

ourpick Map p54; ☎ 661-3322; 1285 Front St; plates $4-14; 🕑 10:30am-10pm

Forget tourist traps. This is the Hawaii you came to find: friendly, open-air and right on the beach. The food's first-rate, the prices affordably local. For a thoroughly Hawaiian experience, order the Ali'i Plate, packed with *laulau, kalua* pig, *lomilomi* salmon, poi and *haupia* (see the food glossary, p265) and, of course, two scoop rice. On your next visit tackle the awesome coconut prawns.

SUNRISE CAFÉ
Café $

Map p57; ☎ 661-8558; 693A Front St; mains $6-11; 🕑 6am-6pm

The dawn patrol loves this cozy mom-and-pop hole-in-the-wall near the harbor. Breakfasts have pizzazz: smoked salmon with eggs, Maui onions and lemon caper hollandaise, or maybe a croissant with cheese and fresh fruit. Lunch covers the gamut of gourmet sandwiches to roast beef plates.

BRADDA TIKIS
Shave Ice $

Map p57; ☎ 661-9999; 884 Front St; shave ice $4, plate lunches $8-10; 🕑 9:30am-9:30pm

Search out this hip eatery tucked into a quiet courtyard to find Lahaina's best shave ice in cool tropical flavors like piña colada, mango and coconut. There's also an attached grill that sweeps in surfers with its tasty fish kebab and pineapple fried rice plate lunches.

PENNE PASTA CAFÉ
Italian $$

Map p57; ☎ 661-6633; 180 Dickenson St; mains $7-17; 🕑 11am-9:30pm Mon-Fri, 5-9pm Sat & Sun

OK, there's no view, but that's the key to this place. To keep prices down, renowned chef Mark Ellman, who also operates upscale Mala, chose a side-street location off the main drag and streamlined the menu to pastas, pizzas and sandwiches. That said, the food's anything but boring: garlic *'ahi* atop a bed of pesto linguine, roasted squash with almonds, warm focaccia. And, of course, creamy tiramisu for dessert.

COOL CAT CAFÉ
Café $$

Map p57; ☎ 667-0908; Wharf Cinema Center, 658 Front St; mains $9-15; 🕑 11am-10pm

The burgers may have tacky names – like the Marilyn (chili hot) – but they're made fresh daily with 100% Angus beef and rate as the best on Maui. The view overlooking Banyan Tree Sq isn't bad either.

THAI CHEF
Thai $$

Map p57; ☎ 667-2814; Old Lahaina Center, 880 Front St; mains $10-16; 🕑 lunch Mon-Fri, dinner daily

Hidden in the back of an aging shopping center, this place looks like a dive from the outside, but the food's incredible. Start with the fragrant ginger coconut soup and the fresh summer rolls and then move on to savory curries that explode with flavor. It's a BYOB place – pick up a bottle from the nearby Foodland.

SMOKEHOUSE
BBQ GRILL
Comfort Food $$

Map p57; ☎ 667-7005; 930 Waine'e St; mains $7-20; 11:30am-9pm Mon-Fri, 3-9pm Sat & Sun

Kiawe-smoked meats slow-cooked to perfection are the specialty at this casual family-run joint. The tender, meaty baby-back ribs are the obvious first choice, but Smokehouse offers more than just ribs. The *kalua* pork sandwiches are also killer and the warm cornbread served with mac-nut honey is not to be missed.

LAHAINA FISH CO
Seafood $$

Map p57; ☎ 661-3472; 831 Front St; lunch $9-15, dinner $13-29; 11am-10pm

Sit on the deck above crashing waves and enjoy some of Lahaina's freshest fish. There's no skimping on the serving size either, so it's little wonder this place consistently packs a crowd. There are lots of fish preparations to choose from, but if you want to walk away with the best value, order the fish and chips for just $13. Come early for a good table at sunset.

LAHAINA STORE GRILLE
& OYSTER BAR
Seafood $$$

Map p57; ☎ 661-9090; 744 Front St; mains $9-30; 11am-10pm

The crowd's as fashionable as the food at this stylish restaurant and oyster bar serving briny delights from the sea. Oysters take on all sorts of incarnations, from fresh on the half shell to shooters in tequila. The house *poke* is another knockout. Don't like it raw? The exhibition kitchen here grills things up nicely too.

KIMO'S
Hawaiian $$$

Map p57; ☎ 661-4811; 845 Front St; lunch $8-13, dinner $17-30; 11am-10:30pm

At this Hawaiian-style standby, you'll find reliable food, a superb water view and a family-friendly setting. Dishes include fresh fish, oversized prime rib cuts and good ol' teriyaki chicken. And you get your money's worth: all dinners come with Caesar salad and warm carrot muffins. Lunch ranges far and wide, from sandwiches and salads to catch of the day.

MALA
Eclectic $$$

Map p54; ☎ 667-9394; 1307 Front St; mains $15-32; 11am-10pm Mon-Fri, 9am-10pm Sat, 9am-9pm Sun

Mediterranean and Pacific influences fuse brilliantly at Mark Ellman's signature bistro. Sophisticated tapas include a tasty lamb tzatziki and seared tombo bruschetta. Anything with fish is a sure pleaser, and everyone raves over the decadent 'caramel miranda' dessert. The best time to come is at sunset, when you can watch turtles feeding in the water below you, and the tiki torches on the lanai add a romantic touch.

🦐 PACIFIC'O
Hawaii Regional $$$

Map p54; ☎ 667-4341; 505 Front St; lunch $13-16, dinner $26-38; 11:30am-4pm & 5:30-10pm

Contemporary cuisine with added bling jumps off the menu at this chic seaside restaurant. The food is bold and innovative – where else can you try a crispy coconut roll with seared scallops and lime pesto? Lunch is a tamer affair, with salads and sandwiches, but the same in-your-face ocean view. Live dinnertime jazz on the weekends cranks the hip atmosphere up a notch.

🦐 I'O
Hawaii Regional $$$$

our pick Map p54; ☎ 661-8422; 505 Front St; mains $28-38; dinner

If you're looking for Lahaina's best fine dining in a waterfront setting, stop the search here. I'O is the handiwork of Maui's most acclaimed chef, James McDonald. The nouveau Hawaii cuisine includes scrumptious creations like seared fresh catch in lobster curry, island-raised filet mignon with tempura Maui onions and guava-glazed coconut cheesecake. McDonald is so obsessed with freshness that he started a farm in Kula to grow his own veggies. There's a fierce martini menu, too.

LAHAINA GRILL
Hawaii Regional $$$$

Map p57; ☎ 667-5117; 127 Lahainaluna Rd; mains $28-45; dinner

Beautiful people, beautiful food – this is Lahaina's most sophisticated dining scene. The menu relies on fresh local ingredients given innovative twists. Seafood standouts include the Maui onion seared 'ahi served with vanilla-bean jasmine rice and the Big Island prawns in roasted Kula corn salsa.

Although the food gets rave reviews, seating is limited and service can be rushed, so be prepared to hold on to your plates.

Need to stock up? **Foodland** (Map p57; ☎ 661-0975; Old Lahaina Center, 880 Front St; ☺ 6am-midnight) and **Safeway** (Map p54; ☎ 667-4392; Lahaina Cannery Mall, 1221 Honoapi'ilani Hwy; ☺ 24hr) supermarkets both have everything you'll need for self-catering, as well as good delis.

DRINKING

PIONEER INN
Map p57; ☎ 661-3636; 658 Wharf St; ☺ 11am-10pm
You couldn't be more in the middle of the action at this century-old landmark overlooking the harbor. With its whaling-era atmosphere and breezy veranda, it makes for great people watching. The afternoon happy hour (3pm to 6pm) keeps it light on the wallet.

ALOHA MIXED PLATE
Map p54; ☎ 661-3322; 1285 Front St; ☺ 10:30am-10pm
This beachside shack at the north side of town is pure fun. Let the sea breeze whip through your hair while lingering over a heady mai tai – come between 2pm and 6pm and they're half price. It really gets atmospheric after sunset, when you can listen to Old Lahaina Luau's music beating next door.

LAHAINA COOLERS
Map p57; ☎ 661-7082; 180 Dickenson St; ☺ 8am-2am
An eclectic open-air café, Lahaina Coolers attracts the thirtysomething crowd who come to mingle, munch *pupu* (snacks) and sip wine coolers. As the town's late-night bar, it's the place to head after the dance floor has emptied.

COOL CAT CAFÉ
Map p57; ☎ 667-0908; Wharf Cinema Center, 658 Front St; ☺ 11am-10pm
The breezy open-air setting and cool '50s decor would make Elvis feel right at home. Whether you're looking for fountain drinks or hard-hitting cocktails, this is the perfect spot to wet the whistle as the sun sets over the harbor. Live music nightly.

BAMBOO SPORTS BAR
Map p54; ☎ 667-0361; 505 Front St; ☺ 11am-2am
This self-acclaimed place 'where locals hang loose' is Lahaina's version of a *Cheers* bar. Visitors and locals alike come to watch sports on the big-screen TV, shoot a game of pool and feast on sushi.

FRONT STREET GRILL
Map p57; ☎ 662-3003; 672 Front St; ☺ 11am-10pm
This balcony bar near the harbor is a hit with young sailors and a college-age crowd who come to listen to live music in the afternoon and have a few cold ones.

Grab a drink at the landmark Pioneer Inn

GREG ELMS

LAHAINA

ENTERTAINMENT

After the sun drops down, Lahaina springs to life. Front St is the center of the action. Check the entertainment listings in the free weeklies *Lahaina News* and *MauiTime Weekly*, or just stroll the streets. Typically, nightspots in Lahaina don't have a cover charge unless there's a big-name performer. In addition to places listed here, many of Lahaina's waterfront restaurants have live music at dinnertime.

Live Music

MOOSE McGILLICUDDY'S

Map p57; ☎ 667-7758; 844 Front St

This vibrant bar-cum-restaurant attracts a rock-on party crowd, out to drink and dance till they drop. With two dance floors, Moose jams with live music Friday to Sunday and with DJs nightly. Happy hour (3pm to 6pm) features piña coladas for a mere $2.

MULLIGANS AT THE WHARF

Map p57; ☎ 661-8881; Wharf Cinema Center, 658 Front St; ⏰ 11am-midnight

Lahaina's friendly Irish pub has live music – typically Irish, folk or Hawaiian – every night of the week. Want to play your own tunes? Swing by at 10pm on Wednesday, when it's open mic.

HARD ROCK CAFÉ

Map p57; ☎ 667-7400; Lahaina Center, 900 Front St

There's not much that's Hawaiian about this rock-themed chain restaurant, but it does get jiggy to the island's best reggae on Monday from 10pm.

CHEESEBURGER IN PARADISE

Map p57; ☎ 661-4855; 811 Front St

Just follow your ears to this energetic

open-air place on the waterfront. No surprise, the music's Jimmy Buffett–style, and the setting is pure tropics, from the rattan decor to the frosty margaritas. Live soft rock from 4:30pm to 10:30pm nightly.

LONGHI'S

Map p57; ☎ 667-2288; 888 Front St

With its art deco decor and koa-wood dance floor, this upscale Italian restaurant attracts a well-heeled crowd with live jazz and dancing on Friday nights.

BJ'S

Map p57; ☎ 661-0700; 730 Front St

Live music is in store from 7:30pm to 10pm nightly at this ocean-view pizza joint. Incidentally, this was where the legendary 1970s Blue Max club partied.

Luau, Hula & Theater

When it comes to hula, Lahaina offers the real deal. Its two luau have few rivals anywhere in Hawaii and catching one is a sure bet to highlight a vacation. You can also enjoy free hula shows performed by children's hula troupes at **Lahaina Cannery Mall** (Map p54; 1221 Honoapi'ilani Hwy) at 1pm Saturday and Sunday and 7pm Tuesday and Thursday, and at **Hale Kahiko** (p59) at 2:30pm Wednesday and 3:30pm Friday.

OLD LAHAINA LUAU

ourpick Map p54; ☎ 667-1998; www.oldlahaina luau.com; 1251 Front St; adult/child 2-12 $92/62; ⏰ 5:15-8:15pm Oct-Mar, 5:45-8:45pm Apr-Sep

No other luau on Maui even comes close to matching this one for its authenticity, presentation and all-around aloha. The hula troupe and music are first-rate and the feast is outstanding, with high-quality Hawaiian fare and none of the long lines you'll find at a resort-hotel luau. It's held on the beach at the north side of town. One caveat: it often sells out a month in advance, so book ahead.

🌺 FEAST AT LELE

ourpick Map p54; ☎ 667-5353; www.feastatlele .com; 505 Front St; adult/child 2-12 $110/80; ⏰ 5:30-8:30pm Oct-Mar, 6-9pm Apr-Sep

Food takes center stage at this intimate Polynesian luau held on the beach in front of I'O restaurant. Dance performances in Hawaiian, Maori, Tahitian and Samoan

Growing in popularity, Maui-grown coffee has a rich and earthy flavor   NED FRIARY

styles are each matched to a food course. With the Hawaiian music, you're served *kalua* pork and taro; with the Maori, duck salad with poha berry dressing; and so on. A true gourmet feast.

'ULALENA
Map p57; ☎ 661-9913; www.ulalena.com; Old Lahaina Center, 880 Front St; adult $60-100, child 3-12 $40-70; ⏱ 6:30-8pm Mon-Sat

This Cirque du Soleil–style extravaganza has its home at the 700-seat Maui Theatre. The theme is Hawaiian history and storytelling; the medium is modern dance, brilliant stage sets, acrobatics and elaborate costumes. All in all, an entertaining, high-energy performance.

SHOPPING

Classy boutiques, tacky souvenir shops and flashy art galleries run thick along Front St. You'll find lots of shops under one roof at the **Wharf Cinema Center** (Map p57; ☎ 661-8748; 658 Front St) and **Lahaina Cannery Mall** (Map p54; ☎ 661-5304; 1221 Honoapi'ilani Hwy).

LAHAINA ARTS SOCIETY
our pick Map p57; ☎ 661-0111; 648 Wharf St

A nonprofit collective representing nearly 100 island artists, this extensive gallery covers two floors in the Old Lahaina Courthouse. Works range from avant-garde paintings to traditional weavings. Many of Maui's best-known artists got their start

here, and there are some gems among the collection, so it's the perfect place to start any art browsing.

🐾 MAUIGROWN COFFEE
Map p57; ☎ 661-2728; 277 Lahainaluna Rd; ⏱ 6:30am-5pm Mon-Sat

This shop next to the old sugar mill's smokestack sells West Maui's newest homegrown crop, Ka'anapali Estate coffee. Buy it by the pound or test it by the cup. Curious to see what a coffee tree looks like? Just wander out to the north side of the shop.

LAHAINA PRINTSELLERS
Map p54; ☎ 667-5815; 505 Front St

Hawaii's largest purveyor of antique maps, including fascinating originals dating back to the voyages of Captain Cook. The shop also sells affordable reproductions if you don't have a large wad of cash on you.

VILLAGE GIFTS & FINE ARTS
Map p57; ☎ 661-5199; cnr Front & Dickenson Sts

This one-room shop in the Masters' Reading Room sells prints, wooden bowls and glasswork, with a portion of the proceeds supporting the Lahaina Restoration Foundation.

Other recommendations:
Aloha Shirt Museum (Map p57; ☎ 661-7172; 780 Front St) Quality new (from $25) and vintage (up to $4500) aloha shirts.
Crazy Shirts (Map p57; ☎ 661-4775; 865 Front St)

Stylish Hawaii-motif T-shirts for sale and cool whaling-era artifacts for browsing.

Lahaina Scrimshaw (Map p57; ☎ 669-0018; 845A Front St) Contemporary and antique artwork on fossil walrus teeth, mammoth ivory and bone.

Maui Hands (Map p57; ☎ 667-9898; 612 Front St) Excellent selection of island-made crafts.

Needlework Shop (Map p54; ☎ 662-8554; 505 Front St) Hawaiian quilt kits (free quilting lessons) and gorgeous tropical print fabrics.

Quiksilver Boardriders Club (Map p57; ☎ 661-3505; 849 Front St) Threads for surfers and wannabes in hip motifs.

Serendipity (Map p57; ☎ 667-7070; 752 Front St) Brilliant sarongs for women; several notches above the competition.

SLEEPING

Despite the throngs of tourists filling its streets, Lahaina is surprisingly sparse on places to stay. All of West Maui's resort hotels are to the north, where the beaches are better. On the plus side, Lahaina's accommodations tend to be small and cozy. The nearest campground (p78) is in Olowalu, 5 miles south of town. See p79 for midrange B&Bs between Lahaina and Ka'anapali.

MAKAI INN   Condo $$
Map p54; ☎ 662-3200; www.makaiinn.net; 1415 Front St; r $100-175; (P) (💻)

This family-run place is a gem, albeit not a highly polished one. It's an older condo complex and the furnishings could use a bit more luster, but the oceanside setting shines. The tropical garden in the central courtyard would be the envy of any top-end resort. All units have full kitchens and louvered windows to catch the breeze. The price difference largely reflects the distance from the ocean, but even the cheapest rooms are a mere stone's throw from the water.

LAHAINA INN   Boutique Hotel $$
Map p57; ☎ 661-0577, 800-669-3444; www .lahainainn.com; 127 Lahainaluna Rd; r $145-165; (P) (💥)

Crazy Shirts founder Rick Ralston spent millions painstakingly restoring this century-old streetside inn. With just a dozen rooms it's now one of Maui's most acclaimed boutique hotels. The charm of an earlier era – hardwood floors, hand-stitched Hawaiian quilts and wooden rocking chairs – offers a classic touch beyond the imagination of any cookie-cutter resort. To keep the period ambience intact, guestrooms are sans TV and radio, but you'll find these in the guest lounge.

PIONEER INN   Independent Hotel $$
Map p57; ☎ 661-3636, 800-457-5457; www .pioneerinnmaui.com; 658 Wharf St; r $150-215; (💥) (🛒)

Between the ship figureheads and swinging saloon doors, this historic harborfront hotel packs so much whaling-era personality you almost expect Herman Melville to mosey in. While the common space abounds in character, the rooms are disappointingly bland and lacking water views. But heck, you're in the hub of Lahaina, so who's hanging out in a room?

PLANTATION INN   Boutique Hotel $$$
Map p57; ☎ 667-9225, 800-433-6815; www.the plantationinn.com; 174 Lahainaluna Rd; r incl breakfast $166-235, ste $255-280; (P) (💥) (🛒)

Central yet quiet, this plantation-style inn fuses period elegance with modern amenities. The guest rooms are decked out in frilly Victorian decor, with antique four-poster beds and matching upholstery and wallpaper. French doors open to spacious balustraded verandas. A hot tub and Lahaina's deepest swimming pool are in the garden courtyard.

LAHAINA SHORES   Condo $$$
Map p54; ☎ 661-3339, 800-642-6284; www .lahainashores.com; 475 Front St; studio/1br from $210/290; (P) (💥) (🛒)

Adjacent to some of Lahaina's hottest restaurants, this is the only oceanfront condo complex in central Lahaina to be operated hotel-style with a front desk and full services. The adjacent beach is a good place for beginner surfers and a venue for nighttime entertainment. All the units are roomy, and even the studios have full kitchen and lanai.

Other options:

Aina Nalu (Map p57; ☎ 667-9766, 800-688-7444; www.outrigger.com; 660 Waine'e St; studio/2br from $185/275; (P) (💻)) Sprawling nondescript apartment complex, though recent renovations and online deals can add up to good value.

ISLAND VOICES

NAME: KAREN CAMARA
OCCUPATION: PLEIN-AIR ARTIST; LAHAINA ARTS SOCIETY MEMBER
RESIDENCE: LAHAINA

What's it like being an artist on Maui? Everywhere I turn is a painting. The palette for Maui is so much more intense than anywhere else I've ever painted. It's very inspirational. The nice thing about being a plein-air artist on Maui is I can go all year round. And not only bright sunny days; I also paint the rain a lot. Being an outdoor painter, I'm prepared – I have my umbrella. It's a very satisfying lifestyle.

What are your favorite locations? I love Lahaina Harbor, all the sailboats. I'm inspired every time I look. Sometimes I paint right out the window here (from the Lahaina Arts Society gallery – p56). Another place I love dearly is Hana (p206). Hana is magical. My plein-air group has an outing there once a year. We stay in the funky Wai'anapanapa State Park (p198) cabins. That's as close as I ever come to camping. But it's good – we can all sling our paints around and feel comfortable.

What's the Lahaina Arts Society about? It's run by artists for artists. I love our mission statement: the emphasis on instilling a love for art in young people. Part of all our sales benefit our children's art and scholarship programs. We have kids' classes here, and one of the jail cells downstairs displays kids artwork.

How can visitors enjoy the Maui art scene? Every Wednesday my plein-air group (www .pleinairpaintersofhawaii.com) gets together to paint. We paint all over the place – in winter maybe Lahaina Harbor or Makena, the dry side of the Island. Usually anywhere from five people to 25 or more. Visitors are invited to come along, too, to join us in painting or just watch us paint. We get people from the mainland, from other islands. It's really casual. People bring lunch along and make a day of it. And the Lahaina Arts Society has all sorts of events: weekend art shows under the banyan tree and a big annual juried show in mid-December. There's always things for people to plug into.

Patey's Place (Map p57; ☎ 667-0999; www .accommodationshawaii.com; 761 Waine'e St; dm $25, r $55-80; P ☐) Very basic dorm beds. Skip the over-priced private rooms.
Penny's Place Inn Paradise (Map p54; ☎ 661-1068, 877-431-1235; www.pennysplace.net; 1440 Front St; r incl breakfast $98-148; P ⚡ ☐) Pleasant B&B rooms but in a busy location with traffic noise.

GETTING THERE & AWAY

The Honoapi'ilani Hwy (Hwy 30) connects Lahaina with Ka'anapali and points north, with Ma'alaea to the south and with Wailuku to the east. Ferries to Lana'i (p216) and Moloka'i (p228) dock at Lahaina Harbor.

GETTING AROUND
To/From the Airport

To get to Lahaina from the airport in Kahului, take Hwy 380 south to Hwy 30; the drive takes about 45 minutes. If you're not renting a car, **Executive Shuttle** (☎ 669-2300, 800-833-2303) provides the best deal on taxi service between Lahaina and the airport, charging $39 for one person, $45 for two and $4 more for each additional person.

LAHAINA

Lahaina's waterfront bustles with activity, day and night

GREG ELMS

Bicycle

For bike rentals head to **West Maui Cycles** (Map p54; ☎ 661-9005; 1087 Limahana Pl; per day $15-50; ☺ 9am-5pm Mon-Sat, 10am-4pm Sun), which has quality hybrid and mountain bikes, as well as cheaper cruisers that are fine for just kicking around town.

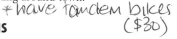

have tandem bikes ($30)

Bus

The **Maui Bus** (p289) connects Kahului and Lahaina ($1, one hour) with a stop at Ma'alaea, where connections can be made to Kihei and Wailea. Another route connects Lahaina and Ka'anapali ($1, 30 minutes). Both routes depart from the Wharf Cinema Center hourly from 6:30am to 8:30pm.

Car & Motorcycle

If it's got two wheels and a motor, you'll find it at **Aloha Toy Store** (Map p57; ☎ 662-0888;

640 Front St; ☺ 8am-5pm), which rents Vespa mopeds ($65 per day), Kawasaki classic 800 motorcycles ($119) and Harleys ($149), and even offers tours on Segways (p63).

Front St has free on-street parking, but there's always a line of cruising cars competing for spots. Your best bet is the large parking lot at the corner of Front and Prison Sts, where there's free public parking with a three-hour limit. There are also several private parking lots, averaging $8 per day, with the biggest one being Republic Parking on Dickenson St. Otherwise, park at one of the shopping centers and get your parking ticket validated for free by making a purchase.

Taxi

For a taxi in Lahaina, call **Ali'i Cab** (☎ 661-3688), **LA Taxi** (☎ 661-4545) or **Paradise Taxi** (☎ 661-4455).

WEST MAUI

Splash on suntan cream – you're going to the beach.
From showy Ka'anapali to exclusive Kapalua, West Maui rolls out one fabulous beach after another: pampering resort strands, private niches, scurry-down-the-cliff surfer haunts. When you've had enough splashy fun, turn your eyes away from the sea and you'll find amazing things on land as well. Those mountains looming inward hold adventures of their own, from serene hiking trails to heart-pounding ziplines. And if you're beginning to think West Maui is all about resort life, just wait till you see the remote north side, a tasty slice of old Hawaii with wild ocean vistas and untouched landscapes.

WEST MAUI
ITINERARIES

IN TWO DAYS *This leg: 8 miles*

❶ KA'ANAPALI BEACH (p80) There's no better way to begin than by jumping into the water at West Maui's hottest sand and sun spot. When you're up for a snorkel, swim toward Pu'u Keka'a and head for the tip of the rock, home to abundant fish and colorful coral.

❷ TERALANI SAILING (p82) Next, get a different angle on the sea and the sand by hopping aboard a catamaran for a motor-free cruise of the spectacular West Maui coast. Teralani's open bar goes down smoothly, too.

❸ KA'ANAPALI BEACH WALK (p82) Finish off your day by strolling this looooong and lovely beach, swinging by the **cliff-diving (p85)** and torch-lighting ceremony off Pu'u Keka'a and popping into the Ka'anapali Beach Hotel's **hula show (p85)** for an authentic slice of aloha. Top off your beach walk with a tropical drink at beachside **Leilani's (p84)**.

❹ GAZEBO (p90) You had a busy day yesterday. Wake up with a splash on day two at this waterfront gem in unspoiled Napili. The pineapple pancakes, perhaps?

❺ KAPALUA ADVENTURE CENTER (p94) Now it's time to get airborne. Strap on a harness and fly like a bird above the treetops on Maui's longest zipline.

IN FOUR DAYS *This leg: 20 miles*

❻ KAHEKILI HIGHWAY (p95) If you have four glorious days in West Maui, plan your first two as above. Then start day three by heading off around the rugged northern tip of the island on West Maui's most adventurous road trip. And be sure to bring good walking shoes – there's a lot more than roadside views on this one!

❼ WAIHE'E RIDGE TRAIL (p98) Get out of the car and stretch your legs big time on this lofty ridgeline trail with misty mountain views. This is one of those hikes that produces I-want-to-go-back memories.

❽ KAPALUA GOLF (p94) On day three, follow in the footsteps of Tiger Woods by knocking around the green greens of Maui's premier golf course. Not much of a golfer? The **Village Walking Trails (p93)** let you tramp a former golf course that's been turned into a nature trail with knockout views.

❾ ONELOA BEACH (p92) Bring a beach towel and find your way to this hidden gem, uncrowded and as pretty as they come.

❿ PINEAPPLE GRILL (p94) Cap off your stay in West Maui at Kapalua's hottest restaurant, dining on what may well be the best Hawaiian fusion fare on the island. And one fab view to go with it!

FOR GREENIES

❶ MAUNALEI ARBORETUM TRAIL (p93)
Head off into the wilderness on the lightly
trodden trails of West Maui's most exotic
forest – a wonderland of tropical trees
planted a century ago by famed arborist
DT Fleming.

❷ HONOLUA BAY (p93) Grab a snorkel
and join the dolphins and other wildly
abundant marine life at this unspoiled
nature preserve. If the winter swells are
rolling in, watch the surfers ride monster
waves instead.

❸ FARMERS MARKET DELI (p88) Pick
up organic Maui-grown picnic supplies at
this earth-friendly deli and head to **Kapalua**

Beach **(p92)**, a scene so pristine that even
Hawaiian monk seals sun on the sand.

❹ PAPAWAI POINT (p78) Don't forget
the binoculars. Not that you'll need them
to see the 40-ton humpbacks that breach
straight up out of the water right off this
cliffside vantage point. And the sunsets
here are spectacular.

**❺ MASTERS OF HAWAIIAN SLACK KEY
GUITAR CONCERT SERIES (p90)** Attend-
ing one of these old-style slack key guitar
jams will make you feel like you're part of
the musicians' *'ohana* (family). It's a rare
cultural beauty you won't want to miss.

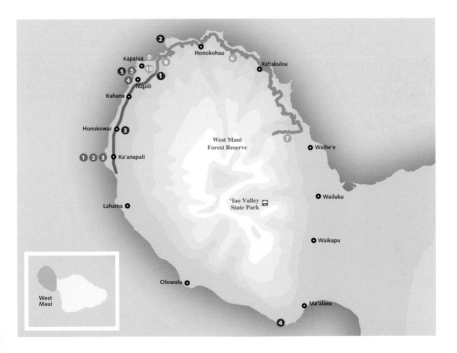

WEST MAUI

WEST MAUI

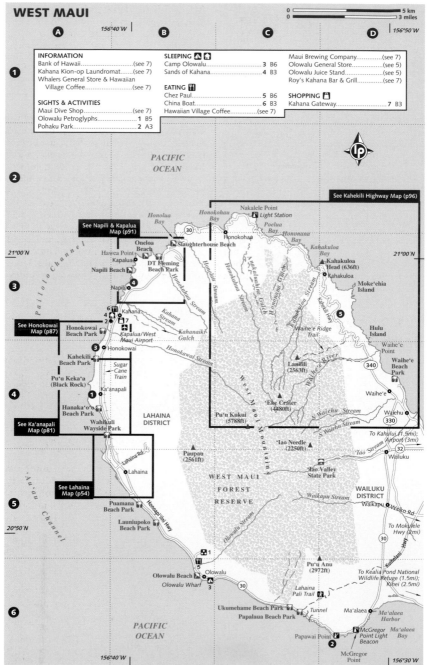

HIGHLIGHTS

❶ **BEST BEACH:** Ka'anapali Beach (p80)
❷ **BEST VIEW:** Papawai Point (p78)
❸ **BEST ACTIVITY:** Swimming at Kahekili Beach Park (p81)
❹ **BEST HAWAIIAN ENTERTAINMENT:** Masters of Hawaiian Slack Key Guitar Concert Series (p90)
❺ **BEST SCENIC ROUTE:** Kahekili Hwy (p95)

Highlights are numbered on the map on p76.

LAHAINA TO MA'ALAEA

The drive between Lahaina and Ma'alaea (p115) offers fine mountain scenery, but during winter everyone is craning their necks toward the ocean to spot humpback whales cruising just offshore.

Puamana & Launiupoko Beach Parks

Shady **Puamana Beach Park** (Map p76), 1.5 miles south of Lahaina, is rocky but sometimes has good conditions for beginning surfers – otherwise it's mostly a quick stop for a seaside view, particularly at sunset.

A better stop is **Launiupoko Beach Park** (Map p76), where even the restrooms glow with murals of young surfers hitting the waves. The south side of the beach has small waves ideal for beginning surfers, while the north side ratchets it up a notch for those who have honed their skills. It's also an ideal spot for families – *keiki* (children) have a blast wading in the large rock-enclosed shoreline pool and good picnic facilities invite you to linger. Launiupoko is at the traffic lights at the 18-mile marker.

Olowalu

The West Maui Mountains form a scenic backdrop, giving Olowalu its name, which means 'many hills.' The tiny village is marked by the Olowalu General Store and a fine chef-driven French restaurant, both at the 15-mile marker.

SIGHTS & ACTIVITIES

You'll notice snorkelers taking to the water near the 14-mile marker. Don't waste your time. The coral reef is shallow and silty, and the 'Sharks May Be Present' signs lining the beach are the real thing – people have been chomped on here.

OLOWALU PETROGLYPHS

A short walk behind the general store will lead you to **petroglyphs** (Map p76), ancient Hawaiian stone carvings. Park just beyond the water tower at the back of the store and look for the signposted gate. It's a quarter-mile walk up an open road to the petroglyph site. The path is easy to follow; just keep the cinder cone straight ahead of you as you go.

As with most of Maui's petroglyphs, these figures are carved into the vertical sides of cliffs rather than on horizontal lava like on the Big Island. Most of the Olowalu figures have been damaged, but you can still make some out.

EATING & SLEEPING

🍴 **OLOWALU JUICE STAND**   Food Truck $
Map p76; Olowalu Village Rd; smoothies $5;
⏱ 9am-5:30pm
Getting thirsty? Tropical fruit smoothies made with squeezed-on-the-spot sugarcane juice are whipped up at this food truck at the north side of Olowalu General Store. Fresh fruit is for sale, too.

CHEZ PAUL   French $$$$
Map p76; ☎ 661-3843; 820 Olowalu Village Rd;
mains $29-44; ⏱ dinner
This fine French provincial restaurant may be in the middle of nowhere, but it attracts diners from far and wide. While old-world artwork and white linen add ambience, it's the classic dishes like rack of lamb and

Top Picks

COOL DRINKS
- **Bikini Blond lager at Maui Brewing Company** (p89)
- **Guava smoothies at Olowalu Juice Stand** (above)
- **Blue Hawaiis at Hula Grill & Barefoot Bar** (p84)

WEST MAUI

WEST MAUI

WHALE SPOTTING

This is the road that gave rise to Maui's popular bumper sticker 'I brake for whales.' During the winter, humpback whales occasionally breach as close as 100yd from the coast, and 40 tons of leviathan suddenly exploding straight up through the water can be a real show-stopper!

Beach parks and pull-offs along the road offer some great vantages for watching the action. The very best is ☙ **Papawai Point** (Map p76), a cliffside perch jutting into the western edge of Ma'alaea Bay, and a favored humpback nursing ground (not to mention a great place to catch a sunset). During winter, the Pacific Whale Foundation posts volunteers at the parking lot to share their binoculars and point out the whales. Papawai Point is midway between the 8- and 9-mile markers. Note that the road sign reads simply 'scenic point,' not the full name, but there's a turning lane into it, so slow down and you won't miss it.

caramelized salmon in Grand Marnier that packs those pretty tables. Reservations are recommended.

CAMP OLOWALU   Camping $
Map p76; ☎ 661-4303; www.campolowalu.com; 800 Olowalu Village Rd; campsites per person $10
Oceanfront camping and a friendly care-taker make this the best camping option in West Maui. Facilities are *Robinson Crusoe* simple – cold-water showers, outhouses, picnic tables and drinking water – but that's part of the fun. And hey, if you want to splurge, Chez Paul is just a half-mile away.

Papalaua Beach Park & Around

At the 12-mile marker is **Ukumehame Beach Park** (Map p76). Shaded by ironwood trees, this sandy beach is OK for a quick dip, but because of the rocky conditions most locals stick with picnicking and fishing. Dive and snorkel boats anchor offshore at **Coral Gardens**. This reef also creates **Thousand Peaks**

toward its west end, with breaks favored by long-boarders and beginning surfers.

Midway between the 12- and 11-mile markers is **Papalaua Beach Park** (Map p76), a lackluster county park squeezed between the road and the ocean, though it does have fire pits, toilets and tent camping (for per-mit information, see p272) under thorny kiawe trees. Campers take note: this place buzzes all night with traffic noise – it's bet-ter to skip it and head to Camp Olowalu (above), a few miles north.

The pull-off for the western end of the **Lahaina Pali Trail** (p116) is just south of the 11-mile marker, on the inland side of the road.

LAHAINA TO KA'ANAPALI

The stretch between Lahaina and Ka'anapali offers a couple of roadside beach parks plus West Maui's best B&Bs.

Wahikuli Wayside Park

Two miles north of Lahaina, this park (Map p76) occupies a narrow strip of beach flanked by the busy highway. With a gift for prophecy, the Hawaiians named it Wahikuli, meaning 'noisy place.' Al-though the beach is mostly backed by a black-rock retaining wall, there's a small

Sunset at Ukumehame Beach Park

sandy area. Swimming conditions are usually fine, and when the water's calm, you can snorkel near the lava outcrops at the park's south end. The park has showers and restrooms.

SLEEPING

The following B&Bs are near each other in a residential neighborhood between Lahaina and Ka'anapali, inland of Hwy 30. You're not on the beach but it's just a five-minute drive away.

GUEST HOUSE   B&B $$
Map p76; ☎ 661-8085, 800-621-8942; www.maui guesthouse.com; 1620 'Ainakea Rd; s/d incl breakfast $149/169; P ⬚ ▯ ⬚
The amenities here put the nearby resorts to shame. Every room has its own hot tub and a 42-inch plasma TV. Stained-glass windows and rattan furnishings reflect a tropical motif. The long list of free perks runs from sunblock and beach gear to a guest shower you can use before your midnight flight home.

HOUSE OF FOUNTAINS   B&B $$
Map p76; ☎ 667-2121, 800-789-6865; www .alohahouse.com; 1579 Lokia St; r incl breakfast $150-180; P ⬚ ⬚
A Hawaiian theme resonates throughout, with hula rattles and warrior masks

Top Picks

SANDY BEACHES
- **Ka'anapali Beach** (p80)
- **Kahekili Beach** (p81)
- **Kapalua Beach** (p92)
- **Oneloa Beach** (p92)
- **Slaughterhouse Beach** (p93)
- **Napili Beach** (p90)

brimming from every corner, and even a hand-carved outrigger canoe hanging from the living room ceiling. The six guest rooms are nicely fitted with queen beds, refrigerators and DVD players. It's a kid-friendly place – the owners have kids of their own. German is spoken.

Hanaka'o'o Beach Park

This long, sandy beach (Map p76), extending south from Ka'anapali Beach Resort, has a sandy bottom and water conditions that are usually safe for swimming. However, southerly swells, which sometimes develop in summer, can create powerful waves and shorebreaks, while the occasional *kona* storm can kick up rough water conditions in winter. Snorkelers head down to the second clump of rocks on the

WEST MAUI

GREG ELMS

south side of the park, but it really doesn't compare with sites further north. The park has full facilities and is one of only two beaches on the entire West Maui coast that has a lifeguard. Hanaka'o'o Beach is also called 'Canoe Beach,' as West Maui outrigger canoe clubs practice here in the late afternoon.

KA'ANAPALI

You're on your honeymoon, right? Or having a family reunion? Maybe looking for some beachside action? Maui's flashiest resort destination boasts three miles of sandy beach, a dozen oceanfront hotels, two 18-hole golf courses and an ocean full of water activities. Here you can sit at a beachfront bar with an umbrella-clad drink in hand, soak up the gorgeous views of Lana'i and Moloka'i across the channel and listen to guitarists strum their wiki-wacky-woo.

It's hard to imagine this same area was nothing but quiet cane fields until the late 1950s, when sugar giant Amfac pulled 600 acres out of production and transformed it into Hawaii's first major resort outside of Waikiki. Now it's sweet in other ways.

Beaches

KA'ANAPALI BEACH

The generous sandy strand fronting the Ka'anapali resort hotels is the most happening beach in West Maui. Dubbed 'Dig-Me Beach' for all the well-waxed strutting that

SOULS LEAP

According to traditional Hawaiian beliefs, Pu'u Keka'a, the westernmost point of Maui, is a place where the spirits of the dead leap into the unknown to be carried to their ancestral homeland. The rock is said to have been created during a scuffle between the demigod Maui and a commoner who questioned Maui's superiority. Maui chased the man to this point, then froze his body into stone and cast his soul out to sea.

A different kind of soul jumps into the water today. You'll often find a line of daring teens waiting for their turn to leap off the rock for a resounding splash into the cool cove below.

takes place, it's a vibrant scene with surfers, boogie boarders and parasailers ripping across the water, and sailboats pulling up on shore. Check with the hotel beach huts before jumping in, however, as water conditions vary with the season and currents are sometimes strong.

You'll find the best underwater sights off **Pu'u Keka'a**, also known as Black Rock, the lava promontory that protects the beach in front of the Sheraton. Novices snorkel along the sheltered southern side of Pu'u Keka'a, but the shallow coral in these waters has been stomped to death. If you're a confident swimmer, the less-frequented horseshoe cove cut into the tip of the rock is the real prize, teeming with tropical fish,

Kahekili Beach Park

GREG ELMS

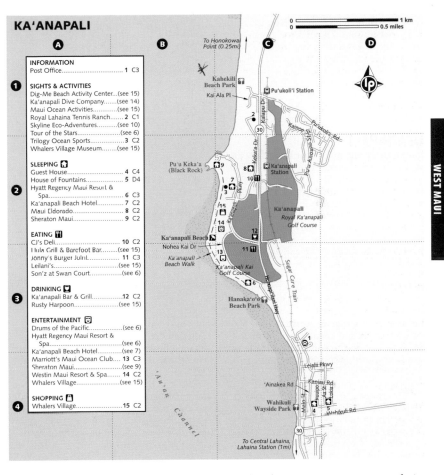

KA'ANAPALI

INFORMATION
Post Office.................................. **1** C3

SIGHTS & ACTIVITIES
Dig-Me Beach Activity Center...(see 15)
Ka'anapali Dive Company.......(see 14)
Maui Ocean Activities.............(see 15)
Royal Lahaina Tennis Ranch....... **2** C1
Skyline Eco-Adventures............(see 10)
Tour of the Stars.....................(see 6)
Trilogy Ocean Sports................. **3** C2
Whalers Village Museum........(see 15)

SLEEPING
Guest House............................. **4** C4
House of Fountains................... **5** D4
Hyatt Regency Maui Resort &
Spa...................................... **6** C3
Ka'anapali Beach Hotel............ **7** C2
Maui Eldorado......................... **8** C2
Sheraton Maui........................ **9** C2

EATING
CJ's Deli................................ **10** C2
Hula Grill & Barefoot Bar........(see 15)
Jonny's Burger Joint................ **11** C3
Leilani's.................................(see 15)
Son'z at Swan Court...............(see 6)

DRINKING
Ka'anapali Bar & Grill.............. **12** C2
Rusty Harpoon........................(see 15)

ENTERTAINMENT
Drums of the Pacific.................(see 6)
Hyatt Regency Maui Resort &
Spa......................................(see 6)
Ka'anapali Beach Hotel............(see 7)
Marriott's Maui Ocean Club..... **13** C3
Sheraton Maui.........................(see 9)
Westin Maui Resort & Spa....... **14** C2
Whalers Village.......................(see 15)

SHOPPING
Whalers Village...................... **15** C2

WEST MAUI

colorful coral and sea turtles. There's often a current to contend with off the point, which can make getting to the horseshoe a bit tricky, but when it's calm you can swim right in. Pu'u Keka'a is also a popular shore-dive spot; any of the beach huts can set you up.

KAHEKILI BEACH PARK

Even Ka'anapali has its secrets. To leave the see-me crowd behind, head to this idyllic golden-sand beach at Ka'anapali's less-frequented northern end. The swimming's better, the snorkeling's good and you'll find plenty of room to stretch without bumping into anyone else's beach towel. The park has everything you'll need for a day at the beach – showers, restrooms, a covered picnic pavilion and barbecue grills. All you need to do is pack a picnic. Access is easy and there's lots of free parking.

Snorkelers will find plenty of coral and marine life right in front of the beach. Sea turtle sightings are common. If you want to go a bit further afield, you can swim north to Honokowai Point and then ride the mild current, which runs north to south, all the way back.

The wide beach, backed by swaying palms and flowering morning glory, is also ideal for strolling. It's a 15-minute walk south to Pu'u Keka'a. Or you could walk north along the beach for about 20 minutes to **Honokowai Point** and have lunch in the village.

WEST MAUI

To get to the beach from the Honoapi'ilani Hwy, turn *makai* (toward the ocean) 0.2 miles north of the 25-mile marker onto Kai Ala Dr, then bear right.

Sights

WHALERS VILLAGE MUSEUM

our pick ☎ 661-5992; Level 3, Whalers Village, 2345 Ka'anapali Pkwy; admission free; ☾ 9am-10pm

Don't let the shopping center location fool you. Simply put, this is one of the best whaling museums anywhere. Authentic period photographs, whaling ship logs and intriguing interpretive plaques sound the depths of whaling history. It's all rounded out with exhibits of harpoons, whale jawbones and a wild array of scrimshaw. A lot of the character of the whalers comes through, and you'll get a feel for how rough and dirty the work really was. Wages were so low that sailors sometimes owed the ship money by the time they got home and had to sign up for another four-year stint just to pay off the debt. No wonder so many jumped ship when they reached Maui!

Interest piqued? You'll find a full-size **sperm whale skeleton** hanging at the front entrance to the shopping center to round out the experience.

KA'ANAPALI BEACH WALK

Smell the salt air, take in the opulent resort sights and check out the lively beach scene along the mile-long walk that runs between the Sheraton and Hyatt hotels. In addition to all the action on the beach, both the Hyatt and the Westin are worth a detour for their dazzling garden statuary and landscaping replete with free-form pools, rushing waterfalls and swan ponds. A walk through the Hyatt's rambling lobbies is a bit like museum browsing – the walls are hung with everything from heirloom Hawaiian quilts to meditative Buddhas and Papua New Guinean war shields.

At the southern end of the walk the graceful 17ft-high bronze sculpture *The Acrobats*, by Australian John Robinson, makes a dramatic silhouette at sunset. If you walk along the beach in the early evening, you'll often be treated to entertainment, most notably from the beachside restaurants at Whalers Village (p84) and

Top Picks

WEST MAUI FOR KIDS

- Keiki swimming hole at Launiupoko Beach Park (p77)
- Hula show at Ka'anapali Beach Hotel (p85)
- Divers at Pu'u Keka'a (p85)
- Whalers Village Museum (left)

from the Hyatt, which holds its luau (p85) on the oceanfront.

Activities

AT SEA

Teralani Sailing (☎ 661-1230; www.teralani.net; Whalers Village, 2345 Ka'anapali Pkwy; outings $59-119; ☾ hours vary) offers a variety of catamaran sails from Ka'anapali Beach, including morning snorkel sails, sunset sails and whale-watch outings. No matter which sail you take you'll find a friendly crew, an open bar and decent food.

If you've never been diving before, **Ka'anapali Dive Company** (☎ 667-4622; www.kaanapalidiveco.com; Westin Maui Resort & Spa; 1-tank dives $65; ☾ 9am-5pm) are the people you want to see. Their introductory dive ($89) for novices starts with instruction in a pool and moves on to a guided dive from the beach. They also offer beach dives for certified divers.

Dig-Me Beach Activity Center (☎ 661-5552; Whalers Village, 2345 Ka'anapali Pkwy; snorkel sets & boogie boards per hr/day $5/12; ☾ 8am-5pm), on the beach near Leilani's, has the best prices on beach gear rentals and arranges all manner of water activities.

Ka'anapali Beach   NED FRIARY

The pros at **Trilogy Ocean Sports** (☎ 661-7789; Ka'anapali Beach Walk; ☼ 8am-5pm), in a beach hut in front of the Ka'anapali Beach Hotel, can get you up riding a board with a two-hour surfing lesson ($70), and rent snorkel sets and boogie boards for $15 a day.

ON LAND

Skyline Eco-Adventures (☎ 662-1500; www.skyline hawaii.com; Fairway Shops; 4hr outing $148; ☼ departs 7am, 8am, 9am, 11am, noon & 1pm), Ka'anapali's new zipline, takes you 2 miles up the wooded cliffsides and sets you off on a free-glide above waterfalls, stream beds and green valleys. The scenery's not as wild as Skyline's popular Haleakalā zipline (p160), but if this is the only one you can book, you won't be disappointed.

Ka'anapali Golf Courses (☎ 661-3691; www.kaana pali-golf.com; 2290 Ka'anapali Pkwy; greens fee $175 205, after 1pm $85-110; ☼ first tee time 6:30am) consists of two courses. The more demanding Royal Ka'anapali Golf Course, designed by Robert Trent Jones, is tournament grade with greens that emphasize putting skills. The Ka'anapali Kai Golf Course is shorter and more of a resort course. The setting isn't as spectacular as the courses in Kapalua, but it tends to be less windy down this way and the rates are a relative bargain.

Treat yourself to stellar stargazing at the Hyatt resort's rooftop **Tour of the Stars** (☎ 667-4727; 200 Nohea Kai Dr; admission $25-30). These 50-minute viewings are limited to 14 people, use a 16in-diameter telescope and are held at 8pm, 9pm and 10pm on clear nights. Romantic types should opt for the couples-only viewing at 11pm Friday and Saturday, which rolls out champagne and chocolate-covered strawberries.

Royal Lahaina Tennis Ranch (☎ 667-5200; 2780 Keka'a Dr; per person per day $10, child under 18 free with playing adult; ☼ 8am-7pm) is the largest tennis complex in West Maui, with six courts lit for night play. Racquets and shoes can be rented. Private lessons and group clinics are available.

Courses

Whalers Village (☎ 661-4567; www.whalersvillage .com; 2435 Ka'anapali Pkwy) offers free lei-making classes and hula lessons. The schedule, which changes throughout the year, is printed in the shopping center's free magazine.

Ziplining above West Maui DOUGLAS BOWSER

Festivals & Events

Na Mele O Maui (www.kaanapaliresort.com) The 'Song of Maui' features children's choral groups singing Native Hawaiian music honoring Hawaii's last monarch, Queen Lili'uokalani, who was a renowned music composer and cultural revivalist. This aloha-rich event is held in January at the Hyatt Regency Maui Resort & Spa.

Maui Onion Festival (www.whalersvillage.com) This festival highlights everything that can be done with Maui's celebrated onions. Held at Whalers Village on the first weekend in August, things heat up with raw-onion-eating contests (participants get free breath mints!) and cooking demonstrations by Maui's top chefs.

Maui Chefs Present (www.visitlahaina.com) Gourmets have their day on the first Friday in September, with a dozen of the island's top chefs whipping up dishes for an elegant themed meal. It's a precursor event for the celebrated A Taste of Lahaina & Best of Island Music Festival (p64).

Hula O Na Keiki (www.kbhmaui.com) Children take center stage at this hula dance competition in November, which features some of the best *keiki* dancers in Hawaii.

Eating

Don't limit yourself to Ka'anapali's restaurants. Many of Maui's top chefs are just a skip down the road in Lahaina.

JONNY'S BURGER JOINT   Sandwiches $
☎ 661-4500; 2291 Ka'anapali Pkwy; burgers $7-10; ☼ 11:30am-2am
Shoot a game of pool while your burger is flipped at this combo eatery-bar at the

entrance to Ka'anapali. The huge burgers, hand-formed and served with caramelized Kula onions, are among the best you'll find on Maui. Forget the fried dishes – Jonny's is all about the burgers.

CJ'S DELI
Café $
☎ 667-0968; Fairway Shops, 2580 Ka'anapali Pkwy; mains $6-12; ⊙ 7am-11pm

This New York–style deli-café is the latest addition to the Ka'anapali dining scene and it's already stacking up a loyal following. The giant chalkboard menu includes all the expected classics, like hot pastrami on rye and cream-cheese bagels. Diners will find affordable egg and pancake fare in the morning and heaped servings of meatloaf and other comfort food in the evening.

HULA GRILL & BAREFOOT BAR
Hawaii Regional $$$
☎ 667-6636; Whalers Village, 2345 Ka'anapali Pkwy; grill menu $9-18, dinner mains $19-34; ⊙ 11am-10:30pm

Sure, it's a bit contrived, but heck, this is Ka'anapali and who doesn't want to dine on the beach? So grab a seat under one of the coconut-frond umbrellas and watch the swimsuit parade pass by as you dine on fun *pupu* (snacks) like coconut calamari or mac-nut wontons. Dinner kicks it up a notch with spicy kiawe-grilled seafood. Wash it down with a Blue Hawaii made with fresh pineapple juice.

SON'Z AT SWAN COURT
Eclectic $$$$
☎ 667-4506; Hyatt Regency Maui Resort & Spa, 200 Nohea Kai Dr; mains $30-48; ⊙ dinner

Between the waterfalls, the swan pond and the tiki torches, this is Ka'anapali's most romantic night out. The award-winning cuisine goes beyond the expected fine-dining steak and lobster offerings to island touches

like Maui goat-cheese ravioli. Incredible wine list, too.

Drinking

LEILANI'S
☎ 661-4495; Whalers Village, 2345 Ka'anapali Pkwy

This open-air bar and restaurant right on the beach is the place to linger over a cool drink while catching a few rays. It also has a good grill and *pupu* menu.

RUSTY HARPOON
☎ 661-3123; Whalers Village, 2345 Ka'anapali Pkwy

Long happy hours (2pm to 6pm) and hard-hitting daiquiris attract the crowds at this seaview bar, as do the big-screen TVs broadcasting the day's sporting events.

KA'ANAPALI BAR & GRILL
☎ 667-7480; 2290 Ka'anapali Pkwy

If you don't want to get caught up in the beach scene, this open-air bar overlooking the golf course is the best place for a sunset drink and light eats.

Entertainment

There's always something happening at the Ka'anapali hotels, ranging from music in the lounges and restaurants to luau and hula shows.

LIVE MUSIC
In addition to the other places listed here, both Leilani's (above) and Hula Grill & Barefoot Bar (above), adjacent beachside restaurants at Whalers Village, have live music throughout the afternoon and evening. It's typically Jimmy Buffett–style guitar tunes, but is occasionally spiced up with some ukulele strumming.

HYATT REGENCY MAUI RESORT & SPA
☎ 661-1234; 200 Nohea Kai Dr

A free torch-lighting ceremony at 6:15pm is followed by live music until 9:30pm in the Weeping Banyan Lounge.

WESTIN MAUI RESORT & SPA
☎ 667-2525; 2365 Ka'anapali Pkwy

The hotel's poolside bar and grill comes

Don't Miss

- Swimming with sea turtles at Kahekili Beach Park (p81)
- A walk out to Dragon's Teeth (p92)
- Sperm whale skeleton at Whalers Village (p82)
- Julia's banana bread in Kahakuloa (p97)

ISLAND VOICES

NAME: MALIHINI KEAHI-HEATH
OCCUPATION: GUEST SERVICES AGENT AT KA'ANAPALI BEACH HOTEL
RESIDENCE: LAHAINA

Is your family from West Maui? My grandfather Jacob Keahi from Moloka'i was a kahuna *lapa'au*, a medicine kahuna (priest), for all Lahaina. He was the kind who took care of someone if they were ailing in spirit. My grandmother – his wife, Emily – lived in Kanaha Valley above Lahainaluna and her father, my great-grandfather, was chosen by Queen Keopuolani to be her feather gatherer.

Did you grow up here? I was born and raised in Lahaina. I was born at the Pioneer Mill hospital, where the Hard Rock Café is now. My father used to play guitar at Ka'anapali Beach Hotel (p86) when I was a little girl. I grew up at this hotel. My mother was a hula dancer. I started dancing hula here when I was 8 years old.

What do you do now at the hotel? I've had this job as guest services agent since 1993. I do all the hands-on crafts (*lauhala* weaving, lei making, *lau* printing, *ti*-leaf skirt making, poi pounding and more). Everything is culturally based. When I lead the garden tours, I teach about the fruits of the land. I focus on the medicinal use of the native plants. *Noni* helps keep your system clean. Taro heals infections. A lot of people are looking for resources to cure them – that's my thing. I lead the tours. Then I dance hula in the evening.

What do you hope visitors take away with them? The tourists today are looking for things in essence. They're different now. They're not just looking for hula lessons. Many of them also want to take the next step and learn more about our culture and history. I hope visitors go away having learned something, something they can do back home. Tradition cannot live on unless you pass it on and carry it on in different places. Before they leave, I give them that last hug so they can embrace what they've learned here.

alive with live Hawaiian music from 3pm to 9pm.

MARRIOTT'S MAUI OCEAN CLUB

☎ 667-1200; 100 Nohea Kai Dr

The Marriott's Longboards lounge has a solo guitarist from 5:30pm to 9pm Friday to Monday, usually accompanied by sunset hula dancing.

HULA, LUAU & THEATER

KA'ANAPALI BEACH HOTEL

☎ 661-0011; 2525 Ka'anapali Pkwy

Maui's most Hawaiian hotel cheerfully entertains anyone who chances by between 6:30pm and 7:30pm with a free hula show. There's also music and dancing nightly in the hotel's Tiki Courtyard.

SHERATON MAUI

☎ 661-0031; 2605 Ka'anapali Pkwy

Everybody swings by to watch the torch-lighting and cliff-diving ceremony from Pu'u Keka'a that takes place at sunset. There's also music with hula dancing from 6pm to 8pm at the hotel's Lagoon Bar.

DRUMS OF THE PACIFIC

☎ 667-4727; Hyatt Regency Maui Resort & Spa, 200 Nohea Kai Dr; adult/child 6-12 $86/45; 5-8pm

Ka'anapali's best luau includes an *imu* ceremony (the unearthing of a roasted pig

WEST MAUI

Hula dancers at the Ka'anapali Beach Hotel

GREG ELMS

from an underground oven), an open bar, a Hawaiian-style buffet dinner, and a flashy South Pacific dance and music show.

WHALERS VILLAGE
☎ 661-4567; 2435 Ka'anapali Pkwy
Ka'anapali's shopping center hosts free hula and Polynesian dance performances from 6:30pm to 8pm on Monday, Wednesday and Saturday.

Shopping

You'll find more than 50 shops at the **Whalers Village** (☎ 661-4567; 2435 Ka'anapali Pkwy; ⏱ 9:30am-10pm) shopping center:

ABC Store (☎ 667-9700) Stop here for beach mats and sunblock.

Gecko Store (☎ 661-1114) Everything from T-shirts to toys crawls with friendly Hawaiian geckos. You'll be amazed at what geckos can do.

Honolua Surf (☎ 661-5455) The place to pick up Maui-style board shorts and other casual beachwear.

Honolua Wahine (☎ 661-3253) Get your bikinis here.

Martin & MacArthur (☎ 661-0088) Museum-quality Hawaiian-made wood carvings, paintings and other crafts.

Sand People (☎ 662-8785) Eclectic island-made souvenirs, from papaya soap to jewelry.

Sleeping

All the following accommodations are either on the beach or within walking distance of it. In addition to these resorts, there are recommendable B&Bs (p79) nearby between Ka'anapali and Lahaina.

🌺 KA'ANAPALI BEACH HOTEL
Resort $$$
our pick ☎ 661-0011, 800-262-8450; www.kbhmaui.com; 2525 Ka'anapali Pkwy; r incl breakfast from $220; P ✕ ☲
If you're looking for aloha over ritz, this is the place. The rooms at this older hotel may not pack the same punch as the fancier neighbors but it's got an enviable location on a gorgeous stretch of beach, and nightly hula shows and welcoming Hawaiian staff remind guests why they came to Maui in the first place. Heaps of family-friendly activities, from lei-making to ukulele singalongs, assure that the *keiki* will never be bored.

MAUI ELDORADO
Condo $$$
☎ 661-0021, 800-688-7444; www.outrigger.com; 2661 Keka'a Dr; studio/1br from $280/330; P ✕ ☐ ☲
Don't bother paying extra for the ocean view – this one's all about the greens. You can literally step off your lanai and onto the fairways at this quiet condo complex bordering the Royal Ka'anapali Golf Course. Best deal are the studios, which are very large and have kitchens set apart from the bedroom area. Online discounts abound.

SHERATON MAUI
Resort $$$$
☎ 661-0031, 866-716-8109; www.sheraton-maui.com; 2605 Ka'anapali Pkwy; r from $320; P ✕ ☲
This sleek resort breathes elegance and enjoys a prime beach location, smack in front of Pu'u Keka'a (Black Rock). The

rooms have rich wood tones and Hawaiian prints, and the grounds have night-lit tennis courts, a fitness center and a lava-rock swimming pool.

HYATT REGENCY MAUI
RESORT & SPA   Resort $$$$

☎ 661-1234, 800-233-1234; www.maui.hyatt.com; 200 Nohea Kai Dr; r from $400; ℗ 🏊 🛏
Ka'anapali's eye-candy resort. The lobby atrium is tricked out with cockatoos in palm trees and extravagant artwork, the grounds given over to gardens and swan ponds. Kids of all ages will thrill in the water world of meandering pools, swim-through grottos and towering water slides.

Getting Around

The Maui Bus (p289) connects the Whalers Village shopping center in Ka'anapali with the Wharf Cinema Center in Lahaina hourly from 6:30am to 8:30pm, and runs north up the coast to Kahana and Napili hourly from 6am to 8pm.

The free **Ka'anapali Trolley** (☎ 667-0648) runs between the Ka'anapali hotels, Whalers Village and the golf course about every 20 minutes between 10am and 10pm.

Ride with the top down in a cool antique convertible with **Classy Taxi** (☎ 665-0003), which charges $10 for a ride from Whalers Village to Lahaina.

The resort hotels offer free beach parking, but it's largely a token gesture and the spaces allotted are so limited they commonly fill by mid-morning. Your best bet for beach parking is at the south end of the Hyatt, which has more slots than other hotels. Another option is the pay parking at Whalers Village (three hours free with a $10 purchase and ticket validation).

HONOKOWAI

Condo-laden Honokowai may not have the glamour of pricier Ka'anapali to the south, but it has its virtues. It's convenient, affordable and low-rise, and the ocean views are every bit as fine as in the upscale resorts. The accommodations here are on a more intimate scale, with most perched right on the waterfront. Another perk: in winter this is the best place in West Maui to spot passing whales right from your room lanai.

Orientation

North of Ka'anapali, the road forks. If you want to zip up to the northern beaches, bypassing the condos and resorts, the main road is Honoapi'ilani Hwy (Hwy 30). The parallel shoreline road is Lower Honoapi'ilani Rd, which leads into Honokowai.

Beaches

HONOKOWAI BEACH PARK
The real thrills here are on land, not in the water. This family-friendly park in the

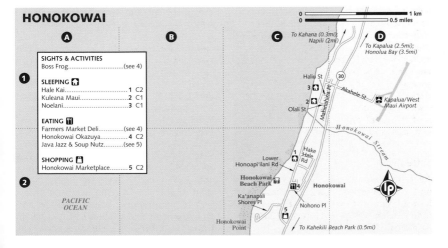

HONOKOWAI

SIGHTS & ACTIVITIES
Boss Frog.............................(see 4)

SLEEPING 🏠
Hale Kai...................................1 C2
Kuleana Maui...........................2 C1
Noelani....................................3 C1

EATING 🍴
Farmers Market Deli..............(see 4)
Honokowai Okazuya..................4 C2
Java Jazz & Soup Nutz...........(see 5)

SHOPPING 🛍
Honokowai Marketplace............5 C2

PACIFIC OCEAN

center of town has cool playground facilities for kids and makes a nice spot for a picnic. Forget swimming, though. The water is shallow and the beach is lined with a submerged rock shelf. Water conditions improve at the south side of town, and you could continue walking along the shore down to lovely **Kahekili Beach Park** (p81) at the northern end of Ka'anapali. Rent a snorkel from **Boss Frog** (☎ 665-1200; 3636 Lower Honoapi'ilani Rd; per day from $3; 8am-5pm) before you set off.

Eating

FARMERS MARKET DELI   Deli $
☎ 669-7004; 3636 Lower Honoapi'ilani Rd; takeout items $5-7; 7am-7pm

Stop here to pick up healthy takeout fare for your beach outing. The salad bar includes organic goodies and hot veggie dishes, the smoothies are first-rate and Maui-made ice cream is sold by the scoop. The place becomes even greener on Monday, Wednesday and Friday mornings, when vendors sell locally grown produce in the parking lot.

HONOKOWAI OKAZUYA   Plate Lunch $$
our pick ☎ 665-0512; 3600 Lower Honoapi'ilani Rd; mains $8-14; 10am-9pm Mon-Sat

No credit cards, the counter service is abrupt and the prices are high for a plate lunch. So why the crowd? It's all about the cooking. Plate lunch takes a gourmet turn here, with fragrant sauces. The mahimahi lemon caper sauté is always a sure winner.

Lunch à la Honokowai Okazuya   GREG ELMS

A strip of stools lines the wall if you want to chow down on the spot – or take it to the park across the street for an instant picnic.

JAVA JAZZ & SOUP NUTZ   Eclectic $$
☎ 667-0787; Honokowai Marketplace, 3350 Lower Honoapi'ilani Rd; breakfast & lunch $6-12, dinner $10-28; 6am-9pm Mon-Sat, to 5pm Sun

With a menu as eclectic as its decor, this arty café never disappoints. Breakfast packs 'em in with everything from bagels to frittata; lunch revolves around Greek salads and innovative sandwiches. Dinner gets downright meaty with the tastiest flame-grilled filet mignon you'll find anywhere on Maui.

Sleeping

KULEANA MAUI   Condo $$
☎ 669-8080, 800-367-5633; www.kuleanaresorts.com; 3959 Lower Honoapi'ilani Rd; 1br/2br from $145/225;

The most bang for the buck in Honokowai. The rooms are a bit small but not claustrophobic, and they're well fitted with full kitchens and entertainment centers. You'll find plenty of space to stretch out on the extensive palm-shaded grounds. Go for the upper floor, which has the best views.

NOELANI   Condo $$
☎ 669-8374, 800-367-6030; www.noelani-condo-resort.com; 4095 Lower Honoapi'ilani Rd; studios $157, 1br/2br/3br from $200/290/360;

This ocean-kissing condo is so close to the water you can sit on your lanai and watch turtles swimming in the surf. The 50 units cover a wide range, from cozy studios to three-bedroom suites. All are kept to a benchmark that's a cut above the competition.

HALE KAI   Condo $$
☎ 669-6333, 800-446-7307; www.halekai.com; 3691 Lower Honoapi'ilani Rd; 1br/2br/3br $160/210/310;

This friendly place abounds in Hawaiian accents, from the room decor to the lava-rock exterior. It's perched on the water's edge: you can step off your lanai and onto the sand. If you have a group, grab the three-bedroom corner unit, which has a cool loft, wraparound ocean-view windows and all the character of a Hawaiian beach house.

Top Picks

WEST MAUI RESTAURANTS

- **Gazebo** (p90)
- **Honokowai Okazuya** (opposite)
- **Pineapple Grill** (p94)
- **Sansei Seafood Restaurant & Sushi Bar** (p94)
- **Roy's Kahana Bar & Grill** (below)

KAHANA

Trendy Kahana, the village north of Honokowai, boasts million-dollar homes, upscale beachfront condominiums and Maui's only microbrewery. It's a popular place to head for a night out.

Information

The following places are all located in the **Kahana Gateway** (Map p76; 4405 Honoapi'ilani Hwy) shopping center, which also has a gas station.

Bank of Hawaii (Map p76; ☎ 669-3922)

Hawaiian Village Coffee (Map p76; ☎ 665-1114; per min 15¢; ⏰ 6am-9pm) Online computers.

Kahana Koin-op Laundromat (Map p76; ☎ 669-1587; ⏰ last wash 8pm)

Whalers General Store (Map p76; ☎ 669-3700; ⏰ 6:30am-11pm) For basic groceries and sundries.

Beaches & Activities

The sandy **beach** fronting the village offers reasonable swimming. Park at seaside **Pohaku Park** (Map p76) and walk north a couple of minutes to reach the beach. Pohaku Park itself has an offshore break called S-Turns that attracts surfers. **Maui Dive Shop** (☎ 669-3800; Kahana Gateway, 4405 Honoapi'ilani Hwy; 2-tank dives $130, snorkel rentals per day $8; ⏰ 8am-9pm) offers a full range of dives and rents snorkel gear.

Eating & Drinking

HAWAIIAN VILLAGE COFFEE   Café $

Map p76; ☎ 665-1114; Kahana Gateway, 4405 Honoapi'ilani Hwy; snacks $2-6; ⏰ 6am-9pm

This little shop's all about local flavor, with Maui-grown coffee, Maui-made Roselani ice cream (try the coconut *haupia*) and homemade baked goods.

CHINA BOAT   Chinese $$

Map p76; ☎ 669-5089; 4474 Lower Honoapi'ilani Rd; mains $9-22; ⏰ lunch & dinner

If you want to see where islanders bring the kids for an affordable dinner, come here. The menu includes both tame Mandarin and fiery Szechuan favorites, with nearly a hundred choices, from candied walnut shrimp to kung pao chicken.

MAUI BREWING COMPANY   Pub $$$

Map p76; ☎ 669-3474; Kahana Gateway, 4405 Honoapi'ilani Hwy; lunch $9-15, dinner mains $20-36; ⏰ 11am-1am

At this classy microbrewery the food goes way beyond the usual pub menu, adding the likes of oysters Rockefeller, grilled fresh fish and raspberry-glazed duck. Beers range from the light Bikini Blonde lager to Wild Hog, a robust black stout with a creamy finish – sample them all with six 3.5oz glasses ($6). Live music nightly.

ROY'S KAHANA BAR & GRILL   Hawaii Regional $$$$

Map p76; ☎ 669-6999; Kahana Gateway, 4405 Honoapi'ilani Hwy; mains $29-40; ⏰ dinner

Renowned chef Roy Yamaguchi, a driving force behind the Hawaii Regional Cuisine movement (see p261), operates a little empire of restaurants. His Maui flagship rakes in a crowd with savory dishes such as sashimi-like blackened *'ahi* (tuna) with Chinese mustard and coriander pork chops in plum-wine sauce. Roy's signature hot chocolate soufflé is pure decadence – ask for two spoons and share it with a friend.

Sleeping

SANDS OF KAHANA   Condo $$

Map p76; ☎ 669-0423, 888-669-0400; www.sands-of-kahana.com; 4299 Lower Honoapi'ilani Rd; 1br/2br/3br from $150/265/375;

This beachside condo is an excellent value for this area. The huge one-bedrooms have more space than the average two-bedroom elsewhere – four people could happily co-exist, as the living room sofa bed is a far 25ft from the bedroom. Room amenities include a washer/dryer and ocean-view lanai; the grounds have tennis courts and a fitness center.

WEST MAUI

NAPILI ✳

Sweet Napili kisses a beautiful little bay. Somewhat ironically, this seaside village owes its low-key allure to its early history of resort development. Napili Kai Beach Resort was built in 1962 as Maui's first hotel north of Ka'anapali. To protect the bay, and its investment, Napili Kai organized neighboring landowners and persuaded the county to pass a zoning bylaw restricting all Napili buildings to the height of a coconut tree. The law passed in 1964, long before the condo explosion took over the rest of West Maui, and as a result Napili has preserved an intimate scale that's been lost elsewhere.

Beaches

The deep golden sands and gentle curves of **Napili Beach** offer good beachcombing at any time and excellent swimming and snorkeling when it's calm. Big waves occasionally make it into the bay in winter, and when they do it's time to break out the skimboards – the steep drop at the beach provides a perfect run into the surf.

Eating

GAZEBO   Café $
our pick ☎ 669-5621; Outrigger Napili Shores, 5315 Lower Honoapi'ilani Rd; meals $6-11; ⏰ 7:30am-2pm
A rare find, this open-air restaurant – literally a gazebo on the beach – sports the most incredible waterfront setting. Sweet tooths love the white chocolate mac-nut pancakes. Get there early to beat the breakfast queue. Meal-size salads, hearty sandwiches and the *kalua* pig plate steal the scene at lunch.

FISH & POI   Comfort Food $$
☎ 442-3700; Outrigger Napili Shores, 5315 Lower Honoapi'ilani Rd; mains $9-20; ⏰ 11am-9pm
Hawaiian comfort food goes upscale here with tempura-style fish and chips, oversize burgers dripping with melted cheddar and warm pineapple upside-down cake topped with vanilla ice cream. The dining room overlooks a serene koi pond, adding a meditative touch.

SEA HOUSE RESTAURANT   Hawaii Regional $$$
☎ 669-1500; Napili Kai Beach Resort, 5900 Lower Honoapi'ilani Rd; dinner mains $22-34; ⏰ dinner
Breezy seaside dining is enhanced by tiki torches. The head chef earned his toque opening the Lahaina Store Grille & Oyster Bar and still works his finest creations with seafood. Favorites include the Hawaiian snapper with bananas and coconut curry and the taro-crusted sea bass pan-seared with miso peanut sauce.

Entertainment

🎵 **MASTERS OF HAWAIIAN SLACK KEY GUITAR CONCERT SERIES**
our pick ☎ 669-3858; www.slackkey.com; Napili Kai Beach Resort, 5900 Lower Honoapi'ilani Rd; admission $46; ⏰ 7:30pm Wed

Crescent-shaped Napili Beach   GREG ELMS

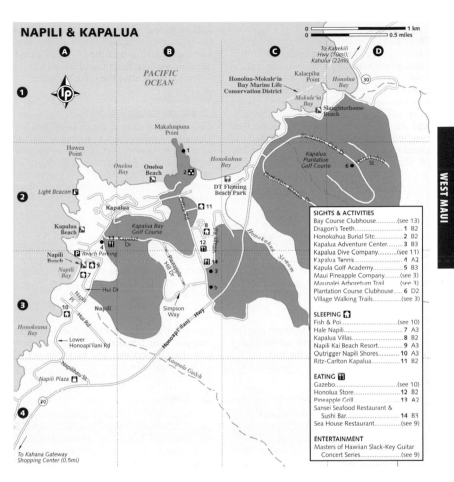

NAPILI & KAPALUA

SIGHTS & ACTIVITIES
Bay Course Clubhouse	(see 13)
Dragon's Teeth	**1** B2
Honokahua Burial Site	**2** B2
Kapalua Adventure Center	**3** B3
Kapalua Dive Company	(see 11)
Kapalua Tennis	**4** A2
Kapula Golf Academy	**5** B3
Maui Pineapple Company	(see 3)
Maunalei Arboretum Trail	(see 3)
Plantation Course Clubhouse	**6** D2
Village Walking Trails	(see 3)

SLEEPING
Fish & Poi	(see 10)
Hale Napili	**7** A3
Kapalua Villas	**8** B2
Napili Kai Beach Resort	**9** A3
Outrigger Napili Shores	**10** A3
Ritz-Carlton Kapalua	**11** B2

EATING
Gazebo	(see 10)
Honolua Store	**12** B2
Pineapple Grill	**13** A2
Sansei Seafood Restaurant & Sushi Bar	**14** B3
Sea House Restaurant	(see 9)

ENTERTAINMENT
Masters of Hawaiian Slack-Key Guitar Concert Series	(see 9)

WEST MAUI

Top slack key guitarists Cyril Pahinui, Ledward Kaapana and Dennis Kamakahi are monthly guests at this exceptional concert series, and George Kahumoku Jr, a slack key legend in his own right, is the weekly host. As much a jam session as a concert, this is a true Hawaiian cultural gem that's worth going out of your way to experience. Seating is limited so call ahead for reservations.

Sleeping

HALE NAPILI
Condo $$

ourpick ☎ 669-6184, 800-245-2266; www.hale napilimaui.com; 65 Hui Dr; studios from $160, 1br $260

The aloha of the Hawaiian manager ensures lots of repeat guests at this well-maintained condo smack on the beach. The place is a welcome throwback to an earlier era, when everything in Maui was small and personable. The 18 neat-as-a-pin units have tropical decor, full kitchens and oceanfront lanai.

OUTRIGGER NAPILI SHORES
Condo $$$

☎ 669-8061, 800-688-7444; www.outrigger.com; 5315 Lower Honoapi'ilani Rd; studios from $199, 1br $289;

This condo complex boasts a palm-filled resort setting with solar-heated pools, a hot tub and two of Napili's most interesting restaurants. Freshly renovated, just about everything in the units is spanking new.

**NAPILI KAI
BEACH RESORT**   Independent Hotel $$$
☎ 669-6271, 800-367-5030; www.napilikai.com;
5900 Lower Honoapiʻilani Rd; r/studios from
$240/295; ⚙ 🖵 🐾

Spread across several acres at the northern end of Napili Bay, this pampering resort offers classic appeal. The units, which tastefully blend Polynesian decor with Asian touches, have oceanview lanai and, in most cases, kitchenettes.

KAPALUA & NORTHERN BEACHES

Everyone knows Kapalua's a world-class golf destination – but how about those folks who aren't on the greens? Kapalua is making an all-out effort to broaden its appeal. Even if you don't have an extra million to buy into a timeshare, there's reason aplenty to head up here. An awesome zipline is taking people skyward for new thrills, trails in

DETOUR ➡

DRAGON'S TEETH

Has Harry Potter been here? It looks like a dragon has been turned to stone. Hmm… turns out those 3ft-high spikes that bear an uncanny resemblance to pointed teeth are lava rock that's been cut by whipping surf. Known locally as the Dragon's Teeth, this curious formation atop Makaluapuna Point is a cool site to walk to and takes about only 15 minutes round-trip.

En route you'll pass the **Honokahua burial site**, a 13.6-acre native burial ground. You can skirt along the outside of this area but don't enter any sites marked 'Please Kokua' (please respect), which are easily visible islets of overgrown stones bordering the Ritz's manicured golf greens.

To start your detour drive north to the very end of Lower Honoapiʻilani Rd, where you'll find parking and a plaque giving details on the burial site. The trail to the Dragon's Teeth leads down from the plaque along the north edge of the golf course.

a once-restricted forest have opened, and the dining scene is among the island's best. The nightlife doesn't exactly sizzle, but the beaches do.

Beaches
KAPALUA BEACH
This gorgeous strand gets the seal of approval! Not only do tourists sun on the beach here, but endangered monk seals occasionally haul out on the soft white sand to snooze the afternoon away as well.

And what good taste they have. This crescent-shaped beach, with its clear view of Molokaʻi across the channel, is a sure bet for a fun day in the water. Long rocky outcrops at both ends of the bay make Kapalua Beach the safest year-round swimming spot on this coast. You'll find colorful snorkeling on the right side of the beach, with abundant tropical fish and orange slate-pencil sea urchins.

Take the drive immediately north of Napili Kai Beach Resort to get to the beach parking area, where there are restrooms and showers. Look for the tunnel that leads from the parking lot north to the beach.

ONELOA BEACH
Even though it extends half a mile – Oneloa means 'long sand' – tourists seldom find their way to this beach. That's largely because it's backed by gated resort condos and restricted golf greens.

But this white-sand jewel is too pretty to leave to the jet set. Fringed by low sand dunes covered in beach morning glory, it's a fine place to soak up a few rays. On calm days swimming is good close to shore, as is snorkeling in the protected area along the rocky point at the north side of the beach. When there's any sizable surf, strong rip currents can be present.

The beach access requires a sharp eye; turn onto Ironwood Lane and immediately turn left into the parking lot opposite the Ironwoods gate. A footpath across the street leads down to the beach.

DT FLEMING BEACH PARK
No matter what you might think of Dr Beach, when he declares a place 'America's Best Beach,' you're not going to just drive by, are you? Untouristed DT Fleming

Beach took the award in 2006. Surrounded by ironwood trees and backed by an old one-room schoolhouse, this sandy beach appears like an outpost from another era. In keeping with its Hawaiian nature, the beach is the domain of wave riders. Experienced surfers and bodysurfers find good action here, especially in winter. The shorebreaks can be brutal, however, and this beach is second only to Ho'okipa for injuries. The reef on the right is good for snorkeling in summer when it's very calm.

Fleming has restrooms, showers and a lifeguard. The access road is off Honoapi'ilani Hwy (Hwy 30), immediately north of the 31-mile marker.

SLAUGHTERHOUSE BEACH & HONOLUA BAY

our pick Talk about dual personalities. This marine conservation district not only has two bays but also has amazing mood swings: wild and wicked in the winter, calm and tranquil in the summer. But no matter what its mood, it's always ideal for some sort of activity.

Slaughterhouse Beach (Mokule'ia Bay) and Honolua Bay are separated by the narrow Kalaepiha Point and together form the Honolua–Mokule'ia Bay Marine Life Conservation District.

Like O'ahu's famed North Shore, Honolua Bay is a surfer's dream. It, too, faces northwest and when it catches the winter swells it has some of the most gnarly surfing

Island Insights

Until 1960 a cattle slaughterhouse stood above Mokule'ia Bay, and to this day everyone still calls it Slaughterhouse Beach.

anywhere in the world. It's so hot it's been cover material for surfing magazines.

In summer snorkeling is excellent in both bays, thanks in part to prohibitions on fishing in the preserve. Honolua Bay is the favorite, with thriving reefs and abundant coral along its rocky edges. As an added treat, spinner dolphins sometimes hang near the mouth of the bays, swimming just beyond snorkelers. When it's calm, you can snorkel around Kalaepiha Point from one bay to the other, but forget it if there have been heavy rains: Honolua Stream empties into Honolua Bay and the runoff clouds the water.

When the waters are calm the bays offer superb kayaking. Slaughterhouse Beach is also a top-rated bodysurfing spot during the summer. Its attractive white-sand crescent is good for sunbathing and beachcombing – look for glittering green olivine crystals in the rocks at the south end of the beach.

Just north of the 32-mile marker, there's public parking and a concrete stairway leading down the cliffs to Slaughterhouse Beach. A half-mile past the 32-mile marker there's

WEST MAUI

HIKERS WELCOME

Good news! Kapalua has been opening up new hiking trails to the public. The most remarkable is the **Maunalei Arboretum Trail**, which cuts through a forest planted by DT Fleming, the arborist who developed Maui's pineapple industry. When he wasn't knee deep in pineapple, Fleming was roaming the world in search of tree species suited to Hawaii's climate. Now you can go see what he found. This previously inaccessible forest sits above an exclusive gated development and access is strictly via a free **shuttle** (☎ 665-9110) that departs from the Kapalua Adventure Center (p94) at 8am, 10am and noon and returns from the trailhead at 10:20am, 12:20pm and 2:20pm. Choose between the 2.5-mile ridge trail offering spectacular views, or a pair of loop trails (1 mile and 0.5 mile) that meander through the arboretum. A walk on these virgin trails is well worth planning your morning around.

The resort has also turned a former golf course into a walking trail. Before you say 'yuk,' listen up: the old Village Golf Course, now quaintly overgrown and reincarnated as the **Village Walking Trails**, offers stunning scenery as it rises up the mountain slopes. For the best views, follow it all the way to the end, where there's a lake loop; it takes about two hours and covers 3.5 miles. Just check in at the Kapalua Adventure Center, where the trails start, sign the liability waiver and pick up a map.

room for about half a dozen cars to park adjacent to the path down to Honolua Bay.

Activities

Kapalua Adventure Center (☎ 665-4386; Office Rd; 2hr zip $130; ⌚ 7am-7pm) is the jumpoff point for zipline tours that soar across nearly 2 miles of the West Maui Mountains. The experience includes eight ziplines in all, two of them extending a breathtaking 2000ft in length. The tour differs from other Maui ziplines in that it has a dual track allowing you to zip side by side with a friend.

🏌 **Kapalua Golf** (☎ 669-8044, 877-527-2582; www.kapaluamaui.com; Bay/Plantation greens fee before 2pm $215/295, after 2pm $130/150; ⌚ first tee time 7am) boasts two of the island's top championship golf courses, both certified by Audubon International as sanctuaries for native plants and animals. How's that for green greens? The **Bay course** (300 Kapalua Dr) is the tropical ocean course, meandering across a lava peninsula. The challenging **Plantation course** (2000 Plantation Club Dr) sweeps over a rugged landscape of hills and deep gorges.

Want to hone your golf skills? **Kapalua Golf Academy** (☎ 669-6500; 1000 Office Rd; 1hr clinic $30, lessons per hr $110; ⌚ 7am-4:30pm), staffed by PGA pros, is Hawaii's top golf academy.

Kapalua Dive Company (☎ 669-3448; www .kapaluadive.com; Ritz-Carlton Kapalua, 1 Ritz-Carlton Dr; dives from $75, kayak tours $70; ⌚ 9am-5pm) offers a range of water activities, including kayak tours that take you snorkeling, and a full menu of dive outings.

Kapalua Tennis (☎ 665-9112; 100 Kapalua Dr; per person per day $16, racquet rental $6; ⌚ 8am-6pm Mon-Fri, 8am-4pm Sat & Sun) is Maui's premier full-service tennis club, with 10 Plexipave courts and an array of clinics. If you're on your own, give the club a ring and they'll match you with other players for singles or doubles games.

Tours

Maui Pineapple Company (☎ 665-4386; Office Rd; 2½hr tour $40; ⌚ departs 9am & 11:45am Mon-Fri) opens its dusty red fields for pineapple-plantation tours led by seasoned workers. They'll give you the lowdown on the pineapple biz and let you harvest a pineapple to take home. Reservations are required, as are covered shoes…those spines are sharp!

Festivals & Events

Mercedes-Benz Championship (www.pgatour.com) Watch Tiger and friends tee off at the PGA Tour's season opener in early January at the Plantation course, vying for a multimillion-dollar purse.

Celebration of the Arts (www.celebrationofthearts .org) This festival in early April at the Ritz-Carlton celebrates traditional Hawaiian culture with storytelling, hula demonstrations, arts and music.

Kapalua Wine & Food Festival (www.kapaluamaui .com) A culinary extravaganza held over four days in late June at the Ritz-Carlton, the festival features renowned winemakers and Hawaii's hottest chefs in cooking demonstrations and wine tastings.

Billabong Pro Maui (www.billabongpro.com/maui) This annual women's title race, held at Honolua Bay when the surf's up in mid-December, showcases the world's top *wahine* (female) surfers. And as the final event of the surfing professionals World Championship Tour, it may determine the world's champ.

Eating

HONOLUA STORE   Plate Lunch $
☎ 669-6128; 502 Office Rd; lunches $5-7; ⌚ store 6am-8pm, deli to 2:30pm

A nod to normalcy in the midst of lavish exclusiveness, this general store's deli serves sandwiches and plate lunches. It's all takeout but there are picnic tables on the porch where you can chow down alongside the brawny construction workers who flock here at lunchtime. A small farmers market selling local organic veggies sets up out front from 11am to 2pm on Thursdays.

SANSEI SEAFOOD RESTAURANT & SUSHI BAR   Japanese $$$
☎ 669-6286; 600 Office Rd; sushi $3-15, mains $17-32; ⌚ dinner

The innovative sushi menu is reason enough to dine here, but the nonsushi house specials shouldn't be overlooked. The tempura rock shrimp in garlic aioli flawlessly blends Japanese and French flavors, and the spicy Dungeness crab ramen with truffle broth is another prize. Order before 6pm and all food is discounted by 25%.

PINEAPPLE GRILL   Hawaii Regional $$$
our pick ☎ 669-9600; Kapalua Bay Golf Course clubhouse, 300 Kapalua Dr; lunch $10-16, dinner mains $27-40; ⌚ lunch & dinner

The misty, mountainous backdrop to the beaches of West Maui   GREG ELMS

This beauty's got it all, from a sweeping hilltop view to a sleek exhibition kitchen that whips up creative fusion fare. Tantalize the taste buds with the likes of lobster-coconut bisque, wasabi-seared fish and Maui-coffee roasted duck breast. A well-matched wine list rounds it all out. Come before 6pm to take advantage of the three-course sunset dinner specials ($32).

Sleeping

KAPALUA VILLAS   Condo $$$$
☎ 669-8088, 800-545-0018; www.kapaluavillas
.com; 500 Office Rd; 1br/2br from $299/419; 🌀 🌊
Budget really isn't part of the vernacular in Kapalua, but if you have a small group this is the most affordable way to go. Three luxury condominium complexes comprise Kapalua Villas, with some units on the golf course and others overlooking the beach. The one-bedroom units sleep up to four; the two-bedroom units sleep six. Amenities include free tennis and discounted golf.

RITZ-CARLTON KAPALUA   Resort $$$$
☎ 669-6200, 800-262-8440; www.ritzcarlton.com;
1 Ritz-Carlton Dr; r incl breakfast from $425;
🌀 🌊
Fresh off a $200 million renovation, this luxe hotel's low-key elegance attracts the exclusive golf crowd. On a hillside fronting the greens and the sea, the hotel has a heated multilevel swimming pool shaded by palm trees, a spa and a fitness club. Rooms boast oversize marble bathrooms, goose-down pillows...you get the picture.

KAHEKILI HWY

One of Maui's most adventurous drives, and undisputedly its most challenging, this razor-thin road traverses the rugged northern tip of the island.

The area's so ravishingly rural that it's hard to imagine trendy West Maui could hold such untouched countryside. The key to its preservation is the Kahekili Hwy ('highway' – ha!), which narrows to the width of a driveway, keeping construction trucks and tourist buses at bay.

Not for the faint of heart, sections slow to just 5mph as the road wraps around hairpin curves, and a 2-mile stretch around the village of Kahakuloa is a mere one lane with cliffs on one side and a sheer drop on the other – if you hit oncoming traffic here you may be doing much of your traveling in reverse! But heck, if you can handle that, this largely overlooked route

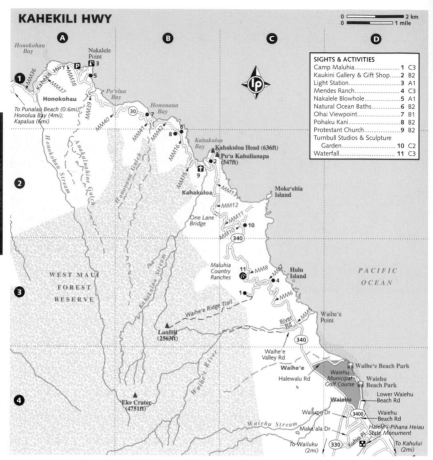

KAHEKILI HWY

SIGHTS & ACTIVITIES	
Camp Maluhia	**1** C3
Kaukini Gallery & Gift Shop	**2** B2
Light Station	**3** A1
Mendes Ranch	**4** C3
Nakalele Blowhole	**5** A1
Natural Ocean Baths	**6** B2
Ohai Viewpoint	**7** B1
Pohaku Kani	**8** B2
Protestant Church	**9** B2
Turnbull Studios & Sculpture Garden	**10** C2
Waterfall	**11** C3

offers all sorts of adventures, with horse and hiking trails, mighty blowholes and delicious banana bread. But you've gotta earn these treats!

Don't be fooled by car rental maps that show the road as a dotted line – it's paved and open to the public the entire way. There are no services, so gas up before heading off, and give yourself a good two hours' driving time, not counting stops.

Punalau Beach

As you head north beyond Kapalua, the development ceases and the scenery gets wilder as you make your way toward the island's northernmost point. Ironwood-lined

Punalau Beach, 0.7 miles after the 34-mile marker, makes a worthy stop if you're up for a solitary stroll. Swimming is a no-go though, as a rocky shelf creates unfavorable conditions for water activities.

Nakalele Point

Continuing on, the terrain is hilly, with rocky cattle pastures punctuated by tall sisal plants. At a number of pull-offs, you can stop and explore. Lush pastures beg you to traipse down the cliffs and out along the rugged coastline.

At the 38-mile marker, a mile-long trail leads out to a **light station** at the end of windswept Nakalele Point, where you'll

Nakalele Blowhole   NED FRIARY

find a coastline of arches and other formations worn out of the rocks by the pounding surf.

The **Nakalele Blowhole** roars when the surf is up but is a sleeper when the seas are calm. To check on its mood park at the boulder-lined pull-off 0.6 miles beyond the 38-mile marker. It's a 15-minute walk down to the blowhole. You can get a glimpse of the action, if there is any, just a few hundred yards beyond the parking lot.

Eight-tenths of a mile after the 40-mile marker look for the **Ohai Viewpoint**, on the *makai* side of the road. The viewpoint won't be marked but there's a sign announcing the start of the Ohai Trail. Don't bother with the trail – it's not particularly interesting. Instead, bear to the left and walk out to the top of the point just two minutes away for a jaw-dropping coastal view that includes a glimpse of the Nakalele Blowhole. If you have kids, be careful – the crumbly cliff has a sudden drop of nearly 800ft!

Ocean Baths & Bellstone

After the 42-mile post the markers change; the next marker is 16 and the numbers go down as you continue on from here.

One-tenth of a mile before the 16-mile marker, look seaward for a large dirt pull-off and a well-beaten path that leads 15 minutes down lava cliffs to **natural ocean baths** on the ocean's edge. Cut out of slippery lava rock and encrusted with olivine minerals, these incredibly clear pools sit in the midst of roaring surf. Some have natural steps, but if you're tempted to go in, size it up carefully – people unfamiliar with the water conditions here have been swept into the sea and drowned. If the rocks are covered in silt from recent storm runoffs, or the waves look high, forget about it – it's dangerous.

That huge boulder with concave marks on the inland side of the road just before the pull-off is **Pohaku Kani**, a bellstone. If you hit it with a rock on the Kahakuloa side, where the deepest indentations are, you might be able to get a hollow sound. It's a bit resonant if you hit it just right, though it takes some imagination to hear it ring like a bell.

Kahakuloa

Like Hana at the other side of the island, the village of Kahakuloa retains a solidly Hawaiian character. As you've no doubt discovered by now, it's no easy task getting here. Kahakuloa's isolation has protected it from the rampant development found elsewhere on Maui. Cradled in a tidy valley and embraced by towering sea cliffs, the village has a real Polynesian charm. Farmers tend taro patches, poi dogs wander across the road, and a missionary-era **Protestant church** marks the village center. One of Hawaii's most accomplished ukulele players, Richard Ho'opi'i, is the church minister.

You won't find any stores here, but villagers set up roadside stands selling fruit and snacks to day-trippers. For shave ice, hit Ululani's hot-pink stand. For 'ono (delicious) banana bread stop at Julia's lime-green sugar shack. In this one-road town, you can't miss 'em.

Heading into the valley, a pull-off above town provides a bird's-eye view of the village and the surrounding coast. The rise at the backdrop of Kahakuloa Bay is **Kahakuloa Head** (636ft), once a favorite cliff-diving spot of chief Kahekili.

Kahakuloa to Waihe'e

On the outskirts of Kahakuloa, near the 14-mile marker, the hilltop **Kaukini Gallery & Gift Shop** (☎ 244-3371; 🕑 10am-5pm) has works by island artists, with watercolors, native-fiber baskets, pottery and more. Past the 10-mile marker look for **Turnbull Studios & Sculpture Garden** (☎ 244-9838; 🕑 10am-5pm Tue-Fri), where you can view Bruce Turnbull's ambitious bronze and wood creations, as well as the works of other area artists... very cool stuff.

Continuing around beep-as-you-go hairpin turns, the highway gradually levels out atop sea cliffs. To spot an Eden-like scene, stop at the pull-off 0.1 miles north of the 8-mile marker and look down into the ravine below, where you'll see a cascading **waterfall** framed by double pools.

For a real *paniolo* (cowboy) experience, saddle up at **Mendes Ranch** (☎ 871-5222; www.mendesranch.com; 3530 Kahekili Hwy; 2hr rides $110; 🕑 rides 8:15am & 12:15pm), a working cattle ranch near the 7-mile marker. Take a camera – the picture-perfect scenery on these rides includes everything from jungle valleys to lofty seacliffs and waterfalls.

Waihe'e Ridge Trail

🌺 **our pick** This lightly trodden trail slices along a ridgetop deep into the West Maui Mountains, rewarding hikers with breathtaking views. The well-defined trail is 5 miles roundtrip and takes about three hours. It crosses forest reserve land and is a bit steep, but it's a fairly steady climb and not overly strenuous. Consider packing a lunch as there's a picnic spot with an unbeatable view waiting at the end.

Starting at an elevation of 1000ft, the trail climbs a ridge, passing from pasture to cool forest. Guava trees and groves of rainbow eucalyptus are prominent along the way, and if you look closely you can usually find thimbleberries. From the 0.75-mile post, panoramic views open up, with a scene that sweeps clear down to the ocean along the Waihe'e Gorge and deep into pleated valleys. As you continue on, you'll enter ohia forest with native birds and get distant views of waterfalls cascading down the mountains. The ridgetop views are similar to those you'd see from a helicopter, though the stillness along this route can be appreciated only by those on foot.

The trail ends at the 2563ft peak of Lanilili, where you'll enjoy awesome views in all directions.

To get to the trailhead, take the one-lane paved road that starts on the inland side of the highway just south of the 7-mile marker and leads up to the Boy Scouts' Camp Mahulia. The drive winds through open pasture, so keep an eye out for cattle that mosey across the road. The trailhead, marked with a Na Ala Hele sign, is a mile up on the left just before the camp.

Waihe'e to Wailuku

Soon after the Waihe'e Ridge Trail, the Kahekili Hwy runs through the sleeper towns of Waihe'e and Waiehu before arriving in Wailuku (p109). There's not much to do here, but if you're up for a round of golf, the county-run **Waiehu Municipal Golf Course** (☎ 243-7400; 200 Halewaiu Rd; greens fee $45, optional cart $16) offers an affordable and easily walkable 18 holes on the coast.

CENTRAL MAUI

Let it rip! Once all but overlooked by travelers, this wind-whipped region has hit the map big time, morphing into action-central for anything with a sail. Kanaha Beach takes home gold for kitesurfing and windsurfing, bursting into color each day in a glorious mile-long sea of sails. But you don't have to get all your thrills on the water. Central Maui has exceptional green treats, most notably lush 'Iao Valley, a sight so spectacular it was once reserved for royalty; two rare waterbird sanctuaries; and the most dazzling tropical aquarium you'll ever see. Bustling Kahului boasts Maui's largest farmers market and homespun Wailuku serves up the island's tastiest lunch scene.

CENTRAL MAUI
ITINERARIES

IN ONE DAY *This leg: 28 miles*

❶ 'IAO VALLEY STATE PARK (p113) Start your day in this magical state park ogling the island's most photographed landmark, 'Iao Needle. Follow your photo snaps with a walk along the park's cool streamside trails in search of the perfect swimming hole.

❷ WAILUKU (p109) Lucky you – there's no better place to be at lunchtime. The only hard part is choosing. Organic café fare, hot Vietnamese or those famous Sam Sato's noodles. Work off your lunch with a poke around the town's antique shops and a visit to the Bailey House Museum (p110).

❸ KANAHA BEACH PARK (p103) What? You weren't planning on taking up kite-surfing? That's OK. Just go sit on the beach and watch the show. It takes maybe all of five minutes of oohing and aahing (Look how fast she's going! Look how high he's jumping!) before you find yourself signing up for lessons.

❹ KANAHA POND BIRD SANCTUARY (p103) Mellow out at this unexpectedly peaceful respite. Unexpected because it's right along the highway where cars and trucks barrel along, yet once you walk through the gate into the wetlands it's all zen. Just you and some of the rarest birds on the planet.

❺ MAUI ARTS & CULTURAL CENTER (p107) An evening show here might well be one of the highlights of your trip. Amazing ukulele virtuosos, Willie Nelson at his finest – crikey, even whirling dervishes take to the stage.

IN TWO DAYS *This leg: 35 miles*

❻ KEALIA POND NATIONAL WILDLIFE REFUGE (p115) Plan your first day in Central Maui as above, then start day two meandering along Maui's longest boardwalk, getting a close-up look at the fascinating ocean, marsh and pond sights unfolding at your feet.

❼ PU'UNENE (p114) Roll down your windows and smell the sweet air of Maui's sugar town. Start at the Alexander & Baldwin Sugar Museum (p114) to get up to speed, then drive around the back of the sugar mill for a little detour (p114) to discover the remains of a forgotten plantation town.

❽ MAUI OCEAN CENTER (p115) Come eye to eye with huge stingrays, menacing reef sharks and pulsating jellyfish. A glass tunnel takes you right through the center of the tank – how cool is that? Lots of bubbly charm. Whether you're five or 95, you're gonna love the place.

❾ THE WATERFRONT (p116) Top off day two with a sunset dinner at Central Maui's best seafood restaurant. Sit on the breezy lanai and gaze out at Ma'alaea Harbor, where fishing boats pull up each afternoon and unload their catch. What to order? Catch of the day, natch.

FOR OCEAN ADVENTURES

❶ **WINDSURFING (p105)** Grab a sail and let the wind whip you across expansive Kahului Bay. Windsurf fanatics from all over the world come to Maui to test themselves. Most of them start right at **Kanaha Beach Park (p103)**. Now it's your turn.

❷ **KITESURFING (p105)** Strap yourself to a kite and fly. **Kite Beach (p103)**, at the southwest end of Kanaha Beach Park, is center stage for this exciting extreme sport. If you've never tried it before, you can learn the ropes from some of the very pros who've made kitesurfing Hawaii's hottest new wave ride.

❸ **SNORKELING AT MOLOKINI (p116)** It's time to take your adventures beneath the surface. Hop a boat at Ma'alaea Harbor for a snorkel cruise to the awesome volcanic crater of Molokini, renowned for its crystal waters and wildly abundant sealife. For the calmest water and best chance of seeing dolphins along the way, catch an early boat.

❹ **SHARK DIVE MAUI (p115)** The sharks are circling – some 20 of them, to be exact. Blacktip reef sharks, gray reef sharks, hammerheads and, gasp, a tiger shark. And if you're a certified diver, you can join the toothy beasts on a daredevil's plunge into Maui Ocean Center's 750,000-gallon deep-ocean tank as aquarium visitors gaze on in wonder.

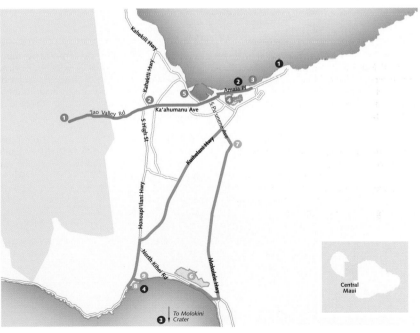

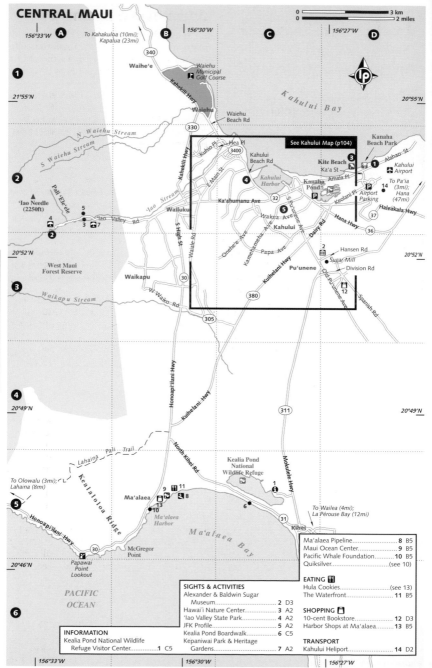

CENTRAL MAUI

SIGHTS & ACTIVITIES
Alexander & Baldwin Sugar
  Museum.....................................2 D3
Hawai'i Nature Center................3 A2
'Iao Valley State Park.................4 A2
JFK Profile.................................5 A2
Kealia Pond Boardwalk..............6 C5
Kepaniwai Park & Heritage
  Gardens.................................7 A2

Ma'alaea Pipeline........................8 B5
Maui Ocean Center.....................9 B5
Pacific Whale Foundation..........10 B5
Quiksilver..............................(see 10)

EATING
Hula Cookies.........................(see 13)
The Waterfront........................11 B5

SHOPPING
10-cent Bookstore....................12 D3
Harbor Shops at Ma'alaea.........13 B5

TRANSPORT
Kahului Heliport.......................14 D2

INFORMATION
Kealia Pond National Wildlife
  Refuge Visitor Center...............1 C5

HIGHLIGHTS

❶ **BEST BEACH:** Kanaha Beach Park (below)
❷ **BEST VIEW:** 'Iao Valley State Park (p113)
❸ **BEST ACTIVITY:** Windsurfing (p105)
❹ **BEST ENTERTAINMENT VENUE:** Maui Arts & Cultural Center (p107)
❺ **BEST PLACE TO MEET THE LOCALS:** Maui Swap Meet (p108)

Highlights are numbered on the map on p102.

KAHULUI

pop 20,150

All roads lead to Kahului. It's home to the island's gateway airport and the Superferry and cruise-ship harbors. Just about everything that enters Maui comes through this workaday town that's thick with warehouses and shopping centers. Need a Costco fix? This is the place. OK, perhaps that's sounding a bit too much like what you left back home. Well, there's more to Kahului. The gnarly windsurfing mecca of Kanaha Beach, the farmers proudly selling a cornucopia of goodies at the Maui Swap Meet – the deeper you dig the better Kahului looks.

History

Fronted by the island's deepwater port, Kahului has long been the commercial heart of Maui. In the 1880s it became headquarters to Hawaii's first railroad, built to haul sugar from the refineries to Kahului Harbor. In 1900 an outbreak of bubonic plague hit Kahului, and the settlement that had grown up around the harbor was deliberately burned to the ground.

Present-day Kahului is a planned community that was developed in the early 1950s by the Alexander & Baldwin sugar company. It was called 'Dream City' by cane workers who had long dreamed of moving away from the dusty mill camps and into a home of their own. These first tract houses are still found at the southern end of town.

Orientation & Information

Ka'ahumanu Ave (Hwy 32) is Kahului's main artery, connecting the town to neighboring Wailuku. Dairy Rd, to the south, links to both Lahaina (take Hwy 380) and Kihei (take Hwy 311).

Bank of Hawaii (☎ 871-8250; 27 S Pu'unene Ave)
Borders Books & Music Café (☎ 877-6160; Maui Marketplace, 270 Dairy Rd; ⌚ 9am-10pm Sun-Thu, to 11pm Fri & Sat) Good selection of maps, Hawaiiana books and international newspapers.
Kahului Public Library (☎ 873-3097; 90 School St; ⌚ 1-8pm Tue, 10am-5pm Wed-Sat) Internet access.
Kinko's (☎ 871-2000; Dairy Center, 395 Dairy Rd; per min 20¢; ⌚ 7am-10pm Mon-Fri, 9am-9pm Sat, 9am-6pm Sun) Fast internet access with no minimums.
Longs Drugs (☎ 877-0041; Maui Mall, 70 E Ka'ahumanu Ave; ⌚ 7am-midnight) The town's largest pharmacy
Maui Memorial Medical Center (☎ 244-9056; 221 Mahalani St; ⌚ 24hr) Actually on the fringes of the neighboring town of Wailuku, this is the island's main hospital.
Maui Visitors Bureau (☎ 872-3893; www.visitmaui .com; Kahului airport; ⌚ 7:45am-9:45pm) A staffed booth in the airport's arrivals area with tons of free tourist brochures.
Post office (☎ 871-2487; 138 S Pu'unene Ave, Kahului, HI 96732)

Beaches

KANAHA BEACH PARK

This mile-long beach is surf city, with hundreds of brilliant sails zipping across the waves. Both windsurfing and kitesurfing (also known as kiteboarding) are so hot here that the beach is divvied up, with kitesurfers converging at the southwest end, known as **Kite Beach**, and windsurfers hitting the water at the northeast end. There's no better place to learn both sports (see p105).

A section in the middle of the beach is roped off for swimmers, but this place is really all about wind power. Facilities include restrooms, showers and shaded picnic tables.

Sights

🏵 KANAHA POND BIRD SANCTUARY

Hwy 37; admission free; ⌚ dawn-dusk

This easy-access roadside sanctuary provides a haven for rare Hawaiian birds,

CENTRAL MAUI

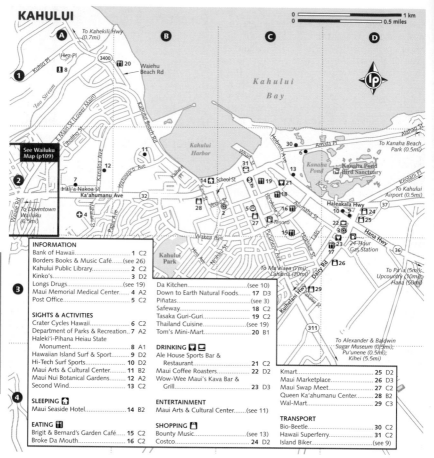

KAHULUI

including the *ae'o* (black-necked stilt), a wading bird with long orange legs that feeds along the pond's marshy edges. Even though this graceful bird has a population of just 1500 in the entire state, you can count on spotting it here.

An observation deck just a short walk beyond the parking lot offers the ideal lookout for seeing stilts, native coots and black-crowned night herons. Close the gate and walk into the preserve quietly; you should be able to make several sightings right along the shoreline.

MAUI NUI BOTANICAL GARDENS
249-2798; 150 Kanaloa Ave; admission free; 8am-4pm Mon-Sat

Those expecting a landscape of exotic tropical flowers in riotous colors may be disappointed. But if you're interested in the more subtle beauty of Hawaiian plants, this garden is precious. Come here to identify native plants you've heard about but haven't yet seen: *wauke* (paper mulberry, used to make tapa), *'iliahi* (sandalwood) and the medicinal *noni*. Don't leave without seeing *koki'o ke'oke'o*, a rare white hibiscus whose sole native habitat is the cliff face along Moloka'i's towering north shore, an area so remote that *National Geographic* filmed a scientist rappelling down ropes to study the rare blooms. And all you have to do is take a garden stroll!

MAUI ARTS & CULTURAL CENTER

MACC; ☎ 242-2787; www.mauiarts.org; 1 Cameron Way; admission free; 🕐 tour 11am Wed

Maui's pride and joy, MACC is the island's state-of-the-art concert venue. Free tours (reservations required) include both the concert halls and the grounds, which have the remains of a heiau. The center's **Schaefer International Gallery** (🕐 11am-5pm Tue-Sun) has changing exhibits of works by island and international artists.

Activities

Kahului is Maui's kitesurfing and windsurfing center. For more information on both, see the Outdoor Activities & Adventures chapter (p27).

KITESURFING

Also known as kiteboarding, kitesurfing has taken off big-time in Kahului. The action centers on Kite Beach, the southwest end of Kanaha Beach Park – go down and see what it's all about if you're thinking of giving it a fly. Vans set up right at the beach to offer lessons. Expect to pay about $300 for a half-day intro course.

Recommended operators:

Action Sports Maui (☎ 871-5857; www.actionsportsmaui.com)

Aqua Sports Maui (☎ 242-8015; www.mauikiteboardinglessons.com)

Kiteboarding Lessons of Maui (☎ 205-5558; www.kiteboardinglessonsmaui.com)

Kiteboarding School of Maui (☎ 873-0015; www.ksmaui.com)

WINDSURFING

Windswept Kahului is the base for Maui's main windsurfing operations. Board-and-rig rentals start around $50/300 per day/week. Introductory windsurfing classes last a couple of hours and cost around $85. The business is competitive, so ask about discounts.

Top-of-the-line shops that rent gear and arrange lessons:

Hawaiian Island Surf & Sport (☎ 871-4981, 800-231-6958; www.hawaiianisland.com; 415 Dairy Rd; 🕐 8:30am-6pm)

Hi-Tech Surf Sports (☎ 877-2111; www.htmaui.com; 425 Koloa St; 🕐 9am-6pm)

Second Wind (☎ 877-7467, 800-936-7787; www.secondwindmaui.com; 111 Hana Hwy; 🕐 9am-6pm)

Top Picks

NATURE SPOTS

- **'Iao Valley State Park** (p113)
- **Maui Nui Botanical Gardens** (opposite)
- **Kealia Pond Boardwalk** (p115)
- **Kanaha Pond Bird Sanctuary** (p103)
- **Maui Ocean Center** (p115)

HELICOPTER TOURS

Several companies, including **AlexAir** (☎ 871-0792), **Blue Hawaiian** (☎ 871-8844), **Mauiscape** (☎ 877-7272) and **Sunshine** (☎ 871-5600), offer helicopter tours of Maui and Moloka'i. All operate out of the **Kahului Heliport** (Map p102; 1 Kahului Airport Rd), at the southeast side of Kahului Airport. For details on tours and prices, see p35.

Festivals & Events

Neil Pryde Slalom (www.mauiwindsurfing.org) Top windsurfers take to the waves at this windsurfing slalom competition at Kanaha Beach Park in early June.

our pick **Ki Ho'alu Slack Key Guitar Festival** (www.mauiarts.org) Held at the Maui Arts & Cultural Center in late June, this festival showcases big-name slack key guitarists from throughout Hawaii. A cool scene with both old-time music and jazzed-up contemporary picking. Plenty of food booths selling local grinds, so plan to spend the day.

Maui Marathon (www.mauimarathon.com) This 26.2 mile race held in mid September begins at Queen Ka'ahumanu Center.

Eating

TASAKA GURI-GURI   Ice Cream $

☎ 871-4513; Maui Mall, 70 E Ka'ahumanu Ave; scoop/quart 50¢/$4.50; 🕐 10am-6pm Mon-Thu & Sat, to 8pm Fri, to 4pm Sun

For the coolest treat in town, queue up at this hole-in-the-wall shop dishing up homemade pineapple sherbet. The *guri-guri*, as it's called, is so popular that locals pick up quarts on the way to the airport to take to friends on neighboring islands.

PIÑATAS   Mexican $

☎ 877-8707; 395 Dairy Rd; mains $5-10; 🕐 10:30am-8pm Mon-Sat, from 11am Sun

Hey amigos, join the surfers at this serape-draped cantina serving good Mexican fare

CENTRAL MAUI

Top Picks

CENTRAL MAUI FOR KIDS
- **Maui Ocean Center** (p115)
- **Hawaii Nature Center** (p113)
- **Snorkeling trip to Molokini** (p116)

at honest prices. If you're starving, order the oversized 'kitchen sink burrito,' stuffed with beef, beans, guacamole, sour cream and nearly everything else you'd find in a Mexican kitchen except the sink.

DA KITCHEN   Hawaiian $
☎ 871-7782; 425 Koloa St; plate lunches $8-12; ◷ 9am-9pm

Hawaiian decor and unbeatable island grinds make this a favorite meal stop. The *kalua* pork is, as they say, 'so tender it falls off da bone,' and the more expensive plate lunches are big enough to feed two. Expect a crowd at lunch but don't be deterred as the service is quick.

THAILAND CUISINE   Thai $$
☎ 873-0225; Maui Mall, 70 E Ka'ahumanu Ave; mains $9-15; ◷ 10:30am-3:30pm & 5-9:30pm

Maui News readers voted this family-run eatery as Maui's best ethnic restaurant. And yes, it lives up to the reputation. Just be sure to get here early for dinner to beat the lines. Start with the shrimp summer rolls, then move on to aromatic green curries or perhaps the ginger grilled mahimahi.

BRIGIT & BERNARD'S GARDEN CAFE   Eclectic $$
☎ 877-6000; 335 Ho'ohana St; mains $10-20; ◷ lunch Mon-Fri, dinner Wed-Sat

The 'garden' is laughable – this little café overlooks a busy road in an industrial center. But the food is damn good and if you swing by at lunchtime you'll need to hustle just to find an empty table. The extensive menu runs from fresh Kula salads and grilled local fish to authentic German dishes like Wiener schnitzel.

Eating in? **Down to Earth Natural Foods** (☎ 877-2661; 305 Dairy Rd; ◷ 7am-9pm Mon-Sat, 8am-8pm Sun) has a full range of organic goodies, from a robust salad bar to deli

fare and groceries. For more conventional shopping, stop at **Safeway** (☎ 877-3377; 170 E Kamehameha Ave; ◷ 24hr) supermarket. For dessert, pick up Maui's best chocolate *haupia* (coconut pudding) pie at **Broke Da Mouth** (☎ 873-9255; 190 Alamaha St; ◷ 6am-7pm Mon-Fri, 7am-5pm Sat).

Drinking

WOW-WEE MAUI'S KAVA BAR & GRILL
☎ 871-1414; 333 Dairy Rd; ◷ 6am-9pm Sun-Thu, to midnight Fri & Sat

This hip café is *the* place to try kava drinks served in a coconut shell. Mildly intoxicating, this spicy elixir made from the roots of the *Piper methysticum* plant was a favored ceremonial drink in old Hawaii. And yes, it's legal. Wow-Wee Maui's famed chocolate bars will also make you swoon.

MAUI COFFEE ROASTERS
☎ 877-2877; 444 Hana Hwy; ◷ 7am-6pm Mon-Fri, 8am-5pm Sat, 8am-2:30pm Sun

Both the vibes and java are first-rate at this coffee shop where locals linger over lattes while surfing on free wi-fi. Need to jumpstart your day? Step up to the bar and order a Sledge Hammer – a quadruple espresso with steamed half and half.

ALE HOUSE SPORTS BAR & RESTAURANT
☎ 877-9001; 355 E Kamehameha Ave

A bit of a *Cheers* bar, wash-ashores from the mainland and locals alike gather here to watch major-league sports on big-screen TVs. And to make sure everyone shows up, they offer $2.50 draft beers whenever a big game is on.

Wow-Wee Maui's Kava Bar   GREG ELMS

CENTRAL MAUI

Entertainment

MAUI ARTS & CULTURAL CENTER
MACC; ☎ box office 242-7469; www.mauiarts.org;
1 Cameron Way

There's always something happening at this snazzy performance complex, which boasts two indoor theaters and an outdoor amphitheater, all with excellent acoustics. As Maui's main venue for music, theater

ISLAND VOICES

NAME: ROBBY NAISH
OCCUPATION: PRO WINDSURFER, BIG WAVE SURFER, KITESURFING PIONEER
RESIDENCE: HAIKU

Why is Maui special? As a wind- and ocean-minded local, Maui's unique in that the valley between the two mountain ranges creates a venturi effect – an acceleration – of the trade winds. So if we have normal 10- to 15-knot trades in most of the state, Maui's North Shore will be 15 to 25 knots. The consistency, year-round really, makes it a paradise for sports. It's almost guaranteed to have good wind and waves. So it's become really world-famous as being the spot where windsurfers dream of going once in their lives. And kiteboarders now as well.

Is Maui the best? It's probably the most famous wind, wave, water spot in the world. There are other good spots but they're often in Third World countries. The beauty about the North Shore is you've got the wind and waves, you've got really good places to eat and things to do, and a hospital close by in case you get into trouble.

What are the best spots on Maui? There's Kanaha Beach Park (p103), which for a recreational windsurfer is one of the best places in the world. With its sandy beach and constant trade winds, it's a great place for the average guy to go windsurfing. Then there's Hoʻokipa (p145), which is the premier spot for high-performance windsurfing. That's where the world's best professionals train year-round. A couple miles further up the coast we've got Jaws (p148), which during the 10 or 15 days during the year that it breaks is one of the most spectacular rideable big waves in the world.

How long does it take to learn kitesurfing basics? Normally one lesson. The learning curve is extremely quick. Of all the extreme sports, it's probably the most accessible. You can start when you're 50 and in a month be jumping and spinning and having the time of your life.

Any advice for beginners? Number-one thing is take a lesson. Go to a good windsurfing school or kitesurfing school – there are many on Maui. They quickly teach you the dos and don'ts, where to go, how to go…and from there the sky's the limit.

Do you go out daily? I go to Hoʻokipa nearly every day if I'm here. I still travel a good four months of the year, so I don't have the luxury of going day after day after day. But when I'm on Maui I'll be there.

How will we recognize you? I'll have the pink and red sail with US1111. Hopefully I'll be the guy really ripping!

CENTRAL MAUI

Maui Arts & Cultural Center   TONY NOVAK-CLIFFORD

and dance, it hosts everything from ukulele jams to touring rock bands. Check the schedule online.

Shopping

🌺 MAUI SWAP MEET
ourpick ☎ 877-3100; Pu'unene Ave; admission 50¢; ❂ 5:30am-1pm Sat

For a scene that glows with aloha, spend a Saturday morning chatting with local farmers and craftspeople at Maui's largest outdoor market. You'll not only find fresh organic Hana fruits, Kula veggies and homemade banana bread, but it's also a fun place to souvenir shop for everything from Hawaiian quilts to Maui-designed Ts.

BOUNTY MUSIC
☎ 871-1141; 111 Hana Hwy

Hawaiian music lovers, take note. Here you'll find all sorts of ukuleles, from $100 imported models to $4000 handcrafted masterpieces.

Kahului hosts Maui's big-box discount chains and the lion's share of its malls. Mainland discount stores like **Wal-Mart** (☎ 871-7820; 1011 Pakaula St; ❂ 6am-11pm), **Costco** (☎ 877-5241; 540 Haleakala Hwy; ❂ 11am-8:30pm Mon-Fri, 9:30am-6pm Sat, 10am-6pm Sun) and **Kmart** (☎ 871-8553; 424 Dairy Rd; ❂ 8am-11pm) are all on or near Dairy Rd. The island's largest malls, **Queen Ka'ahumanu Center** (☎ 877-4325; 275 Ka'ahumanu Ave; ❂ 9:30am-9pm Mon-Fri, to 7pm Sat, to 5pm Sun) and the **Maui Marketplace** (☎ 873-0400; 270 Dairy Rd; ❂ 10am-9pm Mon-Sat, to 7pm Sun), are nearby.

Sleeping

If you have some dire need to spend the night in Kahului, the better of its aging hotels is the **Maui Seaside Hotel** (☎ 877-3311, 800-560-5552; www.seasidehotelshawaii.com; 100 W Ka'ahumanu Ave; r from $120; 🅿 🖥 🌊). It's a Plain Jane but the rooms are clean. Forget camping at Kanaha Beach Park (p103) – planes rumble overhead from dawn to midnight, and folks down on their luck hang out here, making personal safety a real issue.

Getting There & Around
TO/FROM THE AIRPORT
Kahului airport is at the east side of town. Most visitors pick up rental cars (see p290) at the airport. 🌺 **Bio-Beetle** (☎ 873-6121, 877-873-6121) offers a green alternative to the scene, with Volkswagens that run on recycled vegetable oil. See p288 for shuttle and taxi information.

BICYCLE
Island Biker (☎ 877-7744; 415 Dairy Rd; per day/week $40/140; ❂ 9am-5pm Mon-Fri, to 3pm Sat) rents quality mountain bikes and road-racing bikes.

BUS
The Maui Bus (p289) connects Kahului with Ma'alaea, Kihei, Wailea and Lahaina; each route costs $1 and runs hourly. There are also free hourly buses that run around Kahului and connect to Wailuku.

Ukeleles at Bounty Music   GREG ELMS

Don't Miss

- The intoxicating combination of kava and chocolate at Wow-Wee Maui's (p116)
- Duke Kahanamoku's surfboard at Bailey House Museum (p110)
- The 'lava lamp' of pulsating jellyfish at Maui Ocean Center (p115)
- Organic Kula strawberries at Maui Swap Meet (opposite)

HALEKI'I-PIHANA HEIAU STATE MONUMENT

Overgrown and nearly forgotten, Haleki'i-Pihana Heiau (Map p104; Hea Pl; admission free; ☼ sunrise-sunset) holds the hilltop ruins of two of Maui's most important temples. The site was the royal court of Kahekili, Maui's last ruling chief, and the birthplace of Keopuolani, wife of Kamehameha the Great. After his victory at the battle of 'Iao

in 1790, Kamehameha marched to this site to worship his war god Ku, offering the last human sacrifice on Maui.

Haleki'i, the first heiau, has stepped stone walls that tower above 'Iao Stream, the source for the stone used in its construction. The pyramid-like mound of Pihana Heiau is a five-minute walk beyond, but a thick overgrowth of kiawe makes it harder to discern.

From Waiehu Beach Rd (Hwy 340), turn inland onto Kuhio Pl, then take the first left onto Hea Pl.

WAILUKU
pop 12,300

Wailuku is an enigma. It boasts more sights on the National Register of Historic Places than any other town on Maui but sees the fewest tourists. As the county capital, its central area wears a modern facade of mid-rise office buildings, while its backstreets hold an earthy mishmash of pawnshops, galleries and antique shops that just beg browsing.

CENTRAL MAUI

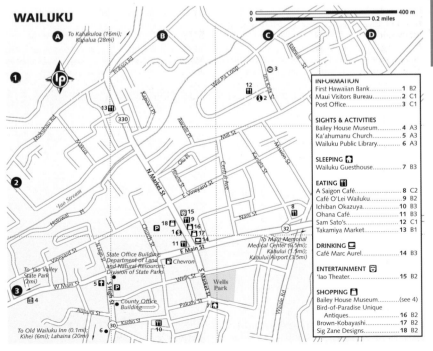

WAILUKU

0 ___ 400 m
0 ___ 0.2 miles

INFORMATION
First Hawaiian Bank.................1 B2
Maui Visitors Bureau................2 C1
Post Office...............................3 C1

SIGHTS & ACTIVITIES
Bailey House Museum............4 A3
Ka'ahumanu Church...............5 A3
Wailuku Public Library.......... 6 A3

SLEEPING 🏠
Wailuku Guesthouse...............7 B3

EATING 🍴
A Saigon Café.........................8 C2
Café O'Lei Wailuku.................9 B2
Ichiban Okazuya...................10 B3
Ohana Café...........................11 B3
Sam Sato's............................12 C1
Takamiya Market...................13 B1

DRINKING 🍺
Café Marc Aurel....................14 B3

ENTERTAINMENT 🎭
'Iao Theater..........................15 B2

SHOPPING 🛍️
Bailey House Museum...........(see 4)
Bird-of-Paradise Unique
    Antiques..........................16 B2
Brown-Kobayashi..................17 B3
Sig Zane Designs...................18 B2

Long a sleeper when it came time to eat, Wailuku's dining scene is evolving into a real eye-opener. Cafés sporting green and organic labels are blooming. Any excuse to find yourself in this town at lunchtime will do.

Orientation & Information

The county and state office buildings are adjacent on S High St, near its intersection with Main St.

First Hawaiian Bank (☎ 877-2377; 27 N Market St)
Maui Visitors Bureau (MVB; ☎ 244-3530, 800-525-6284; www.visitmaui.com; 1727 Wili Pa Loop; ☺ 8am-4:30pm Mon-Fri) Essentially an administrative office – you'll find better information and more brochures at the airport booth.
Post office (☎ 244-1653; 250 Imi Kala St; ☺ 8am-4:30pm Mon-Fri, 9am-noon Sat)

Dangers & Annoyances

One caution: the town can get rough at night. The public parking lot on W Main St is an after-dark hangout rife with drug dealing and fights that gets more police calls than any other spot on Maui.

Sights

If you love period architecture, pick up a copy of the free Wailuku Historic District walking map at the Bailey House Museum and stroll S High St. The c 1928 **Wailuku Public Library** (251 S High St), for instance, was designed by Maui native CW Dickey, Hawaii's best-known architect, who borrowed from Mediterranean styles to create a distinctive Hawaii regional design.

BAILEY HOUSE MUSEUM

☎ 244-3326; 2375 W Main St; adult/child under 12 $5/1; ☺ 10am-4pm Mon-Sat
This superb museum occupies the 1833 home of Wailuku's first Christian missionary, Edward Bailey. The second story, decorated with Bailey's spare furnishings, reflects his era. But downstairs, the Hawaiian section is the real prize. The intriguing collection of native artifacts includes shark-tooth daggers and other weapons used in the bloody battles at nearby 'Iao Valley. Don't miss the 10ft redwood surfboard, in the exhibit near the parking lot,

that surfing legend Duke Kahanamoku once rode.

KA'AHUMANU CHURCH

cnr W Main & S High Sts
This handsome 1832 missionary church is named for Queen Ka'ahumanu, who cast aside the old gods and allowed Christianity to flourish. The clock in the steeple, brought around the Horn in the 19th century, still keeps accurate time. Hymns ring out in Hawaiian at Sunday morning services, but at other times it's a look-from-outside site, as the church is usually locked.

Festivals & Events

Maui County Fair (www.mauicountyfair.com) Get a feel for Maui's agricultural roots at this venerable fair held in late September at the War Memorial Complex, with farm exhibits, ethnic foods and a dazzling orchid display.
E Ho'oulu Aloha (www.mauimuseum.org) This old-Hawaii-style festival held in November at the Bailey House Museum features hula, ukulele masters, crafts, food and more. You won't find a friendlier community scene.

Eating

TOM'S MINI-MART   Shave Ice $

our pick Map p104; ☎ 244-2323; 372 Waiehu Beach Rd; shave ice $2; ☺ 7am-6pm Mon-Sat
Search out this little neighborhood shop in the middle of nowhere for supersmooth

Ka'ahumanu Church   NED FRIARY

Top Picks

LOCAL SWEET TREATS

- **Manju at Sam Sato's** (below)
- **Chocolate haupia pie at Broke Da Mouth** (p106)
- **Pineapple guri-guri at Tasaka Guri-Guri** (p105)
- **Mango shave ice at Tom's Mini-Mart** (opposite)

shave ice ripe with tropical fruit syrups. You gotta try the mango.

TAKAMIYA MARKET   Hawaiian $
☎ 244-3404; 359 N Market St; ✆ 5:30am-6:30pm Mon-Sat
The king of local takeout, this old-time grocery store specializes in all things Hawaiian. *'Ahi poke, laulau, kalua* pig (see the food glossary on p265), Japanese-style meals – at lunchtime there are literally hundreds of items, all wrapped and ready to go.

SAM SATO'S   Japanese $
☎ 244-7124; 1750 Wili Pa Loop; mains $4-8; ✆ 7am-2pm Mon-Sat
Don't even think of coming during the noon rush – islanders flock here from far and wide for Sato's steaming bowls of saimin-like dry noodles. Maui's number-one noodle house also makes amazing *manju* (Japanese cakes filled with sweet bean paste), which are sold for takeout at the counter until 4pm.

A Saigon Café   GREG ELMS

ICHIBAN OKAZUYA   Plate Lunch $
☎ 244-7276; 2133 Kaohu St; mains $6-7; ✆ 10am-2pm & 4-7pm Mon-Fri
Little more than a tin-roofed shed, this place tucked behind the government buildings has been dishing out tasty Japanese-style plate lunches to office workers for half a century, so you'd better believe it has the recipes down pat. It's takeout, but there's an inviting picnic table shaded by an old mango tree out back.

🌿 OHANA CAFÉ   Café $
☎ 244-5950; 2010 Main St; mains $5-9; ✆ 8am-2pm Mon-Fri
Wailuku's greenest meals sizzle on the grill in front of your eyes at this cozy café. Wake up to mac-nut French toast with organic maple syrup or swing by at lunch for the seared *'ahi* wrap with brown rice and local greens. The word 'organic' precedes most everything on the luscious menu.

CAFÉ O'LEI WAILUKU   Hawaii Regional $
☎ 986-0044; N Market St; mains $6-12; ✆ 7:30am-3pm Mon-Fri, 7am-1pm Sat
Sophisticated decor, waitstaff in black… Wailuku has never looked so smart. The food's on par with top-end restaurants and the average price is less than $10. Stars include the mac-nut–crusted chicken on foccacia and their signature blackened mahimahi topped with fresh papaya salsa.

A SAIGON CAFÉ   Vietnamese $$
our pick ☎ 248-9560; cnr Main & Kaniela Sts; mains $7-20; ✆ 10am-9:30pm Mon-Sat, to 8:30pm Sun
If anyone tells you this isn't the best Vietnamese food on Maui, you can bet they didn't find the place. And that's the challenge – there's no sign and it's hidden on a backstreet. But you'll be well rewarded for your effort. Menu stars include the Buddha rolls in spicy peanut sauce and the aromatic lemongrass curries. To get there take Central Ave to Nani St and turn south on Kaniela St.

Drinking & Entertainment

🌿 CAFÉ MARC AUREL
☎ 244-0852; 28 N Market St; ✆ 7am-at least 9pm Mon-Sat
Proof positive that down-home Wailuku has its hip corners, this 'green certified' café

CENTRAL MAUI

The historic 'Iao Theater   GREG ELMS

brews organic espresso by day and morphs into a wine bar with jazz at night.

'IAO THEATER
☎ 242-6969; www.mauionstage.com; 68 N Market St
Beautifully restored after years of neglect, this 1928 art deco theater, which once hosted big names such as Frank Sinatra, is now the venue for community theater productions.

Shopping
Wailuku's best shops:
Bailey House Museum (☎ 244-3326; 2375 W Main St) Fine local crafts and a good selection of books about Maui.

Island Insights

Olympian gold-medal swimmer Duke Kahanamoku (1890–1968) revived the ancient art of surfing. A full-blooded Hawaiian, he traveled the world with his surfboard in hand, introducing the sport to people in Australia, Europe and the US mainland. Today he's considered the father of modern surfing.

Bird-of-Paradise Unique Antiques (☎ 242-7699; 56 N Market St) Poke around here for vintage Hawaiiana.
Brown-Kobayashi (☎ 242-0804; 38 N Market St) Museum-quality Asian antiques.
Sig Zane Designs (☎ 249-8997; 53 N Market St) Original aloha shirts and women's wear that's beautiful to behold.

Sleeping
WAILUKU GUESTHOUSE   Guesthouse $
☎ 877-986-8270; www.wailukuhouse.com; 210 S Market St; r $80-95; 🖵
This affordable family-run guesthouse offers Hawaiian-style hospitality with simple, clean rooms, each with their own bathroom and private entrance. There's a refrigerator and coffeemaker in the rooms, and guests have access to a barbecue grill.

OLD WAILUKU INN   B&B $$
our pick ☎ 244-5897, 800-305-4899; www.mauiinn.com; 2199 Kaho'okele St; r incl breakfast $150-190; 🖵
Step back into the 1920s in this elegant period home built by a wealthy banker. Authentically restored, the inn retains the antique appeal of earlier times while discreetly adding modern amenities. Each room has its own personality, but all are large and comfy with traditional Hawaiian quilts warming the beds. Hands-down the finest place to lay your head in Central Maui.

Getting There & Around
The Maui Bus (p289) runs free buses between Wailuku and Kahului hourly from 7:30am to 8:30pm. Wailuku stops include the state office building and the post office.

WAILUKU TO 'IAO VALLEY STATE PARK
'Iao Valley's unspoiled natural beauty belies its brutal past. Filled as it is today with sightseers and picnickers, it's hard to imagine this was once the site of Maui's bloodiest battle. In 1790 Kamehameha the Great invaded Kahului by sea and routed the defending Maui warriors up into precipitous 'Iao Valley. Those unable to escape over

the mountains were slaughtered along the stream. The waters of 'Iao Stream were so choked with bodies that the area was called Kepaniwai (Dammed Waters).

Today a steady stream of cars and tour buses marches up 'Iao Valley Rd along the same streamside route to Maui's most celebrated sight, 'Iao Needle.

Sights

KEPANIWAI PARK & HERITAGE GARDENS
Map p102; 875 'Iao Valley Rd; ☾ 7am-7pm

Two miles west of Wailuku, this family-oriented park pays tribute to Hawaii's ethnic heritages. Sharing the grounds are a traditional Hawaiian *hale* (house), a New England–style missionary home, a Filipino farmer's hut, Japanese gardens with stone pagodas and a Chinese pavilion with a statue of revolutionary hero Sun Yat-sen (who, incidentally, briefly lived on Maui). 'Iao Stream runs through the park, bordered by picnic shelters with barbecue pits. The place is cheerfully alive with families picnicking here on weekends.

✿ HAWAII NATURE CENTER
Map p102; ☎ 244-6500; 875 'Iao Valley Rd; adult/child 5-12 $6/4; ☾ 10am-4pm

At the west end of Kepaniwai Park, this nonprofit educational facility has interactive kid-oriented exhibits that let *keiki* (children) take to the air on the wings of a dragonfly, hear the screech of a Hawaiian owl and the like. For those over 10, more interesting are the center's guided two-hour **rain-forest walks** (adult/child 5-12 $30/20) that climb into an unspoiled wilderness that's otherwise inaccessible; reservations are required.

JFK PROFILE
Map p102; 'Iao Valley Rd

At a bend in the road a half-mile after Kepaniwai Park, you'll likely see a few cars pulled over and their occupants staring off into Pali 'Ele'ele, a gorge on the right where a rock formation has eroded into the shape of a profile. Some legends associate it with a powerful *kahuna* (priest) who lived here during the 1500s, but today it bears an uncanny resemblance to former president John F Kennedy. If parking is difficult, continue on to 'Iao Valley State

Park, as it's only a couple of minutes' walk from there back to the viewing site.

'IAO VALLEY STATE PARK
our pick Every Hawaiian island has a landmark scene of singular beauty that's duplicated nowhere else. On O'ahu it's Diamond Head and on Maui it's unquestionably 'Iao Needle. Rising above a mountain stream in Maui's lush interior, this sensuous rock pinnacle is the focal point of ✿ **'Iao Valley State Park** (Map p102; admission free; ☾ 7am-7pm). The rain-forest park, which starts 3 miles west of central Wailuku, extends clear up to Pu'u Kukui (5788ft), Maui's highest and wettest point.

'Iao Valley State Park   GREG ELMS

CENTRAL MAUI

Island Insights

'Iao Needle

The velvety green pinnacle that rises straight up 2250ft takes its name from 'Iao, the daughter of Maui. 'Iao Needle is said to be 'Iao's clandestine lover cast into stone (see the boxed text on p113).

Whether you believe in legends or not, this place looks like something from the pages of a fairy tale. Clouds rising up the valley form an ethereal shroud around the top of 'Iao Needle. With a stream meandering beneath and the steep cliffs of the West Maui Mountains in the backdrop, it's the most photographed scene on Maui. Just a few minutes' walk from the parking lot, you'll reach a bridge where most people shoot their photos of the needle. A better idea is to take the walkway just before the bridge that loops downhill by the stream; this leads to the nicest photo angle, one that captures the stream, bridge and 'Iao Needle together.

If the water is high you'll see local kids taking bravado jumps from the bridge to the rocky stream below. You might be tempted to join them, but expect to get the stink eye, and the rocks below are potentially spine-crushing for unfamiliar divers. It's better to take your dip from the streamside path below, where there are lovely swimming holes.

Walking Trails

After you cross the bridge you'll come to two short trails that start opposite each other. Both take just 10 minutes to walk and shouldn't be missed. The upper path leads skyward up a series of steps, ending at a sheltered lookout with a close-up view of 'Iao Needle. The lower path leads down along 'Iao Stream, skirting the rock-strewn streambed past native hau trees with their fragrant hibiscus-like flowers. Look around and you'll be able to spot fruiting guava trees as well. The lower path returns to the bridge by way of a garden of native Hawaiian plants, including patches of taro.

PU'UNENE

Pu'unene revolves around sugar. Endless fields of sugarcane expand out from the Hawaiian Commercial & Sugar (C&S) Company's mill that sits smack in the center of the village. If you happen to swing by when the mill is boiling down the sugarcane, the air hangs heavy with the sweet smell of molasses.

Pu'unene's main attraction, the **Alexander & Baldwin Sugar Museum** (Map p102; ☎ 871-8058; cnr Pu'unene Ave & Hansen Rd; adult/child 6-17 $5/2; ⏰ 9:30am-4:30pm Mon-Sat, also Sun Jul & Aug), occupies the former home of the mill's superintendent. Evocative exhibits give the skinny on the sugarcane biz and include a working scale model of a cane-crushing plant. Even more interesting, however, are the images of people. The museum traces how the privileged sons of missionaries wrested control over Maui's fertile valleys

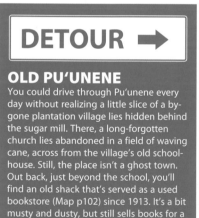

DETOUR ➡

OLD PU'UNENE

You could drive through Pu'unene every day without realizing a little slice of a bygone plantation village lies hidden behind the sugar mill. There, a long-forgotten church lies abandoned in a field of waving cane, across from the village's old schoolhouse. Still, the place isn't a ghost town. Out back, just beyond the school, you'll find an old shack that's served as a used bookstore (Map p102) since 1913. It's a bit musty and dusty, but still sells books for a mere dime. To get there turn off Mokulele Hwy (Hwy 311) onto Hansen Rd and take the first right onto Old Pu'unene Ave, continuing past the old Pu'unene Meat Market building (c 1926) and the mill. Turn left after half a mile, just past a little bridge. Just before the pavement ends, turn right and drive behind the old school to reach the bookstore, which is open 9am to 4pm Tuesday to Saturday.

GREEN POWER

It may be a tiny village but Pu'unene lays claim to one of the world's largest biomass power plants. A thorough recycler, the power plant adjacent to the mill burns residue sugarcane fibers, called bagasse, to run the mill machinery that refines the sugar. With a capacity of 37,000 kilowatts, it's also a significant contributor to the island-wide grid system.

Boardwalk in Kealia Pond NWR NED FRIARY

and dug the amazing irrigation system that made large-scale plantations viable. Representing the other end of the scale is an early-20th-century labor contract from the Japanese Emigration Company stating that the laborer shall be paid $15 a month for working the fields 10 hours a day, 26 days a month.

KEALIA POND NATIONAL WILDLIFE REFUGE

A bird-watcher's oasis, 🐦 **Kealia Pond National Wildlife Refuge** (Map p102; ☎ 875-1582; Mokulele Hwy; ☷ 7:30am-4pm Mon-Fri) harbors native waterbirds year-round and migratory birds in winter. In the rainy season Kealia Pond swells to 400 acres, while in summer it shrinks to half the size, creating a skirt of crystalline salt (Kealia means 'salt-encrusted place').

Birding is excellent from the boardwalk (see the boxed text below) on North Kihei Rd, as well as from the refuge's visitor center off Mokulele Hwy (Hwy 311) at the 6-mile marker. In both places, you're almost certain to spot wading Hawaiian black-necked stilts and Hawaiian coots – endangered species that thrive in this sanctuary.

NEVER BORED ON THE BOARDWALK

You can tread gently *and* directly into a fragile wildlife habitat thanks to a new elevated boardwalk that's turned inaccessible marshland into an exceptional nature walk. The coastal dunes nestling Kealia Pond not only provide feeding grounds for native waterbirds but are also a nesting site for the endangered hawksbill sea turtle. The 2200ft boardwalk begins on North Kihei Rd near the 2-mile marker. Interpretive plaques and benches along the way offer opportunities to stop and enjoy the splendor, and in winter you might be able to spot passing humpback whales. You'll even find a turtle laying eggs at the end of the boardwalk. Say what?! Go take a look…

MA'ALAEA

Wind defines Ma'alaea. Prevailing trade winds sweep from the north, funneling down between the two great rises of Haleakalā and the West Maui Mountains straight at Ma'alaea Bay. It's no coincidence that Maui's first windmill farm marches up the slopes here. By midday you'll need to hold on to your hat.

Sights

MAUI OCEAN CENTER

our pick Map p102; ☎ 270-7000; www.mauiocean center.com; 192 Ma'alaea Rd; adult/child 3-12 $24/17; ☷ 9am-6pm Jul & Aug, to 5pm Sep-Jun

The largest tropical aquarium in the USA showcases Hawaii's dazzling marine life with award-winning style. The exhibits are laid out to take you on an ocean journey, beginning with nearshore reefs teeming with colorful tropical fish like those you see while snorkeling and ending with deep-ocean sealife. For the spectacular grand finale, you walk along a 54ft glass tunnel right through the center of a massive tank as gliding stingrays and menacing tiger sharks encircle you. It's as close as you'll ever get to being underwater without donning dive gear.

Kid-friendly features abound, including interactive displays on whales in the Marine Mammal Discovery Center, a cool touch pool and, best of all, *keiki*-level viewing ports that allow the wee ones to peer into everything on their own.

And how's this for thrills? Certified divers can take a daredevil plunge into the deep-ocean tank with **Shark Dive Maui** (2hr dive $200; 🕐 8:15am Mon, Wed & Fri).

Activities

HIKING

Fine hilltop views of Kaho'olawe and Lana'i are in store along the **Lahaina Pali Trail**, which follows an ancient footpath as it zigzags steeply up through native dryland. After the first mile it passes into open, sun-baked scrub, from where you can see Haleakalā and the fertile central plains. Ironwood trees precede the crossing of Kealaoloa Ridge (1600ft), after which you descend through Ukumehame Gulch. Look for stray petroglyphs and *paniolo* (cowboy) graffiti. Stay on the footpath all the way down to Papalaua Beach and don't detour onto 4WD roads. The 5.5-mile trail should take about 2½ hours each way.

You can hike in either direction, but starting off early from the east side of the mountains keeps you ahead of the blistering sun. The trailhead access road, marked by a Na Ala Hele sign, is on Hwy 30, about 100yd south of the intersection of Hwy 380. If you prefer to start at the west end, the trailhead is 200yd south of the 11-mile marker on Hwy 30.

SNORKELING

Many of the boats going out to Molokini (see p29) leave from Ma'alaea. Afternoon trips are often cheaper, but rougher and murkier. Snorkel gear is included. Bring your own towels and sunscreen.

Pacific Whale Foundation (Map p102; ☎ 849-8811, 800-942-5311; www.pacificwhale.org; Ma'alaea Harbor Village Mall; adult/child 7-12 from $55/35; 🕐 7am-6pm) Led by naturalists, these Molokini outings do it right, with on-boat snorkeling lessons and wildlife talks. Snacks are provided and kids under six travel free.

Quicksilver (Map p102; ☎ 662-0075, 888-700-3764; Slip 103, Ma'alaea Harbor; per person $95) If you want more of a party scene, book a snorkel tour on this sleek double-decker catamaran. Once you're done in the water they crank up Jimmy Buffett and break out a barbecue lunch.

SURFING & WINDSURFING

Wicked winds from the north shoot straight out toward Kaho'olawe, creating some of the best **windsurfing** conditions on Maui. In winter, when the wind dies down elsewhere, windsurfers still fly along Ma'alaea Bay.

The bay also has a couple of hot surfing spots. The **Ma'alaea Pipeline**, south of the harbor, freight-trains right and is the fastest surf break in all Hawaii. Summer's southerly swells produce huge tubes. Ma'alaea Bay is fronted by a continuous 3-mile stretch of sandy beach, running from Ma'alaea Harbor south to Kihei, and can be accessed at several places along North Kihei Rd.

Eating

HULA COOKIES   Ice Cream $
Map p102; ☎ 243-2271; Harbor Shops at Ma'alaea; snacks $2-5; 🕐 10am-6pm Mon-Sat, to 5pm Sun
Reward your inner child with fresh-made cookies and island-made ice cream chock full of macadamia nuts, pineapple and mango.

THE WATERFRONT   Seafood $$$$
Map p102; ☎ 244-9028; Milowai Condominium, 50 Hauoli St; dinner $26-41; 🕐 dinner
Sit on the lanai, listen to the surf and order fresh-off-the-boat seafood at this harborfront restaurant. The type of fish depends on what's reeled in each day, but the preparation choice – nine tempting options – is yours. Maybe you're in a blackened Cajun mood. Perhaps Sicilian with artichoke hearts and roasted garlic. The food, service and wine selection are among Maui's best.

Getting There & Away

Located at a crossroads, Ma'alaea has good connections to the rest of Maui's public bus system. The Maui Bus (p289) connects the Harbor Shops at Ma'alaea shopping center with Lahaina, Kahului, Kihei and Wailea. Service depends on the route, but buses operate hourly from around 6am to 8pm.

SOUTH MAUI

Hungry? The mixed plate of adventures here will sate any intrepid appetite. Snorkel reefs teeming with turtles, kayak remote bays frequented by dolphins or sail off in an outrigger canoe. The coral gardens are so rich you can step in and dive from the shore. The beaches are nothing short of glorious, whether you're looking to hang under a resort cabana or discover your own little pocket of sand. Add reliably sunny weather, lightly trodden coastal trails and a taste-bud-pleasing dining scene and South Maui's a pretty tempting place to settle in. Eventually you'll need to tear yourself off the beach towel and see the rest of Maui but, heck, get your tan first.

SOUTH MAUI
ITINERARIES

IN TWO DAYS This leg: 30 miles

❶ ULUA BEACH (p133) Start your first day shaking off the jet lag at Wailea's favorite snorkeling beach. Get really dazzled by donning a mask and snorkeling north to coral gardens teeming with colorful fish. See if you can identify the *humuhumunukunukuapua'a*, Hawaii's state fish, which has more colors than vowels.

❷ SOUTH KIHEI (p120) There's no better place to be at lunchtime than at **Café O'Lei (p128)**, munching on Maui-centric fare. Now work off those calories by walking in the footsteps of the ancients along the scenic **Kihei Coastal Trail (p121)**.

❸ MAKENA BAY (p137) Start your second day kayaking at **Makena Landing (p137)**, paddling south through waters so thick

with green sea turtles they're dubbed Turtle Town. Back on land mosey over to the **Keawala'i Congregational Church (p139)** for a glimpse of Makena's *paniolo* (cowboy) past.

❹ MAKENA STATE PARK (p138) Take a walk on the wild side at Big Beach, a magnificent stretch of endless sand and surf untouched by development. And if the bathing suit is feeling restrictive, climb the hill to unclad Little Beach.

❺ SANSEI SEAFOOD RESTAURANT & SUSHI BAR (p128) When dinnertime swings around, head back to Kihei. Revel in an explosion of flavors at this hip fusion restaurant, where fiery wasabi meets hot Eurasian cuisine.

IN FOUR DAYS This leg: 35 miles

❻ MALU'AKA BEACH (p138) If you have four days in South Maui, plan your first two as above. Then on day three get an early start before the wind picks up and head down to Turtle Beach, the best place on Maui to swim among honkin' big sea turtles.

❼ MAKENA STABLES (p140) Giddyup on a sunset ride up the slopes of 'Ulupalakua Ranch with a Maui-born cowboy whose stories are as fascinating as the terrain.

❽ MAUI DREAMS DIVE COMPANY (p124) All that snorkeling got you craving something deeper? Take the plunge with this personable dive outfit. Never been before? No problem. They can set you up with an introductory dive from shore.

❾ KEAWAKAPU BEACH (p120) Lucky you – all of South Maui faces the sunset. On your last evening, pack a picnic and watch the orange orb drop into the sea from Kihei's loveliest strand.

Big Beach in Makena State Park

NED FRIARY

FOR FAMILIES

❶ HAWAIIAN SAILING CANOE ADVENTURES (p134) Hop aboard a traditional outrigger canoe for a Hawaiian-style sail. Chants, stories and a chance to slip over the side for a swim assure a good time.

❷ LOCAL BOYS SHAVE ICE (p125) Cool off with a rainbow-striped cone of soft shaved ice drenched in sweet Hawaiian flavors. Top choice among the local boys: Maui pineapple, naturally.

❸ KALEPOLEPO BEACH PARK (p122) Little tots will love splashing around this protected beach within the walls of an ancient fishpond. After drying off, stroll over to the adjacent **Hawaiian Islands Humpback Whale National Marine Sanctuary (p123)** to see the cool whale sights.

❹ GRAND WAILEA RESORT HOTEL & SPA (p136) If you gave your kids a choice of where to unpack their bags, they'd choose this splashy hotel without a pause. Waterworld thrills with nine pools, white-water rapids, towering slides and shrieks galore.

❺ ESKIMO CANDY (p127) Ahoy matey. The pirate decor and Captain Kid's menu spells fun at dinnertime, and the casual setting lets the *keiki* (children) hang loose. Popeye burger, anyone?

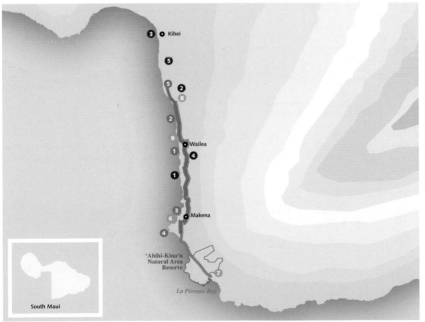

SOUTH MAUI

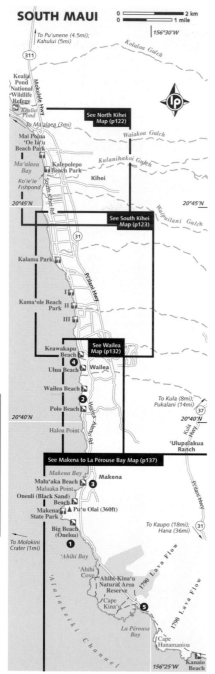

SOUTH MAUI

See North Kihei Map (p122)

See South Kihei Map (p123)

See Wailea Map (p132)

See Makena to La Pérouse Bay Map (p137)

SOUTH MAUI

KIHEI

pop 19,850

Fringed with 6 miles of sun-kissed beaches, and loaded with affordable accommodation options, it's easy to see why Kihei has boomed into the island's largest tourist destination. The strip-mall development is not Maui's finest look, but it's just two skips to the beach from nearly every condo and hotel. You'll find everything you need for an enjoyable seaside vacation close at hand.

Orientation & Information

The Pi'ilani Hwy (Hwy 31) runs parallel to and bypasses the stop-start traffic of S Kihei Rd. Half a dozen crossroads connect the two, making it easy to zip in and out of Kihei efficiently.

Bank of Hawaii (Map p122; ☎ 879-5844; Azeka Mauka, 1279 S Kihei Rd)

Coffee Store (Map p122; ☎ 875-4244; Azeka Mauka, 1279 S Kihei Rd; per min 20¢; ⏰ 6am-6pm Mon-Sat, to 5pm Sun) Internet café with good java.

Kihei Police District Station (Map p123; ☎ 244-6400; Kihei Town Center, 1881 S Kihei Rd; ⏰ 7:45am-4:30pm Mon-Fri)

Lipoa Laundry Center (Map p122; Lipoa Center, 40 E Lipoa St; ⏰ 8am-9pm Mon-Sat, to 5pm Sun)

Longs Drugs (Map p122; ☎ 879-2033; 1215 S Kihei Rd; ⏰ 7am-midnight) Kihei's largest pharmacy.

Post office (Map p122; ☎ 879-1987; 1254 S Kihei Rd)

Urgent Care Maui Physicians (Map p122; ☎ 879-7781; 1325 S Kihei Rd; ⏰ 7am-10pm) This clinic accepts walk-in patients.

Beaches

The further south you go, the better the beaches get. At the northern end of Kihei, swimming is not advised, but kayaking is good in the morning and windsurfers set off in the afternoon.

KEAWAKAPU BEACH

our pick Map p123

The star of Kihei's public beaches, this sparkling stretch of sand extends from southern Kihei to Wailea's Mokapu Beach. Less visible than Kihei's main roadside beaches, Keawakapu Beach is also less crowded.

With its cushiony soft sand, it's a favorite for people doing sunrise yoga and wake-up

HIGHLIGHTS

❶ **BEST BEACH:** Big Beach (p138)
❷ **BEST VIEW:** Wailea Beach Walk (p133)
❸ **BEST ACTIVITY:** Snorkeling (p138)
❹ **BEST SUNSET SWIM:** Keawakapu
Beach (opposite)
❺ **BEST LAVA LANDSCAPE:** La Pérouse
Bay (p140)

**Highlights are numbered on the map
on p120.**

strolls, and is the perfect spot for a sunset swim. Mornings are the best time for snorkeling: head to the rocky outcrops that form the northern and southern ends of the beach. During winter keep an eye out for humpback whales, which come remarkably close to shore here.

There are three beach access points, all with outdoor showers. To get to the south end, go south on S Kihei Rd until it deadends at a beach parking lot. Near the middle of the beach, there's a parking lot at the corner of Kilohana and S Kihei Rd; look for a blue shoreline access sign on the *makai* (seaward) side of the street. At the northern end, beach parking can be found at the side of Mana Kai Maui.

Keawakapu Beach   GREG ELMS

KAMA'OLE BEACH PARKS
Map p123

Kama'ole is one long beach divided into three sections by rocky points. Known locally as Kam I, II and III, all three are pretty golden-sand beaches with full facilities, lifeguards included.

Water conditions vary with the weather, but swimming is usually good. For the most part, these beaches have sandy bottoms with a fairly steep drop, which tends to create good conditions for bodysurfing, especially in winter.

For snorkeling, the south end of Kama'ole Beach Park III has some near-shore rocks harboring a bit of coral and a

DETOUR ➡

KIHEI COASTAL TRAIL

Leave the crowds at the beach and follow this new trail (Map p123) along coastal bluffs ideal for whale watching and quiet meditation. At the start of the trail look for the burrows of *'ua'u kani* (wedge-tailed shearwaters), ground-nesting seabirds that return to the same sites each spring. The birds lay a single egg and remain until November, when the fledglings are large enough to head out to sea.

The lightly trodden trail starts beyond the grassy lawn at the south end of Kama'ole Beach Park III and winds half a mile south to Kihei Surfside condos, just beyond Kihei Boat Ramp. The easy-to-follow path is of packed gray gravel outlined in white coral. Curiously, when the trail was being built, a storm washed hundreds of yards of bleached coral onto the shore here. The coral was not originally planned for the trail construction, but the volunteers building the trail consulted with a Hawaiian kahuna (priest) and were told ancient trails often were outlined in white coral so they could be followed at night. The Hawaiian gods were thanked for the gift of coral, which was then incorporated into the trail. Benches set in pretty places and interpretive plaques identifying native plants enhance the experience.

SOUTH MAUI

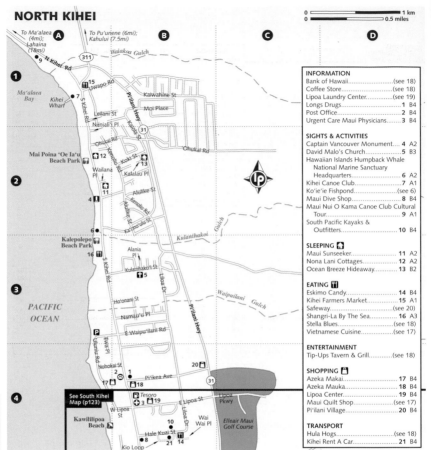

NORTH KIHEI

INFORMATION	
Bank of Hawaii	(see 18)
Coffee Store	(see 18)
Lipoa Laundry Center	(see 19)
Longs Drugs	**1** B4
Post Office	**2** B4
Urgent Care Maui Physicians	**3** B4

SIGHTS & ACTIVITIES	
Captain Vancouver Monument	**4** A2
David Malo's Church	**5** B3
Hawaiian Islands Humpback Whale National Marine Sanctuary Headquarters	**6** A2
Kihei Canoe Club	**7** A1
Ko'ie'ie Fishpond	(see 6)
Maui Dive Shop	**8** B4
Maui Nui O Kama Canoe Club Cultural Tour	**9** A1
South Pacific Kayaks & Outfitters	**10** B4

SLEEPING	
Maui Sunseeker	**11** A2
Nona Lani Cottages	**12** A2
Ocean Breeze Hideaway	**13** B2

EATING	
Eskimo Candy	**14** B4
Kihei Farmers Market	**15** A1
Safeway	(see 20)
Shangri-La By The Sea	**16** A3
Stella Blues	(see 18)
Vietnamese Cuisine	(see 17)

ENTERTAINMENT	
Tip-Ups Tavern & Grill	(see 18)

SHOPPING	
Azeka Makai	**17** B4
Azeka Mauka	**18** B4
Lipoa Center	**19** B4
Maui Quilt Shop	(see 17)
Pi'ilani Village	**20** B4

TRANSPORT	
Hula Hogs	(see 18)
Kihei Rent A Car	**21** B4

few colorful fish, though it pales in comparison to the snorkeling at beaches further south.

CHARLEY YOUNG BEACH
Map p123
Out of sight from sightseers cruising the main drag, this side-street neighborhood beach is the least-touristed strand in Kihei. It's a real jewel in the rough: broad and sandy, and backed by swaying coconut palms. You're apt to find fishers casting their lines, families playing volleyball and someone strumming a guitar. It also has some of the better bodysurfing waves in Kihei. Beach parking is on the corner of S Kihei Rd and Kaia'u Pl. To get to the beach,

simply walk to the end of Kaia'u Pl and follow the steps down the cliff.

PUNAHOA BEACH
Map p123
This discreet postage-stamp-sized beach, embraced by a rocky lava shoreline, is Kihei's best bet for swimming with turtles. Forget it, however, if it's not a calm day. The beach is reached via shoreline access at the north side of Punahoa condos. Park streetside on Ili'ili Rd and it's just a minute away.

KALEPOLEPO BEACH PARK
Map p122
Keiki, this one's for you. The park is fronted

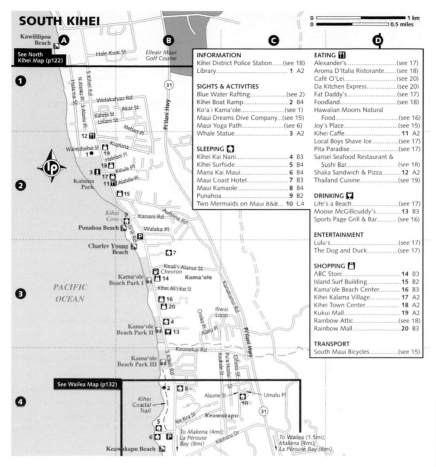

SOUTH KIHEI

INFORMATION
Kihei District Police Station......(see 18)
Library..**1** A2

SIGHTS & ACTIVITIES
Blue Water Rafting...................(see 2)
Kihei Boat Ramp........................**2** B4
Ko'a i Kama'ole.........................(see 1)
Maui Dreams Dive Company...(see 15)
Maui Yoga Path..........................(see 6)
Whale Statue..............................**3** A2

SLEEPING
Kihei Kai Nani..........................**4** B3
Kihei Surfside............................**5** B4
Mana Kai Maui...........................**6** B4
Maui Coast Hotel.......................**7** B3
Maui Kamaole............................**8** B4
Punahoa.....................................**9** B2
Two Mermaids on Maui B&B..**10** C4

EATING
Alexander's...............................(see 17)
Aroma D'Italia Ristorante.......(see 18)
Café O'Lei..................................(see 20)
Da Kitchen Express..................(see 20)
Fat Daddy's................................(see 17)
Foodland....................................(see 18)
Hawaiian Moons Natural
    Food....................................(see 16)
Joy's Place.................................(see 15)
Kihei Caffe.................................**11** A2
Local Boys Shave Ice...............(see 17)
Pita Paradise............................(see 17)
Sansei Seafood Restaurant &
    Sushi Bar.............................(see 18)
Shaka Sandwich & Pizza..........**12** A2
Thailand Cuisine.......................(see 19)

DRINKING
Life's a Beach...........................(see 17)
Moose McGillicuddy's...............**13** B3
Sports Page Grill & Bar............(see 16)

ENTERTAINMENT
Lulu's..(see 17)
The Dog and Duck....................(see 17)

SHOPPING
ABC Store.................................**14** D3
Island Surf Building..................**15** B2
Kama'ole Beach Center.............**16** B3
Kihei Kalama Village.................**17** A2
Kihei Town Center....................**18** A2
Kukui Mall.................................**19** A2
Rainbow Attic............................(see 18)
Rainbow Mall............................**20** B3

TRANSPORT
South Maui Bicycles..................(see 15)

by the ancient **Ko'ie'ie Fishpond** (p124), whose stone walls create a shallow swimming pool, with calm waters perfect for kids.

MAI POINA 'OE IA'U BEACH PARK
Map p122
This long sandy beach at the northern end of Kihei is a popular morning launch for outrigger canoes and kayaks. After the wind picks up in the afternoon, it's South Maui's main venue for windsurfing.

KALAMA PARK
Map p123
A retaining wall runs along most of the shoreline, so the action here is best suited for landlubbers. This expansive park has

ball fields, tennis and volleyball courts, a playground, picnic pavilions, restrooms and showers. You will find a small beach behind a whale statue, but a runoff ditch carries wastewater here after heavy rains so best take your swim elsewhere.

Sights

HAWAIIAN ISLANDS HUMPBACK WHALE NATIONAL MARINE SANCTUARY
our pick Map p122; 879-2818, 800-831-4888; www.hawaiihumpbackwhale.noaa.gov; 726 S Kihei Rd; admission free; 10am-3pm Mon-Fri
The marine sanctuary headquarters is a great place to get acquainted with Hawaii's

Island Insights

In ancient Hawaii, coastal fishponds were built to provide a ready source of fish for royal families. The most intact fishpond remaining on Maui is the 3-acre 🌺 **Ko'ie'ie Fishpond** (Map p122), now on the National Register of Historic Places. This fascinating fishpond borders both Kalepolepo Beach Park and the Hawaiian Islands Humpback Whale National Marine Sanctuary headquarters.

spectacular marine life. The center overlooks an ancient fishpond and its oceanfront lookout is ideal for sighting the humpback whales that frequent the bay during winter. There are even free scopes set up for viewing. Displays on whales and sea turtles offer interesting background on the creatures you might spot here. And there's always a whale poster, coloring book or other free handout for the kids. Want to take it deeper? Swing by at 11am on Tuesday and Thursday for the center's free '45-Ton Talks' on whales.

DAVID MALO'S CHURCH
Map p122; 100 Kulanihako'i St
Philosopher David Malo, who built this church in 1853, wore many collars. He was the first Hawaiian ordained to the Christian ministry, coauthor of Hawaii's first Constitution and an early spokesperson for Hawaiian rights. While most of Malo's original church has been dismantled, a 3ft-high section of the walls still stands beside a palm grove. Pews are lined up inside the stone walls, where open-air services are held at 9am Sunday by Trinity Episcopal Church-by-the-Sea.

Activities
CANOEING & KAYAKING
our pick South Pacific Kayaks & Outfitters (Map p122; ☎ 875-4848, 800-776-2326; www.southpacific kayaks.com; 95 Hale Kuai St; 1-/2-person kayaks per day $40/50, tours $65-100; ☼ 6am-9pm) is a topnotch operation that leads kayak-and-snorkel tours. It also rents kayaks for those who want to go off on their own, and will deliver them to Makena Landing (see p137).

Kihei Canoe Club (Map p122; www.kiheicanoeclub .com; Kihei Wharf; donation $25) invites visitors to share in the mana by joining members in paddling their outrigger canoes on Tuesday and Thursday mornings. No reservations are necessary; just show up at the wharf at 7:30am. The donation helps offset the cost of maintaining the canoes and entitles you to join them each Tuesday and Thursday for the rest of the month.

🌺 **Maui Nui O Kama Canoe Club Cultural Tour** (Map p122; ☎ 242-8536; 1191 N Kihei Rd; outing $40; ☼ 7:30am) offers memorable 90-minute narrated outrigger canoe rides led by a Native Hawaiian. Much more than just a canoe ride, the tour emphasizes cultural aspects, including chanting and a paddle to an ancient Hawaiian site. Reservations are required.

DIVING & SNORKELING
our pick 🌺 Maui Dreams Dive Company (Map p123; ☎ 874-5332, 888-921-3483; www.mauidreamsdiveco .com; Island Surf Building, 1993 S Kihei Rd; 1-/2-tank dives from $60/90; ☼ 7am-6pm) is a first-rate five-star PADI operation specializing in shore dives. With this family-run outfit, a dive trip is like going out with friends. Nondivers, ask about the introductory dive ($79). And if you really want to have fun zooming underwater, check out their scooter dive ($89).

Maui Dive Shop (Map p122; ☎ 879-3388; www .mauidiveshop.com; 1455 S Kihei Rd; 2-tank dives $130, snorkel rentals per day $8; ☼ 6am-9pm), the main outlet of this island-wide diving chain, is a good spot to rent or buy water-sports gear, including boogie boards, snorkels and wetsuits.

Blue Water Rafting (Map p123; ☎ 879-7238; www .bluewaterrafting.com; Kihei Boat Ramp; Molokini/Kanaio

Canoes at Kihei Canoe Club   GREG ELMS

Top Picks

POST-DIVE LUNCH SPOTS

- **Da Kitchen Express** (p126)
- **Joy's Place** (below)
- **Café O'Lei** (p128)
- **Fat Daddy's** (p127)
- **Stella Blues** (p127)

Keiki **love Local Boys Shave Ice**   GREG ELMS

trip $45/100; 🕒 departure times vary) has a Molokini Express trip that's perfect for those who want to zip out to the crater, snorkel and be back within two hours. An adventurous half-day trip heads southward on a motorized raft to snorkel among sea turtles and dolphins at remote coves along the Kanaio coast.

YOGA

If you need to loosen up after that long flight, Maui Yoga Path (Map p123; ☎ 874-5545; 2960 S Kihei Rd; class $20; 🕒 9-10:30am Sun-Fri) has sessions at Mana Kai Maui resort that focus on the relaxing stretches and breathing exercises of Iyengar hatha yoga.

Festivals & Events

Whale Day Celebration (www.greatmauiwhalefestival .org) Kihei's top family-oriented festival, this big bash celebrates Maui's humpback whales with a parade, live music, and craft and food booths. Fun things for kids include a whale regatta (Maui's version of a rubber duck race), a children's carnival and storytelling. It's held at

Island Insights

Before setting out in their canoes for a day of fishing, Hawaiians would leave offerings, perhaps a shell or fishhooks, at a *ko'a* (fishing shrine). When they returned, the first catch of the day would be placed at the shrine to thank the gods for their favors. When ground was broken for construction of the Kihei library, an ancient stone fishing shrine, **Ko'a i Kama'ole** (Map p123), was unearthed; the mound of rocks is marked by an interpretive plaque at the front of the library parking lot.

Kalama Park, next to the big whale statue, on a Saturday in mid-February.

Maui Ohana Pride (www.mauigayinfo.com) Maui's gay and lesbian community gets together to party at Kalama Park on the first Sunday in June, with drag races (kings and queens), a barbecue dinner and volleyball on the beach.

Eating

Odds are if you're staying in Kihei, you've got a place with a kitchen. Still, there's no need to slave behind the stove every meal – Kihei has lots of tasty choices.

LOCAL BOYS SHAVE ICE   Shave Ice $
Map p123; Kihei Kalama Village, 1913 S Kihei Rd; shave ice $4; 🕒 10am-9pm
A hot day at the beach deserves a cool treat. This stall conveniently located opposite Kalama Park dishes up soft shaved ice drenched in a rainbow of sweet syrups. Go tropical with passion fruit, pineapple and lemon-lime.

KIHEI CAFFE ✳   Café $
Map p123; ☎ 879-2230; 1945 S Kihei Rd; mains $5-10; 🕒 5am-3pm
If jet lag has you up before sunrise, head here for the killer cinnamon rolls fresh out of the oven. Breakfast burritos and eggs in every conceivable preparation highlight the menu. Best of all, the jolting coffee comes with a free refill.

❊ JOY'S PLACE   Café $
Map p123; ☎ 879-9258; Island Surf Building, 1993 S Kihei Rd; mains $6-10; 🕒 10am-3pm Mon-Sat
Just a hole in the wall – blink and you'd

SOUTH MAUI

miss it, but what a shame that'd be. Joy takes pride in her little kitchen. The operative words are organic, free range and local harvested. The healthiest takeout salads ($7) you'll find anywhere in South Maui, wrap sandwiches made to order and daily specials like fresh fish tacos on Saturdays attract a loyal following.

ALEXANDER'S
Seafood $

Map p123; ☎ 874-0788; Kihei Kalama Village, 1913 S Kihei Rd; meals $8-13; ☼ 11am-9pm

If you're hanging at the beach, scoot over here for fish and chips, made with your choice of mahimahi, *'ahi* (tuna) or *ono* (wahoo). The fried fare is a bit greasy but the grilled fish is absolute perfection. The food is prepared for takeout, but you can eat at picnic tables at the side.

DA KITCHEN EXPRESS
Hawaiian $

Map p123; ☎ 875-7782; Rainbow Mall, 2439 S Kihei Rd; meals $8-12; ☼ 9am-9pm

It's all about the plate lunches – tasty and huge – at this quintessentially Hawaiian diner. The local favorite is Da Lau Lau Plate (with steamed pork wrapped in taro leaves), but you won't go wrong with any choice, from charbroiled teriyaki chicken to gravy-laden *loco moco* (rice, fried egg and hamburger patty).

SHAKA SANDWICH & PIZZA
Pizza $$

Map p123; ☎ 874-0331; 1770 S Kihei Rd; mains $6-21; ☼ 10:30am-9pm Sun-Thu, 10:30am-10pm Fri & Sat

Come here for Maui's best pizza, including a sweet Hawaiian version topped with ham and Maui-grown pineapple. Good

---

ISLAND VOICES

NAME: KIMOKEO KAPAHULEHUA

OCCUPATION: LEADER OF 'AO'AO O NA LOKO I'A O MAUI, MAUI'S FISHPOND ASSOCIATION

RESIDENCE: KIHEI

What's the history of Ko'ie'ie Fishpond? The fishpond (p124) was built around the 16th century. It's 3 acres and has a 1100ft rock wall, and one sluice gate in the middle. We're revitalizing it in the traditional way. Everything is being done as it would have been done in ancient times – no mechanical equipment at all. We use only hand tools.

How's the restoration of the fishpond walls progressing? All the rocks are there. We're picking up every rock hand by hand, trying to find the old footing and restacking them back the way they were before.

Can anyone help? We welcome everyone. All ages, genders and nationalities can work on the fishpond. Everyone can help in some way – that's *holomua*, to move forward. No experience is needed. Volunteers can help remove invasive plants, revitalize the fishpond wall, help restore cultural sites such as heiau, walking paths. People can call us (☎ 276-7219) or email us (www.mauifishpond.com) and set up times. They'll definitely get wet!

You're also restoring the nearby dunes? We're planting kou, milo, *'a'ali'i* (Hawaiian hopseed bush) and *pahoehoe* (beach morning glory), and removing some of the kiawe. You cannot make everything native anymore. If you remove all the nonnative plants, the native plants won't be able to fill in fast enough.

Do you have any advice for visitors? Give something back to Maui. Whether you're here a day or a week, do something cultural, something environmental, get involved. *Malama 'aina, malama moana* – take care of the land, take care of the ocean.

cheesesteak sandwiches, too. And if you want to hang around your condo's lanai for the sunset, they'll deliver.

VIETNAMESE CUISINE   Vietnamese $$
Map p122; ☎ 875-2088; Azeka Makai, 1280 S Kihei Rd; mains $8-14; ⏱ 10:30am-9:30pm
It doesn't look like much from the outside but the Vietnamese chef-owner works wonders in the kitchen. The curried lemongrass chicken with jasmine rice awakens the senses. Or have some fun with your food and order *banh hoi*, a roll-your-own Vietnamese version of fajitas that come with mint leaves, assorted veggies and grilled shrimp.

ESKIMO CANDY   Seafood $$
Map p122; ☎ 891-8898; 2665 Hale Kuai St; meals $7-16; ⏱ 10:30am-7pm Mon-Fri
Tucked into a side street between the beach and the highway, Eskimo Candy is a fish market with a takeout counter and a few tables. Fresh-fish fanatics should key in on the *poke* (cubed, marinated raw fish), *'ahi* wraps and fish tacos. Bring the little ones; they'll love the pirate theme and you'll love the $4 kids menu.

THAILAND CUISINE   Thai $$
Map p123; ☎ 875-0839; Kukui Mall, 1819 S Kihei Rd; mains $9-15; ⏱ lunch Mon-Sat, dinner nightly
The solid menu of well-prepared Thai dishes includes aromatic Panang curries redolent with lime and sweet basil, and a spicy vegetarian 'evil prince tofu' that will fire up your taste buds. Cool it all down with a dish of homemade coconut ice cream.

SHANGRI-LA BY THE SEA   Indian $$
Map p122; ☎ 875-4555; Menehune Shores, 760 S Kihei Rd; lunch $8-12, dinner $12-25; ⏱ 10:30am-9pm
Made-from-scratch Indian fare is served in a knockout waterfront setting overlooking an ancient Hawaiian fishpond. Go with the tandoori grill side of the menu for delicious clay-oven cooked dishes served with warm naan bread.

FAT DADDY'S   Comfort Food $$
Map p123; ☎ 879-8711; Kihei Kalama Village, 1913 S Kihei Rd; mains $8-17; ⏱ 11:30am-9pm Mon-Sat, to 2pm Sun
Big plates of tangy barbecued ribs with all

THE VANCOUVER CONNECTION

Captain Cook never set foot on Maui, but his enterprising first mate, George Vancouver, did. After returning to the Islands in command of his own ship, Vancouver came ashore at the small settlement of Kihei in 1792. When he returned the next year, he dropped off the first cattle and horses ever to set foot (or hoof, rather) in Hawaii.

An enlightened explorer, Vancouver at first tried to make peace between the warring *ali'i* (chiefs) on Maui and refused to trade with them in arms or ammunition. Eventually he became an advisor to Kamehameha the Great, who was so impressed by Vancouver's talk of the British Empire that he adopted the Union Jack into his royal flag.

The **Captain Vancouver Monument** (Map p122), a small totem pole on the beach in North Kihei, commemorates Vancouver's landing. In between trips to Hawaii, the captain sailed north to 'discover' British Columbia, a journey now done in reverse by thousands of Canadian tourists who flock to Kihei each year.

the fixings are the specialty at this smart Texas-style smokehouse. Here, Southwest takes on a Hawaiian accent with Maui Cattle Company beef on the grill and Maui-brewed beers on tap.

STELLA BLUES   Eclectic $$
Map p122; ☎ 874-3779; Azeka Mauka, 1279 S Kihei Rd; breakfast $6-10, lunch & dinner $8-27; ⏱ 7:30am-11pm
This jazzy Kihei favorite is one place that never skimps. The omelets start with three eggs, the salads are Maui grown and the fish is fresh off the boat. The eclectic menu offers something for every mood, from Hawaiian-style macadamia-nut pancakes and grilled taro burgers to juicy steaks.

PITA PARADISE   Mediterranean $$
Map p123; ☎ 875-7679; Kihei Kalama Village, 1913 S Kihei Rd; mains $7-22; ⏱ 11am-9:30pm
One of the more unusual places to find gourmet fare is at this patio café hidden in

SOUTH MAUI

the back of a shopping arcade. Talk about fresh: owner John Arabatzis goes out and catches his own fish, which is served in everything from pita sandwiches to grilled dinners. Wonderful kebabs too, and a baklava ice-cream cake to die for.

AROMA D'ITALIA
RISTORANTE
Italian $$$

Map p123; ☎ 879-0133; Kihei Town Center, 1881 S Kihei Rd; mains $10-23; ☺ dinner

Just like Mama used to make…if yo mama was Italian. This place has it all – classy service, old-world decor and a chef-owner who relies upon her traditional family recipes to create delicious pastas, mouthwatering eggplant parmigiana and superb antipasti.

CAFÉ O'LEI
Hawaii Regional $$$

our pick Map p123; ☎ 891-1368; Rainbow Mall, 2439 S Kihei Rd; lunch $6-13, dinner $15-33; ☺ 10:30am-10pm Tue-Sun

If you eat at only one place in Kihei make it here. Sophisticated atmosphere, innovative Hawaii Regional Cuisine and honest prices separate this place from other upscale Kihei dining spots. For a tangy treat, order the blackened mahimahi with fresh papaya salsa. Unbeatable lunch deals for under $10, and a raw bar and sushi chef after 4:30pm. Famous martinis, too.

SANSEI SEAFOOD
RESTAURANT & SUSHI BAR
Japanese $$$

Map p123; ☎ 879-0004; Kihei Town Center, 1881 S Kihei Rd; appetizers $3-15, mains $17-32; ☺ dinner

The line runs out the door, but you'll be well rewarded for your patience. The innovative appetizer menu rolls out everything from traditional sashimi to blue-crab ravioli. Hot Eurasian fusion dishes include

Fresh farmers market fare   GREG ELMS

the likes of Peking duck in a foie gras demi. And despite its popularity, Sansei offers deals – between 5:30pm and 6pm all food is discounted by 25%.

Need to stock up the condo? Kihei has two 24-hour supermarkets: **Foodland** (Map p123; ☎ 879-9350; Kihei Town Center, 1881 S Kihei Rd) and **Safeway** (Map p122; ☎ 891-9120; Pi'ilani Village, 277 Pi'ikea Ave). **Hawaiian Moons Natural Foods** (Map p123; ☎ 875-4356; Kama'ole Beach Center, 2411 S Kihei Rd; ☺ 8am-9pm) makes a good place to pack a healthy picnic lunch. 🌺 **Kihei Farmers Market** (Map p122; ☎ 875-0949; 61 S Kihei Rd; ☺ 8am-4pm Mon-Thu, to 5pm Fri) sells island-grown fruits and vegetables – a bit pricey but fresh.

Drinking

MOOSE MCGILLICUDDY'S
Map p123; ☎ 891-8600; 2511 S Kihei Rd

Moose's open-air lanai is a fine place to head for a sunset drink. If you come on Friday or Saturday nights you can hang around and do some dancing to DJ tunes.

LIFE'S A BEACH
Map p123; ☎ 891-8010; Kihei Kalama Village; 1913 S Kihei Rd

Directly opposite the beach, this brightly painted, Bob Marley–lovin' shack with neon palm trees draws a crowd, offering $1 mai tais from 4pm to 7pm and live music or DJs after 9pm.

SPORTS PAGE GRILL & BAR
Map p123; ☎ 879-0602; Kama'ole Beach Center, 2411 S Kihei Rd

If life won't be complete without the playoffs on 16 big-screen TVs, tip your glass here.

Don't Miss

- **Whale-watching scopes at Hawaiian Islands Humpback Whale National Marine Sanctuary** (p123)
- **Avant-garde sculptor Fernando Botero's rotund bronzes in the Grand Wailea Resort lobby** (p136)
- **Charley Young Beach** (p122)
- **Outrigger canoe ride** (p124)

SOUTH MAUI

Entertainment

LULU'S

Map p123; ☎ 879-9944; 1941 S Kihei Rd

Kihei's top party venue is open-air on three sides, loud, lively and full of people having fun. Come here to have a sunset-view drink, shoot some pool or dance the night away. Salsa, reggae bands or DJs command the floor at night.

THE DOG AND DUCK

Map p123; ☎ 875-9669; Kihei Kalama Village, 1913 S Kihei Rd

This cheery Irish pub attracts a younger crowd – yes, they have sports TV, but it's a side show, not blaring from every corner. Decent spuds and pub grub to go along with that heady Guinness draft, and Irish music several nights a week.

TIP-UPS TAVERN & GRILL

Map p122; ☎ 874-9299; Azeka Mauka, 1279 S Kihei Rd

This cozy bistro offers a more sophisticated scene. Sip the perfect martini while listening to live or DJ music from 10pm nightly. On Mondays it hosts Kihei's main gay night out.

Shopping

PI'ILANI VILLAGE

Map p122; 225 Pi'ikea Ave

Kihei's largest shopping center has scores of stores perfect for stocking up on gifts to cart home. Highlights include Tropical Disc (☎ 874-3000), with a fine selection of Hawaiian music and headphone setups for previewing; Crazy Shirts (☎ 875-6440) for quality Hawaiian-motif shirts; and Hilo Hattie (☎ 875-4545) for kitschy souvenirs.

KIHEI KALAMA VILLAGE

Map p123; ☎ 879-6610; 1913 S Kihei Rd

Some 50 shops and stalls are clustered under one roof at this shopping arcade, where you'll find everything from cheapo T-shirts and erotic sex toys to classy sarongs.

Other recommendations:

ABC Store (Map p123; ☎ 879-6305; 2349 S Kihei Rd) Convenience store selling liquor, beach mats, sunblock and other tourist needs.

Maui Quilt Shop (Map p122; ☎ 874-8050; Azeka

MAUI TUNES

To soak up the Maui mood, listen to these:

- *Maui Hawaiian Sup'pa Man,* performed by Israel Kamakawiwo'ole on *Facing Future* (Big Boy Record Company)
- *Haleakalā Kū Hanohano,* performed by Hapa (Barry Flanagan and Keli'i Kaneali'i) on *Hapa* (Coconut Grove Recording Company)
- *Maui Medley,* performed by Barney Isaacs and George Kuo on *Hawaiian Slack Key Guitar Masters, Instrumental Collection* (Dancing Cat Records)
- *Ka'anapali,* performed by Ali'i Manu O Kai on *A Gift of Aloha* (Paradise Productions)
- *Highway to Hana,* performed by Led Kaapana on *Black Sand* (Dancing Cat Records)

Makai, 1280 S Kihei) Hawaiian fabrics and quilt kits. Quilting classes, too.

Rainbow Attic (Map p123; ☎ 874-0884; Kihei Town Center, 1881 S Kihei Rd) The place to find quality secondhand aloha shirts.

Sleeping

Condos line up cheek by jowl in Kihei, whereas hotels and B&Bs can be counted on one hand. Some condominium complexes maintain a front desk or a daytime office that handles bookings, but others are booked only via rental agents. In many places along S Kihei Rd the traffic is noisy, so when you book, avoid rooms close to the road.

The following rental agents handle Kihei condos:

Bello Realty (☎ 879-3328, 800-541-3060; www.bello maui.com)

Kihei Maui Vacations (☎ 879-7581, 800-541-6284; www.kmvmaui.com)

Resort Quest Maui (☎ 879-5445, 866-774-2924; www.resortquestmaui.com)

OCEAN BREEZE HIDEAWAY   B&B $

Map p122; ☎ 879-0657, 888-463-6687; www.hawaiibednbreakfast.com; 435 Kalalau Pl; r incl breakfast $95-115; ⊠ ▣

The friendly couple who run this B&B are a treasure trove of insider tips. Their home has two comfortable guest rooms, one with

SOUTH MAUI

a queen bed and ceiling fans, the other with a king bed and air-con. Both have a private entrance and a refrigerator.

NONA LANI COTTAGES   Cottages $$
Map p122; ☎ 879-2497, 800-733-2688; www
.nonalanicottages.com; 455 S Kihei Rd; r $115, cottages from $130; ⌷
Those who prefer old-fashioned simplicity to glitzy resort amenities will feel at home in these sweet retro cottages. They're compact but squeeze in everything you'll need: a full kitchen, a living room with daybed and a bedroom with a queen bed. Don't want to feel squeezed? Book one of the commodious guest rooms in the main house, which is set in a fragrant plumeria grove.

TWO MERMAIDS ON MAUI B&B   B&B $$
Map p123; ☎ 874-8687, 800-598-9550; www
.twomermaids.com; 2840 Umalu Pl; studio/1br incl breakfast $115/140; ⌷ ⌷ ⌷
The women operating this B&B add lots of personal touches. The units have kitchenettes and cheerful tropical decor, a breakfast of organic island fruit is provided and families are welcome – the backyard pool even has a shallow section just for kids. One of the 'mermaids' is a justice of the peace and can arrange wedding packages.

MAUI SUNSEEKER   Boutique Hotel $$
Map p122; ☎ 874-3131, 800-532-6284; www
.mauisunseeker.com; 551 S Kihei Rd; studios from $165; ⌷ ⌷
Catering to gay and lesbian travelers, this place consists of two adjacent properties. Opt for the rear one, known formerly as Wailana Inn, as its studios beam with tasteful decor that outshines other places in this price range. Amenities include kitchenette and lanai, and there's a clothing-optional rooftop deck with a hot tub and broad ocean views.

KIHEI KAI NANI   Condo $$
Map p123; ☎ 879-9088, 800-473-1493; www
.kiheikainani.com; 2495 S Kihei Rd; 1br $140; ⌷ ⌷ ⌷
Don't be fooled by the affordable price – this inviting low-rise condo has all the amenities of the big boys. It's an older complex with furnishings that are comfortably worn, but it offers plenty of room to move and a convenient setting opposite the golden sands of Kama'ole Beach Park II. The staff are cheery and accommodating, and that's not always a hallmark of Kihei condos.

PUNAHOA   Condo $$
Map p123; ☎ 879-2720, 800-564-4380; www
.punahoabeach.com; 2142 Ili'ili Rd; studios/1br $150/263
A rare find in bustling Kihei, this classy boutique condo lies hidden on a quiet side street fronting a quiet beach. Every unit has a clear-on ocean view, perfect for watching sunsets and whales. There's no pool, but who needs one when the ocean's at your doorstep? Surfers, bring your boards – Kihei's best waves are just a few minutes' walk away.

MAUI KAMAOLE   Condo $$$
Map p123; ☎ 874-5151, 800-367-5242; www.crh
maui.com; 2777 S Kihei Rd; 1br/2br from $225/270; ⌷ ⌷ ⌷
Bougainvillea draped over the balconies and birdsong in the gardens set the tone at this luxurious condo. Everything is low-rise, the units are spacious and it's got a quiet location opposite Kama'ole Beach Park III. No surprise, the place has a loyal following of return guests.

MANA KAI MAUI   Condo $$$
Map p123; ☎ 879-2778, 800-367-5242; www.crh
maui.com; 2960 S Kihei Rd; r/1br from $175/280; ⌷ ⌷ ⌷
Perched on a point overlooking Keawakapu Beach, this complex offers great sunset views. And you can swim and snorkel from the beach right outside the door. You'll find all the conveniences of a condo as well as the pluses of a hotel, with a front desk and a full-service restaurant. Request an upper floor for the best views.

KIHEI SURFSIDE   Condo $$$
Map p123; ☎ 879-5445, 800-822-4409; www
.kiheisurfside.com; 2936 S Kihei Rd; 1br/2br from $220/325; ⌷
The rooms are standard fare, but step onto your lanai and you've got the finest ocean view in Kihei. Grab a drink and watch the whales swim past. Out the back door lies fabulous Keawakapu Beach. On the downside, the place can be noisy from the buzz of families, and with no air-conditioning your windows will be open.

MAUI COAST HOTEL   International Hotel $$$
Map p123; ☎ 874-6284, 800-895-6284; www
.mauicoasthotel.com; 2259 S Kihei Rd; r/ste from
$245/275; 💱 🖥 📶
Among the handful of hotels in condo-laden
Kihei, this is the best. It's clean and com-
fortable with plenty of perks, from guest
computers to free laundry facilities, and
the set-back-from-the-road location makes
it quieter than other places on the strip.
Rooms are big, though the decor has an
out-of-the-box blandness, a letdown from
the upbeat tropical theme in the lobby.

Getting There & Around
TO/FROM THE AIRPORT
Almost everyone rents a car at the airport
in Kahului. Otherwise, expect to pay about
$30 for a shuttle service or $45 for a taxi.

BICYCLE
Bike lanes run along both the Pi'ilani Hwy
and S Kihei Rd, but cyclists need to be cau-
tious of inattentive drivers making sudden
turns across the lanes.
    South Maui Bicycles (Map p123; ☎ 874-0068; Is-
land Surf Building, 1993 S Kihei Rd; per day $22-60, per
week $100-250; ⏲ 10am-6pm Mon-Sat) rents top-
of-the-line Trek road bicycles and quality
mountain bikes, as well as basic around-
town bikes – no matter what you opt for,
you can bet it'll be well maintained.

BUS
The Maui Bus (p289) serves Kihei with
two routes. One route connects Kihei
with Wailea and Ma'alaea; stops include
Kama'ole Beach Park III, Pi'ilani Village
shopping center, and Uwapo and S Kihei
Rds. From Ma'alaea you can connect with
buses bound for Lahaina and Kahului. The
other route primarily serves the northern
half of Kihei, with a half-dozen stops along
S Kihei Rd. Both routes operate hourly from
around 5:30am to 7:30pm and cost $1.

CAR & MOTORCYCLE
A family-owned operation, Kihei Rent A Car
(Map p122; ☎ 879-7257, 800-251-5288; www.kihei
rentacar.com; 96 Kio Loop; per day/week from $30/175)
rents cars and jeeps to those aged over 21,
accepts cash deposits and includes free
mileage.
    Hula Hogs (Map p122; ☎ 875-7433, 877-464-7433;
www.hulahogs.com; 1279 S Kihei Rd; per day from $115)
are the folks to see if you want to pack
your saddlebags and tour Maui on a Harley-
Davidson Road King. Helmets and rain
gear are included.

Morning calm at Kihei's Mai Poina 'Oe Ia'u Beach

© BILL BROOKS / ALAMY

SOUTH MAUI

WAILEA

pop 5400

Well-manicured Wailea, South Maui's most elite haunt, stands in sharp contrast to Kihei. Don't even bother looking for a gas station or fast-food joint. Wailea is all about swank beachfront resorts, low-rise condo villas, emerald golf courses and a tennis club so chic it's dubbed 'Wimbledon West.'

One look at Wailea's beaches and it's easy to see why it's become such hot real estate. The golden-sand jewels sparkling along the Wailea coast are postcard material, offering phenom swimming, snorkeling and sunbathing. So grab a beach mat, pack the snorkel and enjoy the good life.

Orientation & Information

If you're heading to Wailea from Lahaina or Kahului, be sure to take the Pi'ilani Hwy (Hwy 31) and not S Kihei Rd, which can be a tediously slow drive through congested traffic. Wailea's main road is Wailea Alanui Dr, which turns into Makena Alanui Dr after Polo Beach and continues south to Makena.

Shops at Wailea (3750 Wailea Alanui Dr; ☯ 9:30am-9pm) has an ATM, as do many of the hotels.

Beaches

Wailea's fab beaches begin with the southern end of Keawakapu Beach (p120) in Kihei and continue south toward Makena. All of the beaches that are backed by resorts

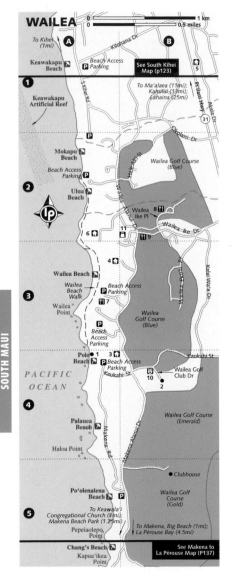

INFORMATION	
ATM	(see 11)

SIGHTS & ACTIVITIES	
Hawaiian Sailing Canoe Adventures	**1** A4
Maui Ocean Activities	(see 4)
Wailea Golf Club	**2** B4
Wailea Tennis Club	(see 8)

SLEEPING ⌂	
Fairmont Kea Lani	**3** A4
Grand Wailea Resort Hotel & Spa	**4** A3
Pineapple Inn Maui	**5** B1
Wailea Beach Marriott Resort & Spa	**6** A2

EATING ⊞	
Ferraro's	**7** A3
Joe's Bar & Grill	**8** B2
Longhi's	(see 11)
Matteo's	**9** B2
Waterfront Deli	(see 11)

ENTERTAINMENT ☺	
Four Seasons Resort	(see 7)
Mulligan's on the Blue	**10** B4
Wailea Marriott Resort & Spa	(see 6)

SHOPPING ⌂	
Shops at Wailea	**11** B2

Scuba divers at Ulua Beach   GREG ELMS

have public access, with free parking, showers and restrooms.

ULUA & MOKAPU BEACHES

our pick You'll have to get up early to secure a parking space but it's worth it. Ulua Beach offers Wailea's best easy-access snorkeling. Not only is it teeming with brilliant tropical fish but it's also one of the best spots for hearing humpbacks sing as they pass offshore. Snorkelers should head straight for the coral at the rocky outcrop on the right side of Ulua Beach, which separates it from its twin to the north, Mokapu Beach. Snorkeling is best in the morning before the winds pick up and the crowds arrive. When the surf's up, forget snorkeling – go bodysurfing instead. Beach access is just north of the Wailea Marriott Resort.

WAILEA BEACH

Wailea's premier resort beach, this wide sparkling strand is where most of Wailea's vacationers soak up the rays. It offers a full menu of water activities. The beach slopes gradually, making it a good swimming spot. When it's calm, there's decent snorkeling around the rocky point on the south end. Most afternoons there's a gentle

shorebreak suitable for bodysurfing. Divers entering the water at Wailea Beach can follow an offshore reef that runs down to Polo Beach. The beach access road runs between the Grand Wailea and Four Seasons resorts.

POLO BEACH

At the quieter south end of Wailea, Polo Beach is seldom crowded. When there's wave action, boogie boarders and bodysurfers usually find good shorebreaks here. When calm, the rocks at the northern end of the beach provide good snorkeling. If you arrive at low tide, check out the lava outcropping at the southern end for tide pools harboring spiny sea urchins and small fish. To get to Polo Beach, turn down Kaukahi St after the Fairmont Kea Lani and keep an eye peeled for the beach parking lot on the right.

PALAUEA BEACH

This untouristed sandy stretch to the south of Polo Beach attracts local surfers and boogie boarders. Kiawe trees block the view of the beach from the roadside, but you can

---

WAILEA BEACH WALK

For the perfect sunset stroll, take the 1.3-mile shoreline path that connects Wailea's beaches and the resort hotels that front them. The undulating path winds above jagged lava points and back down to the sandy shore.

Not only is the vista fantastic from here, but in winter this is one of the best places in all of Maui for spotting humpback whales. On a good day you may be able to see more than a dozen of them frolicking in the waters offshore. Forgot your binoculars? Just drop a coin in the telescope in front of the Wailea Marriott Resort.

Some of the luxury hotels you'll pass along the walk are worth strolling through as well, most notably the Grand Wailea Resort, which is adorned with $30 million worth of artwork. In front of the Wailea Point condos you'll find the foundations of three Hawaiian house sites dating to AD 1300; this is also a fine spot to watch the sun drop into the sea.

Po'olenalena Beach   GREG ELMS

find it easily by the line of cars parked along Makena Rd.

PO'OLENALENA BEACH
Beyond all the development of the Wailea resort strip lies this lovely long crescent favored by local families on weekends. Still, it's rarely crowded and the shallow, sandy bottom and calm waters make for excellent swimming. There's good snorkeling off both the southern and northern lava points. Haloa Point, a bit further north, is a popular scuba-diving spot. The beach parking lot is on Makena Alanui Rd, a half-mile south of its intersection with Makena Rd. There are no facilities except a portable toilet.

Activities
AT SEA
Maui Ocean Activities (☎ 667-2001; www.mauiwatersports.com; Grand Wailea Resort, 3850 Wailea Alanui Dr; snorkel/kayak/hobie-cat rental per hr $8/15/59; ⏰ 8am-4pm) has water-sports rentals and gives surfing lessons ($70) and windsurfing lessons ($90).

Hawaiian Sailing Canoe Adventures (☎ 281-9301; www.mauisailingcanoe.com; adult/child 5-12 $100/80; ⏰ tours 8am & 10am) shares insights into native traditions on two-hour sails aboard a Hawaiian-style outrigger canoe.

There's a max of six passengers, so they're able to accommodate requests – including stopping to snorkel with turtles. Tours depart from Polo Beach.

ON LAND
Wailea Golf Club (☎ 875-7450; www.waileagolf.com; 100 Golf Club Dr; greens fee $125-200; ⏰ first tee 7am) consists of three championship courses. The Emerald course is a tropical garden that consistently ranks top; the rugged Gold course takes advantage of volcanic landscapes; and the Blue course is marked by an open fairway and challenging greens. For the cheapest fees, tee off after 1pm, when 'twilight' rates are in effect.

Wailea Tennis Club (☎ 879-1958; www.waileatennis.com; 131 Wailea Ike Pl; court fees from $30; ⏰ 7am-7pm), nicknamed 'Wimbledon West,' is an award-winning complex with 11 Plexipave courts, lessons, clinics and equipment rentals.

Festivals & Events
Hollywood celebs galore show up for the Maui Film Festival (www.mauifilmfestival.com), a five-day extravaganza in mid-June. Sit with the stars under the stars at various locations around Wailea, including at the open-air 'SandDance Theater' right on Wailea Beach.

Eating
WATERFRONT DELI   Deli $
☎ 891-2039; Shops at Wailea, 3750 Wailea Alanui Dr; meals $6-10; ⏰ 7am-8pm
Wailea's sole budget option, this deli inside the Whalers General Store serves up salads, chicken burgers and all sorts of sandwiches. It's takeout but there are tables next to the store where you can eat – or have them pack it for the beach.

Top Picks
SOUTH MAUI FOR KIDS
- Ko'ie'ie Fishpond (p140)
- Ulua Beach (p133)
- Hawaiian Islands Humpback Whale National Marine Sanctuary (p123)

SOUTH MAUI

MATTEO'S   Italian $$
☎ 874-1234; 100 Wailea Ike Dr; pizzas $11-19;
🕑 11am-9pm Mon-Fri, 5-9pm Sat & Sun
This family-style Italian eatery is Wailea's most affordable sit-down restaurant. The thin-crust pizzas are surprisingly good and Matteo's makes it fun for kids by letting them add any topping combo that strikes their fancy.

LONGHI'S   Eclectic $$$$
☎ 891-8883; Shops at Wailea, 3750 Wailea Alanui Dr; breakfast & lunch $6-18, dinner $24-40; 🕑 8am-10pm
Locals flock here for breakfast to get the hot-from-the-oven pastries and the perfect frittata. At dinner Longhi's grills up Wailea's best steak. Excellent wine list, too.

JOE'S BAR & GRILL   Comfort Food $$$$
☎ 875-7767; 131 Wailea Ike Pl; mains $20-42;
🕑 dinner
A sister operation of the famed Hali'imaile General Store, Joe's is celebrated in its own right. Forget razzle-dazzle – at Joe's the emphasis is on large portions and homestyle simplicity. Think roast beef prime rib with whipped potatoes, slow-cooked chicken in a crock and pumpkin-seed-crusted fresh fish.

FERRARO'S   Italian $$$$
☎ 891-8883; Four Seasons Resort, 3900 Wailea Alanui Dr; lunch $18-24, dinner $36-50; 🕑 11am-9pm
No other place in Wailea even comes close to this breezy restaurant for romantic seaside dining. Lunch strays into fun selections, like *kalua* pig quesadillas with mango poi, while dinner gets more serious, showcasing a rustic Italian menu with wood-fired bruschetta and an award-winning lobster risotto.

Entertainment
All of the Wailea hotels have some sort of live music, most often jazz or Hawaiian, in the evening.

MULLIGAN'S ON THE BLUE
☎ 874-1131; 100 Kaukahi St
Rising above the golf course, Mulligan's offers entertainment nightly, anything from Irish folk music to European jazz. It's also

---

Top Picks
SNORKEL SPOTS
- **Ulua Beach** (p133)
- **Malu'aka Beach** (p138)
- **'Ahihi-Kina'u Natural Area Reserve** (p140)

a good place to knock back an ale while enjoying the distant ocean view.

FOUR SEASONS RESORT
☎ 874-8000; 3900 Wailea Alanui
The lobby lounge has Hawaiian music and hula performances from 5:30pm to 8:30pm nightly, and jazz or slack key guitar later in the evening.

WAILEA MARRIOTT RESORT
☎ 879-1922; 3700 Wailea Alanui; adult/child 6-12 $88/43; 🕑 5-8pm Mon, Thu, Fri & Sat
It's a bit of a tourist-resort-luau cliché but the Marriott still runs the best luau this side of Lahaina, and it's right on the oceanfront lawn.

Shopping
Shops at Wailea (☎ 891-6770; 3750 Wailea Alanui Dr; 🕑 9:30am-9pm) has dozens of stores, most flashing designer labels like Prada and Gucci, but there are some solid island choices, too:
Blue Ginger (☎ 891-0772) Women's clothing in cheery colors and tropical motifs.
Honolua Surf Co (☎ 891-8229) Hip surfer-motif T-shirts, board shorts and aloha shirts.
Martin & MacArthur (☎ 891-8844) Museum-quality Hawaiian-made woodwork and other crafts.
Maui Waterwear (☎ 891-1939) Tropical swimwear you'll love to flaunt.
Na Hoku (☎ 891-8040) Hawaiian jeweler specializing in island floral and marine-life designs.

Sleeping
PINEAPPLE INN MAUI   Inn $$
☎ 298-4403, 877-212-6284; www.pineappleinn maui.com; 3170 Akala Dr; r/cottages from $140/215;
This sweet boutique inn has rooms as nice as those found at the exclusive resorts, but at a fraction of the cost. It's not on the

water, but every room has an ocean-view lanai and you can watch the sunset from the pool. The rooms have kitchenettes. For serious cooking, consider the two-bedroom cottage, which has a full kitchen.

WAILEA BEACH MARRIOTT RESORT & SPA
Resort $$$$
☎ 879-1922, 800-367-2960; www.waileamarriott
.com; 3700 Wailea Alanui Dr; r from $380;

Perched between two of Wailea's loveliest beaches, this is the smallest and most Hawaiian of the Wailea resorts. Instead of over-the-top flash, you'll find serene koi ponds, swaying palm trees and tropical decor.

GRAND WAILEA RESORT HOTEL & SPA
Resort $$$$
☎ 875-1234, 800-888-6100; www.grandwailea
.com; 3850 Wailea Alanui Dr; r from $500;

It's unbridled extravagance, from the million-dollar artwork in the lobby to the guest rooms decked out in Italian marble. But don't think it's all highbrow. Just follow your ears to the shrieks coming from the pool: the Grand Wailea boasts the most elaborate water-world wonders in Hawaii, an awesome series of nine interconnected pools with swim-through grottos and towering water slides.

FAIRMONT KEA LANI
Resort $$$$
☎ 875-4100, 800-659-4100; www.kealani.com; 4100 Wailea Alanui Dr; ste/oceanfront villa from $500/1350;

To stargaze Hollywood style, head to this swank resort. With its Moorish-style

architecture, the resort resembles something out of *Arabian Nights,* but what really draws the rich and famous is the privacy. The villas even have their own private plunge pools.

Getting There & Around

The Maui Bus (p289) operates between Wailea and Kahului hourly until 8:30pm. The first bus leaves the Shops at Wailea at 6:30am and runs along S Kihei Rd before heading up to the Pi'ilani Village shopping center and Ma'alaea. From Ma'alaea you can connect to buses bound for Lahaina.

A free shuttle bus (☎ 879-2828) runs around the Wailea area every 30 minutes from 6:30am to 6pm, stopping at the Grand Wailea and Four Seasons resorts, the Shops at Wailea and the golf courses.

MAKENA ✳

The gateway to untamed South Maui, Makena's a handsome sight on land and stunning in the water. Primo snorkeling, kayaking and bodysurfing, plus sea turtles galore, pristine coral, reef sharks and dolphins – how's that for company?

The beaches are magnificent. The king of them all, Big Beach, is an immense sweep of glistening sand and a prime sunset-viewing locale. The secluded cove at neighboring Little Beach is Maui's most popular nude beach. Together these beaches form Makena State Park, but don't be misled by the term 'park,' as they remain in a natural state, with no facilities except for a couple of pit toilets and picnic tables. No one on Maui would have it otherwise.

Kayaking at Makena Landing   GREG ELMS

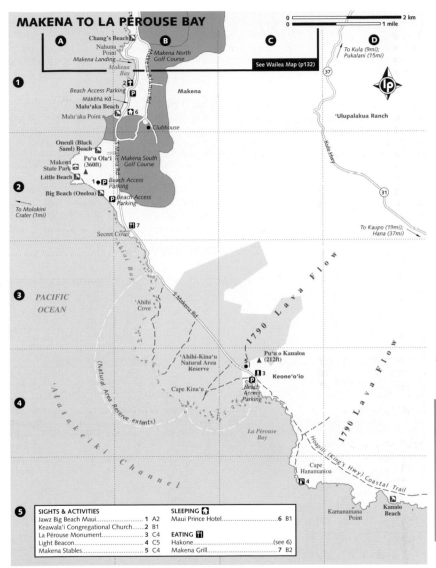

MAKENA TO LA PÉROUSE BAY

SOUTH MAUI

Beaches

MAKENA BAY

This one's all about the water. There's no better place on Maui for kayaking and, when seas are calm, snorkeling is good along the rocks at the south side of Makena Landing, the boat launch that's the center of the action. Makena Bay is also a good place for shore dives; divers will want to head to the north side of the bay.

Kayak-rental companies deliver kayaks to Makena Landing (see p124) – you can either head off on your own or join a tour. Although the norm is to make arrangements in advance (there are no shops here), if there's an extra kayak on the trailer, you might be able to arrange something on the spot. Paddle your kayak south along the lava coastline to Malu'aka Beach, where green sea turtles abound.

MALU'AKA BEACH

our pick Forget the official name – everyone just calls this 'Turtle Beach.' Snorkelers and kayakers flock here to see the sea turtles that frequent this golden-sand beach fronting the Maui Prince Hotel. You'll find terrific coral about 100yd out. Sea turtles feed along the coral and often swim within a few feet of snorkelers. The best action is at the south end of the beach. Come on a calm day – this one kicks up with even a little wind and when it's choppy you won't see anything.

You'll find beach parking lots, restrooms and showers at both ends of the beach. At the north side, the lot's opposite Keawala'i Congregational Church. If it's full take the first right after Maui Prince Hotel, where there's additional parking for about 60 cars.

ONEULI (BLACK SAND) BEACH

Look for the first Makena State Park access sign and the dirt road leading to this little salt-and-pepper-sand beach. Because of a lava shelf along the shoreline, it's not good for swimming, but families come here on the weekends for fishing and picnics. Kayakers take to the water here as well, and it can be a good spot for seeing turtles poking their heads out of the water as they feed along the shore.

BIG BEACH (ONELOA)

our pick The crowning glory of Makena State Park, this untouched beach is arguably the finest on Maui. In Hawaiian it's called Oneloa, literally 'Long Sand.' And indeed the golden sands stretch for the better part of a mile and are as broad as they come. The waters are a beautiful turquoise. When they're calm you'll find kids boogie boarding here, but at other times the breaks belong to experienced bodysurfers, who get tossed wildly in the transparent waves.

In the late 1960s this was the site of an alternative-lifestyle encampment nicknamed 'Hippie Beach.' The tent city lasted until 1972, when police finally evicted everyone. More than a few of Maui's now-graying residents can trace their roots on the island to those days.

The turnoff to the main parking area is a mile beyond the Maui Prince Hotel. A second parking area lies a quarter of a mile to the south. Thefts and broken windshields are unfortunately commonplace; don't leave anything valuable in your car.

The rocky shallows at Secret Cove

LITTLE BEACH

Little Beach, also known as Pu'u Ola'i Beach, is South Maui's *au naturel* beach. Mind you, nudity is officially illegal, though enforcement is at the political whim of the day. Hidden by a rocky outcrop that juts out from Pu'u Ola'i, the cinder hill that marks the north end of Big Beach, most visitors don't even know Little Beach is there. But take the short trail up the rock that links the two beaches and bam, there it is, spread out in front of you. The crowd is mixed, about half gay and half straight.

Little Beach fronts a sandy cove that usually has a gentle shorebreak ideal for body-surfing and boogie boarding. When the surf's up, you'll find plenty of local surfers here as well. When the water's calm, snorkeling is good along the rocky point.

SECRET COVE

Well, once it was secret. Now a favorite for getaway weddings, it's a toss-up whether you'll have this little pocket cove all to yourself or it'll be packed to the brim with tuxes and tulle. But this lovely postcard-size beach of golden sand with a straight-on view of Kaho'olawe is certainly worth a peek. The cove is a quarter-mile after the southernmost Makena State Park parking lot. The entrance is through an opening in a lava-rock wall just south of house No 6900.

GREG ELMS

PANIOLO ROOTS

Sitting beneath the slopes of Upcountry's 'Ulupalakua Ranch (p164), Makena was once a *paniolo* village, home to Hawaiian cowboys who corralled cattle at the landing and loaded them onto barges bound for Honolulu slaughterhouses. To get a glimpse of Makena's roots, stop at the **Keawala'i Congregational Church**, just south of Makena Landing. One of Maui's earliest missionary churches, its 3ft-thick walls were constructed of burnt coral rock. In the seaside churchyard take a look at the old tombstones adorned with cameo photographs of the Hawaiian cowboys laid to rest a century ago. Inside, the *hala* (pandanas) fans and Hawaiian-language hymnals in the pews let you know this church is still true to its Hawaiian heritage.

Festivals & Events

The Xterra World Championship (www.xterraplanet.com), held in late October from the Maui Prince Hotel, is a major off-road triathlon that begins with a 1-mile swim, follows with a 6.8-mile trail run and tops off with a grueling 18.65-mile bike ride up the slopes of Haleakalā.

Eating & Sleeping

JAWZ BIG BEACH MAUI — Food Truck $
Makena State Park; snacks $3-9; ⏱ 11am-3:30pm
Get your beach snacks at this food truck that sets up in the northernmost Big Beach parking lot selling tacos, burritos and shave ice. Other vendors with cold coconuts, pineapples and other fruit can sometimes be found along Makena Alanui Dr opposite Big Beach.

MAKENA GRILL — Takeout $
Makena Alanui Dr; dishes $7-10; ⏱ 11am-4pm
This little roadside smoke grill serves up fish tacos and chicken kebabs. Hours can be irregular but when it's open these are tasty grinds. Take your goodies across the street to Secret Cove, and have a little picnic.

MAUI PRINCE HOTEL — Resort $$$$
☎ 874-1111, 800-321-6248; www.mauiprince.com; 5400 Makena Alanui Dr; r from $380; 🞪 ▣ ▨
Largely a tour-group hotel, the Maui Prince

SOUTH MAUI

looks like a fortress from the outside, but the interior incorporates a fine sense of Japanese aesthetics, with carp ponds and raked-rock gardens. It has a well-regarded Japanese dinner restaurant, Hakone, and an excellent Sunday brunch.

BEYOND MAKENA

Makena Rd continues as a narrow paved road for an adventurous 3 miles after Makena State Park. The road goes through the 'Ahihi-Kina'u Natural Area Reserve before dead-ending at La Pérouse Bay.

'Ahihi-Kina'u Natural Area Reserve

Chalk this one up to Maui's last lava flow, which spilled down to the sea here in 1790, shaping 'Ahihi Bay and Cape Kina'u along the way. The jagged lava coastline and the pristine waters fringing it have been designated a reserve because of its unique marine habitat.

Thanks in part to the prohibition on fishing, snorkeling is incredible. Just about everyone heads to the little roadside cove 0.1 miles south of the first reserve sign – granted, it offers good snorkeling, but there are better (and less-crowded) options. Instead, drive 0.2 miles past the cove and look for a large clearing on the right. Park here and follow the coastal footpath south for five minutes to reach a black-sand beach with fantastic coral, clear water and few visitors. Enter the water from the left side of the beach where access is easy, snorkel in a northerly direction and you'll immediately be over coral gardens teeming with an amazing variety of fish. Huge rainbow parrotfish abound here and it's not unusual to see turtles and the occasional reef shark as well.

La Pérouse Bay

Earth and ocean merge at La Pérouse Bay with a raw desolate beauty that's almost eerie. The ancient Hawaiian village of Keone'o'io flourished here before the 1790 volcanic eruption and its remains – mainly

THE FRENCH CONNECTION

In May 1786 the renowned French explorer Jean François de Galaup La Pérouse became the first Westerner to land on Maui. As he sailed into the bay that now bears his name, scores of Hawaiian canoes came out to greet him. Two years after leaving Hawaii, La Pérouse mysteriously disappeared in the Pacific. While no one knows his fate, some historians speculate that he and his crew were eaten by cannibals in the New Hebrides (now part of Vanuatu). A monument to the explorer is located at the end of the road at La Pérouse Bay.

house and heiau platforms – can be seen scattered among the lava patches. From the volcanic shoreline look for pods of spinner dolphins, which commonly come into the bay during the early part of the day. The combination of strong offshore winds and rough waters rule out swimming, but it's an interesting place to explore on land.

ACTIVITIES

Makena Stables (☎ 879-0244; www.makenastables .com; 3hr trail rides $145-170; ⏰ 8am-6pm), located just before the road ends, offers morning and sunset horseback rides across the lava flows and up the scenic slopes of 'Ulupalakua Ranch.

From La Pérouse Bay, the **Hoapili (King's Highway) Trail** follows an ancient path along the coastline across jagged lava flows. Be prepared: wear hiking boots and bring plenty to drink. It's a dry area with no water and little vegetation, so it can get very hot. The first part of the trail is along the sandy beach at La Pérouse Bay. Right after the trail emerges onto the lava fields, it's possible to take a spur trail for three-quarters of a mile down to the light beacon at the tip of Cape Hanamanioa. Alternatively, walk inland to the Na Ala Hele sign and turn right onto the King's Hwy as it climbs through rough 'a'a lava inland for the next 2 miles before coming back to the coast to an older lava flow at Kanaio Beach.

NORTH SHORE & UPCOUNTRY

Windsurfing capital of the world and the garden belt of Maui. Local as a ton of onions on a pickup truck, a rancher on horseback, a lone surfer beating across the waves. The surf-sculpted North Shore coast stands in sharp contrast to gently rolling pastures and bountiful gardens carpeting the Upcountry slopes. The towns – hip Pa'ia, artsy Makawao and mud-on-your-boots Keokea – boast as much weathered personality as their proud residents. The scenery pulls at your soul; makes you want to hang around and browse the real-estate ads. So do. Hike up a mountainside, zipline over deep gorges, paraglide down the hillsides or ride a horse through a lofty cloud forest.

NORTH SHORE & UPCOUNTRY
ITINERARIES

IN ONE DAY *This leg: 18 miles*

❶ **MAKAWAO (p152)** Start your day off in this tasty town by popping into **Komoda Store & Bakery (p153)** for a mouthwatering cream puff or two. Now take a stroll – the town's numerous art galleries and ranch shops beckon with quirky surprises.

❷ **OLINDA RD (p152)** Head out of town on an adventurous country drive through a spicy eucalyptus forest, stopping to hike the cool paths of **Waihou Springs Trail (p152)**.

❸ **HA'IKU (p156)** Continue your countryside tour by taking the winding backroads to the surfing town of Ha'iku. Poke around. Salivate over the picnic goodies at **Vasi's Deli & Bakery (p156)** and walk out with an armful.

❹ **HO'OKIPA BEACH PARK (p145)** It's afternoon now, so the winds will be on a tear.

Head to Ho'okipa to watch the world's hottest pro windsurfers ride 'em. Remember that picnic lunch? Savor it now while you savor the view.

❺ **TAVARES BEACH (p147)** Grab your beach towel. It's time to catch some serious rays. Watch the dogs and kiddies romp around at this untouristed strand. Then join them in a swim.

❻ **PA'IA (p145)** The late afternoon light plays on the candy-colored plantation shacks that house Pa'ia's eclectic shops and eateries. Take your time – this is a great place to browse. Dinnertime brings the tough choice. If a wafting scent really grabs you, let it happen. Otherwise, check out the night's fish special at **Jacques Northshore Restaurant & Bar (p149)**.

IN TWO DAYS *This leg: 25 miles*

❼ **SURFING GOAT DAIRY (p158)** Plan day one as above. Start day two with a little farm tour, beginning at the source of all that delicious chevre and feta found on Maui.

❽ **ENCHANTING FLORAL GARDENS (p159)** Now it's time to explore Kula's gardens and this place is the most wildly diverse of them all.

❾ **LA PROVENCE (p161)** If you've worked up an appetite with your garden stroll, meander over to this French-accented restaurant and order up a salad of fresh Kula greens and guess-who's goat cheese.

❿ **TEDESCHI VINEYARDS (p164)** There's nothing like an afternoon drive along rolling pastures with sweeping views, especially one that ends at a winery.

⓫ **GRANDMA'S COFFEE HOUSE (p164)** After you've tipped your wine glass, go sip a cup of Upcountry's other favorite homegrown beverage. Folks at this little coffee shop have been growing top-rate beans since grandma's days and they have the deckside coffee trees to prove it.

⓬ **ALI'I KULA LAVENDER (p159)** Just when you think it can't get any prettier, head up the slopes. Soak up the fragrant scents on a stroll through this lavender garden at the foot of a cool cloud forest.

⓭ **HALI'IMAILE GENERAL STORE (p151)** Plantation era meets nouvelle Hawaii cuisine at this remarkable chef-driven restaurant in an atmospheric century-old general store. But get there early – it packs a crowd at dinner.

FOR THRILL SEEKERS

❶ SKYLINE ECO-ADVENTURES (p160)
Soar above treetops and gulches on this
adrenaline-rush zipline along the slopes of
Haleakalā.

❷ PIIHOLO RANCH (p153) Swing into
the saddle and join the ranch hands on
a horseback ride across green pastures at
one of Upcountry's oldest family-run cattle
ranches.

**❸ POLIPOLI SPRING STATE RECREATION
AREA (p162)** Explore trails on foot or on a
mountain bike in this dreamy cloud forest
miles from anywhere.

❹ HO'OKIPA BEACH PARK (p145) If
you're a top-notch boardrider and you're

looking for the best, this is where you'll
find it. Surfers come here in the morning;
windsurfers hit it in the afternoon.

❺ PROFLYGHT PARAGLIDING (p161)
Take to the wing and glide like an eagle on
a 1000ft leap off the edge of Haleakalā – the
term 'bird's-eye view' will never be the same
after this one.

❻ HA BALDWIN BEACH PARK (p147)
Grab your boogie board and wait for the
perfect break at this white-sand beach in
the surfer haunt of Pa'ia.

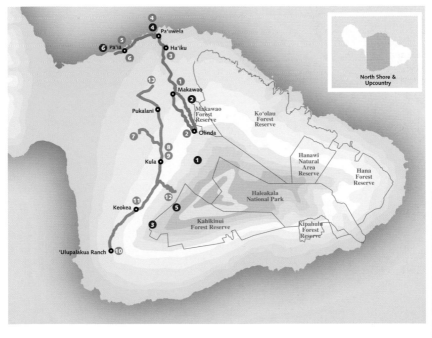

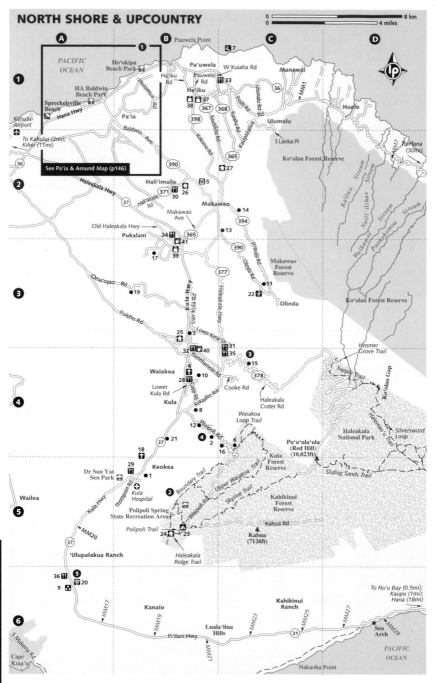

NORTH SHORE & UPCOUNTRY

HIGHLIGHTS

❶ **BEST BEACH:** Ho'okipa Beach (below)
❷ **BEST VIEW:** Polipoli Spring State Recreation Area (p162)
❸ **BEST ACTIVITY:** Skyline Eco-Adventures Zipline (p160)
❹ **BEST PLACE TO BREATHE DEEPLY:** Ali'i Kula Lavender (p159)
❺ **BEST PLACE TO TOAST:** Tedeschi Vineyards (p164)

Highlights are numbered on the map on p144.

PA'IA

This is hands-down the most interesting burg on Maui. Once a thriving sugar town, a century ago Pa'ia boasted 10,000 residents living in plantation camps above the now-defunct sugar mill. During the 1950s there was an exodus to Kahului, shops were shuttered and Pa'ia began to collect cobwebs. Attracted by low rents, hippies seeking paradise landed in Pa'ia in the 1970s.

A decade later, windsurfers discovered Ho'okipa Beach, and Pa'ia broke onto the map big time. Its aging wooden storefronts, now splashed in cheery sunshine yellows and robin's-egg blues, house a wild array of shops and eateries geared to visitors and locals alike.

You never know who you'll find in Pa'ia. Was that Woody Harrelson in the Hemp House? Windsurfer Robby Naish at Jacques? Even the Dalai Lama made an appearance in 2007 to consecrate Pa'ia's new stupa.

Orientation & Information

At Pa'ia's one stoplight, the Hana Hwy (Hwy 36) intersects with Baldwin Ave (Hwy 390), which leads upcountry to Makawao. Everything in Pa'ia is on these two roads, and the whole town is walkable. Traffic backs up along Hana Hwy as commuters shuttle to and from jobs, and whenever the surf is up on the North Shore. For many travelers, Pa'ia is the first stop on the Road to Hana (see p187). It's also the last place to gas up your car before Hana, but that's not a problem as there's a 24-hour gas station in town.

Bank of Hawaii (☎ 579-9511; 35 Baldwin Ave) Has a 24-hour ATM.
Livewire Café (☎ 579-6009; 137 Hana Hwy; per min 15¢, 20min minimum; ☽ 6am-10pm) The place to surf the internet – lots of stations and good munchies.
Pa'ia Laundromat (129 Baldwin Ave; ☽ 5am-8pm)
Post office (☎ 579-8866; 120 Baldwin Ave; ☽ 8:30am-4:30pm Mon-Fri, 10:30am-12:30pm Sat)

Beaches

HO'OKIPA BEACH PARK

Ho'okipa is to gutsy windsurfers what Everest is to climbers. It reigns supreme as the

INFORMATION		
ATM	(see 39)	
Bank of Hawaii	(see 39)	
Coin Laundary	(see 39)	
Public Restrooms	**1**	B5
Pukalani Post Office	(see 39)	

SIGHTS & ACTIVITIES		
Ali'i Kula Lavender	**2**	B4
Enchanting Floral Gardens	**3**	B3
Haleakala ATV Tours	(see 15)	
Haleakala Ranch	(see 15)	
Holy Ghost Church	**4**	B4
Hui No'eau Visual Arts Center	**5**	B2
Hunter Check Station	**6**	C4
Jaws	**7**	C1
Kula Botanical Garden	**8**	B4
Makee Sugar Mill Ruins	**9**	A6
Maui Agricultural Research Center	**10**	B4
Maui Bird Conservation Center	**11**	C3

Maui Polo Club	(see 13)	
O'o Farm	**12**	B4
Oskie Rice Arena	**13**	C2
Piiholo Ranch	**14**	C2
Pony Express	**15**	C4
Proflyght Paragliding	**16**	C4
Pukalani Country Club	**17**	B3
St John's Episcopal Church	**18**	B4
Skyline Eco-Adventures	(see 37)	
Studio Maui	(see 37)	
Surfing Goat Dairy	**19**	B3
Tedeschi Vineyards	**20**	A6
Thompson Ranch	**21**	B4
Waihou Springs Trail	**22**	C3

SLEEPING 🅰 🅖		
Campground	**23**	B5
Housekeeping Cabin	**24**	B5
Kula View Bed & Breakfast	**25**	B3
Peace of Maui	**26**	B2
Pilialoha	**27**	C2

EATING 🍴		
Café 808	**28**	B4
Colleen's	(see 37)	
Foodland	(see 39)	
Grandma's Coffee House	**29**	B5
Hali'imaile General Store	**30**	B2
Kula Sandalwoods Restaurant	**31**	C3
La Provence	**32**	B4
Pa'uwela Café	**33**	C1
Serpico's	**34**	B2
Sunrise Market & Protea Farm	**35**	C4
'Ulupalakua Ranch Store	**36**	A6
Vasi's Deli & Bakery	(see 38)	
Veg Out	(see 38)	

SHOPPING 🛍		
Ha'iku Marketplace	**37**	B1
Ha'iku Town Center	**38**	B1
Pukalani Terrace Center	**39**	B3

TRANSPORT		
Gas Station	**40**	B4
Gas Station	**41**	B3

PA'IA & AROUND

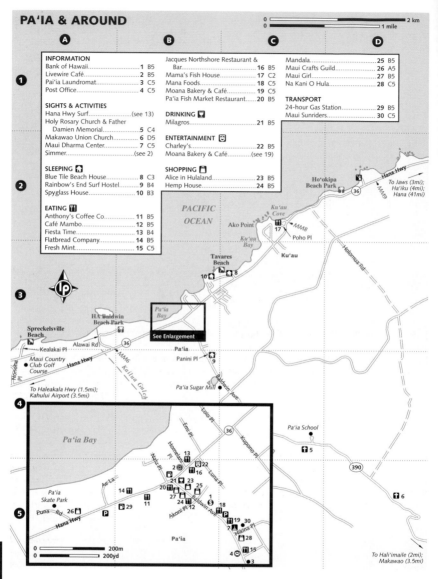

INFORMATION
Bank of Hawaii...................................**1** B5
Livewire Café......................................**2** B5
Pai'ia Laundromat...............................**3** C5
Post Office..**4** C5

SIGHTS & ACTIVITIES
Hana Hwy Surf...........................(see 13)
Holy Rosary Church & Father
  Damien Memorial.............................**5** C4
Makawao Union Church.....................**6** D5
Maui Dharma Center..........................**7** C5
Simmer...(see 2)

SLEEPING
Blue Tile Beach House.........................**8** C3
Rainbow's End Surf Hostel..................**9** B4
Spyglass House.................................**10** B3

EATING
Anthony's Coffee Co..........................**11** B5
Café Mambo......................................**12** B5
Fiesta Time..**13** B4
Flatbread Company............................**14** B5
Fresh Mint...**15** C5

Jacques Northshore Restaurant &
  Bar...**16** B5
Mama's Fish House.............................**17** C2
Mana Foods.......................................**18** C5
Moana Bakery & Café.........................**19** C5
Pa'ia Fish Market Restaurant...............**20** B5

DRINKING
Milagros...**21** B5

ENTERTAINMENT
Charley's...**22** B5
Moana Bakery & Café..................(see 19)

SHOPPING
Alice in Hulaland...............................**23** B5
Hemp House.....................................**24** B5

Mandala...**25** B5
Maui Crafts Guild..............................**26** A5
Maui Girl..**27** B5
Na Kani O Hula.................................**28** C5

TRANSPORT
24-hour Gas Station...........................**29** B5
Maui Sunriders..................................**30** C5

---

world's premier windsurfing beach, with strong currents, dangerous shorebreaks and razor-sharp coral offering the ultimate challenge.

Ho'okipa is also one of Maui's prime surfing spots. Winter sees the biggest waves for board surfers, and summer has the most consistent winds for windsurfers. To prevent intersport beefs, surfers typically hit the waves in the morning and the windsurfers take over during the afternoon.

The action in the water is suitable for pros only. But a hilltop perch overlooking the beach offers spectators a bird's-eye view of the world's top windsurfers doing their death-defying stuff. Ho'okipa is just before the 9-mile marker; to reach the lookout above the beach take the driveway at the east side of the park.

HA BALDWIN BEACH PARK

Bodysurfers and boogie boarders take to the waves at this palm-lined county park about a mile west of Pa'ia, at the 6-mile marker. The wide sandy beach drops off quickly, and when the shorebreak is big, unsuspecting swimmers can get slammed soundly. If you see lots of bodysurfers in the water, it's probably big! Showers, restrooms, picnic tables and a well-used baseball and soccer field round out the facilities. The park has a reputation for drunken nastiness after the sun sets, but it's fine in the daytime when there's a lifeguard on duty.

SPRECKELSVILLE BEACH

Extending west from HA Baldwin Beach, this 2-mile stretch of sand punctuated by lava outcrops is a good walking beach, but its near-shore lava shelf makes it less than ideal for swimming for adults. The rocks do, however, provide protection for young kids. If you walk to the center of the beach, you'll come to a section dubbed 'baby beach,' where local families take the little ones to splash. There are no facilities. To get there, turn toward the ocean on Nonohe Pl, then turn left on Kealakai Pl.

TAVARES BEACH

The best place for swimming in the Pa'ia area, this unmarked sandy beach is quiet during the week but livens up on weekends when local families come here toting picnics, guitars, dogs and kids. A submerged lava shelf runs parallel to the beach about 25ft from the shore and is shallow enough

Surf's up at Ho'okipa Beach   GREG ELMS

for swimmers to scrape over. Once you know it's there, however, the rocks are easy to avoid, so take a look before jumping in. The beach parking lot is at the first shoreline access sign on the Hana side of the 7-mile marker. There are no facilities.

Activities

At **Hana Hwy Surf** (☎ 579-8999; 149 Hana Hwy; surfboards/boogie boards per day $20/10; ☽ 9am-6pm Mon-Sat, 10am-5pm Sun), Pa'ia's surfing headquarters, the staff keep their fingers on the pulse of the surf scene – and even provide a daily recorded surf report.

Simmer (☎ 579-8484; www.simmerhawaii.com; 137 Hana Hwy; sailboards per day/week $45/280; ☽ 9am-7pm) is all about windsurfing and handles everything from repairs to top-of-the-line gear rentals.

The **Maui Dharma Center** (☎ 579-8076; www.mauidharmacenter.org; 81 Baldwin Ave; ☽ 6:30am-6:30pm), the Tibetan Buddhist temple and stupa in the town center, provides good karma, inviting visitors to join in morning meditation, yoga sessions and other spiritual activities.

NORTH SHORE & UPCOUNTRY

Festivals & Events

Aloha Classic Wave Championships (www.aloha classicwindsurfing.com) The final event of the Pro World tour, this tournament brings the world's best sailboarders out to one-up the competition at Ho'okipa Beach during a week in early November. Get there early to get a parking space overlooking the beach.

THE ULTIMATE WAVE

When this monster rears its powerful head, it's big, fast and mean enough to crunch bones. What is it? Jaws (also known to locals as Pe'ahi), Maui's famous big-wave surf spot. A few times a year, strong winter storms off the coast of Japan generate an abundance of energy that races across the Pacific Ocean to Hawaii's shores, translating into the planet's biggest rideable waves.

News of the mammoth swells, which reach as high as a seven-story building, attracts gutsy surfers from all over the state and beyond. With them come scores of spectators. Unfortunately, there's no legitimate public access to the cliffs that overlook Jaws, and the crowds that gather create some big headaches. Photographers, visitors and locals numbering in the thousands have been known to trample the surrounding pineapple fields and hold up harvest for a glimpse of the action, while traffic on Hana Hwy slows to a crawl.

When Jaws is up, it's impossible for surfers to paddle through the break to catch a ride. But where there's a thrill, there's a way. Tow-in surfers work in pairs, using small watercraft known as wave runners to get people and their boards beyond the break. When even a wave runner is outmatched, surfers get dropped into the ocean from a helicopter.

The equation of extreme sport says that thrill doesn't come without its share of danger. There are myriad opportunities for big-wave surfers to get hurt or killed. The insanely powerful waves can wash surfers into rocks, throw them into their wave runners, knock them against their surfboards or simply pummel them with the force of all that moving water. That said, these guys are pros and are very good at skirting the perils.

Hi-Tech/Lopez Split Surfbash (www.mauisurfohana .org) At Maui's largest surf contest, the surfers take over Ho'okipa Beach on the last weekend in November or the first weekend in December, with competing short-boarders, long-boarders and boogie boarders.

Eating

Most of Pa'ia's luscious eateries are clustered around the intersection of Baldwin Ave and the Hana Hwy. Go poke your head in a few places and see what's cookin'. Nothing better awaits you in Hana, so grab your picnic supplies before heading onward.

🍴 MANA FOODS   Takeout $
☎ 579-8078; 49 Baldwin Ave; deli items $4-7;
⏱ 8:30am-8:30pm

Dreadlocked, Birkenstocked or just needing to stock up – everyone rubs shoulders at Mana Foods, a health food store, bakery and deli wrapped in one. Don't miss the luscious walnut cinnamon rolls made fresh every morning. Then look for the hot barbecued chicken and organic salad bar. It's gonna be a *g-o-o-d* picnic!

ANTHONY'S COFFEE CO   Café $
our pick ☎ 579-8340; 90 Hana Hwy; mains $4-11;
⏱ 6am-2pm

The best cup of joe on this side of the island. Fresh-ground organic coffee and a delish variety of goodies, from pastries to lox Benedict. They even pack picnics for the drive to Hana. You know everything's done right – you'll find Anthony himself on the other side of the counter grinding away.

FIESTA TIME   Mexican $
☎ 579-8269; 149 Hana Hwy; mains $4-13;
⏱ lunch & dinner

Surfers line up at this hole-in-the-wall for authentic homecooked Mexican food that's twice as good and half the price as nearby Tex-Mex options. Quesadillas, tostadas, hot tamales – *muy delicioso!*

FRESH MINT   Vietnamese $$
☎ 579-9144; 115 Baldwin Ave; mains $8-13;
⏱ dinner

Authentic Vietnamese fare but totally veg, and the chef-owner of this place takes pride in her artistically presented dishes. Even meat eaters will be blown away by how soy takes on the flavors and texture of the foods it substitutes. In doubt? Just try the spicy ginger soy beef.

CAFÉ MAMBO
Café $$

☎ 579-8021; 30 Baldwin Ave; mains $6-18;
🕑 8am-9pm

This upbeat, arty café adds a splash of innovation to everything it does. Breakfast, served until noon, features create-your-own omelets. At other times choose from fragrant Moroccan stews, mouthwatering duck fajitas and hearty salads. Mambo also packs box lunches in coolers for the road to Hana (for two people $17).

PA'IA FISH MARKET RESTAURANT
Seafood $$

☎ 579-8030; 110 Hana Hwy; meals $9-16;
🕑 11am-9:30pm

Come mealtime the tables here are packed like sardines. Pick your fish from the day's catch staring back at you from the refrigerated display case. The local favorite is fish and chips, but the menu includes plenty of other tempting fish preparations, from charbroiled to Cajun blackened.

Stop at Mana en route to Hana   GREG ELMS

FLATBREAD COMPANY
Italian $$

☎ 579-8989; 89 Hana Hwy; mains $9-20;
🕑 11:30am-10pm Mon-Thu, to 11pm Fri & Sat

Wood-fired pizzas made with organic sauces, nitrate-free pepperoni, Kula onions – you'll never stop at a chain pizza house again. Lots of fun combinations, from vegan to *kalua* pig and local pineapple. The service is as good as the food, and on Tuesday nights a cut of the profits goes to a local environmental cause.

JACQUES NORTHSHORE RESTAURANT & BAR
Seafood $$

our pick ☎ 579-8844; 120 Hana Hwy; mains $14-26; 🕑 dinner Thu-Sun

Don't be fooled by first impressions. This simple open-air place serves the best-value upscale seafood on Maui. Jacques is all about fresh fish, from the top-quality sushi bar to grilled delights like mahimahi with mac-nut pesto. Order the nightly special and you can't go wrong.

MOANA BAKERY & CAFÉ
Eclectic $$$

☎ 579-9999; 71 Baldwin Ave; breakfast & lunch $8-15, dinner $13-35; 🕑 8am-9pm Wed-Sat

The bakery side has slipped since its French pastry chef left, but everything else at this stylish restaurant is spot on. The eclectic menu brims with local flavors   think seared 'ahi (tuna), Moloka'i sweet potatoes and Kula greens. Dishes range from lemongrass prawns to traditional rack of lamb.

MAMA'S FISH HOUSE
Seafood $$$$

☎ 579-8488; 799 Poho Pl; mains $36-50; 🕑 lunch & dinner

Really, this is as good as it gets. Mama's is where you go when you want to propose, or celebrate a big anniversary. The island-caught fish is so fresh your server tells you who caught it, and where! But it's much more than just great food. When the beachside tiki torches are lit at dinnertime, the scene's achingly romantic.

Drinking & Entertainment
MILAGROS

☎ 579-8755; 3 Baldwin Ave

The spot for a late-afternoon beer. The sidewalk tables are perched perfectly for watching all the action on Pa'ia's busiest corner.

CHARLEY'S
☎ 579-9453; 142 Hana Hwy
Don't be surprised to find country-singer legend Willie Nelson at the next table. He's a part-time Pa'ia resident, and this cowboy-centric place is his favorite hang. Charley's has live music most nights – with a little luck it could even be Willie. On Thursdays the twang turns rasta, with Marty Dread, Maui's top reggae musician, taking the stage.

MOANA BAKERY & CAFÉ
☎ 579-9999; 71 Baldwin Ave
If jazz is your thing, this is your place, with live music several nights a week.

Shopping
MAUI CRAFTS GUILD
☎ 579-9697; 43 Hana Hwy
This longstanding collective of Maui artists and craftspeople sells everything from pottery and jewelry to handpainted silks and natural-fiber baskets at reasonable prices.

🌺 NA KANI O HULA
☎ 573-6332; 105 Baldwin Ave
Hula *halau* (troupes) come here for *'uli'uli* (feather-decorated gourd rattles), bamboo

Crafts from Na Kani O Hula — GREG ELMS

nose flutes and other traditional dance and music crafts – any of which would make for a fascinating souvenir.

Other quirky and perky places:
Alice In Hulaland (☎ 579-9922; 19 Baldwin Ave) Kitschy but fun souvenirs.
Hemp House (☎ 579-8880; 16 Baldwin Ave) Sells all things hemp – well, almost all.
Mandala (☎ 579-9555; 29 Baldwin Ave) Lightweight cotton and silk clothing, Buddhas and Asian crafts.
Maui Girl (☎ 579-9266; 12 Baldwin Ave) Get your itty-bitty bikinis here.

Sleeping
Although Pa'ia has no hotels, there are some good sleeping options.

RAINBOW'S END
SURF HOSTEL   Hostel $
☎ 579-9057; www.mauigateway.com/~riki; 221 Baldwin Ave; dm/r $25/65; 🖵
Within walking distance of Pa'ia center, this small hostel in a tightly packed residential neighborhood offers simple clean rooms, a guest kitchen and a TV room. It attracts mostly a surfer crowd and is well suited for early risers – quiet-time rules are strictly enforced after 10pm.

CHAMELEON VACATION
RENTALS MAUI   Cottages $$
☎ 575-9933, 866-575-9933; www.donna chameleon.com; cottages from $89
Only smoke-free places to stay are offered by this eco-minded operation that books everything from rustic cottages to a secluded house on stilts.

BLUE TILE BEACH HOUSE B&B $$

our pick ☎ 579-6446, 888-579-6446; www.beach
vacationmaui.com; 459 Hana Hwy; r incl breakfast
$90-150, ste $250

Slide into your bathing suit, step out the
door of this exclusive oceanfront estate
and you're literally on the beach. Sleeping options range from a small straightforward room to a spacious honeymoon
suite with wraparound ocean-view windows and a four-poster bed. All six rooms
share a living room with fireplace and a
full kitchen.

SPYGLASS HOUSE B&B $$

☎ 579-8608, 800-475-6695; www.spyglassmaui
.com; 367 Hana Hwy; r incl breakfast $110-170

Smack on the beach at the end of a private
road, Spyglass House attracts surfers and
families who prefer salt spray to resort glit-
ter. It was once a favorite haunt of LSD guru
Timothy Leary, and although the psyche-
delics are history this seaside retreat still
maintains an eccentric edge. Stained glass,
porthole windows and a seaside hot tub are
just some of the fun here.

Getting There & Around

You can rent road bikes at **Maui Sunriders**
(☎ 579-8970; www.mauibikeride.com; 71 Baldwin Ave;
per day/week $30/90; 9am-4:30pm). The price
includes a bike rack, so a travel companion
could drop you off at the top of Haleakalā, or
anywhere else, to cycle a one way route.

HIGHWAY 390: PA'IA TO MAKAWAO

Baldwin Ave (Hwy 390) rolls uphill for
seven winding miles between Pa'ia and
Makawao, starting amid feral sugarcane
fields and then traversing pineapple fields
interspersed with little open patches where
cattle graze.

CHURCHES

Two churches grace Baldwin Ave. Two
miles above Pa'ia the **Holy Rosary Church** (Map
p146; 945 Baldwin Ave), with its memorial statue
of Father Damien, comes up on the right.
A mile further along on the left is the attractive c 1916 **Makawao Union Church** (Map
p146; 1445 Baldwin Ave), a stone-block building

with stained-glass windows that's on the
National Register of Historic Places.

HUI NO'EAU VISUAL ARTS CENTER

Map p144; ☎ 572-6560; www.huinoeau.com; 2841
Baldwin Ave; admission free; 10am-4pm

Occupying the former estate of sugar mag-
nates Harry and Ethel Baldwin, Hui No'eau
radiates artistic creativity. The plantation
house with the main galleries was designed
by famed architect CW Dickey in 1917
and showcases the Hawaiian Regional style
architectural features he pioneered. The
prestigious arts club founded here in the
1930s still offers classes in printmaking,
pottery, woodcarving and other visual arts.
You're welcome to visit the galleries, which
exhibit the diverse works of island artists,
and walk around the grounds, where you'll
find stables converted into art studios. The
gift shop sells quality ceramics, glassware
and original prints created onsite. Pick up
a walking-tour map at the front desk. The
center is just after the 5-mile marker.

Hali'imaile

The little pineapple town of Hali'imaile
(meaning 'fragrant twining shrub') is
named for the fragrant maile plants, used
for lei-making, that covered the area before
pineapple took over. The heart of town –
actually the only commercial business in
town – is the old general store (c 1918)
that's been turned into Upcountry's top
restaurant.

Hali'imaile Rd runs through the town,
connecting Baldwin Ave (Hwy 390) with
the Haleakala Hwy (Hwy 37).

EATING & SLEEPING
HALI'IMAILE
GENERAL STORE Hawaii Regional $$$

our pick Map p144; ☎ 572-2666; 900 Hali'imaile
Rd; lunch $10-24, dinner $24-42; lunch Mon-Fri,
dinner daily

Bev Gannon was one of the original forces
behind the Hawaii Regional Cuisine movement (see p261) and a steady flow of in-the-
know diners beat a track to this tiny village
to feast on her inspired creations. At both
lunch and dinner you'll find taste treats like
ginger chili duck tostadas and Cajun-style
fresh fish. The atmospheric plantation-era
decor sets the mood.

Hali'imaile General Store GREG ELMS

PEACE OF MAUI Inn $

Map p144; ☎ 572-5045, 888-475-5045; www.peace ofmaui.com; 1290 Hali'imaile Rd; s/d with shared bathroom $50/55, 2br cottage $120; 🖵

This aptly named place is Maui's top budget sleep. It's in the middle of nowhere yet within an hour's drive of nearly everywhere – a central base if you want to explore the whole island without changing accommodations. Rooms are spotlessly clean and small but comfortable, each with refrigerator and TV. There's a guest kitchen and a hot tub. If you need more space, the cottage is large enough to sleep a family.

MAKAWAO

Paint a picture of Makawao and what you get is a mélange of art haven and cowboy culture, with some chic boutiques and a dash of New Age sensibility thrown in for good measure.

Started as a ranching town in the 1800s, Makawao wears its *paniolo* (cowboy) history in the Old West–style wooden buildings lining Baldwin Ave. And the cattle pastures surrounding town remind you it's more than just history.

But that's just one side of the place. Many of the old shops that once sold saddles and cattle feed now have artsy new tenants who have turned Makawao into the most happening art center on Maui. Its galleries display the works of painters and sculptors who have escaped frenzied scenes elsewhere to set up shop in the inspirational hills around Makawao. If you enjoy art galleries and shopping, just about every storefront is worth poking your head into.

Orientation & Information

Most everything is within a few minutes' walk of the main intersection, where Baldwin Ave (Hwy 390) meets Makawao Ave (Hwy 365).

Makawao library (Map p153; ☎ 573-8785; 1159 Makawao Ave; ⏲ noon-8pm Mon & Wed, 9:30am-5pm Tue, Thu & Sat) Internet access.

Minit Stop (Map p153; ☎ 573-9295; 1100 Makawao Ave; ⏲ 5am-11pm) This gas station has an ATM.

Post office (Map p153; ☎ 572-0019; 1075 Makawao Ave)

Sights & Activities

OLINDA ROAD

For the ultimate country drive head into the hills above Makawao along Olinda Rd, which picks up in town where Baldwin Ave leaves off, drifting up past the **Oskie Rice Arena** (Map p144), where rodeos are held, and the **Maui Polo Club** (Map p144), which hosts matches on Sunday afternoons in the fall. From here the winding road is little more than a path through the forest, with knotty tree roots as high as your car caressing the roadsides. The air is rich with the spicy fragrance of eucalyptus trees and occasionally there's a clearing with an ocean vista. Four miles up from town, past the 11-mile marker, is the **Maui Bird Conservation Center** (Map p144; closed to the public), which breeds nene (native Hawaiian goose) and other endangered birds. To make a loop, turn left onto Pi'iholo Rd near the top of Olinda Rd and wind back down into town.

WAIHOU SPRINGS TRAIL

If you're up for a meditative walk in the woods, don't miss this quiet trail (Map p144), which begins 4.75 miles up Olinda Rd from central Makawao. The forest along the route is incredibly varied, having been planted by the US Forest Service in an effort to determine which trees would produce the best-quality lumber in Hawaii. Thankfully these magnificent specimens never met the woodman's ax. The trail, which begins on a soft carpet of pine needles, passes Monterey cypress and eucalyptus as well as orderly rows of pine trees. After 0.7 miles, you'll be rewarded with a view clear out to the ocean, and up to this point it's easy going. It's also possible to continue steeply downhill for another quarter-mile to reach Waihou Springs, but if it's been raining recently that part of the trail can be a muddy mess.

HORSEBACK RIDING

At **Piiholo Ranch** (Map p144; ☎ 357-5544; www.piiholo.com; Waiahiwi Rd; 2hr ride $120; 🕑 9am-3:30pm Mon-Sat) you can ride with real *paniolo* across the open range of a cattle ranch that's been worked by the same family for six generations. Mountain, valley and pasture views galore.

YOGA

Yoga Awareness (Map p153; ☎ 573-7771; www.yogaawareness.com; 3660 Baldwin Ave; class $20; 🕑 8:30am-7:30pm) welcomes visitors to join the regulars in one of its daily group yoga classes.

Festivals & Events

Upcountry Fair Traditional agricultural fair with a farmers market, arts and crafts, chili cookoff, *keiki* games and good ol' country music; held on the second weekend in June at the Eddie Tam Complex.

Makawao Rodeo More than 300 *paniolo* show up at the Oskie Rice Arena on the weekend closest to Independence Day (July 4) to compete in roping and riding competitions at Hawaii's premier rodeo. Qualifying events occur all day on Thursday and Friday to determine who gets to compete for the big prizes over the weekend. For thrills on Friday night, head up to the arena to see the daredevil bull-riding bash.

Paniolo Parade Held on the Saturday morning closest to July 4, this festive parade goes right through the heart of Makawao; park at the rodeo grounds and take the free shuttle to the town center.

Eating

KOMODA STORE & BAKERY Bakery $

our pick Map p153; ☎ 572-7261; 3674 Baldwin Ave; pastries 70¢-$2; 🕑 7am-5pm Mon, Tue, Thu & Fri, to 2pm Sat

Legendary for its mouthwatering cream puffs and guava-filled *malasadas,* this

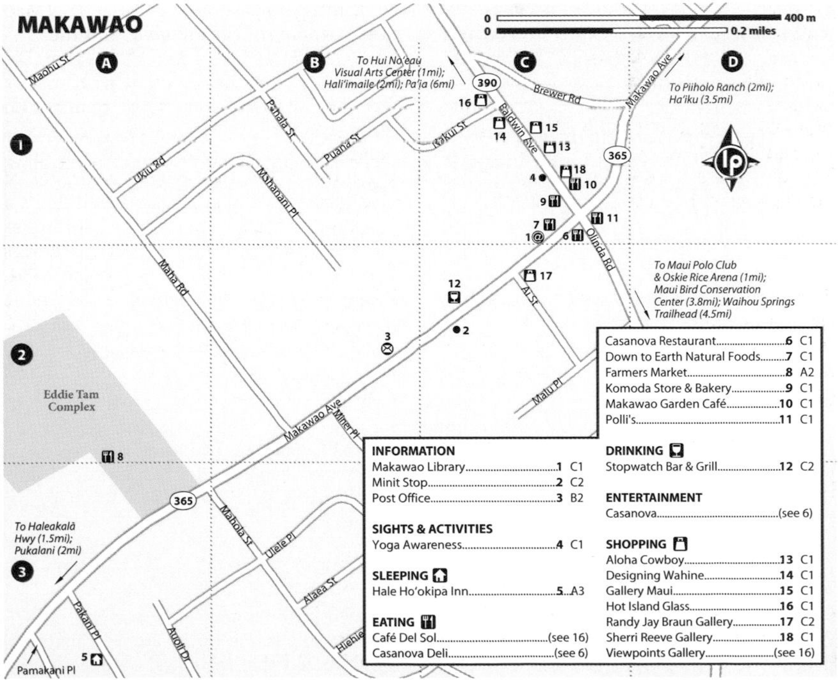
MAKAWAO
0 400 m
0 0.2 miles
To Hui No'eau Visual Arts Center (1mi); Hali'imaile (2mi); Pa'ia (6mi)
To Piiholo Ranch (2mi); Ha'iku (3.5mi)
To Maui Polo Club & Oskie Rice Arena (1mi); Maui Bird Conservation Center (3.8mi); Waihou Springs Trailhead (4.5mi)
To Haleakalā Hwy (1.5mi); Pukalani (2mi)
Eddie Tam Complex
Maohu St
Ukiu Rd
Pahala St
Puana St
Kakui St
Mahanani Pl
Maha Rd
Brewer Rd
Makawao Ave
Baldwin Ave
Olinda Rd
Ai St
Malu Pl
Miner Pl
Mahola St
Ulele Pl
Alaea St
Hiehie
Pakani Pl
Autoli Dr
Pamakani Pl
390
365
INFORMATION
Makawao Library 1 C1
Minit Stop 2 C2
Post Office 3 B2
SIGHTS & ACTIVITIES
Yoga Awareness 4 C1
SLEEPING
Hale Ho'okipa Inn 5 A3
EATING
Café Del Sol (see 16)
Casanova Deli (see 6)
Casanova Restaurant 6 C1
Down to Earth Natural Foods 7 C1
Farmers Market 8 A2
Komoda Store & Bakery 9 C1
Makawao Garden Café 10 C1
Polli's 11 C1
DRINKING
Stopwatch Bar & Grill 12 C2
ENTERTAINMENT
Casanova (see 6)
SHOPPING
Aloha Cowboy 13 C1
Designing Wahine 14 C1
Gallery Maui 15 C1
Hot Island Glass 16 C1
Randy Jay Braun Gallery 17 C2
Sherri Reeve Gallery 18 C1
Viewpoints Gallery (see 16)

Rodeo at Piiholo Ranch   GREG ELMS

multigeneration family bakery is a must-stop. But get there early – they often sell out by noon. You'll find tables and a pot of coffee (honor system) at the side of the store if you can't wait to dig in.

CASANOVA DELI   Deli $
Map p153; ☎ 572-0220; 1188 Makawao Ave; mains $4-8; ⏲ 7am-6pm Mon-Sat, 8:30am-6pm Sun
Makawao's hippest haunt brews heady espressos and buzzes all day with folks munching on buttery croissants, thick Italian sandwiches and hearty Greek salads. Take it all out to the roadside deck for people-watching.

CAFÉ DEL SOL   Café $
Map p153; ☎ 572-4877; 3620 Baldwin Ave; mains $4-10; ⏲ 8am-3:30pm Mon-Sat
Recipe for a perfect morning: grab an outdoor table at this courtyard restaurant and order up the eggs Benedict with homemade hollandaise. In the mood for something lighter? Try the awesome blueberry muffins. Lunch runs from vegan burgers with slabs of Kula onion to blackened chicken sandwiches.

MAKAWAO GARDEN CAFÉ   Café $
Map p153; ☎ 573-9065; 3669 Baldwin Ave; mains $7-10; ⏲ 11am-4pm
On a sunny day there's no better place in town for lunch than this outdoor café

tucked into a courtyard at the north end of Baldwin Ave. It's strictly sandwiches and salads, but everything's fresh, generous and made to order by the owner herself. The mahimahi on homemade focaccia is killer.

POLLI'S   Mexican $$
Map p153; ☎ 572-7808; 1202 Makawao Ave; mains $8-20; ⏲ 7am-10pm Mon-Sat, 8am-10pm Sun
Locals and visitors alike flock to this old standby Tex-Mex restaurant to down a few *cervezas* while munching away on nachos, tacos and sizzling fajitas. The food's just average, but nonstop surf videos and plenty of spirited chatter keep the scene high energy.

CASANOVA RESTAURANT   Italian $$$
Map p153; ☎ 572-0220; 1188 Makawao Ave; lunch $8-14, dinner $12-28; ⏲ lunch & dinner
The one Makawao restaurant that lures diners up the mountain, Casanova offers reliably good Italian fare, attentive service and well-paired wines. The menu ranges from innovative wood-fired pizzas and zesty pastas to juicy Upcountry steaks. Big bang for the buck.

It says something about a town when its biggest grocer is a health food store. At **Down to Earth Natural Foods** (Map p153; ☎ 572-1488; 1169 Makawao Ave; ⏲ 8am-8pm) you'll find all the expected staples as well as takeout fare.

Locals gather to sell their homegrown produce once a week at a small **farmers market** (Eddie Tam Complex; ⊙ 7-9am Sat).

Drinking & Entertainment

CASANOVA

Map p153; ☎ 572-0220; 1188 Makawao Ave
The night scene here is a shadow of what it used to be, but this is still the place to go after dark in the Upcountry. Casanova has a dance floor with live music several nights a week and DJs on others.

STOPWATCH BAR & GRILL

Map p153; ☎ 572-1380; 1127 Makawao Ave
This friendly sports bar brings in Upcountry musicians like the Haiku Hillbillys on weekends. Any other time it's all about the games on TV.

Shopping

Start your exploration by wandering down Baldwin Ave, starting at its intersection with Makawao Ave.

HOT ISLAND GLASS

Map p153; ☎ 572-4527; 3620 Baldwin Ave
Half sightseeing spot, half shop, head here to watch glassblowers spin their red-hot creations (from 10:30am to 4pm) at Maui's oldest handblown glass studio. Everything from paperweights with ocean themes to high-art decorative pieces.

RANDY JAY BRAUN GALLERY

Map p153; ☎ 573-1176; 1152 Makawao Ave
Braun's sepia photographs of traditional hula dancers are among the most recognized

Handblown glass at Hot Island Glass   GREG ELMS

RIDE 'EM, PANIOLO!

The history of *paniolo* (Hawaiian cowboys) dates back at least 50 years before the Wild West cowboys on the mainland climbed into their stirrups.

It all started with Captain Vancouver, who landed the first cattle on the Big Island of Hawai'i in 1793. The herd flourished, thanks to Kamehameha the Great placing a *kapu* (taboo) on their slaughter. A decade later another foreigner by the name of Richard Cleveland brought horses to the Big Island and Maui. By the time Kamehameha III took over, both horses and cows were running rampant on the islands. So the king invited vaqueros from Spanish California to show the first Big Island cowboys the ropes in 1832. In fact, the word *paniolo* is likely a corruption of *español,* meaning Spaniard.

Soon there were working cowboys on every island, rounding up cattle and driving them down the mountainside, then swimming them out past sharks to the cattle boats headed for Honolulu markets. A whole *paniolo* culture developed: slack key guitar music, *palaka* (checked shirts), *lauhala* hats and lei that told where each cowboy was from – pink roses for Maui, orange flowers for Lana'i and kukui nuts for Moloka'i.

It was Ikua Purdy who brought the *paniolo* lasting fame in 1908 when he won the world championship for rodeo steer-roping at Frontier Days in Cheyenne, Wyoming. Even today his record of two steers in 56 seconds has never been bettered. For 25 years Purdy worked as the foreman of Upcountry's 'Ulupalakua Ranch, where he was buried in 1945. A few dozen *paniolo* still follow in his footsteps on the national rodeo circuit, and in 1999 Purdy was inducted into the National Cowboy Hall of Fame.

If you want to know more, *Aloha Cowboy* by Virginia Cowan-Smith and Bonnie Domrose Stone is a captivating account of 200 years of *paniolo* life. Or better yet, go out on a horseback ride with *paniolo* on a working cattle ranch, like **Piiholo Ranch** (p153) on the outskirts of Makawao or **Mendes Ranch** (p98) in Waihe'e, and experience the life for yourself.

photo art in Hawaii today. Also interesting are his shots of Hawaiian cowboys.

VIEWPOINTS GALLERY

Map p153; ☎ 572-5979; 3620 Baldwin Ave

You'll feel like you're walking into a museum at this classy gallery, where a dozen of the island's finest artists hang their works.

SHERRI REEVE GALLERY

Map p153; ☎ 572-8931; 3669 Baldwin Ave

Maui artist Sherri Reeve paints floral watercolors in a pastel palette on everything from T-shirts to full-size canvasses.

Other recommended places:

Aloha Cowboy (Map p153; ☎ 573-8190; 3643 Baldwin Ave) Get your cowboy-themed retro lunch pails and rhinestone-studded leather bags here.

Designing Wahine (Map p153; ☎ 573-0990; 3640 Baldwin Ave) Quality gifts, classic aloha shirts and hand-dyed Ts with *paniolo* themes.

Gallery Maui (Map p153; ☎ 572-8092; 3643 Baldwin Ave) Tucked down an alley, this gallery showcases 20 island painters, sculptors and woodcrafters.

Horse around at Aloha Cowboy   GREG ELMS

Sleeping

HALE HO'OKIPA INN   B&B $$

Map p153; ☎ 572-6698; www.maui-bed-and-breakfast.com; 32 Pakani Pl; r incl breakfast $130-165; 🖳

A short walk from the town center, this Craftsman-style house built in 1924 offers four sunny guest rooms furnished with antiques. If you're feeling romantic go with the Rose Room, which has its own lanai entrance and a claw-foot bathtub just begging a bubbly soak.

HA'IKU

This little town just gets hipper by the day. In some ways it's what Pa'ia was like before the tourists arrived. Like Pa'ia it has its roots in sugarcane – Maui's first 12 acres of the sweet stuff were planted here in 1869, and the village once had both a sugar mill and pineapple canneries. Thanks to its affordability and proximity to Ho'okipa Beach, it's a haunt of pro surfers who have rejuvenated the town. Today the old cannery buildings are once again the heart of the community, housing a yoga studio, several surfboard shops and the kind of eateries that make a detour fun.

Activities

Studio Maui (Map p144; ☎ 575-9390; www.thestudiomaui.com; Ha'iku Marketplace, 810 Ha'iku Rd; classes $13-25; ⏰ 7:30am-10pm) attracts a high-energy, good-karma crowd with a full schedule of yoga classes from Anusara basics to power-flow yoga, as well as ecstatic dance, tango and more. There's the occasional New Age concert, too.

Eating

VASI'S DELI & BAKERY   Deli $

Map p144; ☎ 575-9588; Ha'iku Town Center, 810 Kokomo Rd; mains $5-10; ⏰ 7am-8pm Mon-Sat

You'll be amazed at the delicious goodies that come out of this hole-in-the-wall operation. Order a slice of the mile-high veggie torte and you've got yourself a filling lunch for the beach. The blackened 'ahi sandwich with Thai chili is hot in every way and the *lilikoi* (passion fruit) cheesecake is a must.

GOING LOCAL

Some of the best experiences on Maui are the ones you create yourself; guidebooks can take you only so far. To really get a feel for a place sometimes you need to throw the book aside and make your own spur-of-the-moment discoveries. So how do you get down with island folks, talk story and really get a feel for what life is like on Maui? Grab a newspaper and pore through it, looking for school benefits, church festivals or 4-H livestock competitions. Then go buy some crafts, get a taste of some home cooking or cheer on your favorite heifer. You'll be supporting the local community and will likely make new friends in the process.

VEG OUT   Vegetarian $
Map p144; ☎ 575-5320; Haʻiku Town Center, 810 Kokomo Rd; mains $5-10; ☽ 10:30am-7:30pm Mon-Fri, 11:30am-7:30pm Sat & Sun
Tucked inside an old warehouse, this rasta-casual vegetarian eatery serves up a dynamite burrito with hot tofu, beans and pineapple salsa to the sounds of Ravi Shankar. Not in a Mex mood? The Asian veggie noodles and the taro burgers are also right on the mark.

PAʻUWELA CAFÉ   Café $
Map p144; ☎ 575-9242; 375 W Kuiaha Rd; mains $7-10; ☽ 6am-2:30pm Mon-Sat, to 1pm Sun
If cappuccino is your thing this is your place. Homemade pastries and breakfast burritos start the day. Later it's hearty salads and a *kalua* turkey sandwich that has few rivals anywhere. There are just a handful of tables inside, but when it's sunny the café spills onto the sidewalk, too.

COLLEEN'S   Eclectic $$
Map p144; ☎ 575-9211; Haʻiku Marketplace; 810 Haʻiku Rd; mains $7-14; ☽ 6am-9pm
This is where the surfers get their pre-sunrise breakfast fix and return in the evening to cap things off with a pint of Big Wave Golden Ale. Everything about Colleen's says homegrown. The burgers are made with hormone-free Maui beef, the salads with organic Kula greens, and the beers Colleen pours are Hawaiian microbrews. After 4pm there's pizza by the slice ($3).

Sleeping

PILIALOHA   Cottage $$
ourpick Map p144; ☎ 572-1440; mh@pilialoha .com; 2512 Kaupakalua Rd; d $135
Pilialoha blends countryside charm with all the comforts of a home away from home. The sunny split-level cottage has one pretty setting, nestled in a eucalyptus grove. Everything inside is pretty, too. But it's the warm hospitality and attention to detail – from the fresh-cut roses on the table to the Hawaiian music collection and cozy quilts on the beds – that shines brightest. Breakfast goodies for your first morning and coffee for the entire stay are provided.

PUKALANI & AROUND

True to its name, which means Heavenly Gate, Pukalani is the gateway to the greener pastures. Most visitors just make a quick pass through on the way to Kula and Haleakalā, and unless you need to pick up supplies you won't miss much by sticking to the bypass road. If you do need to gas up, this is your last chance before Haleakalā.

Orientation & Information

Upcountry's largest town, Pukalani is 2 miles from Makawao along Hwy 365. If you're coming from Kahului, take the Haleakala Hwy (Hwy 37), which climbs through cane fields before reaching Pukalani. To reach the business part of town, take the Old Haleakala Hwy exit, where the bypass highway begins. The Old Haleakala Hwy is Pukalani's main street.

Pukalani Terrace Center (Map p144; cnr Old Haleakala Hwy & Pukalani St) has a coin laundry, a **post office** (☎ 572-0019) and a **Bank of Hawaii** (☎ 572-7242) with a 24-hour ATM. A couple of gas stations are on the Old Haleakala Hwy.

Sights & Activities
PUKALANI COUNTRY CLUB
Map p144; ☎ 572-1314; www.pukalanigolf.com; 360 Pukalani St; greens fees $53-68; ☽ 7am-6:30pm
This casual golf course has 18 holes of smooth greens, moderate prices and views sweeping clear down to the coast.

🐐 SURFING GOAT DAIRY

Map p144; ☎ 878-2870; www.surfinggoatdairy
.com; 3651 Oma'opio Rd; admission free, tour $5;
🕑 10am-5pm Mon-Sat, to 2pm Sun

'Feta mo betta' is the motto at this 42-acre farm. And no, the goats may be playful but they can't really surf. They are, however, the source of all that luscious chevre cheese adorning the menus of Maui's top restaurants. The shop here carries an amazing variety of these creamy treats: for island flavor try the mango supreme. Not everything is geared to the connoisseur – your kids will love meeting the goat kids up close in a fun 25-minute dairy tour (minimum three people).

Eating

FOODLAND   Supermarket $

Map p144; ☎ 572-0674; Pukalani Terrace Center,
cnr Old Haleakala Hwy & Pukalani St; 🕑 24hr

This always-open supermarket is a convenient stop for those heading up Haleakalā for the sunrise or coming down for supplies. There's also a good sushi shop and a Starbucks inside the store.

SERPICO'S   Italian $

☎ 572-8498; cnr Aewa Pl & Old Haleakala Hwy;
meals $5-12; 🕑 11am-10pm

In the center of Pukalani, opposite Mc-Donald's, this casual Italian eatery makes New York–style pizzas and pasta dishes, and it makes them well. If you're in a hurry, there are sandwiches and inexpensive lunch specials.

KULA

It's cooler in Kula – refreshingly so. Think of this Upcountry heartland as one big garden, and you won't be far off. The very name Kula is synonymous with fresh veggies on any Maui menu worth its salt. So bountiful is Kula's soil, it produces most of the onions, lettuce and strawberries grown in Hawaii and almost all of the commercially grown proteas. The latest addition, sweet-scented lavender, is finding its niche, too.

The magic is in the elevation. At 3000ft, Kula's cool nights and sunny days are ideal for growing all sorts of crops. Kula's farmers first gained fame during the California gold rush of the 1850s, when they shipped so many potatoes to West Coast miners that Kula became known as 'Nu Kaleponi,' the Hawaiian pronunciation for New California. In the late 19th century Portuguese and Chinese immigrants who had worked off their contracts on the sugar plantations also moved up to Kula and started small farms, giving Kula the multicultural face that it still wears today.

Sights

Get out and smell the roses…and the jasmine, and the lavender and all those other

Take your kids to meet the kids at Surfing Goat Dairy

ABBOT LOW MOFFAT III

ISLAND VOICES

NAME: ALI'I CHANG
OCCUPATION: FARMER; OWNER OF ALI'I KULA LAVENDER
RESIDENCE: KULA

How did you get started? I was in the flower business in Hana. My farm adjoined George Harrison's property. I left there in 1994, but my passion said to come back to farming, so I bought this place. I planted my first lavender plants in 2001.

Why lavender? I was looking for a drought-tolerant plant. Our water is very scarce in the Upcountry. It took me years to figure out what grows here because my mind was set on water. In Hana there's hundreds of inches of rain. When I chose lavender everyone thought I was out of my mind.

Is it difficult to grow? It's organic. No pesticides. It doesn't even require fertilizers. I find lavender is the most low-risk plant I've ever worked with. Bugs don't like it, deer don't like it. It doesn't need water, no irrigation. It fits the area so well here.

Do you make your own products? We collaborate with 25 other island businesses. We supply the lavender and they create the finished products. Three people in the Upcountry make our food products: the dressings, vinegars, jams. Our philosophy is to embrace people instead of competing with each other. It's a win-win for everybody.

What is the best part? When everything is blooming, it's so beautiful. I call this our Monet painting, especially as the sun goes down and it changes everything to a fuchsia hue. The part I like is everybody seems to be happy when they come here. They think they went to heaven. I feel like there's some kind of spiritual change. You cannot believe the number of repeat visitors we get.

sweet-scented blossoms. No two gardens in Kula are alike, and each has its own special charms.

ALI'I KULA LAVENDER

our pick Map p144; ☎ 878-3004; www.aliikula lavender.com; 1100 Waipoli Rd; admission free; 9am-4pm

Everyone who stops here falls under the spell. It starts with a stroll along garden paths where more than 30 varieties of fragrant lavender plants blanket the hillside. Soon you find yourself at the shop dabbing lavender-scented lotion and oil samples all over your body. Next thing you know you're drinking lavender lemonade, eating lavender scones and walking out with armfuls of purple-hued souvenirs. Join a

Lavender Garden Tea Tour ($35; call for reservations) to get the skinny on all things lavender; the tour ends with lavender tea on the lanai, where the views are breathtaking. To get to the parking area, drive pass the farm, go through the Kula Forest Reserve gates and follow the signs.

ENCHANTING FLORAL GARDENS

Map p144; ☎ 878-2531; 2505 Kula Hwy; adult/child 6-12 $7.50/1; 9am-5pm

A labor of love, this colorful garden showcases the green thumb of master horticulturist Kazuo Takeda. Kula has microclimates that change with elevation and this garden occupies a narrow zone where tropical, temperate and desert vegetation all thrive. The sheer variety is amazing. You'll find

Enchanting Floral Gardens   GREG ELMS

everything from flamboyant proteas and orchids to orange trees and kava – all of it identified with Latin and common names. Your garden stroll ends with a sampling of fruits grown here.

MAUI AGRICULTURAL RESEARCH CENTER
Map p144; ☎ 878-1213; 424 Mauna Pl; admission free; ☷ 7am-3:30pm Mon-Thu
This 20-acre garden perched above Waiakoa village is under the jurisdiction of the University of Hawai'i. It's here that Hawaii's first proteas, natives of South Africa, were established in 1965. You can walk through rows of their colorful descendants, as well as new hybrids under development. Named for the Greek god Proteus, who was noted for his ability to change form, the varieties on display here are amazingly diverse – some look like oversize pincushions, others look like feathers and still others have spiny petals. Nursery cuttings from the plants here are distributed to protea farms across Hawaii, which in turn supply florists as far away as Europe. To get here,

take Copp Rd, between the 12- and 13-mile markers on Hwy 37, for half a mile and turn left on Mauna Pl.

KULA BOTANICAL GARDEN
Map p144; ☎ 878-1715; 638 Kekaulike Ave; adult/child 6-12 $7.50/2; ☷ 9am-4pm
Pleasantly overgrown and shady, this mature garden has walking paths that wind through acres of theme plantings, including native Hawaiian specimens and a 'taboo garden' of poisonous plants. Because a stream runs through it, the garden supports water-thirsty plants that you won't find in other Kula gardens. When the rain gods have been generous the whole place is an explosion of color.

HOLY GHOST CHURCH
Map p144; ☎ 878-1261; 4300 Lower Kula Rd; ☷ 8am-5pm
The octagonal Holy Ghost Church, a hillside landmark in Waiakoa, is on the National Register of Historic Places. Built in 1895 by Portuguese immigrants, the church features a beautifully ornate interior that looks like it came right out of the Old World – and indeed much of it did. The gilded altar was carved by renowned Austrian woodcarver Ferdinand Stuflesser and shipped in pieces around the Cape of Good Hope.

Activities
Pony Express, Skyline Eco-Adventures and Haleakala ATV Tours all operate on land belonging to Haleakala Ranch, a working cattle ranch that sprawls across the slopes beneath Haleakalā National Park. The three businesses are clustered together on Hwy 378, 2.5 miles up from Hwy 377.
Pony Express (Map p144; ☎ 667-2200; www.ponyexpresstours.com; Haleakala Crater Rd; trail rides $95-195; ☷ 8am-5pm) offers a variety of horseback rides, beginning with easy nose-to-tail walks across pastures and woods. But the real prize is the ride into the national park's Haleakalā crater that starts at the crater summit and leads down onto the floor of this lunar-like wonder.
ourpick Skyline Eco-Adventures (Map p144; ☎ 878-8400; www.skylinehawaii.com; Haleakala Crater Rd; 1½hr outing $89; ☷ departs 8:30am, 9:30am, 10:30am, 11:30am, 12:30pm, 1:15pm, 2pm & 3pm) lets you unleash your inner Tarzan and soar

Top Picks

NORTH SHORE & UPCOUNTRY FOR KIDS
■ Surfing Goat Dairy farm tour (p158)
■ Hot Island Glass glassblowers (p155)
■ Spreckelsville Beach (p147)

NORTH SHORE & UPCOUNTRY

DETOUR ➡

LA PROVENCE

our pick One of Kula's best-kept secrets, this little courtyard restaurant in the middle of nowhere is the domain of Maui's finest pastry chef. Even if you're not hungry now, do yourself a favor and swing by **La Provence** (Map p144; ☎ 878-1313; 3158 Lower Kula Rd, Waiakoa; pastries $3-4, mains $8-15; ⊙ 7am-3pm Wed-Fri, 7am-2pm Sat, 8am-2pm Sun) to pick up a ham-and-cheese croissant or some flaky chocolate-filled pastries for that picnic further down the road. If you're hungry now, well, grab a seat in the courtyard. Anything for breakfast will do. At lunch the chevre (goat cheese) green salads are a local-grown treat to savor. If it happens to be between May and September, call ahead and ask about dinner as the chef sometimes gets tempted to throw a gastronomic feast – brandied duck anyone?

La Provence is a little tricky to find: look for the low-key sign on the Kula Hwy as you approach Waiakoa. After the highway's 11-mile marker turn east onto Lower Kula Rd and continue 0.1 miles; the restaurant comes up on the left opposite a car repair shop.

above the forest floor. Don your hard hat, strap up to the zipline and let it fly. You glide freestyle along cables strung over five gulches. A half-mile hike and a suspension bridge are tossed in for good measure. One tip: reserve early, as it often books up weeks ahead.

Haleakala ATV Tours (Map p144; ☎ 661-0288; www.atvmaui.com; Haleakala Crater Rd; 2hr tour $115; ⊙ departs 12.30pm) takes you tearing across 6 miles of ATV tracks – goggles, gloves and rain gear provided. And yep, it does get muddy.

If the Skyline ziplines don't get you high enough, try surfing the sky with **Proflyght Paragliding** (Map p144; ☎ 874-5433; www.paraglidehawaii.com; Waipoli Rd; paraglide $75; ⊙ varies with weather). On this one, you strap into a paraglider with a certified instructor and take a running jump off the cliffs beneath Polipoli Spring State Recreation Area. It's a 1000ft

descent with a breathtaking bird's-eye view the entire way. Weight restrictions (230lb) apply and you'll need to be able to run at a fair clip, but once you're skybound the kite inflates and it's all free-flying.

Tours

Whether you're a gardener or a gourmet you're going to love a tour of famed Lahaina chef James McDonald's organic 🌺 **O'o Farm** (Map p144; ☎ 667-4341; www.oofarm.com; Waipoli Rd; lunch tour $50; ⊙ 10:30am-1pm Wed & Thu). Where else can you help harvest your own meal, turn the goodies over to a gourmet chef and feast on the bounty? Bring your own wine.

Festivals & Events

The **Holy Ghost Feast**, at the Holy Ghost Church on the last Saturday and Sunday in May, celebrates Kula's Portuguese heritage and provides a great opportunity for visitors to enjoy the aloha of Upcountry folk. This family-oriented event has games, craft booths, a farmers market and a free Sunday *laulau* lunch for everyone who comes.

Eating

SUNRISE MARKET & PROTEA FARM   Takeout $
Map p144; ☎ 878-1600; Haleakala Crater Rd; simple eats $3-6; ⊙ 7:30am-4pm
A combo food stop and flower garden, Sunrise is conveniently located on the road to Haleakalā, a quarter of a mile up from the Kula Hwy (Hwy 377). Pull over to pick up some post-sunrise java, a breakfast burrito or hot soup. Then take a stroll out back to view the lovely proteas.

CAFÉ 808   Local Food $
Map p144; ☎ 878-6874; Lower Kula Rd, Waiakoa; mains $5-9; ⊙ 6am-8pm
Its motto, 'The Big Kahuna of Island Grinds,' says it all. This unpretentious eatery, a quarter-mile south of the Holy Ghost Church, offers a wall-size chalkboard of all things local, from banana pancakes to gravy-laden plate lunches. Servings are hefty. Breakfast is served to 11am, making it a good choice for an inexpensive eat after sunrise on the mountain.

Top Picks

LOCAL-GROWN TASTES

- **Elk burgers at 'Ulupalakua Ranch Store** (p164)
- **Maui-grown coffee at Grandma's** (p164)
- **Maui Blanc wine at Tedeschi Vineyards** (p164)
- **Lunch tour at O'o Farm** (p161)
- **Lavender scones at Ali'i Kula Lavender** (p159)
- **Goat cheese at Surfing Goat Dairy** (p158)

KULA SANDALWOODS RESTAURANT   Café $

Map p144; ☎ 878-3523; 15427 Haleakala Hwy; mains $7-12; ⊗ 7:30am-3pm

The owner-chef earned her toque from the prestigious Culinary Institute of America. At breakfast she serves up eye-opening espresso and worthy eggs Benedict. Lunch moves into specialty salads and innovative sandwiches on focaccia. The restaurant is less than a mile north of Haleakala Crater Rd.

Sleeping

KULA VIEW BED & BREAKFAST   B&B $$

Map p144; ☎ 878-6736; 600 Holopuni Rd; studio incl breakfast $115

With her *paniolo* roots, this host knows the Upcountry inside out. She provides everything you'll need for a good stay, including warm jackets for the Haleakalā sunrise. The studio unit sits atop her country home and offers sunset ocean views. Breakfast includes fruit from the backyard and homemade muffins.

POLIPOLI SPRING STATE RECREATION AREA

❀ Crisscrossed with lightly trodden hiking and mountain-biking trails, this misty cloud forest on the western slope of Haleakalā takes you deep off the beaten path. The shade from tall trees and the cool moist air add up to a refreshing walk in the woods. Layers of clouds drift in and out; when they

lift, you'll get panoramic views across green rolling hills to the islands of Lana'i and Kaho'olawe. Very zen-like – apart from the symphony of bird calls, everything around you is still.

It's not always possible to get all the way to the park without a 4WD, but it's worth driving part of the way for the view. Access is via Waipoli Rd, off Hwy 377, just under 0.5 miles before its southern intersection with the Kula Hwy (Hwy 37). Waipoli Rd is a narrow, switchbacking, one-lane road through groves of eucalyptus and open rangeland.

The road has some soft shoulders, but the first 6 miles are paved. After the road enters the Kula Forest Reserve, it becomes dirt. When it's muddy, the next four grinding miles to the campground are not even worth trying in a non-4WD vehicle.

Activities

WAIAKOA LOOP TRAIL

The trailhead for the Waiakoa Loop Trail (Map p144) starts at the hunter check station, 5 miles up Waipoli Rd, which is all paved to this point. Walk three-quarters of a mile down the grassy spur road on the left to a gate marking the trail. The hike, which starts out in pine trees, makes a 3-mile loop, passing through eucalyptus stands, pine forest, and scrub land scored with feral pig trails. This is a fairly gentle easy hike, or good moderately strenuous fun on a mountain bike. You can also connect with the Upper Waiakoa Trail at a junction about a mile up the right side of the loop.

UPPER WAIAKOA TRAIL

The Upper Waiakoa Trail (Map p144) is a strenuous 7-mile trail that begins off Waiakoa Loop at an elevation of 6000ft, climbs

Island Insights

Polipoli Spring State Recreation Area was planted during the 1930s by the Civilian Conservation Corps (CCC), a Depression-era work program. Several of the park's trails pass through old CCC camps and stands of redwood, cypress, cedar and pines.

Upcountry view down to the plains of Central Maui   GREG ELMS

1800ft, switchbacks and then drops back down 1400ft. It's stony terrain, but it's high and open, with good views. Bring plenty of water.

The trail ends on Waipoli Rd between the hunter check station and the campground. If you want to start at this end of the trail, keep an eye out for the trail marker for Waohuli Trail, as the Upper Waiakoa Trail begins across the road.

BOUNDARY TRAIL

This 4-mile marked and maintained trail (Map p144) begins about 200yd beyond the end of the paved road. Park to the right of the cattle grate that marks the boundary of the Kula Forest Reserve. It's a steep downhill walk that crosses gulches and drops deep into woods of eucalyptus, pine and cedar, as well as a bit of native forest. In the afternoon the fog generally rolls in and visibility fades.

SKYLINE TRAIL

Also partially in this park is the rugged Skyline Trail (Map p144), which begins near the summit of Haleakalā National Park and drops more than 3000ft, passing cinder cones and craters, and offering clear-on views of West Maui and the islands of Hawai'i, Kaho'olawe and Lana'i before descending into the forest of Polipoli Spring State Recreation Area. For details on this hike, see p180.

Sleeping

To stay in Polipoli is to rough it. Tent camping (Map p144) is free, but requires a

permit from the state. Facilities are primitive, with toilets but no showers or drinking water. Fellow campers are likely to be pig hunters. Otherwise the place can be eerily deserted, and damp. Come prepared – this is cold country, with winter temperatures frequently dropping below freezing at night.

The park also has one housekeeping cabin (Map p144). Unlike other state park cabins, this one has gas lanterns and a wood-burning stove but no electricity or refrigerator. See p269 for details on camping and cabin permits and reservations.

KEOKEA

At the turn of the 20th century, Keokea was home to Hakka Chinese who farmed the remote Kula region. Modest as it may be, Keokea is the last real town before Hana if you're swinging around the southern part of the island. The sum total of the town center consists of a coffee shop, an art gallery, a gas pump and two small stores, the Ching Store and the Fong Store.

Sights & Activities

Built in 1907 to serve the Chinese community, the village's green-and-white **St John's Episcopal Church** (Map p144) still bears its name in Chinese characters. For a time Sun Yat-sen, father of the Chinese nationalist movement, lived on the outskirts of Keokea. A statue of Sun Yat-sen and a small **park** (Map p144) dedicated to him can be found along the Kula Hwy (Hwy 37), 1.7 miles beyond Grandma's Coffee House. The park

Island Insights

So tiny is the crescent volcanic crater of Molokini that King David Kalakaua once wagered it all in a game of poker at 'Ulupalakua Ranch. When he lost, he claimed that he had not bet Molokini, but *'omole kini* (a bottle of gin).

has picnic tables and broad views across to West Maui and its hillside windmills.

Thompson Ranch (Map p144; ☎ 878-1910; Middle Rd; 2hr ride $100; ⊙ departs at 10am) offers horseback rides through the cool Upcountry bordering Polipoli Spring State Recreation Area, at elevations of 4000ft to 6000ft.

Eating

✿ GRANDMA'S COFFEE HOUSE Café $
Map p144; ☎ 878-2140; 9232 Kula Hwy; pastries $2-5, deli fare $6-10; ⊙ 7am-5pm

If you thought Kona was the only place with primo Hawaii-grown coffee, just check out the brew at Grandma's. This cool café also dishes up homemade pastries, sandwiches and salads. The family that owns Grandma's has been growing coffee in Keokea for generations. Take your goodies out on the patio and you can eat right under their coffee trees.

'ULUPALAKUA RANCH

This sprawling ranch has an illustrious history and a progressive future. It was established in the mid-19th century by James Makee, a whaling captain who jumped ship and befriended Hawaiian royalty. King David Kalakaua, the 'Merrie Monarch,' was a frequent visitor who loved to indulge in late-night rounds of poker and champagne. The 20,000-acre ranch is still worked by *paniolo* (note the sign on the ranch store warning cowboys to wipe the shit off their boots before entering!) and has some 6000 head of cattle, as well as a small herd of Rocky Mountain elk.

The ranch is active on environmental fronts. It's staged to host Upcountry's first

wind farm and is restoring a rare native dryland forest on the upper slopes of ranch property.

Hwy 37 winds south through ranch country, offering good views of Kaho'olawe and the little island of Molokini.

After the vineyard, it's another 25 dusty, bumpy miles to Kipahulu along the spectacular Pi'ilani Hwy (p212).

Sights

✿ TEDESCHI VINEYARDS
Map p144; ☎ 878-6058; www.mauiwine.com; Kula Hwy; tours & tastings free; ⊙ 9am-5pm, tours 10:30am, 1:30pm & 3pm

Maui's only winery, in the midst of 'Ulupalakua Ranch, offers up tastings in the historical stone cottage where King David Kalakaua was once a frequent guest. Tell the truth now, when was the last time you had pineapple wine? In the 1970s, while awaiting its first grape harvest, the winery decided to take advantage of Maui's prickly fruit. Today its biggest hit is the sweet Maui Splash, a light blend of pineapple and passion fruit. Other novelties are the dry pineapple Maui Blanc and the sparkling pineapple Hula O'Maui. This is no Napa Valley, however, and the grape wines are a bit of a yawn. Free tours of the grounds and the winery operation are given three times a day.

Don't miss the fascinating little exhibit on 'Ulupalakua Ranch history at the side of the tasting room. Opposite the winery, you can see the stack remains of the **Makee Sugar Mill** (Map p144), built in 1878.

Eating

'ULUPALAKUA RANCH STORE Deli $
Map p144; ☎ 878-2561; burgers $7-8; ⊙ grill 11am-2pm, store 9am-5pm

Sidle up to the life-size wooden cowboys on the front porch and say howdy. Then pop inside and check out the cowboy hats and souvenir T-shirts. Best of all is the lunchtime grill featuring the ranch's own hormone-free beef and elk burgers. The store is opposite the ranch headquarters, 5.5 miles south of Keokea.

HALEAKALĀ
NATIONAL PARK

Omnipresent Haleakalā looms over you like a goddess, taking center stage while you sun on the beach in Kihei or wind down the road to Hana. Whether you come for sunrise or come at the height of the day, by all means get yourself here. You haven't seen Maui – or at least haven't looked into its soul – until you've made the trek to the top of this awe-inspiring mountain. Lookouts on the crater's rim provide breathtaking views of Haleakalā's moonscape surface. But there's a lot more to Haleakalā than just peering down from on high. Trek into the crater on crunchy trails, saddle up and mosey down on horseback, commune with nature – get out there and explore!

HALEAKALĀ NATIONAL PARK
ITINERARIES

IN ONE DAY *This leg: 17 miles*

❶ SUNRISE AT HALEAKALĀ (p171) Start the night before by packing a hearty breakfast and a picnic lunch, then gas up your tank. Set the alarm early to drag yourself up to the top of the mountain for the sunrise.

❷ SLIDING SANDS TRAIL (p177) Burn off the morning chill with an invigorating hike on the sun-warmed cinders of this otherworldly trail. Take the spur trail to Ka Lu'u o ka O'o, checking out the mysterious sights before heading back up Sliding Sands Trail.

❸ PU'U'ULA'ULA (RED HILL) OVERLOOK (p173) Wow, did that work up an appetite! Break out the picnic lunch at the highest point on Maui. Give a wave across the channel to the Big Island, 35 miles away.

❹ KALAHAKU OVERLOOK (p172) Make your way over to this awesome crater-rim overlook for an eye-poppingly wide-angle view of the crater and its multihued cinder cones. Oh, hey, look to the right…there's that trail you were on this morning.

❺ LELEIWI OVERLOOK (p172) Afternoon comes with clouds. There's no better place than Leleiwi to watch their wild, wind-whipped twirls.

❻ HOSMER GROVE TRAIL (p181) You've seen the starkly barren side of Haleakalā – now it's time for its lush green face to shine. Take a walk in this forest brimming with birdsong. Good nene-spotting odds here, too.

IN TWO DAYS *This leg: 8 miles*

❼ KULOA POINT TRAIL (p185) If you have two days for Haleakalā National Park, spend the first day as above. Give the second day over to the wet and wild Kipahulu section of the park. There's no food here, so make sure you bring a big picnic basket. Break it out at the grassy knoll, just minutes from the trailhead, as you savor the sweet ocean view.

❽ 'OHE'O GULCH POOLS (p185) It's time to get that bathing suit wet, and you won't believe your good fortune at the first sight of these gorgeous pools. The only challenge here is deciding which one to jump into first.

❾ MAKAHIKU FALLS (p186) Dry off and hit the trail. The Pipiwai Trail follows the stream uphill from the pools, making its first stop at this 185ft beauty.

❿ WAIMOKU FALLS (p186) Keep going, keep going. There's a magical bamboo forest to walk through and the prize at the end of the trail is this towering 400ft cascade. Here's more good news: you get to walk back through the amazing bamboo forest once again on the return trip.

⓫ KIPAHULU 'OHANA (p186) Want to deep deeper? Join these taro farmers for an ethnobotanical tour to learn first-hand the deeply rooted traditions of this sacred Hawaiian place.

FOR CAMPERS

❶ HOSMER GROVE CAMPGROUND (p182) Maui's best campgrounds are right here in Haleakalā National Park. There's no better place to start than at this gentle green space, fragrant with the sweet spice of eucalyptus. Bonus: you're close to the summit, so it's a cinch getting up for the sunrise.

❷ HOLUA CAMPGROUND (p182) Pack up your gear, strap it to your back and trek down into the crater. Lucky you: the **Supply Trail (p178)** leads right from Hosmer Grove down the crater walls to Holua campground. Pitch your tent here at the base of a spectacular cliff. And how about those sweeping views on the way down!

❸ PALIKU CABIN (p183) If you've played your cards right, you've won the lottery! Hike your way around magnificent cinder cones from Holua to Paliku. The cabin is wonderfully rustic and oh so cozy after a couple of days on the ground. You're allowed two days, so take 'em both and explore the trails at this lightly trodden end of the crater.

❹ KIPAHULU CAMPGROUND (p186) And now for something completely different. Haul yourself down the coast to the other side of this amazing national park. Camp out on an ancient Hawaiian settlement site, perched on the edge of a wild ocean, with the surf as your lullaby. The perfect starlit finale to your Haleakalā experience.

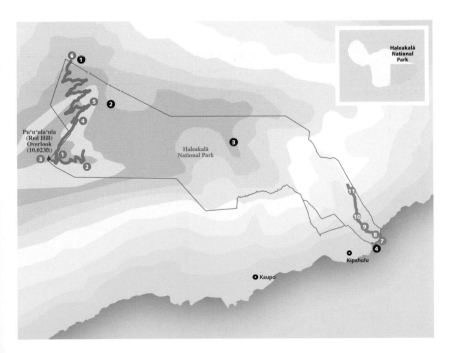

HALEAKALĀ NATIONAL PARK

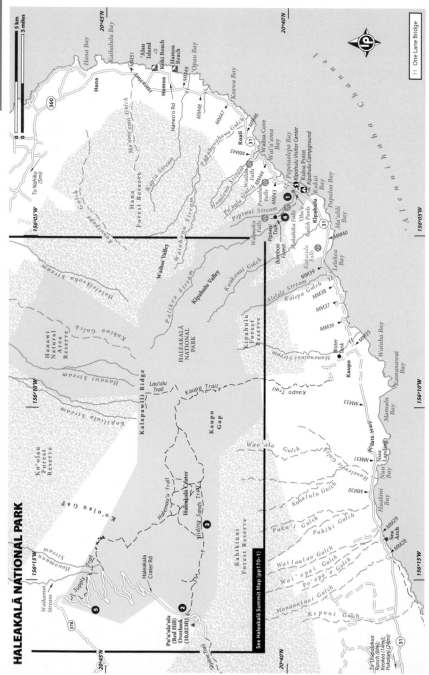

HIGHLIGHTS

❶ **BEST BEACH:** 'Ohe'o Gulch Lower Pools (p185)
❷ **BEST VIEW:** Haleakalā Visitor Center (p173)
❸ **BEST ACTIVITY:** Hiking (p176)
❹ **BEST WATERFALL:** Makahiku Falls (p185)
❺ **BEST NENE SPOTTING:** Park Headquarters Visitor Center (below)

Highlights are numbered on the map on p168.

ORIENTATION

Haleakalā National Park has two sections. The main part of the park is the top of Haleakalā mountain itself, known as the summit area (below) and reached by driving through the Upcountry. The other section is the Kipahulu Area ('Ohe'o Gulch; p184), in East Maui on Haleakalā's southeast slope, 10 miles south of remote Hana. The two sections are visited separately; there is no access between the two.

SUMMIT AREA

🌋 Haleakalā's astonishing volcanic landscape so resembles a lunar surface that astronauts practiced mock lunar walks here before landing on the moon.

Often referred to as the world's largest dormant volcano, the floor of Haleakalā measures a colossal 7.5 miles wide, 2.5 miles long and 3000ft deep. In its prime, Haleakalā reached a height of 12,000ft before water erosion carved out two large river valleys that eventually eroded into each other to form Haleakalā crater. Technically, as geologists like to point out, it's not a true 'crater,' but to sightseers that's all nitpicking. Valley or crater, it's a phenomenal sight like no other in the US National Park system.

HISTORY

Haleakalā was not inhabited by the ancient Hawaiians, but they came up the mountain to worship and built heiau at some of the *pu'u* (cinder cones). The primary goddess of Haleakalā, Lilinoe, also known as the mist goddess, was worshipped at a heiau near the summit. Unfortunately, any evidence of that sacred monument was destroyed during the construction of the Science City observatories.

Prince Jonah Kalanianaole, the man who could have been king if the Hawaiian monarchy hadn't been overthrown (but instead, he became Hawaii's first congressional delegate), proposed Haleakalā as a national park. When the bill was signed into law in 1916, Haleakalā became part of the Hawai'i National Park, along with its Big Island siblings, Mauna Loa and Kilauea. In 1961 Haleakalā National Park became an independent entity and in 1969 it expanded its boundaries down into the Kipahulu Valley. In 1980 the park was designated an International Biosphere Reserve by Unesco.

INFORMATION

Haleakalā National Park (www.nps.gov/hale; 3-day entry pass per car $10, per person on foot, bicycle or motorcycle $5) never closes, and the pay booth at the park entrance opens before dawn to welcome the sunrise crowd. If you're planning several trips, or are going on to the Big Island, consider buying an annual pass ($25), which covers all of Hawaii's national parks.

The **Park Headquarters Visitor Center** (☎ 572-4400; ⏱ 8am-3:45pm), less than a mile beyond the entrance, is the place to pick up brochures, buy nature books and get camping permits. You can also call ahead for recorded information on activities. There are no views at park headquarters; this is simply an information and restroom stop. So once you've taken care of your more earthly needs, hop back into the car and continue on to reach the real wonders.

Occasionally a pair of nene wander around the parking lot. These endangered birds are much too friendly for their own

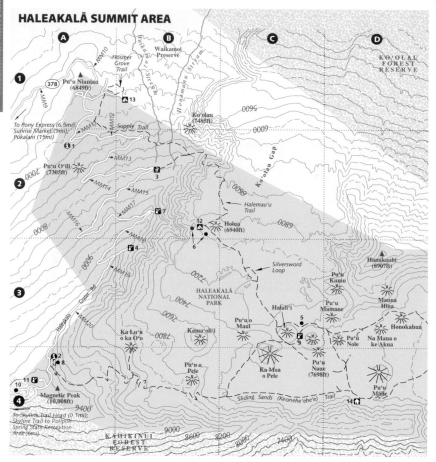

HALEAKALĀ SUMMIT AREA

good; do not feed them, and be careful coming in and out of the parking lot – most nene deaths are the result of being hit by cars.

There's a drinking fountain at park headquarters, so if you need to fill your water bottle, do it here. No bottled water or food is sold anywhere in the park. Be sure to bring something to eat if you're going up for the sunrise; you don't want a growling stomach to send you back down the mountain before you've had a chance to explore the sights.

It's a good idea to check **weather conditions** (☎ 877-5111) before driving up, as it's not uncommon for it to be cloudy at Haleakalā when it's clear on the coast. Or go straight to the crater webcam at **Haleakalā Crater Live Camera** (http://koa.ifa.hawaii.edu/crater).

Maps

National Geographic's *Haleakalā National Park Illustrated Trail Map* makes the perfect companion for hikers, showing elevations and other useful features on the routes. It's waterproof and can be purchased at Haleakalā Visitor Center for $10.

DANGERS & ANNOYANCES

The weather at Haleakalā can change suddenly from dry, hot conditions to cold, windswept rain. Although the general rule

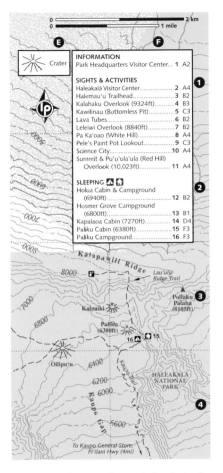

is sunny in the morning and cloudy in the afternoon, fog and clouds can blow in at any time, and the windchill can quickly drop below freezing. Dress in layers and bring extra clothing; don't even think of coming up without a jacket.

At 10,000ft the air is relatively thin, so expect to tire more quickly, particularly if you're hiking. The higher elevation also means that sunburn is more likely.

Visitors rarely experience altitude sickness at Haleakalā summit. An exception is those who have been scuba diving in the past 24 hours, so plan your Haleakalā trip accordingly. Children, pregnant women and those in generally poor health are also susceptible. If you experience difficulty

CATCHING A HALEAKALĀ SUNRISE

ourpick Since ancient times people have been making the pilgrimage up to Haleakalā to watch the sunrise. It's an experience that borders on the mystical. But let's be honest – a rained-out sunrise is an anticlimactic event after tearing out of bed in the middle of the night to drive up a pitch-dark mountain. So check out the **weather report** (☎ 877-5111) the night before to calculate your odds of having clear skies.

Plan to arrive at the summit an hour before the actual sunrise, which will guarantee you a parking space and time to see the world awaken. Around that point the night sky begins to lighten and turn purple-blue, and the stars fade away. Ethereal silhouettes of the mountain ridges appear.

The gentlest colors show up in the fragile moments just before dawn begins. The undersides of the clouds lighten first, accenting the night sky with pale silvery slivers and streaks of pink.

About 20 minutes before sunrise, the light intensifies on the horizon in bright oranges and reds, much like a sunset. Turn around and take a look at Science City (p174), whose domes turn a blazing pink. For the grand finale, at the moment when the disk of the sun appears, all of Haleakalā takes on a fiery glow. It feels like you're watching the earth awaken.

Come prepared – it's going to be c-o-l-d at the top! Temperatures hovering around freezing and a biting wind are the norm at dawn, and there's often frost on the top layer of cinders. If you don't have a winter jacket or sleeping bag to wrap yourself in, bring a warm blanket from your hotel. Tote as many layers of clothes as you can muster – you won't regret it.

The best photo opportunities occur before the sun rises. Every morning is different, but once the sun is up, the silvery lines and the subtleties disappear.

And if you just can't manage to get up that early, sunsets at Haleakalā have inspired poets as well.

Don't Miss

- **Plunking down $1 at Haleakalā Visitor Center for a certificate that says you've climbed 10,000ft in the shortest distance on earth** (opposite)
- **Making the short walk up Pa Ka'oao** (White Hill; opposite)
- **Having your preteen pick up a free Junior Ranger Activity Book at Park HQ** (p169)
- **Getting an up-close look at native silversword at the summit** (opposite)

breathing, sudden headaches and dizziness, or more serious symptoms such as confusion and lack of motor coordination, descend immediately. Sometimes driving down the crater road just a few hundred feet will alleviate the problem. Panicking or hyperventilating only makes things worse.

SIGHTS

For information on driving on Haleakala Crater Rd see Getting There & Around, p183.

Hosmer Grove

Hosmer Grove, off a side road just after the park's entrance booth, is primarily visited by campers and picnickers, but it's also well worth a stop for its forested half-mile loop trail (p181) that begins at the edge of the campground. The whole area is sweetened with the scent of eucalyptus and alive with the red flashes and calls of native birds. Drive slowly on the road in, as this is one of the best places to spot nene.

Waikamoi Preserve

This windswept native cloud forest supports one of the rarest ecosystems on earth. Managed by the Nature Conservancy, the 5230-acre Waikamoi Preserve provides the last stronghold for 76 species of native plants and forest birds. You're apt to spot the 'i'iwi, the 'apapane and the yellow-green 'amakihi flying among the preserve's koa and ohia trees. You might also catch a glimpse of the yellow-green 'alauahio (Maui creeper) or the 'akohekohe (Maui parrotbill), both endangered species found nowhere else.

The only way to see the preserve is to join a guided hike. The National Park Service offers free three-hour, 3-mile guided hikes that enter the preserve from Hosmer Grove campground at 9am on Monday and Thursday. It's best to make reservations, which you can do up to one week in advance by calling ☎ 572-4459. Expect wet conditions; bring rain gear.

Leleiwi Overlook

A stop at Leleiwi Overlook (8840ft), midway between the Park Headquarters Visitor Center and the summit, offers your first look into the crater, and a unique angle on the ever-changing clouds floating in and out. You can literally watch the weather form at your feet. From the parking lot, it's a five-minute walk across a gravel trail to the overlook. En route you'll get a fine view of the West Maui Mountains and the isthmus connecting the two sides of Maui. The trail has plaques identifying native plants, including the silver-leafed *hinahina*, found only at Haleakalā, and the *kukae-nene,* a member of the coffee family.

In the afternoon, if weather conditions are right, you might see the Brocken specter, an optical phenomenon that occurs at high elevations. Essentially, by standing between the sun and the clouds, your image is magnified and projected onto the clouds. The light reflects off tiny droplets of water in the clouds, creating a circular rainbow around your shadow.

Kalahaku Overlook

our pick Whatever you do, don't miss this one. Kalahaku Overlook (9324ft), 0.8 miles beyond Leleiwi Overlook, offers a bird's-eye view of the crater floor and the ant-size hikers on the trails snaking around the cinder cones below. At the observation deck, information plaques provide the skinny on each of the volcanic formations that punctuate the crater floor.

Between May and October the 'ua'u (Hawaiian dark-rumped petrel) nests in burrows in the cliff face at the left side of the observation deck. Even if you don't spot

A LONG DAY

As the legend goes, the goddess Hina was having problems drying her tapa cloth because the days were too short. Her son, the trickster demigod Maui, decided to take matters into his own hands. One morning he went up to the mountaintop and waited for the sun. As it came up over the mountain Maui lassoed the rays one by one and held tight until the sun came to a sliding halt. When the sun begged to be let go, Maui demanded, as a condition for release, that it slow its path across the sky. The sun gave its promise, the days lengthened and the mountain became known as Haleakalā (House of the Sun). To this day there are about 15 more minutes of daylight at Haleakalā than on the coast below.

the birds, you can often hear the parents and chicks making their unique clucking sounds. Of the fewer than 2000 'ua'u remaining today, most nest right here at Haleakalā, where they lay just one egg a year. These seabirds were thought to be extinct until sighted again in the crater during the 1970s.

A short trail below the parking lot leads to a field of rare native silversword ('ahinahina), ranging from seedlings to mature plants.

Haleakalā Visitor Center

our pick OK, it's time to break out the jackets. The **visitor center** (☺ sunrise–3pm) on the rim of the crater (9745ft), half a mile below the actual summit, is the park's main viewing spot. And what a sight it is. The everchanging interplay of sun, shadow and clouds reflecting on the crater floor creates a mesmerizing dance of light and color.

The center has displays on Haleakalā's volcanic origins and details on what you're seeing on the crater floor 3000ft below. Nature talks are given, books on Hawaiian culture and nature are for sale, and there are drinking fountains and restrooms here.

By dawn the parking lot fills with people coming to see the sunrise show (see boxed text, p171), and it pretty much stays packed all day. Leave the crowds behind by taking the 10-minute hike up **Pa Ka'oao (White Hill)**, which begins at the east side of the visitor center and provides stunning crater views.

Haleakalā Summit

PU'U'ULA'ULA (RED HILL) OVERLOOK

Congratulations! The 37-mile drive from sea level to the 10,023ft summit of Haleakalā you've just completed is the highest elevation gain in the shortest distance anywhere in the world. As a matter of fact, it's so high that you need to be cautious if you've come up in the late afternoon in winter, as a sudden rainstorm at this elevation can result in ice-coated roads.

Perched atop Pu'u'ula'ula, Maui's highest point, the summit building provides a top-of-the-world panorama from its wraparound windows. On a clear day you can see the Big Island, Lana'i, Moloka'i and even

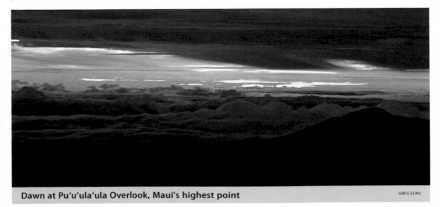

Dawn at Pu'u'ula'ula Overlook, Maui's highest point

GREG ELMS

A GLOWING SUCCESS

Goats ate them by the thousands. Souvenir collectors pulled them up by their roots. They were even used to decorate parade floats, for cryin' out loud. It's a miracle any of Haleakalā's famed silverswords were left at all.

It took a concerted effort to bring them back from the brink of extinction, but Haleakalā visitors can once again see this luminous relative of the sunflower in numerous places around the park.

The silversword (*'ahinahina*) takes its name from its elegant silver spiked leaves, which glow with dew collected from the clouds. The plant lives up to 50 years before blooming for its first and last time. In its final year it shoots up a flowering stalk that can reach as high as 9ft. During summer the stalk flowers gloriously with hundreds of maroon and yellow blossoms. When the flowers go to seed in late fall, the plant makes its last gasp and dies.

Today the silversword survives solely because its fragile natural environment has been protected. After years of effort, the National Park Service has finished fencing the entire park with a 32-mile-long fence to keep out feral goats and pigs. You can do your part by not walking on cinders close to the plant, which damages the silversword's shallow roots that radiate out several feet just inches below the surface.

O'ahu. When the light's right, the colors of the crater from the summit are nothing short of spectacular, with an array of grays, greens, reds and browns. Brief natural and cultural history talks are given at the summit at 9:30am, 11:15am and 12:30pm.

Dozens of silversword have been planted at the overlook, making this the best place to see these luminous, endangered silver-leafed plants in various stages of growth.

MAGNETIC PEAK

The iron-rich cinders in this flat-top hill, which lies immediately southeast of the summit, in the direction of the Big Island, pack enough magnetism to play havoc with your compass. Modest looking as it is, it's also – at 10,008ft – the second-highest point on the island of Maui.

Silversword in full bloom   KARL LEHMANN

Science City

On the Big Island's Mauna Kea, scientists study the stars. Here at Haleakalā, appropriately enough, they study the sun. Science City, just beyond the summit, is off-limits to visitors. It's under the jurisdiction of the University of Hawai'i, which owns some of the domes and leases other land for a variety of private and government research projects.

Department of Defense–related projects here include laser technology associated with the 'Star Wars' project, satellite tracking and identification, and a deep-space surveillance system. The Air Force's Maui Space Surveillance System (MSSS), an electro-optical state-of-the-art facility used for satellite tracking, is the largest telescope anywhere in use by the Department of Defense. The system is capable of identifying a basketball-size object in space 22,000 miles away.

Science City observatories

GREG ELMS

The Faulkes Telescope, a joint University of Hawai'i and UK operation, is dedicated to raising students' interest in astronomy, with a fully robotic telescope that can be controlled in real time via the internet from classrooms in both Britain and Hawaii.

ACTIVITIES

Be sure to stop at the Park Headquarters Visitor Center to see what's happening. All park programs offered by the National Park Service are free. **Ranger talks** on Haleakalā's unique natural history and Hawaiian culture are given at the Haleakalā Visitor Center and the Pu'u'ula'ula (Red Hill) Overlook; the schedule varies, but they typically take place between 7am and 1pm and there's usually half a dozen to choose from each day.

Ranger-led **walks** through Waikamoi Preserve (p172) are held throughout the year.

Evening **stargazing programs** are offered between May and September at Hosmer Grove, typically on Friday and Saturday at 7pm. If you've got a pair of binoculars, bring them along – there's no telescope provided, but the stars themselves are phenomenal here. You can see celestial objects up to the 7th magnitude, free of light interference. If you want to stargaze on your own, pick up a free star map at either visitor center.

For activities that occur on the slopes beneath Haleakalā National Park, including ziplines, paragliding and ATV tours, see p160.

Cycling & Mountain Biking
CYCLING
Those one-way, downhill, group cycle tours that became so popular in recent years are currently banned from the park (see the boxed text on p176). Individual cyclists, however, are still welcome to pedal their way up the mountain. It's a real quad buster but cyclists in prime shape do meet the challenge.

MOUNTAIN BIKING
For experienced mountain bikers Haleakalā's **Skyline Trail** (p180) is the island's ultimate wild ride, plunging some 3000ft in the first 6 miles with a breathtaking 10% grade. The trail starts out looking like the moon and ends up in a cloud forest of redwood and cypress trees that resembles California's northern coast. The route follows a rough 4WD road that's used to maintain Polipoli Spring State Recreation Area. For cripes sake, equip yourself with full pads, use a proper downhill bike and watch that you don't run any hikers down. **Crater Cycles Hawaii** (Map p104; ☎ 893-2020; http://cratercycleshawaii.com; 96 Amala Pl, Kahului; downhill bikes per day $75; ☺ 10am-6pm Mon-Thu, 9am-1pm Fri, 10am-5pm Sat) rents full-suspension downhill bikes, complete with helmet, pads and a bike rack.

BUMPY RIDE

One of the hottest topics on Maui revolves around downhill bicycle tours from Haleakalā National Park. The tours began at the summit at sunrise, with cyclists coasting 38 miles down the mountain for a 10,000ft drop in elevation en route to the coast. In the past decade the number of commercial vans carting cyclists to the top of Haleakalā to catch the sunrise grew exponentially. Not only did this make for a congested sunrise experience – with as many as 1000 people huddled at the crater overlooks – but it brought an outcry from Mauians who felt the bike traffic was overrunning their small communities.

Part of the thrill for cyclists – well, seeing how there's no real pedaling involved in a downhill cruise, perhaps the only thrill – was maneuvering the hairpin twists and turns on the Upcountry's narrow roads.

But for Upcountry residents who travel these roads for more mundane reasons, such as getting to work, it's been a frustration. When a line of cyclists is ahead, drivers are forced to slow to a crawl, waiting for the group to pull over to let them pass. The roads have few shoulders, so the wait can be a long one. And, of course, once one group of cyclists has passed, there's the next one. 'Road rage' finally made it into the vernacular in the otherwise mellow Upcountry.

Just about everyone, including the tour operators, agreed the situation needed a fix. The national park cut the number of cycle-tour vans allowed at sunrise by a third. A group called the Upcountry Citizens for Bike and Traffic Safety advocated for further restrictions, noting that many people taking the tours hadn't ridden a bike in years, and citing accident reports showing ambulance calls for injured downhill cyclists were averaging a few times a week. After two cyclist fatalities in 2007, all bicycle-tour operations were suspended in the park. Studies are currently underway to determine if cycle tours can operate safely. Considering the track record and the road issues, this may be one park activity doomed to extinction.

Cycling Haleakalā   GREG ELMS

Hiking

Strap on a pair of hiking boots and you can climb into the very heart of this otherworldly place. Trails range from short nature walks to treks that take a couple of days. Those who hike the crater will discover a completely different angle on Haleakalā's lunar landscape. Instead of peering down from the rim, you'll be craning your neck skyward at the walls and towering cinder cones. It's a world away from anyplace else. The crater is remarkably still. Cinders crunching underfoot are often the only sound, except for the occasional bark of a *pueo* (Hawaiian owl) or honking of a friendly nene. No matter what trail you take, give yourself plenty of time just to absorb the wonder of it all.

To protect Haleakalā's fragile environment, keep to established trails and don't be tempted off them, even for well-trodden shortcuts through switchbacks.

Be prepared. Hikers without proper clothing risk hypothermia. Remember the climate changes radically as you cross the crater floor. In the 4 miles between Kapalaoa and Paliku cabins, rainfall varies from an annual average of 12in to 300in! Take warm clothing in layers, sunscreen, rain gear, a first-aid kit and lots of water.

HIKING BY THE CLOCK

Here are our recommendations for day hikes, depending on the time you have:

- **Ten hours** If you're planning a full-day outing, and you're in good physical shape, the 11.2-mile hike that starts down Sliding Sands Trail and returns via Halemau'u Trail is the prize. It crosses the crater floor, taking in both a cinder desert and a cloud forest, showcasing the park's amazing diversity. Get an early start.
- **Three hours** For a half-day experience that offers a hearty serving of crater sights, follow Sliding Sands Trail down to the Ka Lu'u o ka O'o cinder cone and back. The easy bit: it takes one hour to get down. However, on the way back, you've got yourself a 1500ft elevation rise, making the return a strenuous two-hour climb.
- **One hour** Take to the forest on the Hosmer Grove Trail and see the green side of Haleakalā National Park.

SLIDING SANDS (KEONEHE'EHE'E) TRAIL

ourpick Sliding Sands (Keonehe'ehe'e) Trail starts at the south side of the Haleakalā Visitor Center parking lot at 9740ft and descends steeply over loose cinders down to the crater floor. If you take this hike after catching the sunrise, you'll walk directly into a gentle warmish wind and the rays of the sunshine.

Even if you're just coming to the summit for a peek at the incredible view, it's worth taking a short hike down Sliding Sands Trail. The visitor center is almost always crowded, and you need a little solitude to really experience the essence of the crater. And its essence gets stranger the longer you look at it, or the further you descend.

The full trail leads 9.2 miles to the Paliku cabin and campground, passing the Kapalaoa cabin at 5.6 miles after roughly four hours.

The first 6 miles of the trail follow the south wall. There are great views on the way down, but virtually no vegetation. About 2 miles down, a steep spur trail leads past silversword plants to Ka Lu'u o ka O'o cinder cone, about a half-mile north. Four miles down, after an elevation drop of 2500ft, the trail intersects with the first of three

Haleakalā's crater seen from the Sliding Sands Trail   ANN CECIL

Sliding Sands Trail GREG ELMS

spur trails leading north into the cinder desert, which after about 1.5 miles meets the Halemau'u Trail.

As you strike out across the crater floor for 2 miles to Kapalaoa, verdant ridges rise on your right, eventually giving way to ropy *pahoehoe* (smooth-surfaced lava). From Kapalaoa cabin to Paliku, the descent is gentle and the vegetation gradually increases. **Paliku** (6380ft) is beneath a sheer cliff at the eastern end of the crater. In contrast to the crater's barren western end, this area receives heavy rainfall, with ohia forests climbing the slopes.

HALEMAU'U TRAIL
If you're not up for a long hike, consider doing just part of the Halemau'u Trail. Even hiking just the first mile gives a fine view of the crater with Ko'olau Gap to the east, and it's fairly level up to this point. If you were to continue on the trail, descending 1400ft along 2 miles of switchbacks, then walk across the crater floor to Holua cabin and campground, the 7.4-mile return would make a good day hike. But start early, before the afternoon clouds roll in and visibility vanishes.

At 6940ft, **Holua** is one of the lowest areas along this hike, and you'll see impressive views of the crater walls rising a few thousand feet to the west. A few large **lava tubes** here are worth exploring: one is up a short, steep cliff behind the cabin and the other is a 15-minute detour further along the trail. According to local legend, the latter tube was a spiritual place where mothers brought the *piko* (umbilical cords) of their newborns to gather mana for the child.

If you have the energy, push on just another mile to the colorful cinder cones, being sure to make a short detour onto the **Silversword Loop**, where you'll see these plants in various stages of growth. If you're here during the summer, you should be able to see the plants in flower, their tall stalks ablaze with hundreds of maroon and yellow blossoms. But be careful – half of all silverswords today are trampled to death as seedlings, mostly by careless hikers who wander off trails and inadvertently crush the plants' shallow, laterally growing roots. The trail continues another 6.3 miles to the Paliku cabin.

The trailhead to Halemau'u is 3.5 miles above the Park Headquarters Visitor Center and about 6 miles below the Haleakalā Visitor Center. There's a fair chance you'll see nene in the parking lot.

If you're camping at Hosmer Grove, you can take a shortcut over to the crater rim via the little-known, and less exciting, **Supply Trail** that follows the old mule path used to get supplies down to the cabins on the crater floor. The trail starts on the campground turnoff road and after 1.5 miles opens up to broad vistas of the volcano's rain-forest slopes and out to sea. After one more mile, the Supply Trail intersects with the Halemau'u Trail down into the crater.

EXPLORING THE CINDER DESERT
Almost all hiking trails lead to the belly of the beast. There's no way to see this amazing area without backtracking. Three major spur trails connect Sliding Sands Trail, from near Kapalaoa cabin, with the Halemau'u Trail between Paliku and Holua cabins. As the trails are not very long, if you're camping you may have time to do them all.

The spur trail furthest west takes in many of the crater's most kaleidoscopic cinder

Are you from this area? I have lived all my life in Kula. I started working at Haleakalā National Park in 1989. Before that I was working at Hawai'i Volcanoes National Park on the Big Island. I came home to Haleakalā.

What are your ranger talks about? They can be anything from geology to Hawaiian culture. My overarching theme is about culture, the evolution of man's interaction with the natural resources in his physical environment. A lot of people define culture as a noun. I define culture as a verb. A verb says it's ongoing, living and growing. It is action, not something that just sits there. I am Native Hawaiian. When I talk about culture, I'm talking about it as an indigenous person.

Why do you chant before your talks? In the morning I chant simply because Hawaiians will ask the environment for the knowledge it holds – to come sit upon their shoulder, almost like a prayer – so that whatever it is I do during the course of the day I do correctly the first time.

Any advice for people visiting Haleakalā? When you come to this park – or any park – make sure to talk to the people who work there. Don't be a tourist. Tourists only cruise. Be a visitor. Go visit with somebody.

cones, and the viewing angle changes with every step. If you prefer stark, black and barren, both of the other spur trails take you through 'a'a (rough, jagged lava) and pahoehoe lava fields, with the one furthest east splattered with rust-red cinders.

All three trails end up on the north side of the cinder desert near **Kawilinau**, also known as the Bottomless Pit. Legends say the pit leads down to the sea, though the National Park Service says it's just 65ft deep. Truth be told, there's not much to see, as you can't really get a good look down the narrow shaft. Don't miss the short loop trail to sit for a while in the saddle of **Pele's Paint Pot Lookout**, the crater's most jaw-dropping vantage point.

LAU'ULU TRAIL
Also known as the Kalapawili Ridge Trail, this trail is overgrown and barely used, but if you're already deep in the crater at Paliku it offers a seldom-trodden adventure. The trouble is finding the trailhead, which is tucked behind the Paliku campground and cabin. From there just keep heading uphill; after an hour or two, the trail empties out onto the high-flying Kalapawili Ridge, which affords broad vistas of Hana out to sea. Since this trail is not well maintained, allow at least five or six hours for the round-trip.

KAUPO TRAIL
The most extreme of Haleakalā's hikes is the Kaupo Trail, which starts at the Paliku campground and leads down to Kaupo on the southern coast. Be prepared for ankle-twisting conditions, blistered feet, intense tropical sun and torrential showers. Your knees will take a pounding as you descend more than 6100ft over 8.6 miles.

The first 3.7 miles of the trail drop 2500ft in elevation before reaching the park

Top Picks

HALEAKALĀ FOR KIDS

- Ranger talks at the Haleakalā Visitor Center (p173)
- Swimming at 'Ohe'o Gulch (p185)
- Pony Express horseback rides (opposite)

boundary. It's a steep rocky trail through rough lava and brushland, with short switchbacks alternating with level stretches. From here you'll be rewarded with spectacular ocean views.

The last 4.9 miles pass through Kaupo Ranch property on a rough jeep trail as it descends to the bottom of Kaupo Gap, exiting into a forest where feral pigs snuffle about. Here trail markings become vague, but once you reach the dirt road, it's another 1.5 miles to the end at the east side of the Kaupo General Store.

The 'village' of Kaupo (p212) is a long way from anywhere, with light traffic. Still, what traffic there is – largely locals in pickup trucks – moves slow enough along Kaupo's rough road to start conversation. If you have to walk the final stretch, it's 8 miles to the 'Ohe'o Gulch campground.

Because this is such a strenuous and remote trail, it's not advisable to hike it alone. No camping is allowed on Kaupo Ranch property, so most hikers spend the night at the Paliku campground and then get an early start.

Having said all that, note that at the time of this book's publication the Kaupo Trail was closed to hikers because of road damage in the Kaupo area. If you're planning on doing the hike, check with the park service to see if it's reopened yet.

SKYLINE TRAIL

Crossing along the incredible crater-dotted spine of Haleakalā, this precipitous trail begins at a lofty elevation of 9750ft in Haleakalā National Park and leads down to the campground at Polipoli Spring State Recreation Area (p162) at 6200ft, a distance of 8.5 miles. It takes about four hours to walk. Get an early start to enjoy the views before clouds take over.

To get to the trailhead, go past Pu'u'ula'ula (Red Hill) Overlook and take the road to the left just before Science City. The road, which passes over a cattle grate, is signposted not for public use, but continue and you'll soon find a Na Ala Hele sign marking the trailhead.

The Skyline Trail starts in barren open terrain of volcanic cinder, a moon walk that passes more than a dozen cinder cones and craters. The first mile is rough lava rock. After three crunchy miles, it reaches the tree line (8500ft) and enters native *mamane* forest. In winter *mamane* is heavy with flowers that look like yellow sweet-pea blossoms.

NENE WATCH

The native nene, Hawaii's state bird, is a long-lost cousin of the Canada goose. By the 1950s, hunting, habitat loss and predators had reduced its population to just 30. Thanks to captive breeding and release programs, it has been brought back from the verge of extinction and the Haleakalā National Park's nene population is now holding steady at about 250.

Nene nest in high cliffs from 6000ft to 8000ft, surrounded by rugged lava flows with sparse vegetation. Their feet have gradually adapted by losing most of their webbing. The birds are extremely friendly and love to hang out where people do, anywhere from cabins on the crater floor to the Park Headquarters Visitor Center. Their curiosity and fearlessness have contributed to their undoing. They don't fare well in an asphalt habitat and many have been run over by cars. Others have been tamed by too much human contact, so no matter how much they beg for your peanut butter sandwich, do not feed the nene. It only interferes with their successful return to the wild.

The nonprofit **Friends of Haleakalā National Park** (www.fhnp.org; PO Box 322, Makawao, HI 96768) helps protect the park's habitats and wildlife, including the nene. Its Adopt-a-Nene program, which costs $30 per adult ($20 for students and seniors), helps protect nene from predators such as mongoose and feral cats. It also coordinates volunteer projects in the park.

Experience Haleakalā on horseback

GREG ELMS

There's solitude on this walk. If the clouds treat you kindly, you'll have broad views all the way between the barren summit and the dense cloud forest. Eventually the trail meets the Polipoli access road, where you can either walk to the paved road in about 4 miles, or continue via the Haleakalā Ridge Trail and Polipoli Trail to the campground. If you prefer treads to hiking boots, the Skyline Trail is also an awesome adventure on a mountain bike (see p175).

HOSMER GROVE TRAIL

our pick Anyone who is looking for a little greenery after hiking the crater will love this shaded woodland walk, and birders wing it here as well.

The half-mile loop trail starts at Hosmer Grove campground, three-quarters of a mile south of the Park Headquarters Visitor Center, in a forest of lofty trees. The exotics in Hosmer Grove were introduced in 1910 in an effort to develop a lumber industry in Hawaii. Species include fragrant incense cedar, Norway spruce, Douglas fir, eucalyptus and various pines. Although the trees adapted well enough to grow, they didn't grow fast enough at these elevations to make tree harvesting practical. Thanks to this failure, today there's a park here instead.

After the forest, the trail moves into native shrubland, with 'akala (Hawaiian raspberry), *mamane, pilo, kilau* ferns and sandalwood. The *'ohelo*, a berry sacred to the volcano goddess Pele, and the *pukiawe*, which has red and white berries and evergreen leaves, are favored by nene.

Listen for the calls of the native *'i'iwi* and *'apapane*, both sparrow-sized birds with bright red feathers that are fairly common here. The *'i'iwi* has a very loud squeaking call, orange legs and a curved salmon-colored bill. The *'apapane*, a fast-moving bird with a black bill, black legs and a white undertail, feeds on the nectar of ohia flowers, and its wings make a distinctive whirring sound.

Horseback Riding

Pony Express (☎ 667-2200; www.ponyexpresstours .com; Haleakala Crater Rd; horseback ride $185; ⏰ 8am-5pm) can get you in the stirrups for the ride of your life on a half-day horseback journey deep into Haleakalā crater. It starts at the crater summit and follows Sliding Sands Trail, offering jaw-dropping scenery the entire way. If you're not hiking down to the crater this is the only other way to get eye to eye with this geological marvel. Book early, as there's a max of nine riders taken. Pony Express is on Hwy 378, 2.5 miles up from Hwy 377.

TOURS

Star Gazers Maui (☎ 281-9158; www.stargazersmaui .com; tour $75; ☺ Wed & Fri) meets at the summit for a light sunset dinner followed by stargazing from a 12in computerized telescope. It's an unbeatable celestial experience if you hit it on a clear night – a rare chance to stargaze in pitch-dark conditions! Down coats and hot chocolate provided.

SLEEPING

To spend the night at Haleakalā is to commune with nature. All of the camping options are primitive; none has electricity or showers. Backcountry campgrounds have pit toilets and limited nonpotable water supplies that are shared with the crater cabins. Water needs to be filtered or chemically treated before drinking; conserve it, as water tanks occasionally run dry. Fires are allowed only in grills and in times of drought are prohibited entirely. You must pack in all your food and supplies and pack out all your trash.

Keep in mind that sleeping at an elevation of 7000ft is not like camping on the beach. You need to be well equipped – without a waterproof tent and a winter-rated sleeping bag, forget it.

Camping

Wake up to the sound of birdsong at **Hosmer Grove campground**, the only drive-up campground in the mountainous section of Haleakalā National Park. Surrounded by lofty trees and adjacent to one of Maui's best birding trails, this campground at an elevation of 6800ft tends to be a bit cloudy, but a covered picnic pavilion offers shelter if it starts to rain. Campers will also find grills, toilets and running water. Camping is free on a first-come, first-served basis. No permit is required, though there's a three-day camping limit per month. It's busier in summer than in winter and is often full on holiday weekends. The campground is just after the park entrance booth.

For hikers, two backcountry campgrounds lie in the belly of Haleakalā Crater. The easiest to reach is at **Holua**, 3.7 miles down the Halemau'u Trail. The other is at **Paliku**, below a rain-forest ridge at the end of Halemau'u Trail. Weather can be unpredictable at both. Holua is typically dry after sunrise, until clouds roll back in the late afternoon. Paliku is in a grassy meadow, with skies overhead alternating between stormy and sunny.

Permits (free) are required for crater camping. They are issued at the Park Headquarters Visitor Center on a first-come, first-served basis between 8am and 3pm on the day of the hike. Camping is limited to three nights in the crater each

Camping at Hosmer Grove   GREG ELMS

Island Insights

On your drive from Maui's coast to the summit of Haleakalā National Park you'll pass through as many ecological zones as you would on a drive from Alaska to central Mexico.

month, with no more than two consecutive nights at either campground. Because only 25 campers are allowed at each site, permits can go quickly when larger parties show up, a situation more likely to occur in summer.

Cabins

our pick Three **rustic cabins** (per cabin with 1-12 people $75) dating from the 1930s lie along trails on the crater floor at Holua, Kapalaoa and Palĭku. Each has a wood-burning stove, two propane burners, cooking utensils, 12 bunks with sleeping pads (but no bedding), pit toilets and a limited supply of water and firewood.

Hiking distances to the cabins from the crater rim range from 4 miles to 9 miles. The driest conditions are at Kapalaoa, in the middle of the cinder desert off the Sliding Sands Trail. Those craving lush rain forest will find Palĭku serene. Holua has unparalleled sunrise views. There's a three day limit per month, with no more than two consecutive nights in any cabin. Each cabin is rented to only one group at a time.

The challenge here is the demand, which is so high that the National Park Service holds a monthly lottery to award reservations! To enter, your reservation request must be received two months prior to the first day of the month of your proposed stay (eg requests for cabins on any date in July must arrive before May 1). Your chances increase if you list alternate dates within the same calendar month and choose weekdays rather than weekends.

Only written (no phone) **reservation requests** (Haleakalā National Park, PO Box 369, Makawao, HI 96768, Attn: Cabins) are accepted for the lottery. Include your name, address, phone number, specific dates and cabins requested. Only winners are notified.

If you miss the lottery, don't write off the cabins completely. Cancellations often result in last-minute vacancies, and occasionally occur a few weeks in advance as well. You can check for vacancies in person at the Park Headquarters Visitor Center at any time, but calls (☎ 572-4459) regarding cancellations are accepted only between 1pm and 3pm, and you'll need to have a credit card handy to secure the cabin. As an added boon, if you get a vacancy within three weeks of your camping date, the cabin fee drops to $60 a day.

GETTING THERE & AROUND

Getting here is half the fun. Snaking up the mountain it's sometimes hard to tell if you're in an airplane or a car – all of Maui opens up below you, with sugarcane and pineapple fields creating a patchwork of green on the valley floor. The highway ribbons back and forth, and in some places as many as four or five switchbacks are in view all at once.

Haleakalā Crater Rd (Hwy 378) twists and turns for 11 miles from Hwy 377 near Kula up to the park entrance, then another 10 miles to Haleakalā summit. It's a good paved road all the way, but it's steep and winding. You don't want to rush it, especially

Haleakalā sandalwood blossoms KARL LEHMANN

HALEAKALĀ NATIONAL PARK

The scenic drive up Haleakala Crater Rd

when it's dark or foggy. Watch out for cattle wandering freely across the road.

The drive to the summit takes about 1½ hours from Pa'ia or Kahului, two hours from Kihei and a bit longer from Lahaina. If you need gas, fill up the night before, as there are no services on Haleakala Crater Rd.

On your way back downhill, be sure to put your car in low gear to avoid burning out your brakes.

KIPAHULU AREA ('OHE'O GULCH)

There's more to Haleakalā National Park than the cindery summit. The park extends down the southeast face of the volcano all the way to the sea. The crowning glory of the Kipahulu section of the park is 'Ohe'o Gulch with its magnificent waterfalls and wide pools, each one tumbling into the next one below. When the sun shines, these cool glistening pools make great swimming holes.

Because there's no access between the Kipahulu section of the park and the main Haleakalā summit area, you'll be visiting the two sections of the park on different days. So hold on to your ticket – it's good for both sections of the park.

HISTORY

Back in the 1970s 'Ohe'o Gulch was dubbed the 'Seven Sacred Pools' as part of a tourism promotion and the term still floats around freely, much to the chagrin of park officials. It's a complete misnomer since there are 24 pools in all, extending from the ocean to Waimoku Falls, and they were never sacred – but they certainly are divine. The waters once supported a sizable Hawaiian settlement of farmers who cultivated sweet potatoes and taro in terraced gardens beside the stream. Archaeologists have identified the stone remains of more than 700 ancient structures at 'Ohe'o.

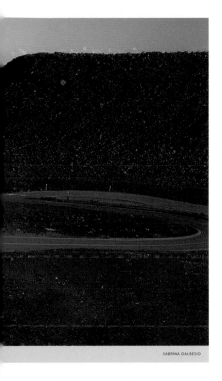

SABRINA DALBESIO

One of the expressed intentions of Haleakala National Park is to manage its Kipahulu area 'to perpetuate traditional Hawaiian farming and *ho'onanea*' – a Hawaiian word meaning to pass the time in ease, peace and pleasure. So kick back and have some fun!

INFORMATION

The national park's **Kipahulu Visitor Center** (Map p168; ☎ 248-7375; www.nps.gov/hale; 3-day entry pass per car $10, per person on foot, bicycle or motorcycle $5; ☺ park 24hr, visitor center 9am-5pm) offers a thin

menu of visitor programs, depending on the season and the staff available. The mainstay is short cultural history talks, usually given on the half hour between 12:30pm and 3:30pm. You'll find restrooms at the parking lot. Food and gas are not available.

SIGHTS & ACTIVITIES
Lower Pools

our pick Even if you're tight on time, you've got to take this 20-minute stroll! The **Kuloa Point Trail**, a half-mile loop, runs from the visitor center down to the lower pools and back. At the junction with Pipiwai Trail go right. A few minutes down, you'll come to a broad grassy knoll with a gorgeous view of the Hana coast. On a clear day you can see the Big Island, 30 miles away across 'Alenuihaha Channel. This is a fine place to stop and unpack your lunch.

The large freshwater pools (Map p168) along the trail are terraced one atop the other and connected by gentle cascades. They're usually calm and great for swimming, their cool waters refreshingly brisk. The second big pool below the bridge is a favorite swimming hole.

However, be aware: conditions can change in a heartbeat. Heavy rains falling far away on the upper slopes can bring a sudden torrent through the pools at any time. If the water starts to rise, get out immediately. Several people have been swept out to sea from these pools by flash floods. Slippery rocks and unseen submerged ledges are other potential hazards, so check carefully before jumping in.

Waterfall Trails

The **Pipiwai Trail** (Map p168) runs up the 'Ohe'o streambed, rewarding hikers with picture-perfect views of waterfalls. The trail starts on the *mauka* (inland) side of the visitor center and leads up to Makahiku Falls (0.5 miles) and Waimoku Falls (2 miles). Or take a little shortcut by picking up the trail from the pedestrian crossing at the highway. To see both falls, allow about two hours return. The upper section is muddy, but boardwalks cover some of the worst bits.

Along the path, you'll pass large mango trees and patches of guava before coming

Top Picks

HALEAKALĀ HIKES
- **Sliding Sands Trail** (p177)
- **Pipiwai Trail** (right)
- **Kuloa Point Trail** (above right)
- **Halemau'u Trail** (p178)
- **Hosmer Grove Trail** (p181)

Island Insights

Did you see something funny in the water? 'Ohe'o Gulch is home to a rare goby fish called *'o'opu*, which spends the first stages of its life in the ocean, but returns to breed in the upper stream. The fish, which has a face that resembles a frog's, works its way up the chain of pools and waterfalls by using its front fins as suction cups as it climbs the rocks.

to an overlook after about 10 minutes. **our pick** **Makahiku Falls** (Map p168), a long bridal-veil waterfall that drops into a deep gorge, is just off to the right. Thick green ferns cover the sides of 200ft basalt cliffs where the water cascades – a very rewarding scene for such a short walk.

To the left of the overlook, a worn path continues up to the top of the waterfall, where there's a remote skinny-dipping pool known to locals as 'last chance pool.' At midday the pool is enjoyable, but by late afternoon the sun stops hitting it and the mosquitoes move in. If you're considering a swim, assess the situation carefully. Rocks above the falls offer some protection from going over the edge as long as the water level isn't high; a cut on one side lets the water plunge over the cliff – don't go near it! Flash floods are not uncommon here. If the water starts to rise, get out immediately – a drop over this sheer 185ft waterfall could (obviously) be fatal.

Continuing along the main trail, you'll walk beneath old banyan trees, cross Palikea Stream (killer mosquitoes thrive here) and enter the wonderland of the **Bamboo Forest** (Map p168), where thick groves of bamboo bang together musically in the wind. Beyond them is **Waimoku Falls** (Map p168), a thin, lacy 400ft waterfall dropping down a sheer rock face. When you come out of the first grove, you'll see the waterfall in the distance. Forget swimming under Waimoku Falls – its pool is shallow and there's a danger of falling rocks.

If you want to take a dip, you'll find better pools along the way. About 100yd before Waimoku Falls, you'll cross a little stream. If you go left and work your way upstream for 10 minutes, you'll come to an attractive waterfall and a little pool about neck deep. There's also an inviting pool in the stream about halfway between Makahiku and Waimoku Falls.

TOURS

For fascinating insights into the area's past, join one of the ethnobotanical tours led by **Kipahulu 'Ohana** (☎ 248-8558; www.kipahulu .org), a collective of Native Hawaiian farmers who have restored ancient taro patches within the park. Tours range from a two-hour outing that concentrates on the farm to a 3½-hour tour that also includes a hike up to Waimoku Falls. The schedule varies, so call ahead.

SLEEPING

If you've got a tent, you're going to love **Kipahulu campground** (Map p168), which has an incredible setting on oceanside cliffs amid the stone ruins of an ancient Hawaiian village. Good mana here! This is a primitive campground. Facilities include pit toilets, picnic tables and grills, but there's no water so bring your own. Permits aren't required. Camping is free but limited to three nights each month. In winter you'll usually have the place to yourself, and even in summer there's typically enough space to handle everyone who shows up. Bring mosquito repellent and gear suitable for rainy conditions. The campground is a quarter of a mile southeast of the Kipahulu Visitor Center.

GETTING THERE & AROUND

The Kipahulu section of Haleakalā National Park is on Hwy 31, 10 scenic miles south of Hana. For more information on the spectacular drive between Hana and Kipahulu see the East Maui chapter (p211).

THE ROAD TO
HANA

You're about to experience the most ravishingly
beautiful drive in Hawaii. The serpentine Hana Hwy delivers one jaw-dropping
view after the other as it winds between jungly valleys and towering cliffs. Along
the way 54 one-lane bridges mark nearly as many waterfalls, some tranquil and
inviting, others so sheer they kiss you with spray as you drive past. But there's a
lot more to this beauty than the drive: short treks lead to Eden-like swimming
holes, and side roads to sleepy seaside villages. If you've never tried smoked
breadfruit, taken a dip in a spring-fed cave or gazed upon an ancient Hawaiian
temple, set the alarm early – you've got a big day coming up.

TWIN FALLS

Heading south from Pa'ia, houses give way to fields of sugarcane and the scenery gets more dramatic with each mile. After the 16-mile marker on Hwy 36 the Hana Hwy changes numbers to Hwy 360 and the mile markers begin again at zero. Just after the 2-mile marker a wide parking area with a fruit stand marks the start of the trail to Twin Falls. Local kids and tourists flock to the pool beneath the lower falls, about a 10-minute walk in. Twin Falls gets a lot of attention as being the 'first waterfall on the road to Hana.' Truth be told, unless you're interested in taking a dip in muddy waters, this one's not worth the time. You'll find more idyllic options en route to Hana.

HUELO

With its abundant rain and fertile soil Huelo once supported more than 50,000 Hawaiians, but today it's a sleepy, scattered community of farms and enviable cliffside homes.

Don't Miss

- **Hidden but awesome Makapipi Falls** (p196)
- **Towering trees along Waikamoi Nature Trail** (p190)
- **Side trip to scenic Ke'anae Peninsula** (p193)
- **Killer view from Wailua Peninsula Lookout** (p195)
- **Black-sand beach at Wai'anapanapa State Park** (p198)

Forget about a sign. Look instead for the double row of mailboxes and green bus shelter that come up after a blind curve 0.5 miles past the 3-mile marker. Turn left onto the one-lane road that leads into the village. The only sight, Kaulanapueo Church, is just a half-mile down.

It's tempting to continue driving past the church, but not rewarding, as the road shortly turns to dirt and dead-ends at gated homes. There's no public beach access.

ROAD TO HANA: TWIN FALLS TO KE'ANAE

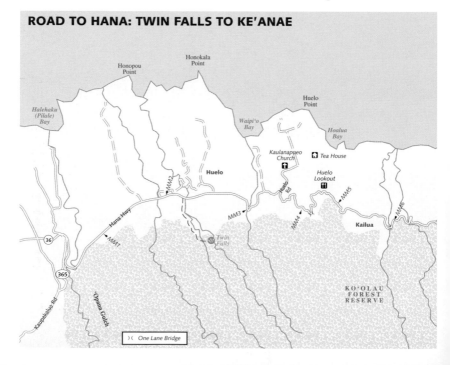

Sights

KAULANAPUEO CHURCH

Constructed in 1853 of coral blocks and surrounded by a manicured green lawn, this immaculately maintained church remains the heart of the village. It's in early Hawaiian missionary style with a spare interior and a tin roof topped with a green steeple. Swaying palm trees add a tropical backdrop. There are no formal opening hours, but the church is typically unlocked during the day. Incidentally, the name Kaulanapueo refers to the *pueo* (Hawaiian owls) that once thrived in the surrounding forest.

Eating & Sleeping

HUELO LOOKOUT   Fruit Stand $

☎ 573-1850; 7600 Hana Hwy; snacks $5; ⏱ 7:30am-6pm

The fruit stand itself is tempting enough: drinking coconuts, smoothies, even real French crèpes…ooh la la. And everything's organic. But it doesn't stop there. Take your

Twin Falls   GREG ELMS

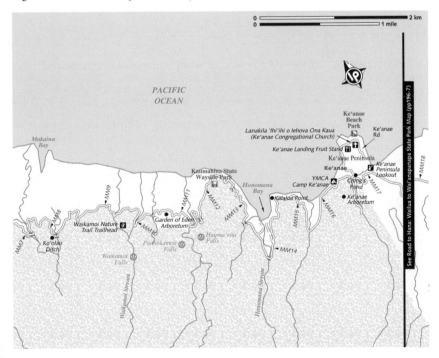

HANA TRIP TIPS

- Beat the crowd – get a sunrise start.
- Fill up the tank in Pa'ia; the next gas station isn't until Hana.
- Bring a picnic and plenty to drink.
- Wear a bathing suit under your clothes so you're ready for impromptu swims.
- Pull over to let local drivers pass – they're moving at a different pace.

goodies down the steps, where you can eat at a café table with a wide-open panorama clear out to the coast.

TEA HOUSE   Cottage $$
☎ 572-5610, 800-215-6130; www.mauiteahouse .com; Huelo Rd; 1br cottages $135
Meditate at a Tibetan-style stupa with a spectacular ocean view at this hidden jewel. The Asian-style cottage is built with walls recycled from a Zen temple and the place is so secluded that it's off the grid, using solar power to stoke up the lights. Guests have a small kitchen and an open-air bath in a redwood gazebo.

KO'OLAU FOREST RESERVE

Now the real adventure begins! As the highway snakes along the edge of the Ko'olau Forest Reserve, the jungle takes over and one-lane bridges appear around every other bend. Ko'olau means 'windward,' and the upper slopes of these mountains squeeze 200in to 300in of rain from passing clouds annually. It's no surprise that this makes for awesome waterfalls as the rainwater rushes down the reserve's abundant gulches and streams.

Kailua

After the 5-mile marker you'll pass through the village of Kailua. This little community of tin-roofed houses is the home base for the employees of the East Maui Irrigation (EMI) company. These EMI workers maintain the extensive irrigation system that carries water from the rain forest to the thirsty sugarcane fields in Central Maui.

After leaving the village, just past the 6-mile marker, you'll be treated to a splash of color as you pass planted groves of painted eucalyptus with brilliant rainbow-colored bark. Roll down the windows and inhale the sweet scent given off by these majestic trees introduced from Australia.

Ko'olau Ditch

For more than a century the Ko'olau Ditch has been carrying up to 450 million gallons of water a day through 75 miles of flumes and tunnels from Maui's rainy interior to the dry central plains. You can get a close-up look by stopping at the small pull-off just before the bridge that comes up immediately after the 8-mile marker. Just 50ft above the road you'll see water flowing through a hand-hewn stone-block section of the ditch before tunneling into the mountain.

WAIKAMOI TRAIL & WATERFALLS

Sights

🌿 WAIKAMOI NATURE TRAIL

our pick Put on your walking shoes and relish the majestic sights and spicy scents along this 30-minute nature trail. A covered table at the top offers one pretty spot to break out that picnic lunch. Look for the signposted trailhead 0.5 miles past the 9-mile marker, where there's a wide dirt pull-off with space for several cars to park.

At the start of this 0.8-mile trail you're welcomed by a sign that reads 'Quiet. Trees at Work' and a strand of grand reddish *Eucalyptus robusta,* one of several types of towering eucalyptus trees that grow along the path. Once you reach the ridge at the top of the loop, you'll be treated to fine views of the winding Hana Hwy.

WAIKAMOI FALLS

There is space for just a few cars before the bridge at the 10-mile marker, but unless it's been raining recently don't worry about missing this one. The East Maui Irrigation Company diverts water from the stream, and as a result the falls are usually just a trickle. After you cross the bridge, bamboo grows almost horizontally out from the cliffs, creating a green canopy over the road.

GARDEN OF EDEN ARBORETUM
☎ 572-9899; 10600 Hana Hwy, 0.5 miles past the 10-mile marker; admission $10; ⊗ 8:30am-3pm

So why pay a steep $10 per person – not per carload, mind you – to visit an arboretum when the entire road to Hana is a garden? Well, it does offer a tamer version of paradise. The winding paths are maintained, the flowers are identified and the hilltop picnic tables sport gorgeous views, including ones of Puohokamoa Falls and of Keopuka Rock, which had a few seconds of fame in the opening shot of *Jurassic Park*. But mostly it's about walking on tidy paths that won't leave you caked in mud. If, however, you prefer your trails *au naturel*, save your money and keep driving.

PUOHOKAMOA FALLS
Immediately after the 11-mile marker you'll pass Puohokamoa Falls. This waterfall no longer has public access, but you can get a glimpse of it from the bridge, or a bird's-eye view of the falls from the Garden of Eden Arboretum (above).

HAIPUA'ENA FALLS
If you're ready for a dip, Haipua'ena Falls, 0.5 miles past the 11-mile marker, provides a gentle waterfall with a zen-like pool deep enough for swimming. Since you can't see the pool from the road, few people know this one's here. Actually, it's not a bad choice if you forgot your bathing suit. There's space for just a couple of cars on the Hana side of the bridge. To reach the falls, simply walk 100yd upstream. Wild ginger grows along the path, and ferns hang from the rock wall behind the waterfall, making an idyllic setting.

KAUMAHINA STATE WAYSIDE PARK
Clean restrooms, much appreciated right about now, and a grassy lawn with picnic tables make this roadside park one family-friendly stop. The park comes up 0.2 miles after the 12-mile marker. Be sure to take the short walk up the hill past the restrooms for an eye-popping view of the coastal scenery that awaits to the south.

For the next several miles, the scenery is absolutely stunning, opening up to a new vista as you turn round each bend. If it's been raining recently, you can expect to see waterfalls galore crashing down the mountains.

HONOMANU BAY
You'll get your first view of this striking stream-fed bay from the 13-mile marker, where there's a roadside pull-off that invites you to pause and take in the scene.

Stunning Honomanu Bay's black-sand beach below the Road to Hana
GREG ELMS

THE ROAD TO HANA

Honomanu Bay's rocky black-sand beach is used mostly by local surfers and fishers. Surfable waves form during big swells, but the rocky bottom and strong rips make it dangerous if you're not familiar with the spot. The sea is usually too turbulent for swimming, but on very calm days it's possible to dive or snorkel here. Keep those rips in mind before you kick out. Honomanu Stream, which empties into the bay, forms a little pool just inland of the beach that's good for splashing around, and on weekends local families take the young'uns here to wade in its shallow water.

If you have a standard-issue rental car, the best way to get to Honomanu Bay is to park at the large turnoff in front of the dirt access road that's 0.5 miles past the 13-mile marker. From there, it's just a five-minute walk to the bay. Be prepared for muddy conditions if it's been raining. The road deposits you on the north side of the stream, but unless the water is high you can wade across to the rock-strewn beach.

Alternatively, just after the 14-mile marker, an inconspicuous road plunges straight down to Honomanu Bay. But this road can be shockingly bad – if you're not in a high-clearance vehicle, send a scout before driving down.

View of the coast at Ke'anae   GREG ELMS

KALALOA POINT
For a fascinating view of the coast stop at the wide pull-off on the ocean side of the highway 0.4 miles past the 14-mile marker. From here you can look clear across Honomanu Bay and watch ant-size cars snaking down the mountain cliffs on the other side. If there's no place to park, there's another pull-off with the same view 0.2 miles further.

KE'ANAE
Congratulations – you've made it halfway to Hana. Here's your reward: dramatic landscapes and the friendliest seaside village on the route.

The views are sweeping. Starting way up at the Ko'olau Gap in the rim of Haleakalā Crater and stretching clear down to the coast, Ke'anae Valley radiates green, thanks to the 150in of rainfall that drenches it each year.

At the foot of the valley lies Ke'anae Peninsula, created by a late eruption of Haleakalā that sent lava gushing all the way down Ke'anae Valley and into the sea. Unlike its rugged surroundings, the volcanic peninsula is flat, like a leaf floating on the water.

You'll want to see Ke'anae up close. But keep an eye peeled, as sights come up in quick succession. After passing the YMCA camp 0.5 miles past the 16-mile marker, the arboretum pops up on the right and the road to Ke'anae Peninsula heads off to the left around the next bend.

Sights
🌿 KE'ANAE ARBORETUM
Up for an easy walk? Ke'anae Arboretum, 0.75 miles past the 16-mile marker, follows the Pi'ina'au Stream past an array of shady trees. Most eye-catching are the painted eucalyptus trees and the golden-stemmed bamboo, whose green stripes look like the strokes of a Japanese *shodo* artist. The arboretum is divided into two sections, with exotic timber and ornamental trees in one area and Hawaiian food and medicinal plants in the upper section.

The 0.6-mile path, which starts on a paved road and then turns to dirt, takes about 30 minutes to walk. It passes ginger

ISLAND VOICES

NAME: SANDRA HUEU
OCCUPATION: BANANA BREAD MAKER
RESIDENCE: KE'ANAE

How did you get started? I opened Ke'anae Landing Fruit Stand (p194) in 1996. Everybody calls me Aunty Sandy. I don't advertise. People tell people. Banana bread is something everybody loves.

Is it a one-person operation? It's a family thing. My daughter Tammy is my partner and she and my granddaughter all help make banana bread. My husband has to peel all the ripe bananas. My son machete opens coconuts for us, and he cleans the yard. During the summer my grandkids work.

How much banana bread do you make? I start off with 80 loaves in the morning and make more as I need. I usually do about 160 loaves a day. We use a lot of bananas, about 400lb a week.

Did you grow up in Ke'anae? My husband was born and raised in Ke'anae. I grew up in 'Aiea, on O'ahu. I moved here in 1976. The first couple years were hard, but Ke'anae has grown on me. I always tell people, I am so blessed to live in Ke'anae. O'ahu is fast paced, everybody's so crazy busy. Ke'anae is so peaceful, so serene. Here you appreciate life more, learn how to slow down.

What's Ke'anae like? Close to 30 people live on the peninsula. Everything we do is family. I take care of the church – I dust the pews, sweep the floors. My husband takes care of the church grounds. Our family has a taro farm, about 24 patches, and we make our own poi. On Ke'anae, you want something, you go pick it. We've got the ocean, the mountains. You can hook fish and dive, and pick bananas, avocado, 'ulu (breadfruit) and grapefruit in your own yard. You can sustain a lot without going to town.

What do you recommend on the road to Hana? Be sure to come to the Ke'anae Peninsula. The lava formations, the waves, the church…this is the most beautiful spot. I have couples who come every year and sometimes they just come to Ke'anae. They don't go all the way to Hana anymore. They come here and just sit by the ocean and watch the waves hitting the rocks.

and other fragrant plants before ending at irrigated patches with dozens of varieties of taro.

KE'ANAE PENINSULA

ourpick A coastline pounded by relentless waves embraces a village so quiet you can hear the grass grow. This rare slice of 'Old Hawaii' is reached by taking the unmarked Ke'anae Rd just beyond Ke'anae Arbore-

tum. Here, families who have had roots to the land for generations still tend stream-fed taro patches.

Marking the heart of the village is **Lanakila 'Ihi'ihi o Iehova Ona Kaua** (Ke'anae Congregational Church), built in 1860. This is one church made of lava rocks and coral mortar whose exterior hasn't been covered over with layers of whitewash. It's a welcoming place with open doors and a guest book to

Island Insights

According to legend, the god Kane thrust his spear into Ke'anae Valley's solid rock walls, and water gushed out to nourish the forest and farms. Thanks to Kane's generosity, to this day Hawaiian farmers continue to grow taro in the wetland patches on Ke'anae Peninsula.

sign. You can get a feel for the community by strolling the church cemetery, where the gravestones have cameo portraits and fresh-cut flowers.

Just past the church is **Ke'anae Beach Park**, with a scenic coastline of jagged black rock and hypnotic white-capped waves. Forget swimming: not only is the water rough, but this is all sharp lava and no beach. You could drive for a couple of minutes more, but it becomes private and the scenery is no better, so be a good neighbor and stop at the park.

The rock islets you see off the coast – **Mokuhala** and **Mokumana** – are seabird sanctuaries.

CHING'S POND

The stream that feeds Ke'anae Peninsula first pauses to create a couple of tempting swimming holes just below the bridge, 0.8 miles after the 16-mile marker. You won't see anything driving by, but there's a good-sized pull-off immediately before the bridge where you can park. Just walk over to the bridge and behold: the water's deep, crystal clear and looks upon a little waterfall. A path at the north side of the bridge leads down to the water. Despite the 'No Trespassing' signs, you'll often see locals swimming here.

KE'ANAE PENINSULA LOOKOUT

You'll get a superb bird's-eye view of the lowland peninsula and village by stopping at the paved pull-off just past the 17-mile marker on the ocean side of the road. There's no sign, but it's easy to find if you look for the yellow tsunami speaker. From here you can see how Ke'anae Peninsula was formed late in the geological game – outlined in a jet-black lava coast, it still wears its volcanic birthmark around the edges. The views of

coconut palms and patchwork taro fed by Ke'anae Stream make one tasty scene. If it's been raining lately, look to the far left to spot a series of cascading waterfalls.

Eating & Sleeping

✦ KE'ANAE LANDING FRUIT STAND
Fruit Stand $

Ke'anae Rd; banana bread $4; ⏰ 9am-3pm Mon-Sat, to noon Sun

'Da best' banana bread on the entire road to Hana is baked fresh every morning, and is so good you'll find as many locals as tourists pulling up here. You can also get fresh coconut, pineapple slices and drinks at this seaside stand.

YMCA CAMP KE'ANAE
Cabins $

☎ 248-8355; www.mauiymca.org; 13375 Hana Hwy; campsite or dm $17, cottages $125

When they're not tied up by groups, the Y's cabins, on a knoll overlooking the coast, are available to individuals as hostel-style dorms. You'll need your own sleeping bag, and cooking facilities are limited to simple outdoor grills. Another option is pitching your tent on the grounds. The Y also has two cottages, each with full facilities, two bedrooms and a lanai with spectacular ocean views. The camp is between the 16- and 17-mile markers.

Roadside banana bread stand   GREG ELMS

WAILUA

After the Ke'anae Peninsula Lookout, you'll pass a couple of roadside fruit stands. A quarter-mile after the 18-mile marker, the unmarked Wailua Rd leads to the left into the village of Wailua.

There's little to see but you will pass **Our Lady of Fatima Shrine**. Also known as the Coral Miracle Church, this blue-and-white chapel was built in 1860 using coral from a freak storm that deposited the material onto a nearby beach. Prior to the storm men from the congregation had to dive to the ocean floor, bringing up chunks of coral one piece at a time: a long and tedious task. After the church was completed, another rogue storm hit the beach and swept all the leftover piles of coral back into the sea...or so the story goes. Since the chapel has just half a dozen little pews, the congregation long outgrew it and now uses the newer church out front.

From Wailua Rd you can also get a peek of the long cascade of **Waikani Falls** if you look back up toward the Hana Hwy. Wailua Rd dead-ends a half-mile down, though you won't want to go that far as blocked-off driveways prevent cars from turning around.

WAYSIDES

WAILUA VALLEY STATE WAYSIDE

Back on the Hana Hwy, just before the 19-mile marker, Wailua Valley State Wayside lookout comes up on the right, providing a broad view into verdant Ke'anae Valley, which appears to be a hundred shades of green. You can see a couple of waterfalls, and on a clear day you can steal a view of Ko'olau Gap, the break in the rim of Haleakalā Crater. If you climb up the

Three Bears Falls NED FRIARY

steps to the right, you'll find a good view of Wailua Peninsula as well. Now, how's that for a package? A word of caution: the wayside is signposted but it comes up quickly after turning round a bend, so be on the lookout.

WAILUA PENINSULA LOOKOUT

For a dynamite view of Wailua Peninsula, stop at the large paved pull-off on the ocean side of the road 0.25 miles past the 19-mile marker. There's no sign but it's not hard to find, as two concrete picnic tables mark the spot. Grab a seat, break out your snack pack and ogle the taro fields and jungly vistas unfolding below.

THREE BEARS FALLS

A real beauty, Three Bears, 0.5 miles past the 19-mile marker, takes its name from the triple cascade that flows down a steep rockface on the inland side of the road. Catch it after a rainstorm and it roars as one mighty waterfall. There's a small turnout with parking for a few cars right before crossing the bridge. It's sometimes possible to scramble down to the falls via a steep rocky trail that begins on the Hana side of the bridge. The stones are moss-covered and slippery; don't try it in loose sandals.

🐷 PUA'A KA'A STATE WAYSIDE PARK

A delightful park with an odd name, Pua'a Ka'a (Rolling Pig) rolls along both sides of the highway 0.5 miles after the 22-mile

---

Top Picks

HOMEGROWN TASTES

■ **Organic fruit crêpes at Huelo Lookout** (p189)

■ **Banana bread at Ke'anae Landing Fruit Stand** (opposite)

■ **Smoked breadfruit at Up in Smoke** (p196)

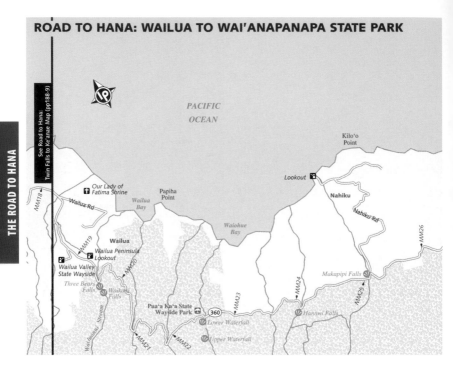

ROAD TO HANA: WAILUA TO WAI'ANAPANAPA STATE PARK

PACIFIC OCEAN

Kilo'o Point

Lookout

Nahiku

Our Lady of Fatima Shrine

Papiha Point

Wailua Rd

Wailua Bay

MM18

Nahiku Rd

Waiohue Bay

MM26

Wailua

MM19

Wailua Peninsula Lookout

Wailua Valley State Wayside

MM20

Three Bears Falls

Waikani Falls

Makapipi Falls

MM24

MM25

Pua'a Ka'a State Wayside Park

360

MM23

Hanawi Falls

Wailuanui Stream

MM21

MM22

Lower Waterfall

Upper Waterfall

---

marker. Some unlucky passersby just see the restrooms on the ocean side of the road and miss the rest. But you brought your beach towel, didn't you? Cross the highway and head inland to find a pair of delicious waterfalls cascading into pools. The best for swimming is the upper pool, which is visible just beyond the picnic tables. To reach it, you'll need to cross the stream, skipping across a few rocks, but it's nothing daunting. To get to the lower falls, which drop into a shallow pool, walk back to the south side of the bridge and then follow the trail upstream. And while you're at it, be sure to catch the scene from the bridge. Just don't hog the view.

HANAWI FALLS

Another waterfall with a split personality, Hanawi sometimes flows gently into a quiet pool and sometimes gushes wildly across a broad rockface. No matter the mood it always invites a picture. The falls are 0.1 miles after the 24-mile marker. There are small pull-offs before and after the bridge.

MAKAPIPI FALLS

Most waterfall views look up at the cascades, but this one offers a rare chance to experience an explosive waterfall from the top. Makapipi Falls makes its sheer plunge right beneath your feet as you stand on the ocean side of the Makapipi Bridge. It's 0.1 miles after the 25-mile marker; you'll find pull-offs before and after the bridge.

NAHIKU

While the village of Nahiku is down on the coast (see Detour, opposite), its little 'commercial' center – such as it is – is right on the Hana Hwy, 0.8 miles past the 28-mile marker. Here you'll find a little café, gallery, fruit stand and barbecue eatery clustered together, begging a stop.

Eating

UP IN SMOKE   Hawaiian $
our pick Hana Hwy; snacks $3-6; 🕙 10am-5pm Fri-Wed
Hawaiian food never tasted so good. This

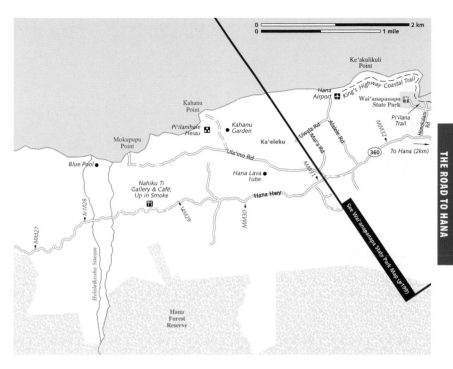

bustling barbecue stand is *the* place to try smoked breadfruit and *kalua* pig tacos, all cooked with kiawe wood right on site. The smoky fragrance will capture you as soon as you open the car door.

NAHIKU TI GALLERY & CAFÉ   Café $

☎ 248-8800; Hana Hwy; snacks $3-5; ⏰ 6am-5pm
This pint-size café brews Maui-grown coffee, whips up fresh fruit smoothies and has simple pastries.

'ULA'INO ROAD

'Ula'ino Rd begins at the Hana Hwy just south of the 31-mile marker. Hana Lava Tube is 0.5 miles from the highway and Kahanu Garden a mile further.

Sights

HANA LAVA TUBE

☎ 248-7308; www.mauicave.com; 'Ula'ino Rd; admission $12; ⏰ 10:30am-4pm Mon-Sat, sometimes Sun
The big kahuna of lava tubes, this mammoth series of caves was formed by an ancient volcanic flow. The caves are so formidable

DETOUR ➡

NAHIKU

All but unseen by most travelers, the rural village of Nahiku was once the site of Hawaii's only rubber plantation. The plantation folded in 1916, but some of the old rubber trees can still be seen along the road, half-covered in a canopy of climbing vines. Be warned, the road is just one lane the entire way and passing traffic requires pulling over and backing up – so this is not a detour for the faint of heart. The turnoff onto the unmarked Nahiku Rd is just east of the 25-mile marker. After winding down 2.5 miles you'll reach the village center with its brightly painted church and smattering of old wooden houses.

THE ROAD TO HANA

TREAD GENTLY

Travelers wanting to explore every nook and cranny sometimes come into conflict with Maui residents who feel their privacy and quality of life is being encroached upon. At no place has this come more to a head than **Blue Pool**, a coastal waterfall and swimming hole off 'Ula'ino Rd. Access to this slice of paradise leads across private property and the rural landowners who cherish their privacy are increasingly at odds with the rising stream of day-trippers cutting across their backyards.

Gentle persuasion has come up short. A signboard posted opposite Hana Lava Tube, which explains how the Blue Pool is of spiritual significance to Native Hawaiians and encourages tourists not to visit, has now been overlaid with a 'Closed to the Public. Trespassers will be Prosecuted' sign. For those who fail to heed the message, heated confrontations are common. If you don't want to get bopped by a coconut, take your dip at one of the many other waterfall pools along the Hana Hwy.

that they once served as a slaughterhouse – 17,000lb of cow bones had to be removed before they were opened to tourists! Winding your way through the extensive underground lava tubes, which reach heights of up to 40ft, you'll find a unique ecosystem of dripping stalactites and stalagmites. Most people take about an hour to explore. The admission includes flashlights and hard hats. Bring a sweater – it's cool down under.

KAHANU GARDEN

ourpick ☎ 248-8912; www.ntbg.org; 'Ula'ino Rd; self-guided tour adult/child under 12 $10/free; ⏱ 10am-2pm Mon-Fri

This one-of-a-kind place delivers a double blast of mana. Hawaii's largest temple and one of its most important ethnobotanical gardens share the 294-acre site. The National Tropical Botanical Garden, which is dedicated to the conservation of rare and medicinal plants from the tropical Pacific, maintains Kahanu. Most interesting is the canoe garden, landscaped with taro and other plants brought to Hawaii by early

Polynesian settlers. The scope is amazing, as the garden holds the world's largest breadfruit tree collection and a remarkable variety of coconut palms.

The garden paths also skirt **Pi'ilanihale Heiau**, an immense lava-stone platform reaching 450ft in length. The history of this astounding heiau is shrouded in mystery, but there's no doubt that it was an important religious site for Hawaiians. Archaeologists believe construction began as early as AD 1200 and the heiau was built in sequences. The final grand scale was the work of Pi'ilani (the heiau's name means House of Pi'ilani), the 14th-century Maui chief who is also credited with the construction of many of the coastal fishponds in the Hana area.

Since visiting Kahanu Garden takes a couple of hours, few day-trippers come this way and you may well have the place to yourself. The site, on Kalahu Point, is 1.5 miles down 'Ula'ino Rd from the Hana Hwy. The road is crossed by a streambed immediately before reaching the gardens; if it's dry you should be able to drive over it OK, but if it's been raining heavily don't even try.

WAI'ANAPANAPA STATE PARK

🌺 ourpick Swim in a cave, sun on a black-sand beach, explore ancient Hawaiian sites – this is one cool park. A sunny coastal trail and a seaside campground make it a tempting place to dig in for awhile. Honokalani Rd, which leads into Wai'anapanapa State Park, is just after the 32-mile marker. The road ends overlooking the jet-black sands at Pa'iloa Bay.

Sights

PA'ILOA BEACH

The park's beach is a stunner – hands down the prettiest black-sand beach on Maui. Walk on down, sunbathe, enjoy. But be cautious before jumping in. It's open ocean with a bottom that drops quickly and water conditions best suited for strong swimmers. Powerful rips are the norm (Pa'iloa means 'always splashing') and there have been drownings here. When it's very calm the area around the sea arch offers good snorkeling.

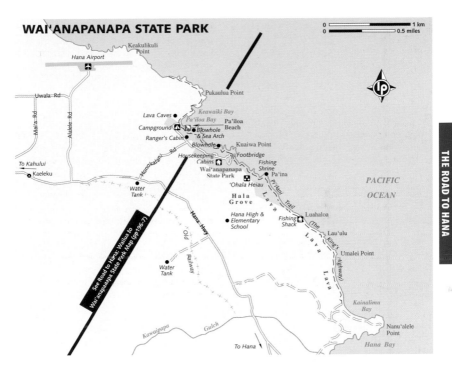

WAI'ANAPANAPA STATE PARK

LAVA CAVES

A 10-minute loop path north from the beach parking lot leads to a pair of impressive lava-tube caves. Their gardenlike exteriors are draped with ferns and colorful impatiens, while their interiors harbor deep spring-fed pools. Wai'anapanapa means 'glistening waters' and the pools' crystal-clear mineral waters reputedly rejuvenate the skin. They certainly will invigorate – these sunless pools are refreshingly brisk!

PI'ILANI TRAIL

This gem of a coastal trail leads 3 miles south from the park to Kainalimu Bay, just north of Hana Bay, offering splendid views along the way. It's one of those trails that packs a lot up front, so even if you just have time to do the first mile, you won't regret it. If you plan to hike the whole trail be sure to bring water, as it's unshaded the entire way, and good hiking shoes, as it gets rougher as you go along.

The route follows an ancient footpath known as the King's Highway that was the main land route between Hana and villages to the north. Some of the worn stepping stones along the path date from the time of Pi'ilani, the king who ruled Maui in the 14th century. The trail begins along the coast just below the camping area and parallels the ocean along lava sea cliffs. Just a few minutes along you'll pass a burial ground, a natural **sea arch** and a **blowhole** that roars to life whenever there's pounding surf. This is

Island Insights

On certain nights of the year, the waters in Wai'anapanapa State Park's lava-tube caves turn red. Legend says it's the blood of a princess and her lover who were killed in a fit of rage by the princess's jealous husband after he found them hiding together here. Less romantic types attribute the phenomenon to swarms of tiny bright-red shrimp called 'opaeula, which occasionally emerge from subterranean cracks in the lava.

Black-sand beach in Wai'anapanapa State Park

GREG ELMS

also the area where you're most likely to see endangered Hawaiian monk seals.

Perched above the sea at 0.7 miles are the remains of **'Ohala Heiau**, a place of worship to the harvest god Lono. A **fishing shrine** ahead on the left affords a good view south of basalt cliffs lined up all the way to Hana. Hala and ironwood encroaches the shoreline past the heiau. Round stones continue to mark the way across lava and a grassy clearing, fading briefly on the way over a rugged sea cliff. A dirt road comes in from the right as the trail arrives at **Luahaloa**, a ledge with a small **fishing shack**. Inland stands of ironwood heighten the beauty of the scenic last mile of cliff-top walking to **Kainalimu Bay**. Stepping stones hasten the approach to the bay ahead, as the trail dips down a shrubby ravine to a quiet black cobble beach. Dirt roads lead another mile from here south to Hana.

Sleeping

Fall asleep to the lullaby of the surf at one of the park's campsites on a shady lawn near the beach. It's a great place to camp but there is one caveat – this is the rainy side of the island, so it can get wet at any time. Plan accordingly. The park also has a dozen basic housekeeping cabins that are extremely popular and usually book up months in advance. See p269 for details on permits, fees and reservations.

EAST MAUI

Where do Mauians go when they want to get away?
Raw and rugged East Maui, the most isolated side of the island. Instead of golf courses and beach resorts, you'll see a face that's barely changed a speck for tourism. It all starts with the awesome Hana Highway, which bends along ocean cliffs, fantastical waterfalls and killer views, tiptoes through the quiet town of Hana, and continues on to yet more waterfalls and stop-for-a-dip swimming holes. The road to Hana is so special we've dedicated an entire chapter to it (p187). This chapter starts with time-honored Hana, where you'll relearn the meaning of s-l-o-w and talk story with people who actually take the time.

EAST MAUI
ITINERARIES

IN ONE DAY *This leg: 9 miles*

❶ **HAMOA BEACH (p212)** Strip down to your bathing suit and see for yourself why the legendary author James Michener called lovely Hamoa the only beach in the North Pacific that actually looked as if it belonged in the South Pacific.

❷ **WAILUA FALLS (p211)** Now *this* is a road trip: hairpin turns, one-lane bridges, everything lush and green, with orchids growing out of the rocks and waterfalls cascading down the cliffs. The star of it all, picture-perfect Wailua Falls, sits right by the roadside waiting to have its picture taken.

❸ **'OHE'O GULCH (p211)** Tromp around 'Ohe'o Gulch – dip into its heavenly pools, hike to its towering waterfalls and take a look at its ancient Hawaiian sites.

❹ **LINDBERGH'S GRAVE (p211)** Soak up the solitude that brought the great aviator to Kipahulu – the visitors at the peaceful churchyard where he's buried are likely to be just you and a sleepy cat curling up on your car hood.

IN TWO DAYS *This leg: 3 miles*

EAST MAUI

❺ **HANA TOWN (p206)** Day two is all about slowing down to experience Hana's aloha. Wander around the town center, taking in the generations-old Hasegawa General Store (p208) and the Wananalua Congregational Church, built of lava rock in 1838. Then stop by the Hana Coast Gallery (p208) to see the museum-quality art.

❻ **KAIHALULU BEACH (p207)** Grab a towel (bathing suit optional) and sneak off to Hana's hidden red-sand beach.

❼ **LYON'S HILL (p208)** Tie up your running shoes and jog up to the top of Lyon's

Hill to watch the sun set over this timeless town.

❽ **HANA BEACH PARK (p207)** Go see what's happening at everyone's favorite hangout. When ex-Beatle George Harrison lived in Hana, he'd occasionally be seen here in the evening strumming a tune with Hana folk. Come see who's here today.

❾ **PANIOLO BAR (p210)** Cap off the evening with a frosty drink and hula dancing at Hotel Hana-Maui's bar.

Coastal trees

SABRINA DALBESIO

FOR OLD HAWAII FLAVOR

❶ MAUI STABLES (p212) Take the reins and ride off into the wilderness on a horseback journey that mixes breathtaking views with Hawaiian storytelling. The Native Hawaiian guides lead you through drippingly luxuriant scenery and past the 400ft Waimoku Falls.

❷ HANA RANCH RESTAURANT TAKE-OUT (p209) Join the *paniolo* (cowboys) chowing down at the ocean-view picnic tables. What's for lunch? Why, barbecued burgers from free-range Hana cattle, of course.

❸ HANA CULTURAL CENTER (p208) Explore this museum inside and out. If it happens to be the first Tuesday of the month, you can watch the tiny period-piece courthouse transform from museum artifact into modern-day court, where Hana residents argue their speeding tickets.

❹ LUANA SPA RETREAT (p208) When was the last time you had a papaya-pineapple scrub followed by an *'awa 'alaea* (kava and red clay) wrap and a *lomi pohaku* (hot stone massage)? Oh, you say it's been a while?

EAST MAUI

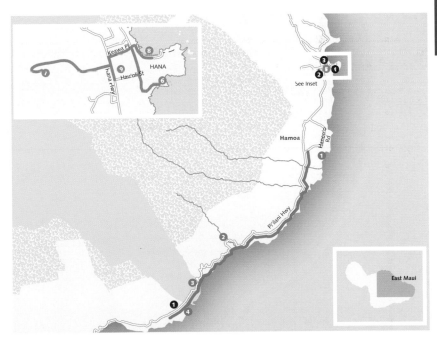

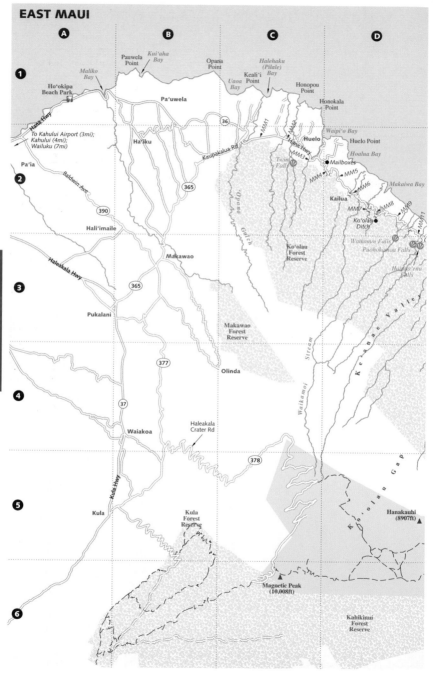

EAST MAUI

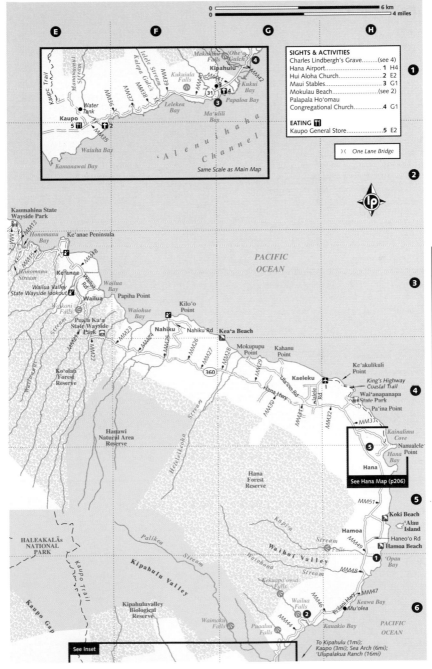

SIGHTS & ACTIVITIES

Charles Lindbergh's Grave	(see 4)
Hana Airport	1 H4
Hui Aloha Church	2 E2
Maui Stables	3 G1
Mokulau Beach	(see 2)
Palapala Ho'omau Congregational Church	4 G1

EATING 🍴

Kaupo General Store	5 E2

)(One Lane Bridge

See Hana Map (p206)

To Kipahulu (1mi);
Kaupo (3mi); Sea Arch (6mi);
'Ulupalakua Ranch (16mi)

See Inset

EAST MAUI

HANA
pop 1855

That long and winding road that separates Hana from the rest of Maui also contributes to its preservation as one of the few authentically Hawaiian communities left in the state. Many of its residents have Hawaiian blood and a strong sense of 'ohana (family). If you listen closely, you'll hear the words 'auntie' and 'uncle' a lot. There's a timeless rural character, and though 'Old Hawaii' is an oft-used cliché elsewhere, it's hard not to think of Hana in such terms.

Separated from Kahului by 54 bridges and almost as many miles, Hana is peaceful and low-key (save for the midday buzz of tourists passing through). Cows graze lazily in green pastures stretching up the hillsides. Neighbors chat over plate lunches at the beach. Even at Hana's famed hotel, the emphasis is on relaxation. Hana doesn't reveal itself in a quick pass-through, however. What's truly special about Hana comes only to those who stop and take the time to unwind.

HIGHLIGHTS

❶ **BEST BEACH:** Hamoa Beach (p212)
❷ **BEST VIEW:** Wailua Falls (p211)
❸ **BEST ACTIVITY:** Horseback riding at Maui Stables (p212)
❹ **BEST SWIMMING HOLE:** 'Ohe'o Gulch (p211)
❺ **BEST TARO PANCAKE BREAKFAST:** East Maui Taro Festival (p208)

Highlights are numbered on the map on pp204–05.

History

It's hard to imagine little Hana as the epicenter of Maui, but this village produced many of ancient Hawai'i's most influential ali'i (chiefs). Hana's great 14th-century chief Pi'ilani marched from here to conquer rivals in Wailuku and Lahaina, and become the first leader of unified Maui.

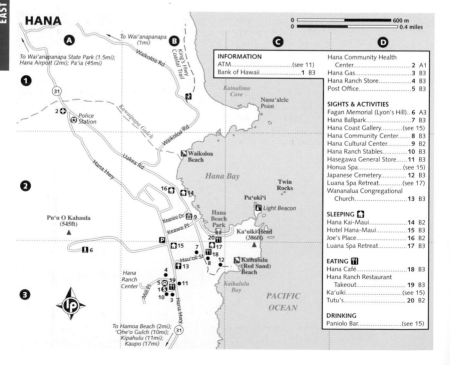

HANA

INFORMATION	
ATM	(see 11)
Bank of Hawaii	**1** B3

Hana Community Health	
Center	**2** A1
Hana Gas	**3** B3
Hana Ranch Store	**4** B3
Post Office	**5** B3

SIGHTS & ACTIVITIES	
Fagan Memorial (Lyon's Hill)	**6** A3
Hana Ballpark	**7** B3
Hana Coast Gallery	(see 15)
Hana Community Center	**8** B3
Hana Cultural Center	**9** B2
Hana Ranch Stables	**10** B3
Hasegawa General Store	**11** B3
Honua Spa	(see 15)
Japanese Cemetery	**12** B3
Luana Spa Retreat	(see 17)
Wananalua Congregational	
Church	**13** B3

SLEEPING	
Hana Kai-Maui	**14** B2
Hotel Hana-Maui	**15** B3
Joe's Place	**16** B2
Luana Spa Retreat	**17** B3

EATING	
Hana Café	**18** B3
Hana Ranch Restaurant	
Takeout	**19** B3
Ka'uiki	(see 15)
Tutu's	**20** B2

DRINKING	
Paniolo Bar	(see 15)

The landscape changed dramatically in 1849 when ex-whaler George Wilfong bought 60 acres of land to plant sugarcane. Hana went on to become a booming plantation town, complete with a narrow-gauge railroad connecting the fields to the Hana Mill. In the 1940s Hana could no longer compete with larger sugar operations in Central Maui and the mill went bust.

Enter San Francisco businessman Paul Fagan, who purchased 14,000 acres in Hana in 1943. Starting with 300 Herefords, Fagan converted the cane fields to ranch land. A few years later he opened a six-room hotel as a getaway resort for well-to-do friends and brought his minor-league baseball team, the San Francisco Seals, to Hana for spring training. That's when visiting sports journalists gave the town its moniker, 'Heavenly Hana.' Hana Ranch remains the backbone of Hana's economy and its hillside pastures graze some 2000 head of cattle worked by *paniolo*.

Orientation & Information

Hana closes up early. If you're going to be heading back late, get gas in advance – the sole gas station, **Hana Gas** (☎ 248-7671; cnr Mill Rd & Hana Hwy; ◔ 7:30am-6:30pm), has limited hours.

Hana Ranch Center (Mill Pl) is the commercial center of town. It has a **post office** (☎ 248-8258; ◔ 8am-4:30pm Mon-Fri); a tiny **Bank of Hawaii** (☎ 248 8015; ◔ 3 4:30pm Mon-Thu, to 6pm Fri); and the **Hana Ranch Store** (☎ 248-8261; ◔ 7am-7:30pm), which sells groceries and liquor. There's no ATM at the bank, but **Hasegawa**

General Store (☎ 248-8231; 5165 Hana Hwy; ◔ 7am-7pm Mon-Sat, 8am-6pm Sun) has one. The **Hana Community Health Center** (☎ 248-8294; 4590 Hana Hwy; ◔ 8am-5pm) is at the north side of town.

Beaches

HANA BEACH PARK

Some towns have a central plaza. Hana's pulse beats from this beach park. Families come here to take the kids for a splash, to picnic on the black-sand beach and to strum their ukuleles with friends.

When water conditions are very calm, snorkeling and diving are good out in the direction of the light beacon. Currents can be strong, and snorkelers shouldn't venture beyond the beacon. Surfers head to **Waikoloa Beach**, at the northern end of the bay.

KAIHALULU (RED SAND) BEACH

A favored haunt of nude sunbathers, this hidden cove on the south side of Ka'uiki Head is a beauty in contrasts, with rich red sand set against brilliant turquoise waters. The cove is partly protected by a lava outcrop, but currents can be powerful when the surf's up (Kaihalulu means 'roaring sea'). Water drains through a break on the left side, which should be avoided. Your best chance of finding calm waters is in the morning.

The path to the beach starts across the lawn at the lower side of **Hana Community Center**, and continues as a steep 10-minute trail down to the cove. En route you'll pass an overgrown **Japanese cemetery**, a remnant of the sugarcane days.

Hana Beach Park

GREG ELMS

EAST MAUI

Island Insights

Ka'uiki Head, the 386ft red cinder hill at the southeast side of Hana Bay, was once the site of a royal fort. The islet at the tip of the point, which now holds a light beacon, is Pu'uki'i (Image Hill), a name that can be traced to a huge deity image that king 'Umi erected here in the 16th century to ward off invaders. Queen Ka'ahumanu, one of the most powerful women in Hawaiian history, was born in a cave here in 1768.

Sights

✿ HANA CULTURAL CENTER

☎ 248-8622; www.hookele.com/hccm; 4974 Uakea Rd; admission $2; ⏱ 10am-4pm

Soak up a little local history at this down-home museum displaying Hawaiian artifacts, wood carvings and hand-stitched quilts. And don't miss the four authentically reconstructed thatched *hale* (houses) at the side of the museum, which can be seen even if you arrive outside of opening hours. The grounds also contain a three-bench courthouse (c 1871).

HANA COAST GALLERY

☎ 248-8638; 5031 Hana Hwy; ⏱ 9am-5pm

Even if you're not shopping, visit this gallery at the north side of Hotel Hana-Maui to browse the fascinating collection of wooden bowls, paintings and Hawaiian featherwork.

Activities

Hana Ranch Stables (☎ 270-5258; Mill Rd; 1hr ride $60), which books through Hotel Hana-Maui, gives horseback riders the option to trot along Hana's black-lava coastline or head for the hills into green cattle pasture.

Other activities, including **kayaking** and **surfing lessons**, can also be arranged through Hotel Hana-Maui. For a good sunset walk, take the 15-minute **hike** to the top of Lyon's Hill, which is topped by a big white cross, a **memorial** to former ranch owner Paul Fagan; the trail begins opposite Hotel Hana-Maui.

Ready for pampering? The posh **Honua**

Spa (☎ 270-5290; Hotel Hana-Maui, 5031 Hana Hwy; treatments $85-240; ⏱ 9am-8pm) can coddle you with massages and hot stone rubs. Or, better yet, take it Hawaiian style at **Luana Spa Retreat** (☎ 248-8855; 5050 Uakea Rd; treatments $50-175; ⏱ by appointment), with *lomilomi* massages and ginger-seaweed wraps in a traditional setting.

Festivals & Events

our pick **East Maui Taro Festival** (www.tarofestival .org) Hana at its finest. This weekend event in April at Hana Ballpark celebrates all things native, with outrigger canoe races, a taro pancake breakfast, hula dancing and some of Hawaii's best slack key guitarists.

Hana Relays (www.virr.com) The ultimate relay road race, held the second Saturday in September, follows the Hana Hwy for 52 breathtaking miles from Kahului to Hana Ballpark.

Eating

Hana has just a couple of stores with limited grocery selections, so if you're staying awhile stock up in Kahului before heading down.

TUTU'S   Plate Lunch $

☎ 248-8224; Hana Beach Park; snacks $3-8; ⏱ 8:30am-4pm

This local-style beach grill serves up shave ice, plate lunches and sandwiches. Grab a table on the sand and you've got yourself an instant picnic at Hana's favorite family beach.

HANA CAFÉ   Café $

5050 Uakea Rd; meals $5-10; ⏱ 10am-4pm

Only a few lucky travelers stumble upon this hidden gem set back from the road

WHO NEEDS A MALL?

For a century, the family-run, tin-roofed **Hasegawa General Store** has been Hana's sole general store, its narrow jam-packed aisles selling everything from fishing gear and machetes to soda pop and bags of poi. This icon of mom-and-pop shops is always crowded with locals picking up supplies, travelers stopping for snacks and sightseers buying 'I Survived the Hana Highway' T-shirts.

ISLAND VOICES

NAME: NANCY PLENTY
OCCUPATION: MASSAGE THERAPIST; OWNER, LUANA SPA RETREAT
RESIDENCE: HANA

How did you get started? I've been doing massage at spas for about 20 years, starting on the Big Island. I got in with the Four Seasons in Wailea when it opened. I was the lead massage therapist there for 11 years.

What brought you to Hana? I met my partner, Barry Chang, through canoe paddling about 10 years ago. He's from a third-generation Hana family. He was living in Kahului but wanted to go back to Hana and do something with the family land. The location, on a hill overlooking Hana Bay, is spectacular and we decided to create a spa retreat there. We started going back and forth on the weekends. It was completely overgrown, nobody had done anything for 30 years. We started in with our machetes, hacking away. We've done everything ourselves on a shoestring.

How is Hana different from Wailea? The really special thing about Hana is that it's still an intact Hawaiian village. The families go back generations. Everybody knows everybody else, whereas Wailea has no historical context – everything is new and manufactured.

What's unique about Luana? We wanted the experience to be culturally authentic. We built a traditional Hawaiian *hale* (house), designed by Francis Sinenci. He's quite well known and has sort of revived the art of *hale* building. Everything was harvested by hand, every leaf tied on individually; there are no nails, it's all handcrafted. The Hawaiian culture is about balance and sustainability. That's what we're trying to emulate with our spa – keeping as small a footprint as possible and sharing that point of view with people.

What's there to do in Hana? A great place to meet local people is the Hana Ranch Restaurant Takeout (below) window – everyone calls it 'the coffee shop.' The guys go up there and get their breakfast. It's the place to hang out. I always recommend Kahanu Garden (p198) – it's such a beautiful place. And the Hana Cultural Center (opposite) is really sweet.

opposite Hana Ballpark. It's just a simple outdoor café, but it serves delish feta quiche and healthy organic salads. On Sunday and Monday there's homemade Thai food worth lining up for.

HANA RANCH RESTAURANT TAKEOUT
Comfort Food $
our pick ☎ 248-8255; Hana Ranch Center, Mill Rd; meals $6-12; ☒ 6:30am-4pm Wed, Fri & Sat, to 7pm Sun-Tue & Thu
This is the busiest spot in town, and for good reason. Everybody comes for the mammoth burgers made of free-range

Hana beef. Vegetarians aren't left out either: the taro burger offers a slice of Hana before ranching took hold. Good breakfast fare and plate lunches, too.

KA'UIKI
Hawaii Regional $$$$
☎ 248-8211; Hotel Hana-Maui, 5031 Hana Hwy; prix fixe dinner $50-60; ☒ lunch & dinner
Don't bother with lunch – all the magic here occurs after sunset. Dinner is a locavore's treat, with Hana-caught fish, Nahiku-grown greens and other goodies harvested locally. Nearly everything is organic. The flavors are an innovative fusion of Hawaiian

and Asian influences. Fridays are casual fun with a buffet spread and hula show.

Drinking & Entertainment

PANIOLO BAR
☎ 248-8211; Hotel Hana-Maui, 5031 Hana Hwy; ⊗ 11am-9:30pm

A classy place to enjoy a drink, this open-air bar at Hotel Hana-Maui has live Hawaiian music most evenings, and on Thursday and Saturday hula dancers as well.

Sleeping

JOE'S PLACE   Inn $
☎ 248-7033; www.joesrentals.com; 4870 Uakea Rd; r with shared/private bathroom $50/60

Hana's only nod to the budget traveler offers a dozen basic rooms. The linoleum is worn and the carpets hail back to another era, but there's a fresh coat of paint on the walls and the place is kept spanking clean.

🌿 LUANA SPA RETREAT   Cottage $$
☎ 248-8855; www.luanaspa.com; 5050 Uakea Rd; d $120

Just you, a yurt and a view. On a hill overlooking Hana Bay, this unique charmer is a cross between camping and a cottage. The yurt sports a well-equipped kitchenette, a comfy queen bed and even a stereo with Hawaiian music. Shower outdoors in a bamboo enclosure, and enjoy the scent of native flowers – all in all, this is aloha 'aina (love of the land) at its finest.

HANA KAI-MAUI   Condo $$$
☎ 248-8426, 800-346-2772; www.hanakai.com; 1533 Uakea Rd; studios from $170

If you were any closer to the water you'd need a life raft. Hana's only condo complex is a stone's throw from Hana's hottest surfing beach. Although the walls are thin, the sound of the surf drowns out neighboring chatter.

HOTEL HANA-MAUI   Boutique Hotel $$$$
☎ 248-8211, 800-321-4262; www.hotelhanamaui .com; 5031 Hana Hwy; r from $395; 🛋

Maui's famed getaway hotel. Everything's airy and open, and rich with Hawaiian accents, from island art in the lobby to hand-stitched quilts on the beds. Rooms have a subdued elegance, with bleached hardwood floors, ceiling fans and French doors opening to trellised patios. Delightfully absent are electronic gadgets – even alarm clocks!

KILLER WEED

According to legend, Hana folks once killed an evil shark-man who lived on a bluff near Mu'olea, the area between mile markers 46 and 47 north of Kipahulu. After burning the shark-man's body, they dropped his ashes into a tide pool, but the shark-man returned – this time in the form of limu make o Hana, the 'deadly seaweed of Hana.' The tide pool where the red seaweed was found was made kapu (taboo), though warriors learned to tip their spears with the toxin to make them more deadly.

Inspired by the legend, which was written down by a Hawaiian scholar in the 19th century, scientists from the University of Hawai'i came to the Mu'olea tide pool to look for limu make o Hana in the early 1960s. The legend said the seaweed resembled 'the suckers of an octopus.' What they found was not a seaweed but a previously unknown type of soft coral, related to the sea anemone. When tested, researchers discovered the toxin it bore, which they named palytoxin, was one of the most deadly substances ever found in nature. Something like palytoxin has since been found in certain toxic fish, and may be related to a symbiotic algae that grows with the coral. The active properties in limu make o Hana are being tested as a possible treatment for cancer.

Maui County, the Trust for Public Lands and the Office of Hawaiian Affairs have jointly purchased 70 acres at Mu'olea Point (Map pp204-05), including the tide pools where the limu is found. The property is culturally important in other ways, too. It includes the ruins of a heiau that seems to be aligned with the Pleiades constellation, plus a summer residence of King David Kalakaua and rare native plants. Hawaiian cultural organizations, including Kipahulu 'Ohana (p186) are hoping to eventually restore the heiau and establish educational programs there.

Top Picks

WATER WINNERS
- **Wailua Falls** (below)
- **Hamoa Beach** (p212)
- **Kaihalulu Beach** (p207)

Getting There & Around

There are two ways to get to Hana: a drive down the winding Hana Hwy (p187) or a prop-plane flight into Hana Airport (p285). Dollar Rent-A-Car (p290) has a booth at the Hana Airport. The Maui Bus doesn't serve East Maui.

BEYOND HANA

South from Hana, the road winds down to Kipahulu, passing 'Ohe'o Gulch, the southern end of Haleakalā National Park. This incredibly lush stretch brims with raw natural beauty. Between its twists and turns, one-lane bridges and drivers trying to take in all the sights, it's a slow-moving 10 miles, so allow yourself an hour.

Wailua Falls

Spectacular Wailua Falls (Map pp204-05) plunges an awesome 100ft just beyond the road. It appears soon after the 45-mile marker and you won't need anyone to point this one out, as tourists are always here snapping photos.

'Ohe'o Gulch

our pick Fantastic falls, cool pools, paths galore. The indisputable highlight of the drive past Hana is 'Ohe'o Gulch (Map pp204-05), aka the Kipahulu section of Haleakalā National Park. See p184 for full details.

Kipahulu

Less than a mile south of 'Ohe'o Gulch lies the little village of Kipahulu. It's hard to imagine this sedate community was once a bustling sugar-plantation town. After the mill shut down in 1922 most people left for jobs elsewhere. Among modest homes, organic farms and back-to-the-landers living off the grid are a scattering of exclusive estates, including the former home of famed aviator Charles Lindbergh.

SIGHTS
LINDBERGH'S GRAVE

Charles Lindbergh moved to remote Kipahulu in 1968. Although he relished the privacy he found here, he occasionally emerged as a spokesperson for conservation issues. When Lindbergh learned he had terminal cancer in 1974, he decided to forgo hospital care on the mainland and came home to Maui to live out his final days. Lindbergh now lies at rest in the graveyard of **Palapala Ho'omau Congregational Church** (Map pp204-05). The 1864 church is also notable for its window painting of a Polynesian Christ draped in the red-and-yellow feather capes that only Hawai'i's highest chiefs wore.

EAST MAUI

Hiking the Kuloa Point Trail (p185), 'Ohe'o Gulch   GREG ELMS

Lindbergh's desire to be out of the public eye may still be at play, because many visitors fail to find his grave, getting the location mixed up with St Paul's Church, which sits on the highway three-quarters of a mile south of 'Ohe'o Gulch. The dirt drive to Palapala Ho'omau church is half a mile beyond that, on the ocean side of the road immediately after the 41-mile marker. The grave, adjacent to the church, is surrounded by lava rocks and a little fence.

ACTIVITIES

our pick **Maui Stables** (Map pp204-05; ☎ 248-7799; www.mauistables.com; 3hr ride $120; ☼ departs 10am), halfway between the 40- and 41-mile markers, offers memorable trail rides that delve into local legends while climbing the scenic slopes above Kipahulu. The stables are Native Hawaiian–owned.

PI'ILANI HIGHWAY

The most remote stretch of Maui, the Pi'ilani Hwy between Kipahulu and 'Ulupalakua Ranch, became even more remote following an October 2006 earthquake that knocked down bridges and destabilized roadside cliffs, closing the highway. At publication time, Kipahulu was the end of the road.

Although moving slowly, there are plans to repair and reopen the road. It's an adventurous 25-mile jaunt that winds like a drunken cowboy through lonesome boonies. Come prepared; there are no services between Hana and the Upcountry.

To see if the road's open, phone the **county public works department** (☎ 248-8254; ☼ 6:30am-3pm Mon-Fri) or contact **Kipahulu Visitor Center** (☼ 248-7375) at 'Ohe'o Gulch.

Kaupo

Near the 35-mile marker is Kaupo, a scattered community of *paniolo*, many of them fourth-generation ranch hands working at Kaupo Ranch. The only commercial venture on the entire road is the **Kaupo General Store** (Map pp204-05; ☎ 248-8054; ☼ irregular).

Kaupo's prettiest site is the whitewashed **Hui Aloha Church** (Map pp204-05), circa 1859, which sits picturesquely above the black-sand **Mokulau Beach** (Map p204-05).

DETOUR ➡

HANEO'O ROAD LOOP

Author James Michener was so taken by the coastal sights along this 1.5-mile loop drive (Map pp204-05) that he compared them to the South Pacific. To see what tickled him, take the turnoff onto Haneo'o Rd just before the 50-mile marker.

At the base of a red cinder hill less than a half-mile from the start of the loop, the chocolate-brown sands of **Koki Beach** attract local surfers. The offshore isle topped by a few coconut palms is **'Alau Island**, a seabird sanctuary. Incidentally, those trees are a green refreshment stand of sorts, planted by Hana residents to provide themselves with drinking coconuts while fishing from the island.

A little further is **Hamoa Beach**, whose lovely gray sands are maintained by Hotel Hana-Maui but are open to all. When surf's up, surfers and boogie boarders flock here, though be aware of rip currents. When seas are calm, swimming is good in the cove. Facilities include showers and restrooms.

Kaupo to 'Ulupalakua Ranch

Near the 31-mile marker a short 4WD road runs down to **Nu'u Bay**, favored by locals for fishing and swimming. If you're tempted to hit the water, stay close to shore, as riptides inhabit the open ocean beyond. In another mile you'll reach dramatic **Huakini Bay**, whipped by violent surf. After the 29-mile marker, keep an eye out for a natural lava **sea arch**; a footpath leads to cliffs for close-up views of the arch and spouting blowholes.

Near the 19-mile marker the road crosses expansive **lava flows** dating from 1790, Haleakalā's last-gasp eruption. This flow, part of the Kanaio Natural Area Reserve, is the same one that covers the La Pérouse Bay area (p140). It's black and barren all the way down to the sea.

As you approach 'Ulupalakua Ranch, groves of fragrant eucalyptus trees take over and you find yourself back in civilization at Tedeschi Vineyards (p164). Cheers!

SIDE TRIPS: LANA'I & MOLOKA'I

Itching to get off the beaten track? Just a ferry skip across the channel, Maui's sister islands of Lana'i and Moloka'i are waiting to be explored. Both have deep roots in farming, but each has taken a different route toward tourism. Lana'i has plowed under its pineapple fields and sprouted two of the most pampering resort hotels in Hawaii. Moloka'i, on the other hand, has barely changed a wink in decades – its leading tourist attraction remains a mule ride. But on both of these slow-paced islands you'll find people with time to sit and talk story, wild landscapes untouched by development and miles of deserted beaches just waiting to be explored. Oh, and enjoy the ferry ride.

LANA'I & MOLOKA'I
ITINERARIES

IN TWO DAYS *This leg: 30 miles*

❶ HULOPO'E BEACH (p221) If you have two days for Lana'i, start your first day swimming and snorkeling at this pristine marine sanctuary with its vibrant coral gardens and colorful fish.

❷ LANA'I CITY (p217) In the afternoon, take a stroll around this classic plantation town. Watch the sun set over the majestic pines at Dole Park and then join the friendly islanders dining on local grinds at **Blue Ginger Café (p219)**.

❸ MUNRO TRAIL (p224) On day two, pick up a walking stick and hit this trail along the spine of Lana'i for panoramic views of everything the island has to offer.

❹ GARDEN OF THE GODS (p224) When you're done hiking take a drive or a mountain-bike ride out to these unusual rock formations, which glow eerily in the late afternoon light. On the way back stroll through **Kanepu'u Preserve (p223)**, the last native dryland forest in Hawaii.

❺ LANA'I CITY GRILLE (p220) Grab a seat by the fireplace in this classic century-old dining room and order up the best Lana'i venison dish you'll ever taste.

IN FOUR DAYS *This leg: 70 miles*

❻ PALA'AU STATE PARK (p237) If you have two days for each island, plan the first two as above. Then fly to Moloka'i and start day three by driving to the end of Hwy 470 to relish the stunning cliff-top view of Kalaupapa Peninsula.

❼ KALA'E, KUALAPU'U & HO'OLEHUA (p235) On the way back get the buzz on Moloka'i's agricultural roots at the **RW Meyer Sugar Mill Museum (p237)** in Kala'e. At lunchtime there's no better place to be than **Kualapu'u Cookhouse (p235)**. Next see what's happening today in the farm biz with a stop at **Purdy's Macadamia Nut Farm (p235)** in Ho'olehua.

❽ PAPOHAKU BEACH PARK (p240) For a long walk on a glorious windswept beach make your way to this unfrequented gem on Moloka'i's West End.

❾ HULA SHORES (p231) Listen to the waves lapping at your feet as you dine on Southern comfort fare and toast the magnificent sunset view with a frosty drink.

❿ KALAUPAPA PENINSULA (p237) You've seen the peninsula from the overlook – now it's time to see it up close. On day four hike or take the **Molokai Mule Ride (p239)** down to one of the most unusual places in the national park system.

⓫ EAST MOLOKA'I (p232) The prettiest darn road in Moloka'i begs a drive in the afternoon.

Bird of Paradise

NED FRIARY

FOR EXPLORERS

❶ HALAWA VALLEY (p233) It's at the end of a one-lane road – and, yep, that means you're sharing the one lane with oncoming traffic – but your first glimpse of this paradisical valley provides ample reward.

❷ KAMAKOU PRESERVE (p235) This treasure doesn't come easy, but if you want to see a radiant slice of raw Hawaii make your way up to this prehistoric forest of rare native trees and remote valleys.

❸ KAUNOLU (p225) You're going to have to hike a mile or two to reach this forgotten Hawaiian village – the road's always a

washout. But what an awesome place to have to yourself.

❹ SHIPWRECK BEACH (p222) Heaven for beachcombers. You can walk this nearly endless beach as far as your thirst for adventure takes you – just bring plenty of water.

❺ POLIHUA BEACH (p224) This one's so remote that green sea turtles nest right on the shore. It's at the end of the road – a rutted and boulder-strewn dirt road, that is – but the occasional surfer makes it here. And if you're a sun worshipper it's the perfect spot to get your all-over tan.

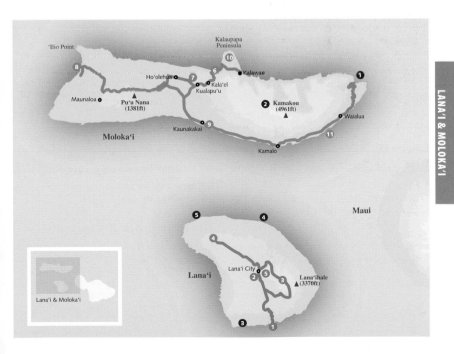

LANA'I & MOLOKA'I

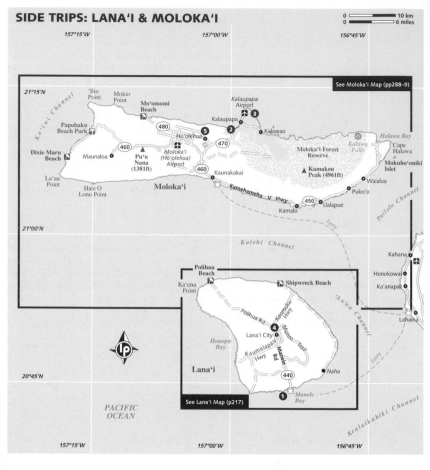

SIDE TRIPS: LANA'I & MOLOKA'I

LANA'I

pop 3300

If you didn't know Lana'i was once the world's largest pineapple plantation, well, you'd never know it now by looking. The island, which is 98% privately owned by Castle & Cooke, has replaced its pineapples with a crop of wealthy vacationers. Almost all of Lana'i's residents still live in Lana'i City, the old plantation town built during the pineapple era. Lana'i's top attraction is gorgeous Hulopo'e Beach at the southern side of the island. Explorers who venture past town will find scores of red-dirt roads,

a handful of archaeological sites, and acres and acres of solitude.

Getting There & Around

Hands down the best island hop between Maui and Lana'i is the **Expeditions** (☎ 661-3756, 800-695-2624; www.go-lanai.com; adult/child one way $25/20) ferry. Spinner dolphins are a common sight with morning sails. The boat leaves Lahaina Harbor (p54) at 6:45am, 9:15am, 12:45pm, 3:15pm and 5:45pm, arriving at Manele Boat Harbor in

HIGHLIGHTS

❶ **BEST BEACH:** Hulopo'e Beach (p221)
❷ **BEST VIEW:** Kalaupapa Overlook (p237)
❸ **BEST ACTIVITY:** Molokai Mule Ride (p239)
❹ **BEST PLANTATION TOWN:** Lana'i City (right)
❺ **BEST HOMEGROWN FARM:** Purdy's Macadamia Nut Farm (p235)

Highlights are numbered on the map on p216.

Lana'i about an hour later. The return boat leaves Lana'i at 8am, 10:30am, 2pm, 4:30pm and 6:45pm. Tickets are sold at Lahaina Harbor between 6am and 4:45pm; at other times, or if boarding at Lana'i, buy your ticket on the boat.

You can also fly to Lana'i, though it'll run you more money and is typically less convenient; see p285 for details.

The only rental company on the island, **Lana'i City Service** (☎ 565-7227, 800-533-7808; 1036 Lana'i Ave, Lana'i City; ⏱ 7am-7pm), is an affiliate of Dollar. Expect to pay $140 a day for a 4WD Jeep Wrangler. And you'll need a 4WD to do any serious exploring, since there are only three paved roads outside of Lana'i City.

Lana'i City Service also provides taxi service for $5 between Lana'i City and the airport, and for $10 between Lana'i City and Manele Harbor.

Expeditions ferry passengers can buy a $10 shuttle ticket at the ferry booth in Lahaina that's good for a return trip between Manele Bay and Lana'i City.

LANA'I CITY

Don't be fooled by the name of this little place – the nearest real city is an island away! Lana'i City glows with small-town charm, its tin-roofed houses and shops scarcely changed since the plantation days. Walk around, soak up the flavor, catch a crimson sunset over the lofty pine trees... there's something truly special here.

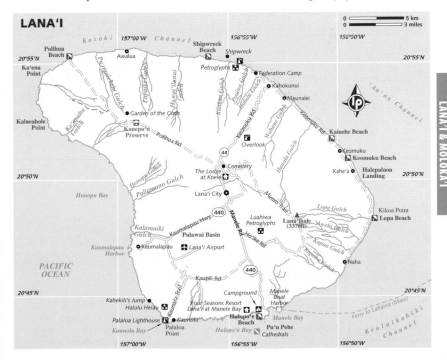

LANA'I & MOLOKA'I

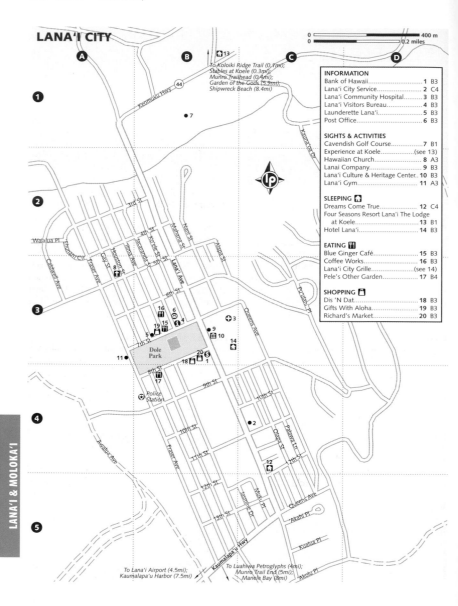

LANA'I CITY

To Koloiki Ridge Trail (0.1mi);
Stables at Koele (0.3mi);
Munro Trailhead (0.4mi);
Garden of the Gods (5.9mi);
Shipwreck Beach (8.4mi)

INFORMATION	
Bank of Hawaii....................	1 B3
Lana'i City Service..............	2 C4
Lana'i Community Hospital......	3 B3
Lana'i Visitors Bureau..........	4 B3
Launderette Lana'i..............	5 B3
Post Office.......................	6 B3

SIGHTS & ACTIVITIES	
Cavendish Golf Course...........	7 B1
Experience at Koele..............	(see 13)
Hawaiian Church.................	8 A3
Lanai Company...................	9 B3
Lana'i Culture & Heritage Center.	10 B3
Lana'i Gym......................	11 A3

SLEEPING	
Dreams Come True................	12 C4
Four Seasons Resort Lana'i The Lodge	
at Koele.......................	13 B1
Hotel Lana'i....................	14 B3

EATING	
Blue Ginger Café.................	15 B3
Coffee Works....................	16 B3
Lana'i City Grille..............	(see 14)
Pele's Other Garden.............	17 B4

SHOPPING	
Dis 'N Dat......................	18 B3
Gifts With Aloha................	19 B3
Richard's Market................	20 B3

Orientation & Information

The town is laid out in a sensible grid pattern, and almost all shops and services border central Dole Park.

Bank of Hawaii (☎ 565-6426; 460 8th St) Has a 24-hour ATM.

Lana'i Community Hospital (☎ 565-6411; 628 7th St) Offers 24-hour emergency medical services.

Lana'i Visitors Bureau (☎ 565-7600, 800-947-4774; www.visitlanai.net; 431 7th St; ⏲ 9am-4pm Mon-Fri)

Launderette Lana'i (☎ 565-7628; cnr Fraser & 7th Sts; ⏲ 6am-9pm) Self-service coin laundry.

Post office (☎ 565-6517; 620 Jacaranda St; ⊙ 9am-4:30pm Mon-Fri, 10am-noon Sat)

Sights

'Sights' are pretty light on the ground, but then again the whole town is a sight in itself and fun to stroll around. Visit the volunteer-run **Lana'i Culture & Heritage Center** (☎ 565-3240; 111 Lana'i Ave; admission free; ⊙ 9am-3pm Mon-Fri) for a peek into Lana'i's past. If you happen to be here on Sunday morning, swing by the **Hawaiian church** (cnr Houston & 5th Sts) and you'll be serenaded with choir music.

Activities

The public **Lana'i Gym** (☎ 565-3939; cnr Fraser Ave & 7th St; admission free; ⊙ 8am-4:30pm Mon & Thu-Sat) has a 75ft-long pool and a couple of tennis courts. The **activities desk** (☎ 565-7300; ⊙ 6:30am-6:30pm) at the Lodge at Koele (p220) rents mountain bikes for $8/40 per hour/day.

GOLF

The Greg Norman–designed **Experience at Koele** (☎ 565-4653; greens fee $185-240; ⊙ 8am-6:30pm) offers world-class golfing with grand vistas. It's as challenging as it is beautiful, with a signature 17th hole dropping 250ft to a wooded ravine.

Just below the manicured greens of Koele, but a world away, lies the **Cavendish Golf Course**, a nine-hole course where the locals tee off. It's open to all, free of dress codes and fees, although there is a donation box where visitors can drop in a few greenbacks.

HIKING

The **Koloiki Ridge Trail**, a 5-mile return hike, leads up to one of the most scenic parts of the Munro Trail (p224). It takes about 2¾ hours return and offers ridge-top views of remote valleys, Maui and Moloka'i.

The trail begins at the rear of the Lodge at Koele on the paved path that leads to the golf clubhouse. From there, follow the signposted path uphill past Norfolk pines until you reach a hilltop bench with a plaque bearing the poem *If* by Rudyard Kipling. Enjoy the view and then continue through the trees until you reach a chain-link fence. Go around the right side of the fence and continue up the hillside toward the power lines.

Top Picks

LANA'I & MOLOKA'I FOR KIDS

- **Tide pools at Hulopo'e Beach** (p221)
- **Pony rides at Stables at Koele** (below)
- **Flying a kite** (p239)
- **Decorating and mailing home a coconut** (p236)

At the top of the pass, follow the trail down through a thicket of guava trees until you reach an abandoned dirt service road, which you'll turn left on. You'll soon intersect with the Munro Trail; turn right on it and after a few minutes you'll pass Kukui Gulch, named for the candlenut trees that grow there. Continue along the trail until you reach a thicket of tall sisal plants; about 50yd after that bear right to reach Koloiki Ridge, where you'll be rewarded with panoramas.

HORSEBACK RIDING

The **Stables at Koele** (☎ 565-7300; trail rides $95; ⊙ departs 9am and 1:30pm) offers two-hour trail rides with scenic views of Maui and Lana'i. And if the *keiki* (children) are ready to cowboy down too, pony rides are available on request for just $10 per 10 minutes.

Festivals & Events

Lana'i's main bash, the **Pineapple Festival** (www.visitlanai.net), is held on the first weekend in July to celebrate the island's pineapple past with local grinds, games and live music at Dole Park.

Eating

COFFEE WORKS   Café $
☎ 565-6962; 604 'Ilima Ave; snacks $2-4; ⊙ 5am-4pm Mon-Fri, 10am-6pm Sat & Sun
Get your java fix here. Along with Kona coffee and jolting espressos, you'll find delicious carrot cake.

BLUE GINGER CAFÉ   Café $
our pick ☎ 565-6363; 409 7th St; breakfast & lunch $5-8, dinner $8-15; ⊙ 6am-8pm
If you need to quiet a growling stomach, or are just looking for a tasty pastry, this

friendly bakery-café will fill the bill. Don't be put off by the cement floors and plastic chairs – the food here is first-rate. For the best in local flavor, order the panko-crusted chicken.

🌺 PELE'S OTHER GARDEN   Café $$
☎ 565-9628; cnr 8th & Houston Sts; lunch $5-8, dinner $10-19; ☺ 11am-3pm & 5-8pm Mon-Sat
This fab little place serves up innovative pastas, gourmet pizzas and a delish garlic shrimp salad made with Lana'i-grown organic greens. Grab one of the tables out on the front porch and watch Lana'i City's traffic trickle by.

LANA'I CITY GRILLE   Hawaii Regional $$$$
☎ 565-7211; Hotel Lana'i, 828 Lana'i Ave; mains $26-36; ☺ dinner Wed-Sun
It may come as a surprise, but the island's best Hawaii Regional Cuisine (see p261) is found sequestered in this century-old hotel, not in the fancy resorts. For real local flavor, order the Lana'i venison with wild mushroom risotto. The fireplaced dining room glows with period charm.

Entertainment

Lana'i shuts the lights out early, but the Lodge at Koele (right) has live music in its 'great hall' nightly and Lana'i City Grille (above) has Hawaiian music on Friday evenings. If you're here on the first Thursday

of the month, join townsfolk at Dole Park for Stars Under the Stars, a free showing of classic movies outdoors on a 20ft screen.

Shopping

Shops and galleries encircle Dole Park, so stroll around and see what catches your fancy. A good place to start is Gifts with Aloha (☎ 565-6589; 363 7th St), which has everything from aloha shirts to ukuleles, or Dis 'N Dat (☎ 565-9170; 418 8th St), a cheery shack with an eclectic collection. Richard's Market (☎ 565-6047; 434 8th St) sells groceries and wine as well as general-store items like T-shirts and sandals.

Sleeping

DREAMS COME TRUE   Inn $$
☎ 565-6961, 800-566-6961; www.dreamscometrue lanai.com; 547 12th St; r $112, 4-bedroom house $450; ☐
This spruced-up plantation house fuses antiques-laden charm with cozy comforts like Jacuzzi baths. Guests have access to a well-equipped kitchen and the yard abounds with fruit just waiting to be picked. The owners can help you arrange activities.

HOTEL LANA'I   Independent Hotel $$
our pick ☎ 565-7211, 800-795-7211; www.hotel lanai.com; 828 Lana'i Ave; r incl breakfast $139-159, cottage $209
Built by Jim Dole in 1923 to house plantation guests, this rustic 10-room lodge retains its original charm, with pedestal sinks and patchwork quilts. It's all very engaging, but those old walls are thin, so earplugs make good friends. If you need more space, there's an atmospheric cottage with a four-poster bed at the rear of the property.

FOUR SEASONS RESORT LANA'I, THE LODGE AT KOELE   Resort $$$$
☎ 565-3800, 800-321-4666; www.fourseasons .com/koele; 1 Keomuku Rd; r/ste from $295/695; ☒ ☐ ☒
Set on a rise above town, this pampering lodge affects the aristocratic demeanor of an English country estate, complete with afternoon tea, lawn bowling and croquet. The 'great hall' lobby brims with antiques and boasts Hawaii's two largest stone fireplaces.

Hulopo'e Beach   KARL LEHMANN

Pu'u Pehe and Sweetheart's Rock

ANN CECIL

MANELE BAY & HULOPO'E BEACH

To snorkel, dive or just spend a day at the beach, head straight to these adjacent bays, 8 miles south of Lana'i City. Crescent-shaped Manele Harbor provides a protected anchorage for sailboats and other small craft. From the harbor, it's just a 10-minute walk to Hulopo'e Beach.

Manele and Hulopo'e Bays are part of a marine-life conservation district, which prohibits the removal of coral and restricts many fishing activities, all of which makes for great snorkeling and diving.

Sights & Activities

HULOPO'E BEACH

our pick Lana'i may have only one easy-access beach, but what a beauty it is. This gently curving white-sand beach is long, broad and protected by a rocky point to the south. Everybody loves it – locals taking the kids for a swim, tourists on daytrips from Maui and the spinner dolphins who frequent the bay during the early morning hours.

For the best snorkeling, head to the left side of the bay, where there's an abundance of coral, large parrotfish and other colorful tropicals. To the left just beyond the sandy beach, you'll find a low lava shelf with tide pools worth exploring. Here, too, is a protected shoreline splash pool ideal for children, with cement steps leading down to it. The park has full facilities, including picnic tables, solar-heated showers and restrooms.

PU'U PEHE

From Hulopo'e Beach, a short path leads south to the end of the point that separates Hulopo'e and Manele Bays. The point is actually a volcanic cinder cone that's sharply eroded, exposing rich rust-red colors with swirls of gray and black. Its texture is bubbly and brittle – so brittle that huge chunks of the point have broken off and fallen onto the coastal shelf below.

Pu'u Pehe is the name of the cove left of the point as well as the rocky islet just offshore.

This islet, also called Sweetheart's Rock, has a tomblike formation on top that figures into Hawaiian legend (see box below).

MANELE HARBOR
This is the jumping-off point for tourists coming from Maui on the ferry or a snorkeling cruise. All the real thrills here are beneath the surface. Coral is abundant near the cliff sides, where the bottom quickly slopes off to about 40ft. Beyond the bay's western edge, near Pu'u Pehe rock, is **Cathedrals**, the island's most spectacular dive site with arches and grottos galore.

GOLF
The **Challenge at Manele** (☎ 565-2222; guests/non-guests $200/250; 🕑 7:10am-6:30pm), designed by Jack Nicklaus, offers spectacular hole plays along seaside cliffs, and receives high ratings from duffers. It's near Four Seasons Resort Lana'i at Manele Bay.

Eating & Sleeping
HARBOR CAFÉ   Café $
Manele Harbor; meals $5-9; 🕑 8am-2pm
This simple harborside café is where the locals who work at the resort come for an affordable bite. In the morning go for the breakfast burritos.

OCEAN GRILL   Café $$$
☎ 565-7700; Four Seasons Resort Lana'i at Manele Bay; lunch $12-27; 🕑 11am-4:30pm
Dine like a millionaire on vacation at this poolside resort restaurant serving crispy crab cakes, leafy salads and tamarind-glazed scallops.

FOUR SEASONS RESORT
LANA'I AT MANELE BAY   Resort $$$$
☎ 565-3800, 800-321-4666; 1 Manele Bay Rd; www.fourseasons.com/manelebay; r/ste from $375/900; 🏊 🖳 🖳
Tropical lobbies adorned with artwork and sculptured gardens with koi ponds set the tone at this luxury hotel perched above the island's finest beach. The hotel boasts top-rated golf and the indulgent Spa at Manele.

Camping is allowed on the lawn at Hulopo'e Beach. Pick up permits from the **Lana'i Company** (☎ 565-2970; 111 Lana'i Ave, Lana'i City; campsites

$20). If the campground's not full you may be able to get a permit without advance reservations, but it's often booked up weeks in advance, especially during summer and on weekends. The maximum stay is three nights.

KEOMUKU ROAD
Keomuku Rd (Hwy 44) heads north from Lana'i City into cool upland hills where fog drifts above grassy pastures. As the road gently slopes down to the coast, the scenery is punctuated by peculiar rock formations sitting atop the eroded red earth, similar to those at Garden of the Gods (p224). Further along, a shipwreck comes into view. After 8 miles, the paved road ends near the coast.

North to Shipwreck Beach
A beachcomber's dream, this windswept stretch of sand extends 9 miles along Lana'i's northeast shore. The beach takes its name from the many ships that its tricky reef has snared. You'll find lots of sun-bleached driftwood, some pieces still bearing witness to their past – hulls, side planks, perhaps even a gangplank with a little imagination.

Take the dirt road north from the end of Hwy 44, park about half a mile in and then walk down to the beach. It's likely to be just you and the driftwood. After walking north

Island Insights
It's said that an island girl named Pehe was so beautiful that her lover decided to make their home in a secluded coastal cave, lest any other young men in the village set eyes on her. One day when he was up in the mountains fetching water, a storm suddenly blew in. By the time he rushed back down, powerful waves had swept into the cave, drowning Pehe. The lover carried Pehe's body to the top of **Pu'u Pehe** (p221), where he erected a tomb and laid her to rest. Immersed in grief, he then jumped into the surging waters below and was dashed back onto the rock, joining his lover in death.

LANA'I SURF BEACHES & BREAKS *Jake Howard*

When it comes to surfing, Lana'i doesn't enjoy quite the bounty of waves as some of the other Islands. Because rain clouds get trapped in the high peaks of Maui and Moloka'i there's very little rain on Lana'i, and thus far fewer reef passes have been carved out by runoff.

Yet on the south shore the most consistent surf comes in around the **Manele Point** (p221) area, where the main break peels off the tip of Manele and into Hulopo'e Bay. Shallow reef and submerged rocks make this a dangerous spot at low tide or in smaller surf conditions; it's probably ideal on a double overhead swell. Not too far away from here, located in front of a deserted old Hawaiian settlement, is a spot called **Naha** (also known as Stone Shack). It offers a fun two-way peak, but does close out when it gets bigger.

Across the island, the north shore's wide-open **Polihua Beach** (p224) is the longest and widest sandy beach on Lana'i. Be careful of the current here, affectionately dubbed 'the Tahitian Express.' The water flowing between Moloka'i and Lana'i in the Kalohi Channel has driven many a ship into the reef, and it could easily take you on a trip to Tahiti if you're not careful.

Jake Howard is a senior writer at Surfer *magazine and lives in San Clemente, CA*

for about a mile, you'll reach a lava-rock point where you'll see the cement foundation of a former lighthouse. From here you'll get a good view of a rusting WWII liberty ship (cargo ship) that's wrecked on the reef. From the lighthouse foundation, a trail leads inland about 100yd to a cluster of petroglyphs. The simple figures are etched onto large boulders on the right side of the path.

The lighthouse site is the turn-around point for most people but it's possible to walk another 6 miles all the way to Awalua, if you enjoy desolate walks without another person in sight. The hike is windy, hot and dry (bring water!).

South to Naha

Keomuku Rd, the bumpy 4WD-only dirt road that heads southward from the end of Hwy 44 to Naha, is best suited for true diehards. It's a barren stretch with a few marginal historical sites, scattered groves of coconuts and lots of kiawe trees. Keomuku Rd is likely to be either dusty or muddy, but if you catch it after it's been graded, it's drivable. Going the full 12 miles to Naha, at the end of the road, can take as long as two hours one way when the road is rough.

About 5.5 miles down is Keomuku, the former site of a short-lived sugarcane plantation. There's little left to see other than an old Hawaiian church and a century-old locomotive abandoned when the sugarcane company went broke in 1901.

Halepalaoa Landing, 2 miles south of Keomuku, was the site of a wharf used to ship the sugarcane to Maui. Another 2 miles brings you to Lopa Beach, which is a decent place to stop for a swim. From here the road to Naha gets rougher and doesn't offer much for the effort, but should you want to continue, it's about 2.5 miles further.

POLIHUA ROAD

Polihua Rd starts between the Lodge at Koele's tennis courts and stables. It's all dirt, but the stretch as far as the Garden of the Gods is a fairly good, albeit dusty, route that generally takes about 20 minutes from town. To travel onward to Polihua Beach is another matter, however; the road to the beach is rocky and suitable only for a 4WD. Depending on road conditions the trip could take anywhere from 20 minutes to an hour.

Kanepu'u Preserve

The 590-acre Kanepu'u Preserve, overseen by the Nature Conservancy, is the last native dryland forest of its kind in Hawaii. Five miles northwest of Lana'i City, the forest is home to 49 species of rare native plants, including endangered Hawaiian sandalwood and fragrant Hawaiian gardenia. You'll get a close-up look at many of them on the self-guided interpretive trail, which takes just 10 minutes to walk.

Dryland forests once covered 80% of Lana'i until introduced goats, deer and pigs made a feast of the foliage, leaving many native species near-extinct. Credit for saving this slice of the forest goes to ranch manager George Munro, who fenced hoofed animals out of this area in the 1920s.

Garden of the Gods

Think rocks, not green. Instead of flowers you'll find a dry, barren landscape of strange wind-sculpted rocks in ocher, pink and sienna. The colors change with the light – pastel in the early morning, rich hues in the late afternoon. How godly the garden appears depends on one's perspective. Some people just see rocks, while others find the formations hauntingly beautiful.

Polihua Beach

Polihua means 'eggs in the bosom' and this broad, 1.5-mile-long white-sand beach at the northwestern tip of the island takes its name from the green sea turtles that nest here. Although the beach itself is gorgeous, strong winds kicking up the sand often make it uncomfortable, and water conditions can be treacherous.

MUNRO TRAIL

our pick This exhilarating 8.5-mile adventure can be hiked, mountain biked or negotiated in a 4WD vehicle. For the best views, get an early start. Those hiking or biking should be prepared for steep grades and allow a whole day. If you're driving and the dirt road has been graded recently, give yourself two to three hours. However, be aware the road can become very muddy after heavy rain and Jeeps often get stuck. It's best to consider this a fair-weather outing.

To start, head north from Lana'i City on Hwy 44. About a mile past the Lodge at Koele, turn right onto the paved road that ends in half a mile at the island's **cemetery**. The Munro Trail starts left of the cemetery, passing through eucalyptus groves and climbing a ridge studded with Norfolk pines. These trees, which draw moisture from the afternoon clouds and fog, were planted in the 1920s as a watershed by naturalist George Munro.

Garden of the Gods   ANN CECIL

Before the Munro Trail was upgraded to a dirt road, it was a footpath. It's along this trail that islanders tried to flee Kamehameha the Great when he went on a rampage in 1778. Lana'ians made their last stand above Ho'okio Gulch, about 2.5 miles from the start of the trail.

The trail looks down on deep ravines cutting across the east flank of the mountain, and passes **Lana'ihale** (3370ft), Lana'i's highest point. On a clear day, you can see all the inhabited Hawaiian Islands, except for distant Kaua'i and Ni'ihau, along the route. Stay on the main trail, descending 6 miles to the central plateau. Keep the hills to your left and turn right at the big fork in the road. Once you hit the cattle grate, pavement is close. The trail ends back on Manele Rd (Hwy 440) between Lana'i City and Manele Bay.

KAUMALAPA'U HIGHWAY

Kaumalapa'u Hwy (Hwy 440) connects Lana'i City to the airport before ending at Kaumalapa'u Harbor, the island's deepwater shipping harbor.

Kaunolu

Perched on a majestic bluff at the southwestern tip of the island, the ancient fishing village of Kaunolu thrived until its abandonment in the mid-19th century. Now overgrown and all but forgotten, Kaunolu boasts the largest concentration of stone ruins on Lana'i, including **Halulu Heiau**. Northwest of the heiau, a natural stone wall runs along the sea cliff. Look for a break in the wall at the cliff's edge, where there's a sheer 80ft drop known as **Kahekili's Jump**. In days past, Kamehameha the Great would test the courage of upstart warriors by having them make a death-defying leap from this spot.

To get to Kaunolu, follow Kaumalapa'u Hwy past the airport, turning left onto the road that circles around the south side of the airport. The turnoff to Kaunolu is marked by a yellow water pipe; turn right onto the dirt road, which leads south toward Palaloa lighthouse. The road washes out after rain storms so expect ruts deep enough to swallow a jeep, but you may be able to make it part of the way and walk the last mile or so.

DETOUR ➡

LUAHIWA PETROGLYPHS

Lana'i's highest concentration of ancient petroglyphs are carved into three dozen boulders spread over three dusty acres on a remote slope overlooking the Palawai Basin.

To get to this seldom visited site, head south from Lana'i City along Manele Rd. Midway between the 7- and 8-mile markers, turn left onto Ho'ike Rd, the wide dirt road that comes up immediately after a roadside shed. Head for the water tower on the ridge, taking a sharp left after 1 mile. Stay on this road for half a mile and then take the jog to the right. About a third of a mile down, you'll come to a large cluster of boulders on the right. Park off to the side.

Many of the rock carvings are quite weathered, but you can still make out linear and triangular human figures, dogs and a canoe. Other than gusts of wind, the place is eerily quiet. You can almost feel the presence of the ancients here – honor their spirits and don't touch the fragile carvings.

Lana'i's coastal trails are rugged! KARL LEHMANN

LANA'I & MOLOKA'I

KAHO'OLAWE

Seven miles southwest of Maui, the uninhabited island of Kaho'olawe (also called Kanaloa) has long been central to the Hawaiian-rights movement. Many consider the island a living spiritual entity, a *pu'uhonua* (refuge) and *wahi pana* (sacred place).

Yet for nearly 50 years, from WWII to 1990, the US military used Kaho'olawe as a bombing range. Beginning in the 1970s, liberating the island from the military became a rallying point for a resurgence of Native Hawaiian pride. Today, the bombing has stopped, the navy is gone and healing the island is considered both a symbolic act and a concrete expression of Native Hawaiian sovereignty.

Kaho'olawe is 11 miles long and 6 miles wide, with its highest point the 1482ft Luamakika. The island and its surrounding waters are now a reserve that is off-limits to the general public because of the wealth of unexploded ordnance that remains on land and in the sea.

Pathway to Tahiti

The channel between Lana'i and Kaho'olawe, as well as the westernmost point of Kaho'olawe itself, is named Kealaikahiki, meaning 'pathway to Tahiti.' When early Polynesian voyagers made the journey between Hawaii and Tahiti, they lined up their canoes at this departure point.

But Kaho'olawe was much more than an early navigational tool. Over 540 archaeological and cultural sites have been identified. They include several heiau (stone temples) and *ku'ula* (fishing shrine) stones dedicated to the gods of fishers. Pu'umoiwi, a large cinder cone in the center of the island, contains one of Hawaii's largest ancient adze quarries.

Prisoners & Smugglers

From the 1830s to 1848, Kaulana Bay, on the island's northern side, served as a penal colony for men from Maui accused of petty crimes. Hanakanaea Bay, on the island's southern side, was so heavily used by smugglers importing illegal Chinese opium that it became known as Smugglers Bay. In more recent times Smugglers Bay served as the site of a US military base camp.

Into the Dust Bowl

Kaho'olawe, today nearly barren, was once a lush, green and forested island.

Considering it good for stock raising, in 1858 the territorial Hawaiian government leased the entire island to ranchers. None was successful, and sheep, goats and cattle were left to run wild. By the early 1900s, tens of thousands of sheep and goats had denuded the better part of the island, turning it into an eroded wasteland (even today, Kaho'olawe looks hazy from dust when seen from Maui).

From 1918 to 1941, Angus MacPhee, a former ranch manager on Maui, ran Kaho'olawe's most successful ranching operation. MacPhee rounded up and sold 13,000 goats, and then built a fence across the width of the entire island to keep the remaining goats at one end. He then planted grasses and ground cover and started raising cattle. It wasn't easy, but MacPhee, unlike his predecessors, was able to turn a profit.

Target Practice

In early 1941, the US military subleased part of the island from MacPhee for bombing practice. Following the December 7, 1941 Pearl Harbor attack, martial law was declared in Hawaii and the military seized control of Kaho'olawe entirely. As well as serving as a target for aerial bombings and torpedoes, it was used to practice mock invasions. Of all the fighting that took place during WWII, Kaho'olawe was the most bombed island in the Pacific – even though the 'enemy' never fired upon it.

After the war, the bombing continued. In 1953 President Eisenhower signed a decree giving the US Navy official jurisdiction over Kaho'olawe, with the stipulation that when Kaho'olawe was no longer 'needed,' the unexploded ordnance would be removed and the island would be returned to Hawaiian control 'reasonably safe for human habitation.'

LANA'I & MOLOKA'I

The Kaho'olawe Movement

In the mid-1960s Hawaii politicians began petitioning the federal government to cease its military activities and return Kaho'olawe to the state. In 1976 a lawsuit was filed against the navy, and in an attempt to attract greater attention to the bombings, nine Native Hawaiian activists sailed across and occupied the island. Despite their arrests, more occupations followed.

During one of the 1977 crossings, group members George Helm and Kimo Mitchell mysteriously disappeared in the waters off Kaho'olawe. Helm had been an inspirational Hawaiian-rights activist, and with his death the Protect Kaho'olawe 'Ohana movement arose. Helm's vision of turning Kaho'olawe into a sanctuary of Hawaiian culture became widespread among islanders.

In 1980, in a court-sanctioned decree, the navy reached an agreement with Protect Kaho'olawe 'Ohana that allowed them regular access to the island. The decree restricted the navy from bombing archaeological sites. In 1981 Kaho'olawe was added to the National Register of Historic Places as a significant archaeological area. For nearly a decade, the island had the ironic distinction of being the only such historic place being bombed by its government.

In 1982 the 'Ohana began to go to Kaho'olawe to celebrate *makahiki,* the annual observance to honor Lono, god of agriculture and peace. That same year – in what many Hawaiians felt was the ultimate insult to their heritage – the US military offered Kaho'olawe as a bombing target to foreign nations during biennial Pacific Rim exercises. This event thrust Kaho'olawe into worldwide attention and international protests over the bombings grew. New Zealand, Australia, Japan and the UK boycotted the Kaho'olawe military exercises and the plan was scrapped.

In the late 1980s Hawaii's politicians became more outspoken in their demands that Kaho'olawe be returned to Hawaii. Then, in October 1990, as Hawaii's two US senators, Daniel Inouye and Daniel Akaka, were preparing a congressional bill to stop the bombing, President George Bush issued an order to immediately halt military activities.

The Navy Sets Sail

In 1994 the US Navy finally agreed to clean up and return Kaho'olawe to Hawaii. In a Memorandum of Understanding, the navy promised to work until 100% of surface munitions and 30% of subsurface munitions were cleared. However, the catch was that the federally authorized cleanup would end in 10 years, regardless of the results.

Ten years later, after spending over $400 million, the navy's cleanup ended, and Kaho'olawe was transferred to the state. The government estimated that only 70% of surface ordnance and a mere 9% of subsurface ordnance had been removed.

The same year, in 2004, Hawaii established the **Kaho'olawe Island Reserve Commission** (KIRC; www.kahoolawe.hawaii.gov) to manage access and use of the island, preserve its archaeological areas and restore its habitats. KIRC's mandate is unique in state law, for it calls for the island to be 'managed in trust until such time and circumstances as a sovereign Native Hawaiian entity is recognized by the federal and state governments.' Although no such entity has yet been recognized, KIRC works in the belief that one day a sovereign Native Hawaiian government will be, and this island will then become theirs.

Helping the 'Ohana

Working with KIRC as official stewards of Kaho'olawe, **Protect Kaho'olawe 'Ohana** (PKO; www.kahoolawe.org) conducts monthly visits to the island to pull weeds, plant native foliage, clean up historic sites, conduct Hawaiian rituals and honor the spirits of the land. It welcomes respectful volunteers who want to help (not just sightsee). Visits last four to five days during or near the full moon; volunteers pay a $100 fee, which covers food and transportation to Kaho'olawe. You'll need your own sleeping bag, tent and personal supplies. PKO's website lists details, schedules and contact information.

LANA'I & MOLOKA'I

MOLOKA'I

pop 7300

According to ancient chants, Moloka'i is a child of Hina, goddess of the moon. Sparsely populated, mostly by Native Hawaiians, Moloka'i's untouched by packaged tourism. This is a place to get in touch with basics. In the morning you can sit on the edge of an 800-year-old fishpond and watch the sun rise over Haleakalā on distant Maui. In the evening you can watch the sun set behind the silhouette of Moloka'i's royal coconut grove.

Getting There & Around

Lahaina's Cruise Company's **Molokai Princess** (☎ 662-3355, 866-440-6284; www.molokaiferry.com; adult/child 4-12 $40/20) operates between Lahaina Harbor and Moloka'i's Kaunakakai Wharf. Departures from Lahaina are at 7:15am and 6pm. The boat leaves Kaunakakai at 5:30am and 4pm. The 90-minute crossing through the Pailolo Channel can get choppy. Buy tickets online, by phone or on the boat a half-hour before departure.

You can also fly to Moloka'i; see p285 for details.

Renting a car is essential if you intend to fully explore the island. All of Moloka'i's highways and primary routes are good, paved roads. Exploring unmarked roads is not advisable. Folks aren't too keen on strangers cruising around on their private turf and can get skittish. On the other hand, if there's a fishpond you want to see, and someone's house is between the road and the water, it's usually easy to strike up a conversation and get permission to cross. If you're lucky they might even share a little local lore and history with you, particularly the old-timers.

Budget (☎ 567-6877) and **Dollar** (☎ 567-6156) both have offices at the airport. **Island Kine Auto Rental** (☎ 553-5242, 866-527-7368; 242 Ilio Rd,

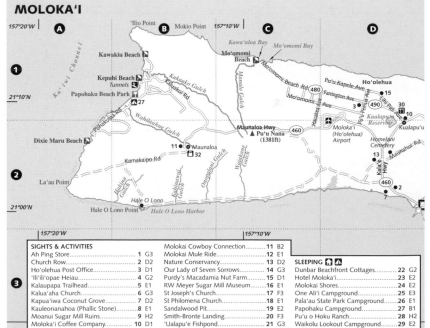

MOLOKA'I

SIGHTS & ACTIVITIES
Ah Ping Store	1	G3
Church Row	2	D2
Ho'olehua Post Office	3	D1
'Ili'ili'opae Heiau	4	G2
Kalaupapa Trailhead	5	E1
Kalua'aha Church	6	G3
Kapua'iwa Coconut Grove	7	D2
Kauleonanahoa (Phallic Stone)	8	E1
Moanui Sugar Mill Ruins	9	H2
Moloka'i Coffee Company	10	D1
Molokai Cowboy Connection	11	B2
Molokai Mule Ride	12	E1
Nature Conservancy	13	D2
Our Lady of Seven Sorrows	14	G3
Purdy's Macadamia Nut Farm	15	D1
RW Meyer Sugar Mill Museum	16	E1
St Joseph's Church	17	F3
St Philomena Church	18	E1
Sandalwood Pit	19	E2
Smith-Bronte Landing	20	F3
'Ualapu'e Fishpond	21	G3

SLEEPING
Dunbar Beachfront Cottages	22	G2
Hotel Moloka'i	23	E2
Molokai Shores	24	E2
One Ali'i Campground	25	E3
Pala'au State Park Campground	26	E1
Papohaku Campground	27	B1
Pu'u o Hoku Ranch	28	H2
Waikolu Lookout Campground	29	E2

Kaunakakai) is a local outfit in the northeast of Kaunakakai. All rent cars and 4WD vehicles.

KAUNAKAKAI

Moloka'i's biggest town takes much of its character from what it doesn't have: not a single traffic light, no shopping centers and no chain eateries. The stores have old wooden false fronts that give Kaunakakai the appearance of a Wild West town. This is a town that hasn't changed its face at all for tourism. It has an almost timeless quality and a nice slow pace.

Orientation & Information

Most of Moloka'i's businesses are lined up along Ala Malama Ave, the town's broad main street.

Bank of Hawaii (☎ 553-3273; Ala Malama Ave) Has a 24-hour ATM.

Laundramat (☎ 567-6734; Makaena Pl; ☷ 7am-9pm) Coin laundry behind the health food store.

Top Picks

HAWAIIAN EATS
- **Lana'i City Grille** (p220)
- **Blue Ginger Café** (p219)
- **Hula Shores** (p231)
- **Mana'e Goods & Grindz** (p233)

Molokai Dispatch (☎ 552-2781; www.themolokai dispatch.com) Pick up this free weekly newspaper anywhere in town.

Molokai Drugs (☎ 553-5790; Moloka'i Professional Bldg, Kamoi St; ☷ 8:45am-5:45pm Mon-Fri, to 2pm Sat) Doubles as the town's bookstore as well as its pharmacy.

Molokai General Hospital (☎ 553-5331; 280 Puali St; ☷ 24hr) Emergency services.

Moloka'i Visitors Association (☎ 553-3876, 800-800-6367; www.molokai-hawaii.com; 2 Kamoi St; ☷ 8am-4:30pm Mon-Fri)

Post office (☎ 553-5845; Ala Malama Ave)

Stanley's Coffee Shop Gallery (☎ 553-9966; Ala Malama Ave; per 10min $1; ☷ 6am-4pm Mon-Fri) Good java at this internet café.

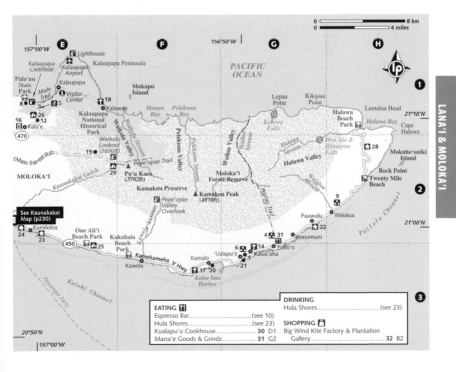

Sights

The days when pineapples were loaded at Kaunakakai Wharf are gone, but the harbor still hums. Kaunakakai has no swimmable beach, but a roped-off area with a floating dock provides a swim area. On the west side of the wharf, near the canoe shed, are the overgrown stone foundations of King Kamehameha V's summer house.

King Kamehameha V had the royal 10-acre Kapua'iwa Coconut Grove (Map pp228-9) planted. Standing tall, about a mile west of downtown, its name means 'mysterious taboo.' Be careful where you walk (or park), because coconuts frequently drop. A falling coconut makes no sound!

Across the highway is Church Row (Map pp228-9). Any denomination that attracts a handful of members receives its own little tract of land here. The number of churches will tell you how big that religion is here.

The downtown softball and baseball fields are perhaps the most active spot on the is-land. For some local flavor, go down and cheer on the Moloka'i Farmers as they compete against their high-school rivals, the Lana'i Pinelads.

Activities

For activities, Molokai Fish & Dive (☎ 553-5926; 61 Ala Malama Ave; ☺ 8am-6pm Mon-Sat, to 2pm Sun) are the folks to see. They can arrange kayaking trips ($90) and scuba diving ($135). They also rent snorkel sets, surfboards, fishing poles – you name it, they've got it.

Molokai Bicycle (☎ 553-3931; 80 Mohala St; per day $15-26; ☺ 3-6pm Wed, 9am-2pm Sat, or by appointment) rents mountain bikes and road bikes.

Festivals & Events

Ka Moloka'i Makahiki Moloka'i's biggest annual event is the celebration of the ancient *makahiki* festival. It takes place in January with Olympics-esque competitions of ancient Hawaiian sports, crafts and activities.

Moloka'i Ka Hula Piko Moloka'i's hula festival takes place in May with hula performances, food and crafts.

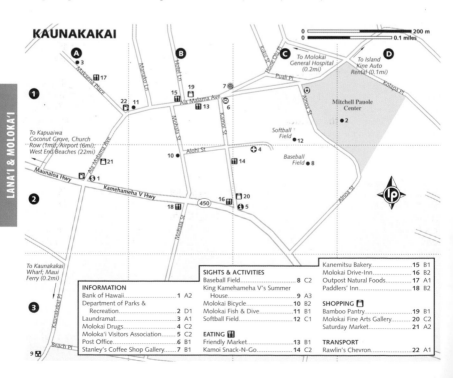

KAUNAKAKAI

To Moloka'i General Hospital (0.2mi)

To Island Kine Auto Rental (0.1mi)

Mitchell Pauole Center

To Kapuaiwa Coconut Grove, Church Row (1mi), Airport (6mi); West End Beaches (22mi)

Softball Field

Baseball Field

To Kaunakakai Wharf; Maui Ferry (0.2mi)

INFORMATION		
Bank of Hawaii	1	A2
Department of Parks & Recreation	2	D1
Laundramat	3	A1
Molokai Drugs	4	C2
Molokai Visitors Association	5	C2
Post Office	6	B1
Stanley's Coffee Shop Gallery	7	B1

SIGHTS & ACTIVITIES		
Baseball Field	8	C2
King Kamehameha V's Summer House	9	A3
Molokai Bicycle	10	B2
Molokai Fish & Dive	11	B1
Softball Field	12	C1

EATING 🍴		
Friendly Market	13	B1
Kamoi Snack-N-Go	14	C2

Kanemitsu Bakery	15	B1
Molokai Drive-Inn	16	B2
Outpost Natural Foods	17	A1
Paddlers' Inn	18	B2

SHOPPING 🛍		
Bamboo Pantry	19	B1
Molokai Fine Arts Gallery	20	C2
Saturday Market	21	A2

TRANSPORT		
Rawlin's Chevron	22	A1

Eating

KANEMITSU BAKERY
Bakery $

☎ 553-5855; Ala Malama Ave; snacks $1-3;
⏲ 5:30am-6:30pm Wed-Mon
Famous for its Moloka'i sweet bread (which is sold statewide), its pastries are decent – the cinnamon apple crisp ($1) is a favorite. Forget the attached restaurant. Here's a local secret: every night but Monday you can slip down the alley to the bakery's back door at 10pm and buy loaves of hot bread fresh from the oven.

KAMOI SNACK-N-GO
Ice Cream $

☎ 553-5790; Moloka'i Professional Bldg, Kamoi St; ice cream cone $3; ⏲ 10am-9pm Mon-Fri, 9am-9pm Sat, noon-9pm Sun
This snack shop sells Honolulu-made Dave's ice cream in tasty Hawaiian flavors like lychee and mango.

MOLOKAI DRIVE-INN
Diner $

☎ 553-5655; Kamehameha V Hwy; meals $3-9;
⏲ 6am-10pm
The Drive-Inn is always packed with folks picking up plate lunches, fried saimin noodles, even Thai spring rolls and oxtail soup. Skip the greasy burgers and fries.

PADDLERS' INN
Eclectic $$

☎ 553-5256; 10 Mohala St, mains $6-18; ⏲ 7am-1am, meals to 9pm
Kaunakakai's most polished eatery, Paddlers' has a fun paniolo (cowboy) decor and a wide-ranging menu that includes burgers, local fish, steaks and more. It also has both an indoor and outdoor bar.

HULA SHORES
Eclectic $$$

our pick Map pp228-9; ☎ 553-5347; Hotel Moloka'i, Kamehameha V Hwy; breakfast & lunch $5-10, dinner $15-22; ⏲ breakfast, lunch & dinner
A hot new chef with a flair for Southern cooking has revived the kitchen at Moloka'i's only waterfront restaurant. Grab a table at the ocean's edge, order up the banana macnut pancakes at breakfast, the charbroiled ribs at dinner…oooh, it's gonna be good. Tiki torches add to the atmosphere after dark.

Of Moloka'i's two grocery stores, Friendly Market (☎ 553-5595; Ala Malama St; ⏲ 8:30am-8:30pm Mon-Fri, to 6:30pm Sat) has the best selection. Outpost Natural Foods (☎ 553-3377; 70 Makaena Pl; ⏲ 9am-6pm Mon-Thu, to 4pm Fri, 10am-5pm Sun) has organic produce, bulk health foods and a vegetarian deli open at lunchtime.

Drinking & Entertainment

The best place to have a sunset drink is the open-air waterfront bar at Hula Shores (above). It's also the most likely spot to find someone strumming a ukulele or guitar after dark. Local kapuna (elders) gather around a table to play Hawaiian music on 'Aloha Fridays' from 4pm to 6pm – don't miss it.

Shopping

Molokai Fine Arts Gallery (☎ 553-8520; 2 Kamoi St) sells a wide selection of quality work from island artists. Bamboo Pantry (☎ 553-3300; 107 Ala Malama Ave) also has Moloka'i-made goods, including some fine locally made pottery. Browse local crafts and pick up fruits and vegetables at the Saturday Market (Ala Malama Ave; ⏲ 8am-1pm Sat) in front of the Moloka'i Center.

Sleeping

MOLOKAI SHORES
Condo $$

Map pp228 9; ☎ 553 5954, 800 535 0085; www .marcresorts.com; Kamehameha V Hwy; 1br/2br from $140/170; 🖳
The oceanfront setting, condo facilities and spacious grounds make this Kaunakakai's top choice for business travelers. However, units are individually owned – some have outlandishly outdated decor, while others are quite nice. Best bet is to ask to see the unit before checking in.

HOTEL MOLOKA'I
Independent Hotel $$

Map pp228-9; ☎ 553-5347, 800-535-0085; www .hotelmolokai.com; Kamehameha V Hwy; r from $159; 🖳 🖳
Fresh off a long-overdue renovation, this hotel has the most character of any place in Moloka'i. Rooms are in a series of two-story Polynesian-style buildings, some with fine sea views. Request an upper-floor room, as the noise from people walking on the creaky wooden floors travels to the lower level. Oh…and step lightly, please.

Camping is permitted at One Ali'i Campground (Map pp228-9) but drawbacks include strong winds, little privacy and late-night carousing. See Camping & Cabins (p269) for permit details.

Getting There & Around

Kaunakakai is a walking town, but **Mid-nite Taxi** (☎ 553-5652) and **Hele Mai Taxi** (☎ 336-0967) service Moloka'i, should you need a lift. **Rawlin's Chevron** (☎ 553-3214; cnr Hwy 460 & Ala Malama Ave; ☒ 6:30am-8:30pm Mon-Thu, to 9pm Fri & Sat, 7am-6pm Sun) is the place to gas up.

EAST MOLOKA'I

The 27-mile road from Kaunakakai to Halawa Valley edges alongside the ocean for much of the drive, with the mountains of east Moloka'i rising up to the north. It's all sweetly pastoral, with small homes tucked into the valleys, horses grazing at the side of the road and silver waterfalls dropping down the mountainsides. There's no gas after Kaunakakai, so check your gauge before setting out.

Kawela to Kalua'aha

In Kawela you'll pass **Kakahaia Beach Park**, a grassy strip wedged between the road and sea, shortly before the 6-mile marker. The park is the only part of the **Kakahaia National Wildlife Refuge** (http://pacificislands.fws.gov) open to the public. Most of the 40-acre refuge is marshland inland from the road.

Kamalo, a small roadside village 10 miles east of Kaunakakai, holds **St Joseph's Church**. Built by Father Damien in 1876, this simple, one-room wooden church has some of its original wavy glass panes. A lei-draped statue of Father Damien and a little cemetery are beside the church.

Three-quarters of a mile past the 11-mile marker, look for a small sign on the *makai* (ocean) side of the road pointing out the **Smith-Bronte Landing**. A little memorial plaque set among the kiawe trees commemorates the first civilian flight from the US mainland to Hawaii. The two pilots were aiming for O'ahu, but safely crash-landed on Moloka'i in 1927.

A half-mile past the 13-mile marker, the impressive **'Ualapu'e Fishpond** lies on the *makai* side of the road. This fishpond has been restored and restocked with mullet and milkfish, two species that were raised here in ancient times. After this, look to your left for the classic, but long closed, c 1930s **Ah Ping Store** and its old gas pump at the roadside.

The ruins of Moloka'i's first church are next at **Kalua'aha**, off the road and inland but (barely) visible. A quarter of a mile later is **Our Lady of Seven Sorrows Church**, a 1966 reconstruction of a Father Damien original. Pull into the church parking lot and you'll get a fine view of an ancient fishpond with the high-rise-studded shores of West Maui as an incongruous backdrop.

'Ili'ili'opae Heiau to Halawa

Quiet **'Ili'ili'opae Heiau** is Moloka'i's biggest ancient stone temple and is thought to be the oldest as well. Once used for human sacrifices, its stones still seem to emanate vibrations of the past. Visiting this heiau is a little tricky, since it's on private property and the trail to it is almost completely overgrown. Check with the **Moloka'i Visitors Association** (☎ 553-3876) to see if there's a local guide available to give you a tour.

The sleepy backwater of **Puko'o** was once the seat of local government – complete with a courthouse, jail, wharf and post office – until the plantation folks shifted everything to Kaunakakai.

About three-quarters of a mile after the 19-mile marker, begin looking for the remains of a stone chimney, a remnant of the **Moanui Sugar Mill**, which processed sugar until the mill burned down in the late 1800s. The ruins are about 50ft inland from the road, just before a stand of tall ironwood trees.

If you want beach over this way, look no further than the 20-mile marker, from where a stretch of white sand called **Twenty Mile Beach** pops up right along the thin roadside. Inside the barrier reef, the waters are calm, but at low tide can be too shallow for much more than a splash.

The pointy clutch of rocks sticking out, as the road swings left before the 21-mile marker, is called, appropriately enough, **Rock Point**. This popular surf spot is the site of local competitions and it's the place to go if you're looking for east-end swells.

After the 21-mile marker, the road starts to wind upwards. Tall grasses right at the edge threaten to reclaim the road, while ironwood trees and spiky sisal plants dot the surrounding hills. It's a good paved road – the problem is there's not always enough of it. In places, including some cliff-hugging curves, this road is only wide enough for one car, and you'll need to do some horn tooting. The road levels out just before the 24-mile marker, where there's a view of the islet of **Mokuho'oniki**, a seabird sanctuary.

One more mile brings you to **Pu'u o Hoku Ranch** (☎ 558-8109). Stop by the ranch store for organic produce or to ask about horseback rides.

EATING & SLEEPING

MANA'E GOODS & GRINDZ   Plate Lunch $
☎ 558-8498; Kamehameha V Hwy, near the 16-mile marker; mains $4-9; ☺ store 8am-5pm, counter 9am-5pm
You'll be amazed at how good the food is at this little shop. It not only serves up the best plate lunches on the island, but also grills excellent burgers and fish sandwiches. The attached market is small but well stocked.

DUNBAR BEACHFRONT COTTAGES   Cottage $$$
☎ 558-8153, 800-673-0520; www.molokai-beachfront-cottages.com; 2br cottages $180
These two cottages on a secluded beach near the 18-mile marker offer plenty of privacy. Each is suitably simple but fitted with a full kitchen, TV, VCR, ceiling fans, a laundry and a lanai. Each sleeps up to four people; the Pu'unana cottage has delicious sea views.

Halawa Valley

After passing the 25-mile marker, the jungle begins to close in, and the scent of eucalyptus fills the air. There are lots of beep-as-you-go hairpin bends. A quarter of a mile after the 26-mile marker there's a turnoff with a panoramic view of Halawa Valley and Moa'ula and Hipuapua Falls.

At the end of the road, **Halawa Beach Park** was a favored surfing spot for Moloka'i chiefs. The beach has double coves separated by a rocky outcrop. When the water is calm, there's good swimming, but both

Halawa Valley

PETER HENDRIE

LANA'I & MOLOKA'I

coves are subject to dangerous rip currents, especially in high surf or when Halawa Stream, which empties into the north cove, is flowing heavily.

CENTRAL MOLOKA'I

Central Moloka'i takes in Mo'omomi Beach, the former plantation town of Kualapu'u and the forested interiors of Kamakou Preserve. On the remote north end of it all is Kalaupapa Peninsula, Hawaii's infamous leprosy colony.

The most trodden route in central Moloka'i is the drive up Hwy 470, past the coffee plantation, restored sugar-mill museum, mule stables and the trailhead down to Kalaupapa Peninsula. The road ends at Pala'au State Park.

Kamakou Area

The mountains that form the spine of Mokola'i's east side reach up to Kamakou, the island's highest peak (4970ft). Few visitors make it up this way. If you're lucky enough to be one of them, you'll be rewarded with amazing views of the island's impenetrable north coast and an opportunity to explore a near-pristine rain forest.

Kamakou is a treasure but not an easily reached one. It's accessed via a narrow rutted dirt road (Maunahui Rd) and you'll need a 4WD. In dry weather some people do make it as far as the lookout in a regular car, but attempt it at your own risk. The turnoff for Kamakou begins between the 3- and 4-mile markers on Hwy 460, immediately east of the Manawainui Bridge. The road is marked with a sign for Homelani Cemetery, but has no street sign.

MOLOKA'I FOREST RESERVE

The 10-mile drive up to Waikolu Lookout takes about 45 minutes, depending on road conditions. A mile before the lookout you'll find the 19th-century Sandalwood Pit, a grassy depression on the left. The pit was dug to the exact measurements of a 75ft-long ship's hold. After being filled with fragrant sandalwood logs, the wood was strapped to the backs of laborers, who hauled it down to the harbor for shipment to China. The sea captains made out like bandits, while Hawaii lost its sandalwood forests.

Waikolu Lookout (3600ft), just before Kamakou Preserve entrance, offers a breathtaking view of remote Waikolu Valley. If it's been raining recently, waterfalls stream down the sheer cliff sides. Morning is the best time for views, as afternoon trade winds commonly bring clouds. A remote, grassy camping (see p269 for information) area is directly opposite the lookout. If you can bear the

Mt Kamakou, the highest point on Moloka'i, viewed from near Kamalo   KARL LEHMANN

Island Insights

mist and cold winds that blow up from the canyon during the afternoon and evening, this could make a base camp for hikes into the preserve. The site has pit toilets but no water supply or other amenities.

KAMAKOU PRESERVE

The preserve's **Pepe'opae Trail** affords a stunning view of Pelekunu Valley. An extensive boardwalk crosses a fragile ecosystem, allowing hikers to access a nearly undisturbed Hawaiian montane bog and a miniature forest of stunted trees and dwarfed plants. From the terminus at **Pelekunu Valley Overlook**, you'll enjoy a view of majestic cliffs, and if it's not too cloudy, you can see down the valley out to the ocean. The area receives about 180in of rain each year, making it one of the wettest regions in Hawaii.

The easiest way to reach the Pepe'opae Trail is to walk from Waikolu Lookout about 2.5 miles along the main 4WD road to the main trailhead. This is a nice forest walk that takes just over an hour. There are some side roads along the way, but they're largely overgrown and it's obvious which is the main road. You'll eventually come to the 'Pepe'opae' sign that marks the start of the trail, which then branches to the left and heads east for 1 mile to the overlook.

A great way to see Kamakou is by joining the guided hikes led by the **Nature Conservancy** (☎ 553-5236; www.nature.org/hawaii; 23 Pueo Pl, Kaunakakai; suggested donation $25) on the first or second Saturday of every month. Transportation is provided to and from the preserve.

Kualapu'u

Moloka'i's second town, Kualapu'u is a small, spread-out farming community with a small town center. Its tiny center has everything a small town needs: a cookhouse, a laundromat, a mom-and-pop grocery store, a beauty parlor and a post office that closes for lunch.

Kualapu'u was a pineapple-plantation town until Del Monte pulled out of Moloka'i in 1982. In 1991 coffee saplings were planted on formerly fallow pineapple fields, and now cover the slopes beneath the town center.

Stop by **Moloka'i Coffee Company** (☎ 567-9064; cnr Hwys 470 & 490; ⊗ 8am-5pm Mon-Fri, to 4pm Sat, to 2pm Sun) gift store for free samples of Moloka'i brews or to take their **Coffee Beans Tour** (adult/child $35/10; ⊗ 8am & 1pm Mon-Fri) in a mule-drawn wagon through their farm.

EATING

ESPRESSO BAR
Café $
☎ 567-9241; cnr Hwys 470 & 490; snacks $2-5; ⊗ 6am-4pm Mon-Fri, 8am-4pm Sat, 8am-2pm Sun
Moloka'i Coffee Company's café sells simple sandwiches, scones and bagels, as well as cups of their homegrown coffee.

KUALAPU'U COOKHOUSE
Eclectic $$
☎ 567-9655; Hwy 490; breakfast & lunch $5-10, dinner $20-27; ⊗ 7am-8pm Tue-Sat, to 2pm Mon
People come from all over Moloka'i to eat at this funky café. At lunch, go with the lemon chicken plate. At dinner, the sautéed *opakapaka* (pink snapper) in *liliko'i* (passion fruit) sauce is heavenly. On Thursday nights the wildly popular prime rib dinners steal the show.

Ho'olehua

Ho'olehua, the dry central plains of Moloka'i, is home to Native Hawaiians living on homestead property and farming the land.

PURDY'S MACADAMIA NUT FARM
☎ 567-6601; admission free; ⊗ 9:30am-3:30pm Tue-Fri, 10am-2pm Sat, tours on the hour 10am-3pm
The Purdy family runs the best little macadamia-nut farm tour in all of Hawaii. Unlike tours on the Big Island that focus on

LANA'I & MOLOKA'I

MAIL HOME SOME ALOHA

This may be the friendliest post office on the planet. Gary, the cheery postmaster of the **Ho'olehua Post Office** (Pu'u Peelua Ave; ☽ 8:30am-4pm Mon-Fri), stocks baskets of free, unhusked coconuts that are collected from the royal coconut grove near Kaunakakai. Colored felt pens are made available so you can jot down a message and address on the coconut husk. You can then mail these 'Post-A-Nuts' as unique (and edible!) 'postcards.' All you pay is the postage, which is typically around $7 to $10, depending on the weight. Other places in Hawaii offer a similar service, but charge for the coconuts and mail them for a much higher price.

processing, Tuddie Purdy takes you into his orchard and personally explains how the nuts grow.

Everything is done in quaint Moloka'i style: you can crack open macadamia nuts on a stone with a hammer, and sample macadamia-blossom honey scooped up with slices of fresh coconut. Macadamia nuts and honey are for sale.

To get to the farm, turn onto Hwy 490 from Hwy 470. After 1 mile, take a right onto Lihi Pali Ave, just before the high school. The farm is a third of a mile up, on the right.

Mo'omomi Beach

🐾 Windswept Mo'omomi Beach, on the western edge of the Ho'olehua Plains, is ecologically unique: it's home to several endangered native plant species and nesting grounds for green sea turtles. Mo'omomi is not lushly beautiful, but windswept, lonely and wild – and that's the appeal. A red-dirt road starts at the end of Farrington Hwy and leads 2.5 miles to the beach.

Mo'omomi Bay, a small sandy beach that is part of Hawaiian Home Lands, is marked by a picnic pavilion with restrooms. The broad, white-sand beach that people call Mo'omomi is at **Kawa'aloa Bay**, a windy 20-minute walk to the west. Because of the fragile ecology of the dunes, visitors should stay along the beach and on trails only.

The **Nature Conservancy** (☎ 553-5236; www .nature.org/hawaii; 23 Pueo Pl, Kaunakakai; suggested donation $25) leads guided hikes of Mo'omomi on the second or third Saturday of the month.

Mule ride to the former leper settlement at Kalaupapa National Historical Park

Transportation is provided to and from the preserve. Reservations are required.

Kala'e

Four miles northeast of Hwy 460 is the sugar mill built by Rudolph W Meyer, an entrepreneurial German immigrant. Meyer was en route to the California gold rush when he stopped off in the Islands, married a member of Hawaiian royalty and landed a tidy bit of property in the process. In 1876 Meyer turned his lands over to sugar, and built a mill. Now on the National Register of Historic Places, this authentically restored mill is the last of its kind. The **RW Meyer Sugar Mill Museum** (☎ 567-6436; adult/child $3.50/1; ☯ 10am-2pm Mon-Sat), behind the mill, has a short video and displays of Moloka'i's history.

Pala'au State Park

our pick **Kalaupapa Overlook**, perched on the edge of a 1600ft cliff, is the highlight of this woodsy park, at the end of Hwy 470. Kalaupapa means 'flat leaf' and the view of the peninsula below is stunning – almost like seeing it from an airplane.

A five-minute walk in the opposite direction leads to **Kauleonanahoa** ('the penis

Send home a Post-A-Nut!   NED FRIARY

of Nanahoa'). Hawaii's premier phallic stone pokes up in a little clearing inside an ironwood grove. Nature has endowed it well, but it's obviously been touched up by human hands. Women who wish to become pregnant leave offerings underneath, and it is said that those who stay overnight return home pregnant.

Camping is allowed in a grassy field near the park entrance, but would-be campers should keep in mind this is one of the wetter parts of the island. See p269 for permit information.

KALAUPAPA NATIONAL HISTORICAL PARK

Wildly beautiful and strikingly isolated, Kalaupapa Peninsula is fronted by rough waters and backed by the world's highest sea cliffs. Still home to leprosy patients, the remote peninsula has been designated a national historical park and is managed by the Hawaii Department of Health and the **National Park Service** (www.nps.gov/kala). A tour of the park at the bottom of the cliffs is Moloka'i's principal attraction.

History

In 1835 doctors diagnosed Hawaii's first case of Hansen's disease (leprosy), one of many diseases introduced by foreigners. Alarmed by the spread of the disease, King Kamehameha V signed a law banishing people with Hansen's to Kalaupapa Peninsula.

Hawaiians call Hansen's disease *mai ho'oka'awale*, which means 'separating sickness,' a disease all the more dreaded because it tore families apart. Some patients arrived

LEE FOSTER

LANA'I & MOLOKA'I

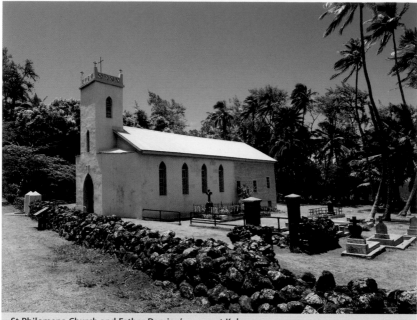

St Philomena Church and Father Damien's grave at Kalawao   LEE FOSTER

at the peninsula in boats, whose captains were so terrified of the disease they dropped patients overboard. Those who could, swam to shore; those who couldn't, drowned.

Once the afflicted arrived on Kalaupapa Peninsula, there was no way out, not even in a casket. Early conditions were unspeakably horrible and lifespans short.

Father Damien (Joseph de Veuster), a Belgian priest, arrived at Kalaupapa in 1873. He wasn't the first missionary to come, but he was the first to stay. A talented carpenter, he built 300 simple houses. Damien also nursed the sick, wrapped bandages on oozing sores, hammered coffins and dug graves. On average, he buried one person a day.

Damien's work inspired others, including Mother Marianne Cope, who stayed 30 years and came to be known as the mother of the hospice movement. Damien died of Hansen's disease in 1889 at the age of 49. In 1995 he was beatified by Pope John Paul II and is now a candidate for sainthood.

Over the years, some 8000 people have come to Kalaupapa Peninsula to live out their lives. The isolation policies in Kalaupapa weren't abandoned until 1969. Today, fewer than 100 patients, all senior citizens, live on Kalaupapa Peninsula. They are free to leave but choose to stay, feeling this is their only home.

Sights

The village looks nearly deserted; the sights you'll see on a tour are mainly cemeteries, churches and memorials. Visitors are not permitted to photograph the residents. Places the residents go, shops and the post office, are pointed out but not stopped at. A park **visitor center** displays period photos of the settlement.

St Philomena Church (better known as Father Damien's Church), in Kalawao, was built in 1872. You can still see where Damien cut open holes in the floor so that the sick, who needed to spit, could attend church without shame. The amazing view from Kalawao could be reason enough to visit the peninsula. It gives you a glimpse of the world's highest sea cliffs, towering 3300ft and folding out in successive verdant ripples.

LANA'I & MOLOKA'I

Tours

No one is allowed to walk around the peninsula alone. Everyone who comes to Kalaupapa must visit the settlement with **Damien Tours** (☎ 567-6171; tours $40; ⊕ Mon-Sat). Make reservations in advance. Tours last 3½ hours; bring your own lunch.

Getting There & Away

The mule trail down the *pali* (cliffs) is the only land route to the peninsula. You can hike the 2 miles down the trail but start early to avoid fresh mule dung. The mules start to descend at 8:30am.

Molokai Mule Ride (☎ 567-6088, 800-567-7550; www.muleride.com; ride $165; ⊕ Mon-Sat) is one of the best-known outings in the Islands. While the mules move none too quickly, there's a certain thrill in trusting your life to these sure-footed beasts as they descend 1600 switchbacking feet. Make reservations well in advance. Lunch and the land tour are included in the rate.

WEST END

The Maunaloa Hwy (Hwy 460) heads west from Kaunakakai, passes Moloka'i Airport and climbs into the high, grassy rangeland of Moloka'i's arid western side. Moloka'i Ranch owns most of the land on this side of the island.

Maunaloa

If something begins to look a bit contrived here, it is. Maunaloa is a yuppified version of a plantation town. Moloka'i Ranch owns this town and it bulldozed many of the original buildings that dated back to Maunaloa's days as a pineapple plantation. New buildings mimicking old, plantation-style homes were erected, resulting in rows of uniform dark-green buildings, and a town devoid of character.

There are some cool things in town nonetheless, including the homespun **Big Wind Kite Factory & Plantation Gallery** (☎ 552-2364; 120 Maunaloa Hwy; ⊕ 8am-5pm Mon-Sat, 10am-2pm Sun), which makes and sells colorful kites in all shapes and styles, and the family-run **Molokai Cowboy Connection** (☎ 552-2900, 877-888-7245; www.molokai-cowboy.us; 100 Maunaloa

Hwy; 1½hr ride $85; ⊕ Mon-Sat), which offers guided horseback rides.

West End Beaches

Off Hwy 460 at the 15-mile marker, a road leads down to Moloka'i's best beaches. The beaches are one after another along the coastal Kaluakoi Rd.

KAWAKIU BEACH

The northernmost of the beaches here is reached by walking north along the coastal golf greens and up over a rocky point. Kawakiu Beach is a white-sand crescent with bright turquoise waters and good swimming when seas are calm, most often in summer.

KEPUHI BEACH

This white-sand beach in front of the defunct Kaluakoi Hotel is okay for sunbathing but swimming conditions are usually dangerous. Not only can there be a tough shorebreak but strong currents can be present even on calm days. Experienced surfers take to the northern end of the beach.

Kepuhi Beach   KARL LEHMANN

MOLOKA'I SURF BEACHES & BREAKS *Jake Howard*

What Moloka'i, one of the most breathtaking islands in Hawaii if not the entire Pacific, possesses in beauty, it lacks in waves. Unfortunately, due to shadowing from the other Islands, there just isn't much in the way of consistent surf. Yet when the surf's up, keep in mind that the Friendly Isle encompasses the ideals of 'old Hawaii' in which family remains the priority, so remember to smile a lot and let the locals have the set waves.

On the western end of Moloka'i, winter swells bring surf anywhere between 2ft and 10ft (and, very rarely, 15ft). The break known as **Hale O Lono** is one such exposed area. It comprises several fun peaks and is the starting point for the annual Moloka'i-to-O'ahu outrigger and paddleboard races. On central Moloka'i's north shore, there are decent waves to be had at Mo'omomi Bay (p236). Being an archaeological site, entry into the area is dependent on approval from the Department of Hawaiian Home Lands. For information ask at the airport when you arrive. **Tunnels**, south of Kepuhi Beach (p239) to the west, is a popular break for bodysurfing and boogie boarding, and is also the only sand-bottom spot on the island.

Jake Howard is a senior writer at Surfer *magazine and lives in San Clemente, CA*

PAPOHAKU BEACH PARK

our pick A beach to die for. The 2.5-mile-long Papohaku Beach could hold the entire population of Moloka'i without getting crowded, although that would be an unlikely scenario. You're more apt to be here all by yourself. So where is everybody? Well, for one, it can be windy, with gusts of sand. But the main drawback is the water itself, which is usually too treacherous for swimming. It is, however, fantastic for long walks.

The beach park is a choice site for **camping** – beautiful and quiet, with the surf lulling you to sleep and the birds waking you up. Facilities include picnic tables, restrooms, outdoor and indoor showers and water fountains. Permits are available through the **Department of Parks & Recreation** (Map p230; ☎ 553-3204; Mitchell Pauole Center, Kaunakakai; ☺ 8am-4pm Mon-Fri).

DIXIE MARU BEACH

This beach at the end of the road is the most protected cove on the west shore, and the most popular swimming area in Moloka'i. Consequently there are usually a fair number of island families here, especially on weekends. The waters are generally calm, except when the surf is high enough to break over the mouth of the bay.

Papohaku Beach Park   NED FRIARY

LANA'I & MOLOKA'I

HISTORY & CULTURE

Maui has wowed 'em from the beginning. The very first Polynesian voyagers to discover this slice of paradise were so enamored by the sight that they journeyed back across 2400 miles of open ocean to tell their friends. So began the perilous Pacific voyages, the Western colonization and the kingdom intrigue, all of which make this island's history so compelling. Today Maui is one of the most ethnically diverse places in the USA. Here you'll find a sushi shop next to a Hawaiian restaurant, a Buddhist temple opposite a missionary church and a rainbow of schoolchildren waiting for the bus. The bond that unites all Mauians is a sense of *aloha 'aina* – love of the land.

HISTORY

ANCIENT HAWAI'I

The earliest Polynesian settlers of Hawai'i came ashore around AD 500. Archaeologists and anthropologists often disagree on exactly where these explorers came from, but artifacts left behind indicate the first were from the Marquesas. The next wave of settlers were from Tahiti and arrived around AD 1000. Unlike the Marquesans, who sparsely settled the tiny islands at the northwest end of the Hawaiian Islands, the Tahitians arrived in great numbers and settled each of the major islands in the Hawaiian chain. Although no one knows what set them on course for Hawai'i, when they arrived in their great double-hulled canoes they were prepared to colonize a new land, bringing with them pigs, dogs, taro roots and other crop plants.

Their discovery of Hawai'i may have been an accident, but subsequent journeys were not. These Tahitians were highly skilled seafarers, using only the wind, stars and wave patterns to guide them. Yet, incredibly, they memorized their route over 2400 miles of open Pacific and repeated the journeys between Hawai'i and the islands to the south for centuries.

And what a story they must have brought back with them, because vast waves of Tahitians followed to pursue a new life in Hawai'i. So great were the Tahitian migrations that Hawai'i's population probably reached a peak of approximately 250,000 by the year 1450. The voyages back and forth continued until around 1500, when all contact between Tahiti and Hawai'i appears to have stopped.

Settlements sprung up all around Maui, with the largest in areas like lush Hana, where fertile soil and abundant rainfall provided ideal conditions for farming. Maui was divided into separate kingdoms, with rival chiefs occasionally rising up to fight for control of the island. It was not until around the 16th century that Pi'ilani, the king of the Hana region, marched north to conquer Lele (now Lahaina) and Wailuku, uniting Maui for the first time under the rule of a single royal family.

Under Pi'ilani's rule Maui experienced a period of prosperity that saw the construction of villages and large stone temples called heiau (see the boxed text on the opposite page). He constructed the *alaloa* (King's Highway), a 138-mile footpath that circled the entire island. Today many of Maui's highways, including the one around the remote southern side of the island, follow the *alaloa* and still bear Pi'ilani's name.

FROM 'DISCOVERY' TO MONARCHY
Here Come the Europeans

On January 18, 1778, an event occurred in the Islands that would change the traditional world of Hawaiians in ways inconceivable at the time. That was the day British naval explorer Captain James Cook, on his third 'Voyage of Discovery' to the Pacific Ocean, sighted Hawai'i while en route to the Pacific Northwest, where he was to search for a possible 'northwest passage' from the Pacific Ocean to the Atlantic Ocean.

Cook's appearance marked the end of Hawai'i's 300 years of complete isolation from the rest of the world. Cook anchored on the Big Island, across the channel from

900,000 years ago	AD 500	1780
The volcano that formed East Maui rises from the sea; eruptions continue until 400,000 BC, building a mountain mass that peaks today at the 10,023ft Haleakalā summit.	Polynesian colonists traveling thousands of miles of open seas in double-hulled canoes arrive in Hawai'i. These migration voyages between the South Pacific and Hawai'i continue for the next 1000 years.	Keopuolani, future wife of Kamehameha the Great and the mother of kings Kamehameha II and Kamehameha III, is born at the royal court at Pihana Heiau in Wailuku.

GODS & TEMPLES

Religion was the cornerstone of ancient Hawaiian society and there was a pantheon of gods and deities that regulated all aspects of daily life. At the top were four main gods: Ku, Lono, Kane and Kanaloa.

Ku was the ancestor god for all generations of humankind: past, present and future. He presided over all male gods while his wife, Hina, reigned over the female gods. When the sun rose in the morning, it was said to be Ku; when it set in the evening it was Hina.

Ku had many manifestations: one as the benevolent god of fishing, another as the god of forests and farming. One of the most fearful of Ku's manifestations was Kukailimoku (Ku, the snatcher of land), the war god that Kamehameha the Great worshipped. The temples built for the worship of Kukailimoku saw sacrifices of food, pigs and chickens, along with the occasional human being.

Lono was the god in charge of the elements that brought rain and an abundant harvest. He was also the god of fertility and peace.

Kane created the first man out of the dust of the earth and breathed life into him (the Hawaiian word for man is *kane*), and it was from Kane that the Hawaiian chiefs were said to have descended.

Kanaloa was the god of the ocean and the god of healing.

Below the four main gods, there were 40 lesser gods. Among those who are still revered today are **Pele**, goddess of volcanoes; **Laka**, goddess of the hula; and **Hina**, goddess of the moon. The Hawaiians had gods for all occupations and natural phenomena. There was a god for the *tapa* (cloth) maker and a god for the canoe builder as well as shark gods and mountain gods.

To praise the major gods the Hawaiians built stone temples, called heiau. There were two types: one a simple rectangular enclosure of stone walls built directly on the ground, the other a more substantial structure built of rocks piled high to form raised terraced platforms. The largest heiau still standing in Hawaii is Pi'ilanihale Heiau (p198), set on the coast just north of Hana.

Inside the heiau were prayer towers, *kapu* (taboo) houses and drum houses. These structures were made of ohia wood and thatched with pili grass. Carved wooden *ki'i* (tiki, or god images) were placed around the prayer towers.

Heiau were built in auspicious sites, often perched on cliffs above the coast or in other places thought to have mana (spiritual power). A heiau's significance focused on the mana of the site rather than the structure itself. When a heiau's mana was gone, it was abandoned.

Maui, and stayed long enough to refresh his food supplies before continuing his journey north.

Cook sighted Maui but never set foot on the island. The first Westerner to land on Maui was French explorer Jean François de Galaup La Pérouse, who sailed into at Keone'o'io Bay (now called La Pérouse Bay) on Maui's southern shore in 1786 (see the boxed text on p140), traded with the Hawaiians and left after two days of peaceful contact.

1786	1790	1793
French explorer Admiral Jean François de Galaup La Pérouse becomes the first Westerner to land on Maui, arriving in the Makena area at Keone'o'io Bay, today known as La Pérouse Bay.	Kamehameha the Great invades Maui, landing his fleet at Kahului and chasing the retreating Maui warriors up 'Iao Valley, where Kamehameha's warriors decimate the Mauians in the bloody battle called Kepaniwai.	British Captain George Vancouver anchors at Lahaina, 15 years after Captain Cook first arrives in Hawai'i, releasing cattle, sheep and goats that later devastate native plant life.

Kamehameha the Great

The last of Maui's ruling chiefs was Kahekili. During the 1780s he was the most powerful chief in all Hawai'i, bringing both O'ahu and Moloka'i under Maui's rule.

In 1790, while Kahekili was in O'ahu, Kamehameha the Great launched a bold naval attack on Maui. Using foreign-acquired cannons and the aid of two captured foreign seamen, Isaac Davis and John Young, Kamehameha defeated Maui's warriors in a fierce battle at 'Iao Valley that was so bloody that the waters of 'Iao Stream ran red for days.

An attack on his own homeland by a Big Island rival forced Kamehameha to withdraw from Maui, but the battle continued over the years. When the aging Kahekili died on O'ahu in 1794, his kingdom was divided among two quarreling heirs. That left a rift that Kamehameha quickly took advantage of.

In 1795 Kamehameha invaded Maui again, with a force of 6000 canoes, and this time he conquered the entire island and brought it under his permanent rule. Later that year Kamehameha went on to conquer O'ahu and unite the Hawaiian Islands under his reign.

In 1810, after two decades of warfare (plus some diplomatic efforts), Kamehameha became the first mo'i (king) of the Kingdom of Hawai'i, named after his native island. He established Lahaina as his royal court, where he built a royal residence made of brick, the first Western-style building in Hawai'i. Lahaina remained the capital of the kingdom until 1845, when King Kamehameha III moved the capital to Honolulu on O'ahu.

Kamehameha the Great is credited for bringing long-term peace and stability to

Whalers Village Museum, Lahaina GREG ELMS

a society that was often in flux because of power struggles among the ali'i (chiefs). While he was a heroic warrior and supreme ruler with absolute powers under the kapu (taboo) system, he was also a just and diplomatic monarch who was greatly admired by his people. Kamehameha ruled for 24 years until his death in 1819.

Whalers & Traders

After Captain Cook's ships returned to England, news of his discovery quickly spread throughout Europe and America, opening the floodgates to a foreign invasion of

1810	1819	1820
Kamehameha the Great takes up residence on Maui and declares Lahaina the royal seat of the Hawaiian kingdom, building a brick palace on the harborfront.	Kamehameha the Great dies and the *kapu* (taboo) system that regulated all aspects of social interaction is cast aside; the old Hawaiian religious beliefs are no longer strictly adhered to.	The first Christian missionaries arrive in Hawai'i from New England, befriend Hawaiian royalty and quickly fill the gap left by the abandonment of the old religion.

explorers, traders, missionaries and fortune hunters.

By the 1820s Hawai'i was becoming a critical link in the growing trade route between China and the USA. British, American, French and Russian traders all used Hawai'i as a mid-Pacific station to provision their ships and to buy Hawaiian sandalwood, which was a highly lucrative commodity in China.

The first whaling ship to ever stop in Maui was the *Balena*, which anchored at Lahaina in 1819. The first missionaries arrived in their wake, and the two groups were soon at odds.

The first whalers were mostly New England Yankees with a sprinkling of Gay Head Indians and former slaves. As more ships arrived, men of all nationalities roamed Lahaina's streets. Most were in their teens or twenties, and ripe for adventure. Lahaina became a bustling port of call with shopkeepers catering to the whalers. Saloons, brothels and hotels boomed.

A convenient way station for whalers of both the Arctic and Japanese whaling grounds, by the 1840s Hawai'i was the whaling center of the Pacific. In Lahaina the whalers could transfer their catch to trade ships bound for America. This allowed whalers to stay in the Pacific for longer periods of time without having to return home with their payload, resulting

A BLOODY CONFRONTATION

In January 1790, American captain Simon Metcalf of the *Eleanora* arrived on Maui, eager to trade Western goods for food, supplies and sandalwood. Late one night, while anchored off Olowalu on Maui's northwestern shore, a group of Native Hawaiians stole the ship's skiff for the purpose of obtaining the iron nails and fittings. In retaliation, Captain Metcalf lured a large group of Hawaiians to his ship, under the pretense of trading with them, but instead he ordered his men to fire every cannon and gun aboard the ship at the Hawaiians, resulting in the massacre of over 100 innocent men, women and children. This tragic event, one of the first contacts between Westerners and Maui islanders, is remembered as the Olowalu Massacre.

in higher profits. At the peak of the whaling era, more than 500 whaling ships were pulling into Lahaina each year.

Whaling brought big money to Maui and the dollars spread beyond Lahaina. Many Maui farmers got their start supplying the whaling ships with potatoes. Hawaiians themselves made good whalers, and sea captains gladly paid a $200 bond to the Hawaiian government for each Hawaiian sailor allowed to join their crew. Kamehameha IV even set up his own fleet of whaling ships that flew under the Hawaiian flag.

Whaling in the Pacific peaked in the mid-19th century and quickly began to burn itself out. In a few short years all but the most distant whaling grounds were being depleted and whalers were forced to go further afield to make their kills. By 1860 whale-oil prices were dropping as an

Island Insights

According to legend, the other Hawaiian Islands didn't even exist until the prankish demigod Maui snagged a fishhook on the ocean floor and yanked them above the surface.

1831	1848	1868
Lahainaluna Seminary, the first secondary school west of the Rocky Mountains, is built in Lahaina. Hawaiian royalty and Californians send their children to study here.	The Great Mahele is passed, creating the first system for the private ownership of land, and casting aside the traditional ownership of land by chiefs.	The first of thousands of Japanese contract laborers arrive on Maui to work the sugarcane fields. They are followed by similar migrations of Portuguese, Koreans and Filipinos.

emerging petroleum industry began to produce a less expensive fuel for lighting.

The last straw for the Pacific whaling industry came in 1871, when an early storm in the Arctic caught more than 30 ships by surprise, trapping them in ice floes above the Bering Strait. Although more than 1000 seamen were rescued, half of them Hawaiian, the fleet itself was lost.

Soul Savers

Shortly after the first missionaries arrived on Maui they made inroads with Hawaiian leaders. By a twist of fate, they arrived at a fortuitous time, when Hawaiian society was in great upheaval after the death of Kamehameha the Great. It made the missionaries' efforts to save the souls of the 'heathen' Hawaiians much easier, especially among the *ali'i* who immediately engaged in the reading and writing lessons offered by the missionaries in the Hawaiian language. By the middle of the 1850s, Hawai'i had a higher literacy rate than the USA.

Lahaina became a center of activity. In 1831 Lahainaluna Seminary (now Lahainaluna High School), in the hills above Lahaina, became the first secondary school to be established west of the Rocky Mountains. Lahaina was also home to the first newspaper – *Ka Lama Hawai'i* – printed west of the Rocky Mountains.

But the New England missionaries also helped to destroy traditional Hawaiian culture. They prohibited the dancing of the hula because of its 'lewd and suggestive movements,' they denounced the traditional Hawaiian chants and songs that paid homage to the Hawaiian gods, and in the late 19th century they managed to prohibit the speaking of the Hawaiian language in schools as another means of turning

Hawaiians away from their 'hedonistic' cultural roots – a major turnaround from the early missionary days when all students were taught in Hawaiian.

The Rise of Sugar

In the 1840s, sugar growing began to emerge as a secondary economic force behind whaling in Hawai'i. Maui's role in sugar had already begun in 1839, when King Kamehameha III issued small parcels of land to individual growers who were required to have their crop processed at a mill in Wailuku built by the king. Half of the crop automatically went to the king. Of the remaining half, one-fifth was taken as a tax to support the government and the other four-fifths went to the grower.

In the heyday of sugar, there were as many as 10 plantations on Maui, cultivating thousands of acres of land in all parts of the island. By 1876 the Hamakua Ditch water system had been built to transport water from the mountains to the dry plains to grow sugar. One of the most prominent and long-lived sugar mills was Pioneer Mill Company, founded in 1863 by entrepreneurs James Campbell and Henry Turton, in partnership with Benjamin Pitman. They cultivated their own land and processed their own crops, as well as crops from other sugar growers. In 1890 the first train to run in West Maui was used to bring freshly cut sugarcane to the mill in Lahaina.

As sugar production grew in the Islands, sugar barons and government officials alike worried about the shortage of field laborers, who were mostly Hawaiian. Introduced diseases, such as typhoid, influenza, smallpox and syphilis, for which the Hawaiians had no immunities, had caused a severe decline in the Native Hawaiian population.

1876	1893	1898
The Hamakua Ditch is completed and the massive irrigation system begins to bring water from Maui's rainy interior to sugar fields in the dry Central Maui plains.	On the eve of proclaiming a new constitution that would restore Native Hawaiian rights, Hawai'i's popular monarch, Queen Lili'uokalani, is overthrown by a contingent of American businessmen, mostly sons of former missionaries.	Against the wishes of the Native Hawaiian people, Hawai'i is annexed by the USA and becomes a US territory. At the time, less than 5% of the population is of American ancestry.

Painting of the god Maui, Alexander & Baldwin Sugar Museum, Pu'unene   GREG ELMS

To expand their operations, plantation owners, with the help of the government, began to look overseas for a cheap labor supply. In 1850 the *Act for the Government of Masters and Servants* was passed, which included rules and regulations for the importation and treatment of foreign labor. Shortly thereafter, plantation owners began recruiting laborers from China. In 1868 recruiters went to Japan, and in the 1870s they brought in Portuguese workers from Madeira and the Azores Islands.

Most of the labor contracts typically lasted for two to three years, with wages as low as $1 per week. Workers lived in ethnically divided 'camps' set up by the plantations that included modest housing, a company store, a social hall and other recreational amenities. These camps provided a strong social-support network for the workers. At the end of their contracts, some returned to their homelands, but most remained in the Islands, integrating into the multicultural mainstream.

After Hawai'i's 1898 annexation, US laws, including racially biased prohibitions against Chinese immigration, were enforced in Hawai'i. Because of these new restrictions on Chinese immigration, plantation owners turned their recruiting efforts to Puerto Rico and Korea. Filipinos were the last group of immigrants brought to Hawai'i to work in the fields and mills, from 1906 to 1946.

The Great Mahele

Throughout the monarchy period, the ruling sovereigns of Hawai'i fought off continual efforts on the part of European and

1901

The Pioneer Inn, Maui's first hotel, is built on the waterfront in Lahaina, with a facade that mimics neighboring whaling-era buildings. Author Jack London is the first of many celebrated guests.

1908

Maui cowboy Ikua Purdy wins the World Rodeo Steer Roping Championship in Cheyenne, Wyoming, establishing Maui as a world-class player in the rodeo circuit.

1927

Road gangs of convict laborers complete the construction of the Hana Hwy along the jungly mountainous cliffs of East Maui. In the process they construct 52 bridges over streams and gullies.

HISTORY & CULTURE

Hawaiian tiki statue at Maui Stables, Kipahulu

GREG ELMS

American settlers to gain control of the kingdom.

In 1848, under pressure from foreign residents who wanted to own their own land, a sweeping land reform act known as the Great Mahele was instituted. This act allowed, for the first time, the ownership of land, which had previously been held exclusively by monarchs and chiefs. The chiefs had not owned the land, in the Western sense, but were considered to be the caretakers of the land, and the commoners who lived on the land worked it, giving a portion of their harvest in return for the right to stay.

The reforms of the Great Mahele had far-reaching implications. For foreigners, who had money to buy land, this meant greater economic and political power. For Hawaiians, who had little or no money, this meant a loss of land-based self-sufficiency and forced entry into the low-wage labor market, primarily run by Westerners.

When King David Kalakaua came to power in 1874, American businessmen had wrested a great deal of control over the economy and they were bent on gaining increasing control over the political scene as well. Kalakaua was an impassioned Hawaiian revivalist, known as the 'Merrie Monarch.' He brought back the hula, reversing decades of missionary repression against the 'heathen dance,' and he composed the national anthem *Hawai'i Ponoi,* which is now the state song. Kalakaua also tried to ensure a degree of self-rule for Native Hawaiians, who had become a minority in their own land.

1937	1941	1959
Workers with the Civilian Conservation Corps build the Kapalaoa, Holua and Paliku cabins on the floor of Haleakalā Crater, one year after the road to Haleakalā summit is completed.	Japanese warplanes attack Pearl Harbor on the island of O'ahu, thrusting the USA into WWII and turning all of Hawai'i into a war zone under martial law.	A plebiscite is held in June and 90% of island residents vote in favor of statehood. On August 21, Hawaii becomes the 50th state of the USA.

OVERTHROW OF THE MONARCHY

When King Kalakaua died in 1891, his sister ascended the throne. Queen Lili'uokalani was a staunch supporter of her brother's efforts to maintain Hawaiian independence.

In January 1893, Queen Lili'uokalani was preparing to proclaim a new Constitution to restore royal powers when a group of armed US businessmen occupied the Supreme Court and declared the monarchy overthrown. They announced a provisional government, led by Sanford Dole, son of a pioneer missionary family.

After the overthrow of the monarchy, the new government leaders pushed hard for annexation, believing that it would bring greater economic and political stability to the Islands, and more profits to Caucasian-run businesses. Although US law required that any entity petitioning for annexation must have the backing of the majority of its citizens through a public vote, no such vote was held in Hawai'i.

Nonetheless on July 7, 1898, President William McKinley signed a joint congressional resolution approving annexation. Many historians feel that Hawai'i would not have been annexed if it had not been for the outbreak of the Spanish-American War in April 1898, which sent thousands of US troops to the Philippines, making Hawai'i a crucial Pacific staging point for the war.

WWII

For the next four decades, Hawai'i's sugar-based economy developed rapidly, bolstered by a burgeoning pineapple industry. A marginal tourism market began to expand as more passenger ships began arriving and new hotels were built. Hawai'i was no longer a sleepy haven for the rich and famous; the Islands were on the move economically, socially and politically.

On December 7, 1941, when Japanese warplanes appeared above the Pearl Harbor area, most residents thought they were mock aircraft being used in US Army and Navy practice maneuvers. Even the loud anti-aircraft gunfire didn't raise much concern. Of course it was the real thing, and by the day's end hundreds of ships and airplanes had been destroyed, more than 1000 Americans had been killed and the war in the Pacific had begun. The impact on Hawai'i was dramatic. The Army took control of the Islands, martial law was declared and civil rights were suspended. Unlike on the mainland, Japanese-Americans in Hawai'i were not sent to internment camps because they made up most of the labor force in the cane fields in Hawai'i's sugar-dependent economy.

The Japanese-Americans' loyalty to the USA was still questioned and they were not allowed to join the armed forces until 1943. When the US government reversed its decision and approved the formation of an all-Japanese combat unit, the 100th Infantry Battalion, more than 10,000 men answered the recruitment call. The 442nd Regimental Combat Team of the battalion, made up largely of Hawai'i's Japanese-American population, eventually saw action in Europe and fought so bravely that they became the most decorated fighting unit in US history.

STATEHOOD

Throughout the 20th century numerous statehood bills were introduced in Congress, only to be shot down. One reason for this lack of support was racial prejudice against Hawai'i's multi-ethnic population. US congressmen from a still-segregated South were vocal in their belief that making Hawai'i a state would open the doors to Asian immigration, and the so-called 'Yellow Peril' threat that was so rampant at the time. Others believed Hawai'i's labor unions were hotbeds of communism.

The fame of the 442nd Regimental Combat Team in WWII went a long way toward reducing anti-Japanese sentiments on the mainland and increasing support for statehood. In March 1959 Congress voted again, this time admitting Hawai'i into the Union. On August 21, President Eisenhower signed the admission bill that officially deemed Hawaii the 50th state.

Statehood had an immediate economic impact on the Islands, most notably in the boosting of the tourism industry. Coupled with the advent of jet airplanes, which could transport thousands of people per week to the Islands, tourism exploded, creating a hotel-building boom previously unmatched in the USA. Tourism quickly became the second-largest industry in the Islands, behind sugar production. By the 1990s tourism had overtaken agriculture as the leading sector of Maui's economy.

THE HAWAIIAN RENAISSANCE

In the 1960s, while tourism brought much-needed cash into the new state, it also brought further erosion of traditional Hawaiian culture, which was increasingly replaced by mainland American culture. Traditional Hawaiian luau became westernized and commercialized, Hawaiian music in Waikiki was replaced by rock and roll, and the Hawaiian language was rarely heard in public. Traditional grass and *ti*-leaf hula

skirts were replaced with glitzy colored cellophane skirts, and fresh flower lei were replaced with fake plastic ones.

But in the 1970s, much of this began to change thanks to two historical events. In 1974 a small group of people committed themselves to building and sailing a replica of a long-distance voyaging canoe. When the Polynesian Voyaging Society completed the *Hokule'a* and sailed it to and from Tahiti in 1976, a new interest in traditional Hawaiian knowledge and activities was born.

The same year, the Protect Kaho'olawe 'Ohana (PKO), a small grassroots group of Hawaiians from Moloka'i, began to protest the bombing of the island of Kaho'olawe, which had been taken by the US government during WWII and used as a practice bombing target (see the box on p226).

The political actions of the PKO, which included the illegal occupation of the island, awakened a new interest in reclaiming not only Kaho'olawe and other military lands, but also many Hawaiian cultural practices, which had nearly been obliterated by American culture. Large numbers of adults began enrolling in hula schools, many new Hawaiian-music groups were formed and Hawaiian-language classes emerged in the schools.

This renaissance also spawned an interest in Hawaiian sovereignty. Today, some groups want Hawaii to secede from the USA and reestablish a monarchy, while others want a nation-within-a-nation model. Some are seeking federal recognition and funding to address Native Hawaiian health and social disparities, and the alienation of Hawaiians, resulting from 100 years of American domination and control. Currently before the US Congress is the Akaka Bill, submitted by Hawaii Senator Daniel Akaka, which calls for such recognition and funding.

1974	2004	2006
The first nonstop flight between the mainland USA and Maui lands at Kahului Airport, beginning a boom in tourism that eventually turns Kahului into the second-busiest airport in Hawaii.	The US Navy returns Kaho'olawe to the people of Hawaii after using the island as a bombing target for nearly 50 years. The Maui-based Protect Kaho'olawe 'Ohana group is given stewardship of the island.	Maui's first commercial wind turbines, rising up the West Maui Mountains from Ma'alaea, connect to the island electricity grid, thrusting the island into the forefront of Hawaii's budding alternative energy movement.

THE CULTURE

ISLAND IDENTITY

Perhaps it's all that sunshine, but people on Maui really do tend to have sunny dispositions. They're more laid-back than their mainland cousins, they certainly dress more casually and they spend a lot more time outside. On weekends everybody can be found hanging on the beach stripped down to T-shirts and bikinis, and wearing those ubiquitous flip-flops known in Hawaii as *slippahs*.

Located 2500 miles from the nearest continent, the Islands are practically another country. On Maui, streets all have Hawaiian names, mixed-race people are the norm and school kids can play the ukulele. Here you'll find no daylight saving time and no significant change of seasons.

The geographical distance puts local, rather than national, news on the front page. Indeed, Washington seems far away, as do Hollywood, New England and especially the Midwest and the South.

People on Maui never walk by anybody they know without stopping to ask how they're doing and looking like they really want to know the answer. Islanders prefer to avoid heated arguments and they generally don't jump into a controversial topic just to argue the point with someone. Politically, most residents are middle-of-the-road Democrats and tend to vote along party, racial, ethnic, seniority and local/nonlocal lines.

To locals, it is best to avoid embarrassing confrontations and to 'save face' by keeping quiet. If you attend community meetings or activist rallies, the chances are that the most vocal, liberal and passionate will be mainland transplants. Of course, as more and more mainlanders settle in Hawaii, the traditional stereotypes are fading.

Mauians tend to be self-assured without being cocky. Though residents in Honolulu may think of the other Hawaiian Islands as 'da boonies,' they generally give a different nod to Maui. In the greater scheme of Hawaiian places Maui is considered the more sophisticated sister, with a more polished scene than, say, the Big Island or Kaua'i. It's no coincidence that the current governor of Hawaii, Linda Lingle, was the former mayor of Maui County.

LIFESTYLE

On Maui, the family (*'ohana*) is central to island lifestyles. *'Ohana* includes all relatives, as well as close family friends. Growing up, the words 'auntie' and 'uncle' are used a lot to refer to those who are dear to you, whether by the bond of blood or friendship. Weekends are typically set aside for family outings – expect to see lots of cookouts on the beach on Sunday afternoons. It's not uncommon for as many as 50 people to be together as a family group on one of these picnics.

People are early risers, often taking a run along the beach or hitting the waves before heading to the office. Most people work a 40-hour week – overtime and the workaholic routine common elsewhere in the USA are the exceptions here.

In many ways, contemporary culture in Maui resembles contemporary culture in the rest of the USA. People in Maui listen to the same pop music and watch the same TV shows as Americans on the mainland. The island has rock bands and classical musicians, junk food and nouvelle cuisine. The wonderful thing about Maui, however, is that the mainland influences largely stand beside, rather than engulf, the culture of the island.

Not only is traditional Hawaiian culture an integral part of the social fabric, but so are the customs of the ethnically diverse immigrants who have made Maui their home. Maui is more than just a meeting place of East and West; it's a place where the cultures merge, typically in a manner that brings out the best of both worlds.

Island Insights

If you spot a Union Jack look-alike in the Hawaii state flag, you're right. It symbolizes the friendship between the British and King Kamehameha I, who commissioned the flag in 1816.

Recent decades have seen a refreshing cultural renaissance in all things Hawaiian. Hawaiian-language classes are thriving, local artists and craftspeople are returning to traditional mediums and themes, and hula classes are concentrating more on the nuances behind hand movements and facial expressions than on the dramatic hip-shaking that sells tickets to dance shows.

Certainly visitors will still encounter a measure of packaged Hawaiiana that seems almost a parody of island culture, from plastic lei to theme-park luau. But fortunately for the visitor, the growing interest in traditional Hawaiian culture is having a positive impact on the tourist industry, and authentic performances by hula students and Hawaiian musicians are now the norm.

The aloha shirt remains appropriate for business and social functions, but only classy ones such as Reyn Spooner designs. The muumuu as street attire has been outmoded since the 1980s, but it's certainly appropriate for hula dancers or Hawaiian *tutu* (grandmothers).

Folks on Maui are quite accepting of other people, which helps explain the harmonious hodgepodge of races and cultures that make up the society. Sexual orientation is generally not an issue and gays and lesbians tend to be accepted without prejudice.

Interested parties probably already know that *pakalolo* (marijuana) remains a top cash crop and that medical marijuana was legalized in 2000. The troublesome drug problem is the use of 'ice' (crystal methamphetamine), which has been rampant in Hawaii since the 1990s, especially in rural communities.

Most locals strive for the conventional 'American dream': kids, home ownership, stable work and ample free time. Generally, those with less-standard lifestyles (eg B&B owners, artists, unmarrieds and world travelers) are mainland transplants.

Maui has the highest housing costs in Hawaii, with the median price of a home hovering around $700,000. That has priced many Mauians out of the market since the median family income of $68,000 barely qualifies for a mortgage. For working-class people, it generally takes two incomes just to make ends meet. The average salary for a hotel maid or retail salesperson is $24,000; for a schoolteacher, $39,000; and for a dentist, $72,000. Considering that food, gasoline and energy costs are about 20% higher than on the mainland, it can be a tough go in paradise. Yet most agree that nothing compares to living on Maui and leave only if absolutely necessary.

POPULATION

Maui's population has increased significantly in recent years, creating pressure on the island's infrastructure, particularly the limited water systems. Still, it's a relatively uncrowded place, with just 118,000 residents.

Ethnically, Hawaii is unique. It's one of only four states in which whites do not form a majority and it has the largest percentage of Asian-Americans in all 50 US states. It also has the highest mixed-race percentage among all states.

People don't live in ethnic enclaves on Maui but remote communities like Hana in

Island identity and culture takes many forms

the south and Kahakuloa in the north tend to retain their traditional ethnic makeup. These are by far the two most Hawaiian communities on Maui – in part because land has stayed within the same families for generations. Elsewhere on Maui, the odds are your neighbors on either side of your house will have different ethnic backgrounds.

Among the US population Hawaii residents have the longest life expectancy: 79.8 years.

MULTICULTURALISM

Hawaii's diversity is both eclectic and narrow at once. That's because Hawaii's unique blend of races, ethnicities and cultures is quite isolated from the rest of the world. On one hand, Hawaii is far removed from any middle-American, white-bread city. On the other, it also lacks major exposure to certain races and ethnicities, particularly blacks and Mexican Hispanics, that are prevalent in the mainland US population.

WHO'S WHO

Haole White person, Caucasian. Often further defined as 'mainland haole' or 'local haole.'

Hapa Person of mixed ancestry, most commonly referring to *hapa haole* who are part white and part Asian.

Hawaiian Person of Native Hawaiian ancestry. It's a faux pas to call a non-native Hawaii resident 'Hawaiian.'

Kama'aina Person who is a resident of Hawaii, literally defined as 'child of the land.'

Local Person who grew up in Hawaii. Locals who move away retain their local 'cred,' at least in part. But longtime transplants never become local. To call a transplant 'almost local' is considered a compliment.

Neighbor Islander Person who lives on any Hawaiian Island other than O'ahu.

Transplant Person who moves to the Islands as an adult.

ABBOT LOW MOFFAT III

Slack key guitar masters at work

HAWAIIAN SLACK KEY GUITAR PRODUCTIONS

Any discussion regarding multiculturalism must address whether we are talking about locals (insiders) or nonlocals (outsiders). Among locals, social interaction has hinged on old plantation stereotypes and hierarchies since statehood. During plantation days, whites were the wealthy plantation owners, and for years afterward minorities would joke about their being the 'bosses' or about their privileges due to race. As the Japanese rose to power both economically and politically, they tended to capitalize on their 'minority' status, emphasizing their insider status as former plantation laborers. But the traditional distinctions and alliances are fading now as the plantation generation dies away.

Of course, any tensions among local groups are quite benign compared with racial strife on the mainland USA. Locals seem slightly perplexed at the emphasis on 'political correctness.' Among themselves, locals good-naturedly joke about island stereotypes: talkative Portuguese, stingy Chinese, goody-goody Japanese and know-it-all haole.

When nonlocals enter the picture, the balance shifts. Generally, locals feel bonded with other locals. While tourists and transplants are welcomed with open arms, they must earn the trust and respect of the locals. It is unacceptable for an outsider to assume an air of superiority and to try to 'fix' local ways. If white, such people will inevitably fall into the category of 'loudmouth haole.'

That said, prejudice against haole is minimal. If called a haole, don't worry. It is generally not an insult or threat (and if it is, you'll know). Essentially, locals are warm and gracious to those who appreciate island ways.

RELIGION

The ancient Hawaiian religion fell to the wayside when the *kapu* system collapsed and Christian missionaries arrived (see p246). But Hawaiians took the traditions underground and today one still sees glimpses of the old religion. Public ceremonies, such as groundbreaking for a new store or housing project, often invite a kahuna (priest) to bless the land. At some ancient historical sites traditionalists perform rituals and leave offerings, such as a *ti* leaf wrapped around a stone and placed on a heiau wall. The spirituality of old Hawai'i also lives in the arts, most notably in the hula, where the intricacies of many dances revere the

SHAKA SIGN

Islanders greet each other with the *shaka* sign, which is made by folding down the three middle fingers to the palm and extending the thumb and little finger. The hand is then held out and shaken back and forth in greeting. On Maui, it's as common as waving.

age-old spirits of the Islands. Hawaiians' activism against development is rooted in *aloha 'aina* (love of the land).

Religion remains quite significant as a social force. Most people in Hawaii are Christians. Sermons often include both Hawaiian and English words, and some hymns are sung solely in Hawaiian. Roman Catholicism is by far the largest denomination. Within Protestant Christianity, the mainstream, less conservative groups – including the Congregational Church (United Church of Christ), which arrived with the early missionaries – are struggling with declining membership. Conversely, nondenominational and often-fundamentalist evangelical churches are growing. Hawaii has the highest statewide percentage of Buddhists in the USA.

ARTS
Music

Contemporary Hawaiian music gives center stage to the guitar, which was first introduced to the Islands by Spanish cowboys in the 1830s. The Hawaiians made it uniquely their own, however. In 1889, Joseph Kekuku, a Native Hawaiian, designed the steel guitar, one of only two major musical instruments invented in what is now the USA. (The other is the banjo.) The Hawaiian steel guitar is usually played with slack key tunings. For the slack key method (*ki ho'alu*, which means 'loosen the key'), the six strings are slacked from their standard tuning to facilitate a full sound on a single guitar – the thumb plays the bass and rhythm chords, while the fingers play the melody and improvisations, in a picked style.

The most influential slack key artist was Gabby Pahinui (1921–80), who launched the modern slack key era with his first recording in 1946. Other pioneering slack key masters were Sonny Chillingworth and Atta Isaacs. Today the tradition lives on in Dennis Kamakahi, Keola Beamer, Led Ka'apana and Cyril Pahinui, among others.

Universally beloved is the ukulele, derived from the *braguinha,* a Portuguese instrument introduced to Hawai'i in the late 19th century. Ukulele means 'jumping flea' in Hawaiian, referring to the way players' deft fingers would swiftly 'jump' around the

TOP HAWAIIAN SOUNDS
Familiarize yourself with the dynamic panoply of Hawaiian music by starting with the following icons:
Genoa Keawe (www.genoakeawe.com) No one epitomizes Hawaii like 'Aunty Genoa,' whose extraordinary signature falsetto sets the standard.
Gregory 'Rocky' Sardinha Versatile, talented Sardinha studied with the late great Jerry Byrd and today performs regularly throughout the Islands.
Israel Kamakawiwo'ole No discussion of Hawaiian music is complete without honoring the late 'Braddah Iz,' whose *Facing Future* is Hawaii's all-time bestselling album. Locals felt kinship to his genuine Hawaiian soul.
Jake Shimabukuro (www.jakeshimabukuro .com) A ukulele virtuoso and exhilarating performer, Shimabukuro is known for lightning-fast fingers and a talent for playing any musical genre on the ukulele. Check his tour schedule online, which often includes Maui.
Keali'i Reichel (www.kealiireichel.com) Charismatic vocalist Reichel is also a *kumu hula* (hula teacher) and the founder of a Hawaiian-language immersion school on Maui. Since recording his award-winning first CD in 1994, he has earned a permanent place in Hawaii's musical pantheon. Check his website for concert details.

strings. Hawaii's ukulele masters include Eddie Kamae, Herb Ohta and contemporary uke whirlwind Jake Shimabukuro.

Both the ukulele and the steel guitar were essential to the lighthearted, romantic music popularized in Hawai'i from the 1930s to the 1950s, of which 'My Little Grass Shack' and 'Lovely Hula Hands' are classics.

In the 1970s Hawaiian music enjoyed a rebirth, and artists such as Cecilio & Kapono and the Beamer Brothers remain icons in Hawaii. Over the years the Hawaiian sound has spurred offshoots like reggae-inspired 'Jawaiian,' but the traditional style lives on in gifted contemporary voices, such as Keali'i Reichel, also a hula master, and Raiatea Helm, who has been scooping up Hawaii's top music awards. Still, the most famous island musician is the late Israel Kamakawiwo'ole, whose *Facing Future* is Hawaii's all-time bestselling album. The genre is now breaking out of the niche market, with online sales mounting and a new Grammy Award for Best Hawaiian

HISTORY & CULTURE

Music Album established in 2005. In that year the award went to a slack key collection that featured Maui's own Jeff Peterson, and Keoki Kahumoku.

To learn more about slack key guitar, start at George Winston's Dancing Cat label (www.dancingcat.com). An online community for guitar and ukulele players is available at www.taropatch.net.

Hula

No art form is more uniquely Hawaiian than the hula. In ancient Hawai'i, hula was not entertainment but a type of religious expression. Dancers used hand gestures, facial expression and rhythmic movement to illustrate historical events, legendary tales and the accomplishments of the great *ali'i*. These were performed to rhythmic chants and drum beatings, serving to connect with the world of spirits. Dancers wore *kapa* (bark cloth), never the stereotypical grass skirts.

There are many hula *halau* (troupes) active on Maui. Some practice in public places, such as school grounds and parks, where visitors are welcome to watch. Although many of the *halau* rely on tuition

fees, others receive sponsorship from hotels or shopping centers and give weekly public performances in return. Two places where you can see authentic hula are at the Lahaina Cannery Mall and Hale Kahiko, both in Lahaina (p68). If you're lucky enough to be in Maui at the time, don't miss the Hula O Na Keiki competition (p83) in Ka'anapali in November.

Hawaiian Arts & Crafts

Ancient crafts have an aesthetic component that reflects the simple stone and shell tools Hawaiians once used to create everything from surfboards to clothing.

Woodworking is an ancient skill that remains popular and commercially viable. In old Hawai'i, the best artisans used giant logs to build canoes. Today, the usual creations are hand-turned wooden bowls and furniture, impossibly smooth and polished, made from a variety of hardwood. Traditionally koa was the wood of choice but, for variety, other gorgeous island woods are also used. Don't be fooled by cheap monkeypod bowls made in the Philippines.

Lei making is a more transitory art form. Although the lei most visitors wear are

Hula dancers at Old Lahaina Luau
GREG ELMS

HAWAIIAN QUILTING

Hawaiian quilts are a unique art form, born of unique circumstances. The concept of patchwork quilting was introduced by the early Christian missionaries but the Hawaiians, who had only recently taken to cotton clothing, didn't have a surplus of cloth scraps to use – and the idea of cutting up new lengths of fabric simply to sew them back together again in small squares seemed absurd.

Instead, Hawaiian women created designs using larger cloth pieces, typically with stylized tropical flora on a contrasting background. The story goes that when the first group of Hawaiian quilters spread their white cloth on the ground, a breadfruit leaf cast its shadow onto the cloth and the outline of the leaf was traced to produce the first native design.

Two places where you can buy Hawaiian quilting kits and materials, and take lessons, are the Needlework Shop (p70) in Lahaina and Maui Quilt Shop (p129) in Kihei.

made of fragrant flowers such as plumeria and tuberose, traditional lei of *mokihana* berries and maile leaves were more commonly worn in old Hawai'i. Both types are still made and sold today.

Lauhala weaving is another traditional craft. Weaving the *lau* (leaves) of the *hala* (pandanus) tree is the fun part, while preparing the leaves, which have razor-sharp spines, is difficult, messy work. Traditionally *lauhala* served as mats and floor coverings, but today smaller items such as hats, placemats and baskets are most common.

Literature

For years, 'Hawaii literature' referred to fiction set in Hawaii, typically by nonlocal writers. Oft-cited examples include *Hawaii*, James Michener's ambitious saga of Hawaii's history, and *Hotel Honolulu*, Paul Theroux's novel about a washed-up writer who becomes the manager of a rundown hotel. Also widely read is Isabella Bird, the 19th-century British adventurer, who captures the exoticism of the Islands for outsiders. Today, however, a growing body of local writers is redefining the meaning of Hawaii literature.

Local literature doesn't consciously highlight Hawaii as an exotic setting but instead focuses on the lives and attitudes of universal characters. **Bamboo Ridge Press** (www .bambooridge.com), which publishes contemporary local fiction and poetry in a biannual journal, *Bamboo Ridge,* has launched many local writers' careers. Some have hit the national scene, such as Nora Okja Keller, whose first novel, *Comfort Woman,* won the 1998 American Book Award, and Lois-Ann Yamanaka, who introduced pidgin to literary circles with *Saturday Night at the Pahala Theatre* – winner of the 1993 Pushcart Prize for poetry – and critically acclaimed novels such as *Behold the Many.*

Much locally written literature features pidgin English, especially in dialogue. If you're new to pidgin, *Growing Up Local: An Anthology of Poetry and Prose from Hawaii* (Bamboo Ridge Press) is a good introduction. This collection is widely used in high school and college ethnic-literature classes nationwide. Also highly amusing are the pidgin writings by Lee Tonouchi, whose books include *Da Word* (short stories), *Living Pidgin: Contemplations on Pidgin Culture* (essays) and, most recently, *Da Kine Dictionary* (pictorial dictionary).

Cinema & TV

Hollywood's love affair with Hawaii began in 1913 and bloomed in the 1930s, when the Islands captured the public's imagination as a sultry, carefree paradise. In film classics such as *Waikiki Wedding* (featuring Bing Crosby's Oscar-winning song, 'Sweet Leilani'), *Blue Hawaii* (an Elvis favorite) and a spate of WWII dramas, including the 1953 classic *From Here to Eternity,* viewers saw Hawaii through foreigners' eyes.

Hundreds of feature films have been shot in Hawaii, including box-office hits such as *Raiders of the Lost Ark, Godzilla, Waterworld, Pearl Harbor,* and *Jurassic Park* and its two sequels. Unless homegrown films are produced, expect to see the same themes and stereotypes (and fake pidgin accents) in Hollywood movies. Essentially, Hawaii is often just a colorful backdrop for mainland characters. Viewers might not even realize they're seeing Hawaii onscreen,

HISTORY & CULTURE

Craftmaking at Old Lahaina Luau ABBOT LOW MOFFAT III

LEARN THE LINGO

The main language of Hawaii is English, although it's liberally peppered with Hawaiian phrases, words borrowed from the various immigrant languages and pidgin slang. The Hawaiian language is still spoken among family members in some homes and many people are studying it as a second language.

Some 85% of all place names in Hawaii are in Hawaiian and often have interesting translations and stories behind them.

The Hawaiians had no written language until the 1820s, when Christian missionaries arrived and wrote down the spoken language in roman letters. The written Hawaiian language has just 12 letters. Pronunciation is easy and there are few consonant clusters. Vowel sounds are about the same as in Spanish or Japanese, more or less as follows:

- **a** – ah, as in 'father,' or uh, as in 'above'
- **e** – ay, as in 'gay,' or eh, as in 'pet'
- **i** – ee, as in 'see'
- **o** – oh, as in 'go'
- **u** – oo, as in 'noon'

as the Islands often serve as stand-ins for Costa Rica, Africa, Vietnam and other such settings.

Surprisingly, Maui is rarely the island seen in these productions. Kaua'i is the celluloid darling, while O'ahu (the site of the current TV hit *Lost* and the past TV hits *Hawaii 5-0* and *Magnum PI*) draws directors with its more advanced facilities. Recent films filmed in part on Maui include *The Hulk* (2003), *Jurassic Park III* (2001) and the James Bond film *Die Another Day* (2002). Two MTV reality series (*Island Fever*, about a group of young folk, and *Living Lahaina*, about the adventures of surf instructors) were shot on Maui in 2006.

For an insider's look at surf culture, don't miss Stacy Peralta's *Riding Giants*, which features three titans in big-wave surfing – Greg Noll, Jeff Clark and Laird Hamilton – hitting the waves on Maui.

For more information about the industry, contact the **Hawaii Film Office** (www.hawaii filmoffice.com).

Written Hawaiian uses both glottal stops and macrons, although in modern print they are often omitted. The glottal stop (') indicates a break between two vowels, producing an effect similar to saying 'oh oh' in English. A macron, a short straight line over a vowel, stresses the vowel. Glottal stops and macrons not only affect pronunciation, but also can give a word a completely different meaning. For example *ai* can mean 'sexual intercourse' or 'to eat,' depending on the pronunciation.

Lonelyplanet.com offers a comprehensive, downloadable **Hawaiian Language & Glossary** supplement for free at www.lonelyplanet.com/hawaiian-language. For now, learn these words: *aloha* (love, welcome, goodbye) and *mahalo* (thank you), which are everyday pleasantries; *makai* (toward the sea) and *mauka* (toward the mountains), commonly used in giving directions; and *kane* (man) and *wahine* (woman), often on toilet doors.

FOOD & DRINK

Foodies, you're in for a treat. Maui has it all, from multistarred chef-driven restaurants that are the darlings of gourmet magazines, to mom-and-pop eateries that are equally famous in their own right. The island's ethnic diversity gives rise to an astounding array of culinary delights. Sensational flavors showcase plantation-era ethnic cuisines, from Japanese teriyaki and Chinese dumplings to Hawaiian *kalua* pork roasted in an underground oven. Then there's the fusion cuisine, the merging of fresh local ingredients and Pacific Rim flavors. Maybe poi isn't for you, but how about a taro burger with a side of crispy taro chips? Or seared *'ahi* with passion fruit salsa? Thought so.

STAPLES & SPECIALTIES

The first thing you'll notice is Hawaii is a rice-eating society. While you might find couscous or mashed potatoes at fancy restaurants, everyday meals are incomplete without sticky white rice. Not flaky rice. Not wild rice. Not flavored rice. And *definitely* not Uncle Ben's. Locals can devour mounds of the sticky stuff.

The top condiment is soy sauce, known on Maui by its Japanese name *shoyu,* which combines well with sharp Asian flavors like ginger, green onion and garlic. You'll invariably find it plopped down on the dining table next to the salt and pepper.

Meat, chicken or fish is often integral to a dish. For quick, cheap eating, locals devour anything tasty, from Portuguese sausage to hamburger steak to corned beef. But the dinner-table highlight is always seafood, especially succulent, fresh-caught fish.

On Maui the local pantry is relatively simple to stock, assuming access to a normal supermarket and a farmers market. If you're seeking premium imported olives, no worries. Maui supermarkets have the same sort of fine-foods aisles you'll find back home – but it would be a shame to rely too much on imports when you're surrounded by gardens and a sea full of fresh fish. And Maui's attempts at nonlocal classics (such as pizza, bagels, croissants and southern barbecue) are disappointing, so stick with *local* local food.

For more on Maui agritourism, see the boxed text on p47.

The classic plate lunch   GREG ELMS

Top Picks

FOOD EXPERIENCES

- **Hawaii Regional Cuisine** Café O'Lei (p128)
- **Shave Ice** Tom's Mini-Mart (p110)
- **Plate Lunch** Da Kitchen (p106)
- **Farm Tour** O'o Farm (p161)
- **Waterfront Breakfast** Gazebo (p90)

Local Food

The distinct style of food called 'local' usually refers to a fixed-plate lunch with 'two scoop rice' and a scoop of macaroni salad, served with mahimahi or teriyaki chicken, and scoffed down with chopsticks. A favorite breakfast combo includes fried egg and spicy Portuguese sausage (or bacon, ham, Spam etc) and, always, two scoops of rice. If it's full of starches, fats and gravies, you're probably eating local.

Pupu is the local term used for all kinds of munchies or 'grazing' foods. Much more than just cheese and crackers, pupu represent the ethnic diversity of the Islands and might include boiled peanuts in the shell, *edamame* (boiled fresh soybeans in the pod), and universal items like fried shrimp. But absolutely not to be missed is *poke,* which is raw fish marinated in soy sauce, oil, chili peppers, green onions and seaweed. It comes in many varieties – sesame *'ahi* (yellowfin tuna) is particularly delicious and goes well with beer.

Hawaii residents love their shave ice, a treat that's as common on the Islands as ice cream is elsewhere. Shave ice is a snow cone taken to the next level. The ice is shaved as fine as powdery snow, packed into a paper cone and drenched with sweet fruit-flavored syrups in eye-popping hues. Kids usually opt for the colorfully striped rainbow shave ice.

Native Hawaiian

Kalua pig, which is traditionally baked in an underground oven, and poi are the 'meat and potatoes' – so to speak – of native Hawaiian food. Poi is served as the main side dish with every Hawaiian-style meal. The purple paste is pounded from cooked taro roots, with water added to make it pudding-like. Its consistency is measured as one-, two- or three-finger poi – which indicates how many fingers are required to scoop it from bowl to mouth. Poi is nutritious and easily digestible, but for many nonlocals it's an acquired taste, largely because of its pasty consistency.

A common Hawaiian main dish is *laulau*, a bundle of pork or chicken and salted butterfish, which is wrapped in a taro leaf that's steamed until it has a soft texture similar to spinach. Other Hawaiian foods popular with visitors include baked *'ulu* (breadfruit), which has a texture similar to a potato – you can try it at Up in Smoke (p196) on the road to Hana – and *haupia*, the standard Hawaiian dessert, which is a delicious pudding made of coconut cream thickened with cornstarch or arrowroot. *Haupia* ice cream made on Maui offers a nice cross between the traditional and the modern.

Hawaii Regional Cuisine

Twenty years ago, foodies sniffed at Hawaii cuisine. Sure, you could slum it on local grinds at the beach, and the multitude of midrange Asian eateries was satisfactory. But fine dining typically meant heavy, European fare that ignored locally grown ingredients and the unique mélange of island flavors.

By the early 1990s, a handful of island chefs had decided to break out of the mold and create their own cuisine, borrowing liberally from Hawaii's various ethnic influences. They partnered with local farmers, ranchers and fishers to feature fresh local fare and transformed their favorite childhood dishes into grown-up, gourmet masterpieces. The movement was dubbed 'Hawaii Regional Cuisine' and the pioneering chefs became celebrities. A trio of those founding chefs with Maui connections are Roy Yamaguchi (Roy's Kahana Bar & Grill in Kahana; p89), Beverly Gannon (Hali'imaile General Store; p151) and Mark Ellman (Mala and Penne Pasta Café in Lahaina; p66 and p65).

The *real* catchwords for Hawaii Regional Cuisine are fresh, organic and locally grown. Think Upcountry greens, Maui chevre (goat cheese), Kula onions,

SPAM A LOT

If you're too embarrassed to eat Spam on the mainland, welcome to Hawaii – the only place you can eat Hormel's iconic canned ham with pride! Here in the Spam capital of the USA, locals consume almost seven million cans per year.

Of course, Spam looks and tastes different in Hawaii. It is always eaten cooked (typically sautéed to a light crispiness in sweetened *shoyu*), not straight from the can, and served as a tasty meat dish – Spam and eggs, Spam and rice, Spam and vegetables.

Spam was first canned in 1937 and introduced to Hawai'i during WWII, when the Hawaiian Islands were considered a war zone. During that period fresh meat imports were replaced by this standard GI ration, and by the time the war was over, Hawaiians had developed an affinity for the fatty canned stuff. Even today, whenever the Islands are threatened by a hurricane or dock-workers' strike, locals stock up on batteries, toilet paper, 20lb bags of rice and...Spam.

The most-common preparation is Spam *musubi:* a block of rice with a slice of fried Spam on top (or in the middle), wrapped with a strip of black sushi nori. Created in the 1960s, it has become a classic, and thousands of *musubi* are sold daily at grocers, lunch counters and convenience stores.

For Spam trivia, recipes, games and more, go to http://spam.com.

A genuine Islands 'delicacy' GREG ELMS

Drinkable coconuts on sale at a roadside stand

NED FRIARY

free-range Hana beef and locally caught fish. The spread of the movement has been a boon to small-scale farmers, who now have an eager commercial market. Some Maui chefs, like James McDonald (Oʻo Farm; p161), have even started their own organic farms. It's all contributing to a greening of Maui's gardens and menus.

DRINKS

Hawaii is the only US state that commercially grows coffee. Both Maui and Molokaʻi have coffee farms, and their final products are certainly worth a try. However, the only Hawaiian coffee with gourmet cachet is the world-renowned Kona coffee, grown on the Big Island. Aficionados rave about Kona coffee's mellow flavor that has no bitter aftertaste. You'll find Kona coffee at cafés and fine restaurants throughout Maui.

IT'S PERFECTLY CLEAR

Here's a riddle: what starts a mile under the waves, costs $35 a bottle and will give you a head-spinning high?

It's Ocean, a distilled-on-Maui vodka made with desalinated water drawn from the depths of the ocean. It's become the hottest spirit in Maui bars and fine restaurants. Passion fruit screwdriver, anyone?

Fruit drinks are everywhere, but inexpensive canned drinks are usually not pure juice. One native Hawaiian juice tonic is *noni* (Indian mulberry), which grows with wild abandon alongside roads. Proponents claim that *noni* reduces inflammation, boosts energy and helps cure everything from arthritis to cancer. *Noni* is pungent, if not repulsive, in smell and taste, so it's typically mixed with other juices.

Traditionally, Hawaiians had no alcoholic drinks, but whalers introduced them to liquor and taught them to make their own, *ʻokolehao*, distilled from the *ti* root. Instead of alcohol, Hawaiians used *ʻawa* (kava) as a mild intoxicant. You can sample the bitter, mouth-numbing beverage at Wow-Wee Maui's Kava Bar & Grill (p106) in Kahului. The lactones in *ʻawa* are believed to relieve anxiety, fatigue and insomnia, while fostering restful sleep and vivid dreams. The effect is mildly narcotic, but not mind-altering. *ʻAwa* is not recommended for pregnant women or for daily use.

In Hawaii, beer is the everyman of drinks. It's cheap, unpretentious and widely available. Maui has its own microbrewery, Maui Brewing Company (p89), which brews a range of beers that will please connoisseurs. It also supplies upscale local restaurants.

At Tedeschi Vineyards (p164) you can sample Maui-made wines, including their ever popular pineapple wine.

And, of course, at every beachside bar you can order one of those colorful tropical drinks topped with a fruit garnish and a little umbrella. Three favorites are piña colada, made with rum, pineapple juice and cream of coconut; mai tai, a mix of rum, grenadine, and lemon and pineapple juices; and Blue Hawaii, a vodka drink colored with blue curaçao.

CELEBRATIONS

The traditional Hawaiian feast marking special events is the luau. Local luau are still commonplace in modern Hawaii for baby christenings, anniversaries and similar events. Typically big bashes that include extended family, co-workers and friends, in spirit these local luau are far more authentic than anything you'll see at a tourist luau, but the short-stay visitor would be lucky indeed to get an invitation to one.

The main dish at any luau is *kalua* pig, which is roasted in a pitlike earthen oven called an *imu*. The *imu* is readied for cooking by building a fire and heating rocks in the pit. When the rocks are glowing red, layers of moisture-laden banana trunks and green *ti* leaves are placed over the stones. A pig that has been slit open is filled with the hot rocks and laid on top of the bed. Other foods wrapped in *ti* and banana leaves are placed around it. It's all covered with more *ti* leaves and a layer of coconut-frond mats and topped with dirt to seal in the heat, which then bakes and steams the food. The process takes about four to eight hours depending on the size of the pig and the amount of food added. Anything cooked in this style is called *kalua*

Food plays center stage in many other Hawaiian celebrations and festivities. On Sundays the beach parks are packed full of large family gatherings, picnic tables stacked high with a massive spread of potluck dishes. On standard American holidays, mainstream foods appear (eg Easter eggs, Super Bowl beer and Thanksgiving turkey) along with nontraditional local fare such as rice (instead of mashed potatoes), sweet-potato tempura (instead of candied yams) and hibachi-grilled teriyaki beef (instead of roast beef).

Maui food festivals such as the East Maui Taro Festival (p208) and Maui Onion

Top Picks
HAWAIIAN COOKBOOKS
- *Roy's Feasts From Hawaii* Roy Yamaguchi
- *The Hali'imaile General Store Cookbook* Beverly Gannon
- *Maui Tacos Cookbook* Mark Ellman
- *Tastes and Flavors of Maui* Mutual Editors
- *What Hawaii Likes to Eat* Muriel Miura and Betty Shimabukuro
- *Hawaii Cooks With Taro* Marcia Zina Mager and Muriel Miura

Festival (p83) showcase homestyle island crops. Gourmet culinary events include A Taste of Lahaina & Best of Island Music Festival (p64) and the Kapalua Wine & Food Festival (p94), which focus on island foods at the hands of Maui's top chefs.

WHERE TO EAT & DRINK

Informal dining is Hawaii's forte and the choices run a wide gamut. If you're looking for a quick meal, takeout plate-lunch–style eateries called *okazu-ya* are good choices and they pack things up tidily so you can carry your meal to a nearby beach for an impromptu picnic lunch. These places get busy at lunchtime but the lines move quickly – just make sure you know what you want when you reach the counter, as the folks in line behind you might get impatient if you dawdle. Lunch vans, known as *kaukau* (food) wagons, are far less common on Maui than on other Hawaiian Islands, but you can occasionally find one at a beach.

Maui has a happening café scene, and these are the best places to relax over a good lunch in an engaging setting and at a fair price. If the setting doesn't matter as much, you'll find plenty of diner-style Asian restaurants with formica tables and vinyl chairs, no view and no decor. They generally offer quick service and often have surprisingly good food at decent prices.

Maui's top-end restaurants are outright impressive and include some of the most highly-rated chef-driven places in Hawaii. Most are set on the beach and forgo the pompous fastidiousness common to up-scale urban restaurants on the mainland. Here you can sit in a casual oceanfront setting and enjoy some of the best gourmet food you'll find anywhere in America.

For groceries, head to farmers markets and locally owned supermarkets. Note that in Hawaii, 75% of groceries are imported from the mainland, including milk and eggs (unless labeled 'Island Fresh'), chicken, pork, produce and most beef. Thus, if absolute freshness matters to you, choose locally raised beef, island-caught fish and Maui-grown produce.

VEGETARIANS & VEGANS

While most locals are omnivores, vegetarians and vegans can feast on Maui, too. That said, vegetarians aren't the target market: a plate lunch without meat or fish is not quite a plate lunch, and high-end restaurants do tend to highlight seafood, though some of the better ones feature at least one vegetarian main dish nightly. Greens and veggies grow so prolifically in the Upcountry that salads have a leading role on menus and the smarter cafés will invariably have meal-size vegetarian salads.

And the Asian influence in local cuisine guarantees lots of vegetable and tofu options – walk into any Thai or Vietnamese restaurant and you'll find a extensive listing of vegetarian dishes on the menu. If you want to be in a totally meat-free space, there are vegetarian-only restaurants in Ha'iku (p156) and Pa'ia (p148).

EATING WITH CHILDREN

Maui's family-oriented, casual atmosphere means *keiki* (children) are welcome almost everywhere. Sit-down restaurants are quick to accommodate kids with high chairs and booster seats.

During the day, eat outdoors! The balmy weather allows for impromptu plate lunches at the beach or fresh fruit at roadside stands. If you really want to act local, buy an inexpensive straw mat at one of those ubiquitous convenience shops, pack a picnic and head to the nearest park.

Locals share a big sweet tooth, so finding treats is easy – perhaps too easy. Premium ice cream, shave ice, home-style cookies and chocolate-covered macadamias are omnipresent temptations. As for main dishes, the local palate tends toward the sweet and straightforward (without too much garlic, bitter greens, pungent cheeses and strong spices), which typically agrees with kid tastes.

You might assume that all fancy restaurants frown on parties that include kids, but many actually cater to them with special menus. Although the trend toward exhibition-kitchen restaurants – one large open area with a loud dining room – is unfortunate, at least kid chatter will blend into the overall din. At hotel luau, kids receive a discount. Commercial luau might seem like cheesy Vegas shows to adults, but kids will enjoy the flashy dances and fire tricks.

For more advice on traveling with children, see p275.

COOKING COURSES

Joy's Place (☎ 879-9258; 1993 S Kihei Rd, Kihei), an owner-run restaurant specializing in local organic food, offers cooking classes several times a year; call for details. **Ali'i Kula Lavender** (☎ 878-3004; 1100 Waipoli Rd, Kula) has cooking courses focused on the use of the herb lavender.

Gorgeously grilled 'ahi　　KENT HWANG

HABITS & CUSTOMS

Locals eat meals early and on the dot: typically 6am breakfast, noon lunch and 6pm dinner. Restaurants are jammed around the habitual mealtimes, but they clear out an hour or two later, as locals are not lingerers. If you dine at 8:30pm you might not have to wait at all! But bear in mind that restaurants also close early and night owls must hunt for places to eat.

Locals tend to consider quantity as important as quality – and the portion sizes are telling, especially at plate-lunch places. If you're a light eater, feel free to split a meal or take home the leftovers.

Home entertainment for local folks always revolves around food, which is usually served 'potluck style' with all the guests adding to the anything-goes smorgasbord. Locals rarely serve dinner in one-at-a-time courses. Rather, meals are served 'family style,' where diners help themselves. Throwaway paper plates and wooden chopsticks make for an easy cleanup, and the rule is 'all you can eat' (and they definitely mean it!).

If you're invited to someone's home, show up on time and bring a dish – preferably homemade, but a bakery cake or Sam Sato's *manju* (p111) are always a certain hit. Remove your shoes at the door. And don't be surprised if you're forced to take home a plate of leftovers.

FOOD GLOSSARY

Island food, with its blend of Pacific influences, is unique enough to require a little translation. In addition to the following food glossary, we offer a free downloadable Hawaiian Language & Glossary at www.lonelyplanet.com/hawaiian-language, which provides more Hawaiian and pidgin terms as well as pronunciation tips.

adobo – Filipino chicken or pork cooked in vinegar, shoyu, garlic and spices
arare – *shoyu*-flavored rice crackers; also called *kaki mochi*
'awa – kava, a native plant used to make an intoxicating drink
bento – Japanese-style box lunch
broke da mout – delicious; literally 'broke the mouth'
char siu – Chinese barbecued pork
crack seed – Chinese-style preserved fruit; a salty, sweet and/or sour snack
donburi – meal-size bowl of rice and main dish
furikake – Japanese condiment typically containing dried seaweed, sesame seeds and bonito flakes
grind – to eat
grinds – food; *ono kine grinds* is good food
guava – fruit with green or yellow rind, moist pink flesh and lots of edible seeds
gyoza – grilled dumpling usually containing minced pork or shrimp
haupia – coconut-cream dessert
hulihuli chicken – rotisserie-cooked chicken
imu – underground earthen oven used to cook *kalua* pig and other luau food
inamona – roasted and ground *kukui* (candlenut), used to flavor *poke*
kalo – Hawaiian word for taro
kalua – Hawaiian method of cooking pork and other luau food in an *imu*
kaukau – food
kamaboko – cake of pureed, steamed fish; used to garnish Japanese dishes
katsu – deep-fried fillets, usually chicken; see *tonkatsu*
laulau – bundle of pork or chicken and salted butterfish, wrapped in taro and *ti* leaves and steamed
li hing mui – sweet-salty preserved plum; type of crack seed; also refers to the flavor powder
liliko'i – passion fruit
loco moco – dish of rice, fried egg and hamburger patty topped with gravy or other condiments
lomilomi salmon – minced, salted salmon, diced tomato and green onion
luau – Hawaiian feast

mai tai – 'tiki bar' drink typically containing rum, grenadine, and lemon and pineapple juices
malasada – Portuguese fried doughnut, sugar-coated, no hole
manapua – Chinese steamed or baked bun filled with *char siu*
manju – Japanese bun filled with sweet bean paste
mochi – Japanese sticky-rice dumpling
nishime – Japanese stew of root vegetables and seaweed
noni – type of mulberry with smelly yellow fruit, used medicinally
nori – Japanese seaweed, usually dried
ogo – crunchy seaweed, often added to *poke; limu* in Hawaiian
ohelo – shrub with edible red berries similar in tartness and size to cranberries
'ono – delicious
'ono kine grinds – good food
pho – Vietnamese soup, typically beef broth, noodles and fresh herbs
pipikaula – Hawaiian beef jerky
poi – staple Hawaiian starch made of steamed, mashed taro
poke – cubed, marinated raw fish
ponzu – Japanese citrus sauce
pupu – snacks or appetizers
saimin – local-style noodle soup
shave ice – cup of finely shaved ice sweetened with colorful syrups
shoyu – soy sauce
soba – buckwheat noodles
star fruit – translucent green-yellow fruit with five ribs like the points of a star and sweet, juicy pulp
taro – plant with edible corm used to make poi and with edible leaves eaten in *laulau; kalo* in Hawaiian
teishoku – fixed, multicourse Japanese meal
teppanyaki – Japanese style of cooking with an iron grill
tonkatsu – breaded and fried pork cutlets, also prepared as chicken *katsu*
tsukemono – Japanese pickled vegetables
ume – Japanese pickled plum

NAME THAT FISH

In Hawaii, most fish go by Hawaiian names (see the Hawai'i Seafood Buyers' Guide at www .hawaii-seafood.org). All of the fish in the following list are good sustainable choices as long as they are caught in Hawaiian waters – ask before ordering, as some fish are imported.

'ahi – yellowfin or bigeye tuna, red flesh, excellent raw or rare
aku – skipjack tuna, red flesh, strong flavor; *katsuo* in Japanese
kajiki – Pacific blue marlin; *a'u* in Hawaiian
mahimahi – dolphin fish or dorado, pink flesh, popular cooked
nairagi – striped marlin; *a'u* in Hawaiian
ono – wahoo, white-fleshed and flaky
opah – moonfish, firm and rich
'opakapaka – pink snapper, delicate flavor, premium quality
'opelu – mackerel scad, pan-size, delicious fried
shutome – swordfish, succulent and meaty
tako – octopus, chewy texture

PLANNING YOUR TRIP

Maui is as tourist-friendly a place as you'll ever come across. Few activities require advance reservations. Hotels and condos are geared for vacationers rather than businesspeople, so you can relax casually no matter where you stay. As a matter of fact, the island's entire infrastructure is set up to handle its main industry – tourism.

That said, Maui is uber-popular, so you'll want to plan a few things ahead, especially your accommodations and car rental, to get good prices and choice. And the closer you are to a major holiday or school break, the more advance planning you should do. Start here.

For itinerary suggestions, see the Island Itineraries chapter (p18).

WHEN TO GO

Well, let's see, how soon can you get away? Simply put, there's no bad time to be on Maui. The busiest seasons are mid-December through March, and June through August, but that has more to do with weather and vacation schedules *elsewhere*. The weather on Maui varies only a little throughout the year. It's a bit rainier in winter, a bit hotter in summer, but pleasant year-round. See Climate (p276) for more information.

In terms of cost, prices can spike around big holidays such as Thanksgiving, Christmas and New Year's, and during special events. Visiting from April to May and September to early December will not only net lower off-season prices but you'll also find sights, restaurants and beaches less crowded as well.

CLIMATE CHANGE & TRAVEL

Climate change is a serious threat to the ecosystems that humans rely upon, and air travel is the fastest-growing contributor to the problem. Lonely Planet regards travel, overall, as a global benefit, but believes we all have a responsibility to limit our personal impact on global warming.

Nearly every form of motorized travel generates CO_2 (the main cause of human-induced climate change), but planes are far and away the worst offenders, not just because of the sheer distances they allow us to travel, but also because they release greenhouse gases high into the atmosphere. The statistics are frightening: two people taking a round-trip flight between Europe and the USA will contribute as much to climate change as an average household's gas and electricity consumption over a whole year.

Climatecare.org and other websites use 'carbon calculators' that allow travelers to offset the level of greenhouse gases they are responsible for with financial contributions to sustainable travel schemes that reduce global warming – including projects in India, Honduras, Kazakhstan and Uganda.

Lonely Planet, together with Rough Guides and other concerned partners in the travel industry, support the carbon offset scheme run by climatecare.org. Lonely Planet offsets all of its staff and author travel. For more information, check out our website, www.lonelyplanet.com.

DON'T LEAVE HOME WITHOUT...

- Sunscreen and your coolest swimsuit
- A snorkel, mask and fins – some of Maui's best sights are in the water
- Binoculars for whale watching and birding
- Broken-in hiking boots or shoes with good traction for wet trails
- Your reservations and your passport
- A warm jacket for Upcountry and Haleakalā
- A sense of adventure, the spirit of aloha and a hang-loose attitude

Maui dining can take a big bite out of your budget, but it doesn't have to   KENT HWANG

Naturally, for certain activities the seasons are a consideration. For instance, if you're a board surfer, you'll find the biggest waves in winter. If you want to go whale watching, that peaks from January to March. Cowboys might want to plan an adventure around Makawao's big rodeo (p153). For details of islandwide festivals and events, see p270.

COSTS & MONEY

The amount of money you'll need depends on your traveling style. Maui is an expensive place, but other than the airfare to get here and your car rental for getting around, it needn't cost a whole lot more to vacation on the island than elsewhere in the USA.

Campers, for instance, can pitch a tent for free in the national park. So if you're camping and preparing your own food, you can probably get by for $75 a day, and most of that outlay is going to be for your car rental. Opting for a B&B or a lower-end hotel and dining on plate lunches, you should be able to get by for under $200 a day. If you're staying at a beachfront resort and dining on haute Hawaii Regional Cuisine (see p261), you could easily spend double that.

Families in particular will want to consider the cost advantages of staying in a condominium. Being able to stock your own refrigerator and prepare some of your own meals can save a bundle. When you do go out, you'll find plenty of restaurants that offer inexpensive kids menus.

The good news for visitors is that lots of things on Maui are free. There are no parking or entrance fees at any beaches or state parks. Entrance fees at museums are reasonable and always discounted for children. And look for discount coupons in the free tourist magazines, which cut costs on all sorts of activities.

HOW MUCH?
- **Aloha shirt** $35–70
- **Pound of poke** $10
- **Pound of Kona coffee** $22
- **Plate lunch** $6
- **Shave ice** $3

For additional price information, see Quick Reference on the inside front cover.

BOOK ACCOMMODATIONS ONLINE

For more accommodation reviews and recommendations by Lonely Planet authors, check out www.lonelyplanet.com/hotels. You'll find the true, insider lowdown on the best places to stay. Reviews are thorough and independent, and best of all, you can book online.

CHOOSING ACCOMMODATIONS

In this book, accommodations are listed in price order, from lowest to highest. Price indicators are $ (under $100 per night), $$ ($100 to $170), $$$ ($170 to $270) and $$$$ (over $270). Room rates are for single (s) and double (d) occupancy; if there's no rate difference for one or two people, the general room (r) or suite (ste) rate is listed. Unless otherwise noted, breakfast is not included and bathrooms are private; rates don't include the whopping 11.41% room tax. (For an explanation of the icons and abbreviations used in this book, see Quick Reference on the inside front cover.)

Room rates are often lower outside of peak season (mid-December to mid-April), but it's wise to reserve in advance almost any time of the year to lock in a good deal. Holiday periods always command premium prices. When demand peaks, including during special events (p270), the best lodgings book up well in advance.

All that said, jockeying for the 'best rate' in Hawaii is a constant game that some elevate to an avocation. Be bold and inquisitive, and work every angle you can think of. For a range of accommodations listings, see **Vacation Rentals by Owner** (www.vrbo.com). You might also take a look at **Trip Advisor** (www.tripadvisor.com) for reviews and traveler advice.

A reservation guarantees your room, but most reservations require a deposit, after which, if you change your mind, there are typically cancellation fees. Note the cancellation policies and other restrictions before making a deposit.

B&Bs, Inns & Guesthouses

Maui offers a scattering of B&Bs and inns, ranging from budget options to smolderingly romantic hideaways. If you're considering a B&B, plan ahead. Most book out weeks in advance, especially in winter. Some require a minimum stay of a few days. Same-day reservations are usually hard to get, though like anyplace else there are sometimes last-minute openings. But always call ahead – B&B owners don't want unannounced visitors disturbing their guests.

In addition to places listed in this book, some B&Bs book only through agencies. A time-honored agency with bookings on Maui is **Bed & Breakfast Hawaii** (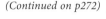 808-822-7771, 800-733-1632; www.bandb-hawaii.com).

There are also informal room rentals or house shares available for longer stays, often at good prices. Check the **Maui News** (www.mauinews.com) classifieds from home, or once on-island check the bulletin boards outside health food stores.

Camping & Cabins

On Maui there's a very clear pecking order in camping. At the top, offering the best and safest options, are the campgrounds at Haleakala National Park. After that, the state parks – most notably Wai'anapanapa State Park – are a better option than the county parks. As a matter of fact, we wouldn't recommend staying at any of Maui's county

(Continued on p272)

Lahaina's Pioneer Inn   GREG ELMS

FESTIVALS & EVENTS
CALENDAR

FEBRUARY

Whale Day Celebration (p125)
mid-February

A whale of a bash, this parade and beach-side celebration in Kihei honors Maui's favorite winter visitors – those splashy humpback whales – with all sorts of fun events.

APRIL

East Maui Taro Festival (p208)
late April

Hana, Maui's most Hawaiian town, throws the island's most Hawaiian party, with everything from outrigger canoe races and hula dances to a topnotch Hawaiian music festival.

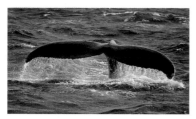

Banyan Tree Birthday Party (p64)
April 24

Celebrate Maui's most renowned tree with a wild birthday party under its sprawling branches, which cover an entire square.

MAY

International Festival of Canoes (p64)
two weeks in May

Maui's signature cultural event honors the island's rich voyaging tradition with two weeks of outrigger canoe carving by master carvers from throughout Polynesia.

JUNE

Maui Film Festival (p134)
mid-June

A movie lover's delight – the beach is transformed into 'SandDance Theater' and Hollywood stars show up for added bling.

Kapalua Wine & Food Festival (p94)
late June

Hawaii's hottest chefs vie for attention in this culinary extravaganza of cooking demonstrations and wine tasting.

Ki Ho'alu Slack Key Guitar Festival (p105)
late June

Slack key guitar music doesn't get any better this – the event brings in all the big-name players from throughout the state.

JULY
Makawao Rodeo (p153)
July 4
Roping contests, daredevil bull-riding events and a colorful parade showcase Upcountry's *paniolo* (cowboy) heritage on Independence Day.

AUGUST
Maui Onion Festival (p83)
early August
Maui's famous pungent bulb takes center stage in cooking events and (gasp) raw-onion-eating contests on the first weekend of August.

SEPTEMBER
Hana Relays (p208)
early September
Perhaps the prettiest relay race on the planet – six-member teams race 52 breathtaking miles along the famed road to Hana.

A Taste of Lahaina & Best of Island Music Festival (p64)
mid-September
The hottest chefs features their top dishes with cooking demonstrations and tasting booths, while the hottest musicians keep the beat.

Maui County Fair (p110)
late September
Maui's a garden land, so it's no surprise its old-fashioned agricultural fair is a bountiful event with orchids, luscious produce and all sorts of good food.

OCTOBER
Halloween in Lahaina (p64)
October 31
Lahaina hosts Maui's biggest street festival on Halloween night, attracting a whopping 20,000 revelers with music, dancing and costume contests.

PLANNING YOUR TRIP

Top Picks

SOUVENIRS

- **Aloha shirts** Aloha Shirt Museum (p69)
- **Lavender body lotions** Ali'i Kula Lavender (p159)
- **Maui-made crafts** Lahaina Arts Society (p69)
- **Maui pineapple wine** Tedeschi Vineyards (p164)
- **Wow-Wee Maui's chocolates** Wow-Wee Maui's Kava Bar & Grill (p106)
- **Ukuleles** Bounty Music (p108)
- **Hand-blown glass** Hot Island Glass (p155)

(Continued from p269)

parks. Kanaha Beach Park, in particular, is outright dangerous after dark.

If you're going to be camping in the Upcountry or in Haleakalā National Park, bring a waterproof tent, a winter-rated sleeping bag, rain gear and layers of warm clothing. Camping on the beach is another matter entirely. A very lightweight cotton bag is the most you'll need. Public campgrounds require campers to use tents – a good idea anyway because of mosquitoes.

NATIONAL PARKS

Haleakalā National Park has excellent drive-up camping at the summit (p182) and in the Kipahulu (p186) section. There are no fees, reservations or permits required for drive-up camping. Haleakalā also offers free backcountry camping on the crater floor with a permit, as well as $75 cabin rentals (p183), though these are in high demand and difficult to score.

STATE PARKS

Maui has state campgrounds and cabins at Wai'anapanapa State Park (p200) on a black-sand beach near Hana and at remote Polipoli Spring State Recreation Area (p163) in the cool Upcountry, as well as tent camping at Pala'au State Park (p237) on Moloka'i. Polipoli, deep in the rain forest, has just one primitive cabin, which is at the end of a rough access road that usually requires a 4WD vehicle. If you're not a pig hunter, you'll find the dozen beachside

cabins at Wai'anapanapa more to your taste. Book well in advance to avoid disappointment! Each state park allows a maximum stay of five consecutive nights per month and permits are required. Tent camping is $5 per night per site while cabins cost $45. For camping permits or cabin reservations, contact the **Division of State Parks** (☎ 984-8109; www.hawaii.gov/dlnr/dsp; 54 S High St, Wailuku, HI 96793; ⊗ 8:30am-3:30pm Mon-Fri).

COUNTY PARKS

Maui County parks permit camping for three consecutive nights at a cost of $3 per day (50¢ for children under 18). Permits are available by mail or in person from the **Department of Parks & Recreation** (☎ 270-7389; www.co.maui.hi.us; 700 Halia Nakoa St, Wailuku, HI 96793; ⊗ 8am-1pm & 2:30-4pm Mon-Fri) at the War Memorial Complex at Baldwin High School. Camping is allowed Thursday through Monday at Kanaha Beach Park (p103) in Kahului and from Friday through Tuesday at Papalaua Beach Park (p78) south of Lahaina.

'Iao Valley State Park, Wailuku

Condominiums

Some vacation destinations on Maui, such as Kihei and Napili, have far more condominiums than hotels. Condos are more spacious than hotel rooms, and furnished with everything a visitor needs, from a kitchen to a washer and dryer. They almost always work out cheaper than hotels, especially if you're traveling with a group. Keep in mind that in most places condo units are individually owned and then placed in a rental pool, so the furnishings and decor usually vary from one unit to the next. Whenever possible, ask to see a few units before settling in. Another advantage of condos over hotels is that many condos have built-in discounts for longer stays: generally the weekly rate is six times the daily rate and the monthly rate three times the weekly.

Don't forget to ask about cleaning fees, which might be tacked onto your bill. Most units have a three- to seven-day minimum stay.

Some condo complexes are booked only through rental agencies. Others operate more like a hotel with a front desk, though even in these places some units are usually handled by rental agencies. The following booking agents handle condos and vacation rentals on Maui:

Bello Realty (☎ 879-3328, 800-541-3060; www .bellomaui.com)

Kihei Maui Vacations (☎ 879-7581, 800-541-6284; www.kmvmaui.com)

Resort Quest Maui (☎ 879-5445, 866-774-2924; www.resortquestmaui.com)

Hostels

There are no Hostelling International (HI) hostels on Maui, but there are a few simple places in older buildings that provide a cheap place to crash. These hostels aren't up to mainland standards, but for travelers on a budget they do provide a dorm bed and kitchen facilities for around $25 per night.

GREG ELMS

SENSORY DELIGHTS

Experience the sights, sounds – yes, even tastes – of Maui on the internet.

- Want to eat Hawaiian-style food before you go? Check out the recipes at www.alohaworld.com/ono and cook up a pre-trip feast.
- To listen to humpback whales swimming along Maui's shores, log on to www.whalesong.net and hear them sing.
- Tune into Hawaiian music at www.alohafriendshawaii.com/hawaiiradio.html.
- Watch kitesurfers riding the waves at www.mauiwebcam.com.
- Want to get married on Maui? For the legal scoop, log on to http://hawaii.gov/health and then check out www.mauiweddings.com.

Hotels

It's very common for hotels, particularly larger beach hotels, to discount their published rack rates, most often when bookings are made via the internet. It really pays to do a little web searching on both the hotel site and the usual travel booking sites. Some hotels discount by the season or day depending on demand, and others throw in a free rental car, so look out for specials.

Within a particular hotel, the main thing that impacts room rates is the view and the floor you're on. An ocean view can cost 50% to 100% more than a parking-lot view, euphemistically called a 'garden view.' And the higher the rate, the quieter the room.

Resorts

Maui resorts don't mess around: they are designed to be pleasure palaces that anticipate your every need and provide 'the best' of everything, hoping to keep you on the property every minute of the day. They provide myriad dining options, multiple swimming pools, children's programs, nightly entertainment and fitness centers. At the priciest ones, beach sands are without blemishes, coconut trees are trimmed of drooping fronds and every aspect of your

experience managed in an oh-so-seamless way. They are intentionally contrived visions of paradise – and once you accept that, they're really quite nice.

INTERNET RESOURCES

Hawaii Visitors & Convention Bureau (www.gohawaii.com) The state's official tourism site.

Lonely Planet (www.lonelyplanet.com) Travel news and features, booking services and links to other useful web resources.

Maui County (www.mauicounty.gov) The official county site, covering Maui, Moloka'i and Lana'i.

Maui News (www.mauinews.com) Maui's main daily newspaper.

Maui Visitors Bureau (www.visitmaui.com) Maui's official tourism site, covering Maui, Moloka'i and Lana'i.

State of Hawaii (www.hawaii.gov) The official state government website.

TRAVEL LITERATURE

Use the long flight to Hawaii for some illuminating background reading and boning up on the rich island culture.

To listen to a Hawaiian king 'talk story,' read *Legends and Myths of Hawaii* by King David Kalakaua, also known as the 'Merrie Monarch.' Of ancient Hawai'i, he writes, 'but a thin veil then divided the living from the dead, the natural from the supernatural,' and he captures this shimmering quality in his evocative tales, which seamlessly mix real history with living mythology.

For an intriguing glimpse of Native Hawaiian culture today, pick up *Voices of Wisdom: Hawaiian Elders Speak* by MJ Harden, which features 24 *kapuna* (elders) speaking about cultural renaissance, from the renewed interest in the Hawaiian language, spirituality and hula, to outrigger navigation. Of particular relevance to Maui visitors is the section on former Haleakalā park ranger Eddie Pu'u, who is rebuilding ancient coastal footpaths on Maui.

Middle Son by Maui author Deborah Iida gives an interesting look at life on Maui in the 1950s through the eyes of a Japanese sugarcane plantation laborer and those of his sons. It includes lots of colorful local insights, from the use of pidgin to multicultural experiences.

DIRECTORY & TRANSPORTATION

CONTENTS

PRACTICALITIES

BUSINESS HOURS

Reviews given in this book only list business hours when they differ from these 'normal' opening hours by a half-hour or more.

Banks From 8:30am to 4pm Monday to Friday; some open to 6pm Friday and 9am to noon or 1pm Saturday.

Bars & Clubs To midnight daily; some to 2am Thursday to Saturday.

Businesses From 8:30am to 4:30pm Monday to Friday; some post offices open 9am to noon Saturday.

Restaurants Breakfast 6am to 10am; lunch 11:30am to 2pm; dinner 5pm to 9:30pm.

Shops From 9am to 5pm Monday to Saturday; some also open noon to 5pm Sunday. Major shopping areas and malls keep extended hours.

CHILDREN

Maui has everything a *keiki* (child) on vacation could dream of: sandy beaches, splashy hotel pools, all sorts of yummy food and tons of outdoor activities. Maui also offers plenty of cross-cultural opportunities, from hula lessons to outrigger canoe rides. Nevertheless, enjoyable family travel entails some logistical gymnastics and juggling to keep boredom at bay. When the going gets tough, bust out the chocolate macadamia nuts or stop for shave ice. Consult Lonely Planet's *Travel with Children*, which has lots of valuable tips and interesting anecdotal stories.

Practicalities

Hawaiians love kids – large families are common and children are a normal part of the scenery. Many restaurants have children's menus with significantly lower prices. High chairs are usually available.

Children are welcome at hotels throughout Maui and those under 17 often stay

PLUGGING INTO MAUI

- Voltage is 110/120V, 60 cycles, as elsewhere in the USA; foreign visitors should bring a universal plug adapter.
- The *Maui News* (www.mauinews.com) is Maui's daily newspaper.
- Several smaller weekly newspapers focus on local issues, including *Lahaina News* and *Haleakala Times*.
- Free tourist magazines such as *This Week Maui* and *Maui Gold* are packed with useful visitor information.
- For the scoop on the island art scene, pick up the free booklet *Art Guide Maui* (www.artguidemaui.com).
- For Hawaiian music with surf reports, turn your radio dial to KPOA 93.5FM.
- All the major US TV networks and cable channels are on Maui TV.
- Video systems use the NTSC standard, which is not compatible with the PAL system.
- As on the US mainland, distances are measured in feet, yards and miles; weights in ounces, pounds and tons.
- Most accommodations have free or inexpensive coin-operated washers and dryers.
- For a recorded island weather forecast, dial ☎ 877-5111.

free when sharing a room with their parents and using existing bedding. Cots and roll-away beds are usually available (for an additional fee) at hotels, but it's wise to ask ahead.

Most car-hire companies lease child-safety seats, but they don't always have them on hand; reserve in advance if you can.

If you're traveling with infants and failed to pack some of your gear, **Baby's Away** (☎ 800-942-9030; www.babysaway.com) rents cribs, strollers and other baby items.

To ditch the kids for an evening out alone, the easiest and most reliable way to find babysitters is through a hotel concierge. If you're not at a hotel, the **Nanny Connection** (☎ 875-4777; www.thenannyconnection.com; first child/each additional child per hr $16/3) arranges sitters with 24 hours' notice.

Before you go, check out **Maui Family Magazine** (www.mauifamilymagazine.com) online for ideas and information on island activities.

Once you arrive on the island pick up a copy of the free magazine at the airport information booth.

Sights & Activities

All of Maui is kid-friendly. Because of their glorious beaches and abundant resort activities, South Maui (p117) and West Maui (p73) are the two top destinations for families. Lahaina (p51) is a good place for kids who want to get out on the water, with surfing lessons and whale-watching cruises, and it's got some fun sights on land as well.

Some activities (like horseback riding, helicopter tours, ziplines and water-sports lessons) require that children be of a certain age, height or weight to participate. Always ask beforehand what restrictions apply. For suggested activities and itineraries geared toward children, see the Keiki Express suggested itinerary (p22) and the Top Picks for Kids boxes throughout the regional chapters. For more on outdoor activities, see p24.

CLIMATE

It's summer year-round and typically warm and sunny – enjoy! Maui is unusually pleasant for the tropics, as near-constant trade winds prevail throughout the year. Near the coast, average highs are about 84°F and lows around 70°F. Average temperatures differ only 8°F between summer and winter, and coastal waters are always warm.

Maui's high volcanic mountains trap the trade winds that blow from the northeast, blocking moisture-laden clouds and bringing abundant rainfall to the windward side of the island. The same mountains block the wind and rain from the west and south sides of the island, so it's there you'll find the driest, sunniest conditions and the calmest waters. It's no coincidence that nearly all of Maui's resorts are found on its leeward side.

Winter sees the most rain and some winter storms can last a few days. In summer, the rain is more likely to come in the form of 'liquid sunshine' – light, brief showers, often followed by rainbows. This doesn't mean winter is a bad time to come to Maui; it just means the weather is slightly more of a gamble.

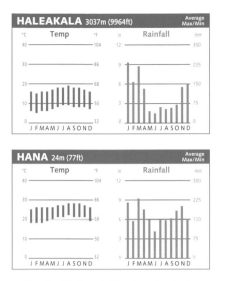

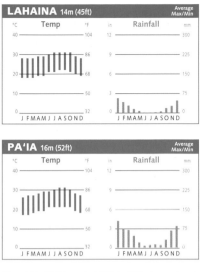

For the National Weather Service's recorded forecast of weather conditions on Maui, call ☎ 877-5111. For a more extensive marine forecast, including surf conditions, winds and tides, call ☎ 877-3477. See also When to Go (p269) and the climate charts (above).

COURSES

Whalers Village (p83) in Ka'anapali offers free classes in lei-making and hula dancing. Some hotels, most notably the Ka'anapali Beach Hotel (p86), offer lessons in a variety of traditional Hawaiian arts to their guests. The hotel concierge is a good source of information not only for your hotel, but for other possibilities in the nearby area.

If you're interested in ukulele or slack key guitar lessons, check at a music shop like Bounty Music (p108) in Kahului. The Hui No'eau Visual Arts Center (p151) schedules a wide range of courses in arts and crafts for both children and adults. Want to learn Hawaiian quilting? The Needlework Shop (p70) in Lahaina and Maui Quilt Shop (p129) in Kihei can teach you. And last but not least, Ali'i Kula Lavender (p159) has awesome cooking courses as well as craft classes using lavender.

CUSTOMS

Each visitor is allowed to bring 1L of liquor and 200 cigarettes into the USA, but you must be at least 21 years old to possess the former and 18 years old to possess the latter. In addition, each visitor to Maui is permitted to bring up to $100 worth of gift merchandise into the US without incurring any duty.

The agricultural laws in Hawaii are set up to protect the Islands' delicate ecosystems. Invasive species are a real threat, so clean your shoes and outdoor gear before you set off on your vacation. Most fresh fruits and plants cannot be brought into Hawaii. Hawaii is a rabies-free state and very strict regarding the importation of pets, so don't plan on bringing your furry friend on a short vacation. For complete details, contact the **Hawaiian Department of Agriculture** (☎ 808-973-9560; www.hawaiiag.org).

FREE HAWAIIAN-LANGUAGE DOWNLOAD

Learn the lingo – for free! Lonely Planet offers a free **Hawaiian Language & Glossary** downloadable PDF at www.lonelyplanet.com/hawaiian-language. Aloha!

DANGERS & ANNOYANCES

Drugs

Pakalolo (marijuana) remains a billion-dollar underground industry throughout Hawaii, and the use of 'ice' (crystal methamphetamine) has been an ongoing social and law-enforcement issue since the 1990s, especially in rural communities. The 'ice epidemic' has abated somewhat recently (as a result of enforcement efforts), but ice-related crimes continue and social-service agencies still struggle to provide treatment for addicts. A lot of the crime on Maui, including theft, is related to addiction to ice. Avoid the seedier parts of towns after dark.

Scams

The main scams directed toward visitors on Maui involve the activity and time-share booths that are ubiquitous in Lahaina. If you make a certain amount of money and own your own home, they'll offer you steep discounts on everything from whale watching to luau. The catch is, you have to subject yourself to a lengthy presentation on time-share properties. For the most part, this is legit, if annoying. But some of the pitches can be aggressive, nasty or dishonest, and some have been known to yank tickets from people who don't show interest in their time-share. If you decide the discounts are worth it, be sure you get your discounted tickets *before* you go to the pitch. Legit operators won't have a problem with this.

Theft & Violence

Maui is notorious for rip-offs from parked rental cars. It can happen within seconds, whether from a secluded parking area at a trailhead or from a crowded hotel parking lot. As much as possible, do not leave anything valuable in your car – ever. If you must, pack things well out of sight *before* you arrive at your destination; thieves wait and watch to see what you put in the trunk.

Otherwise, the most common problem is being hassled by drunks on beaches and in campgrounds, mainly at night. Wherever you are, stay tuned to the general vibe. Also, don't leave anything unattended on a beach. Don't forget your street smarts just because you're on Maui.

Tsunamis

Tsunamis are not common, but when they hit they can be severe. Maui has a warning system, aired through yellow speakers mounted on telephone poles around the island. They're tested on the first working day of each month at 11:45am for about one minute. If you should hear one at any other time and you're in a low-lying coastal area, immediately head for higher ground. The front section of the Maui telephone book shows maps of areas susceptible to tsunamis and safety evacuation zones.

DISCOUNT CARDS

Maui has a multitude of ubiquitous free tourist magazines replete with discount coupons for activities and restaurants. They're well worth perusing, perhaps while you're waiting for your baggage by the airport carousel. However, for hotels, usually the best deals are offered when you book in advance through their websites.

The first time you go into a grocery store, head straight for the customer service booth and ask for a free 'members card' that will allow you to shop at the same discounted prices islanders pay. It takes only a couple of minutes to get a temporary card that you can use immediately.

If you have reached 'that age,' consider joining the nonprofit **American Association of Retired Persons** (AARP; ☎ 888-687-2277; www.aarp .org; 601 E St NW, Washington, DC 20049), which is a good source for travel bargains.

FOOD

Throughout this book, eating reviews are broken down into four price categories: $ (for meals costing $12 or less), $$ (where most main dishes cost $12 to $20), $$$ (from $20 to $28) and $$$$ (over $28). These price estimates do not include taxes, tips or beverages.

For details about Hawaiian specialties and delicacies, see the Food & Drink chapter (p259).

GAY & LESBIAN TRAVELERS

Maui is a popular destination for gay and lesbian travelers. The state has strong legislation to protect minorities and a constitutional guarantee of privacy that extends to sexual behavior between consenting adults. That said, people tend to be private so you won't see much public hand-holding or open displays of affection.

Gay Maui is not terribly organized. There isn't a big, boisterous 'out' scene. Kihei (p120) is the gayest town on Maui, low-key as it is. Although it doesn't have any exclusively gay entertainment venues, some Kihei bars and clubs have a gay night, and Kihei has a gay-oriented hotel, the Maui Sunseeker (p130). For the full scoop on Maui's gay scene, check out **Both Sides Now** (www.mauigayinfo.com) and **Maui Pride** (www.mauipride.com).

For information on gay issues statewide, see the **Gay & Lesbian Community Center** (www.thecenterhawaii.org) website. **Hawaii Gay Travel** (☎ 800-508-5996; www.hawaiiigaytravel.com) arranges packages geared for gay and lesbian travelers.

HOLIDAYS

It's good to make advance reservations around the Christmas and New Year's holidays, as these are the busiest times of the year for hotels and car-rental agencies. When a public holiday falls on the weekend, it's often celebrated on the nearest Friday or Monday instead. These long weekends can also be busy, as people from other Hawaiian Islands often take advantage of the break to visit Maui. Also see the Festivals & Events Calendar (p270).

New Year's Day January 1
Martin Luther King Jr Day Third Monday of January
Presidents Day Third Monday of February
Good Friday March or April
Prince Kuhio Day March 26
Memorial Day Last Monday of May
King Kamehameha Day June 11
Independence Day July 4
Statehood Day Third Friday of August
Labor Day First Monday of September
Columbus Day Second Monday of October
Election Day Second Tuesday of November
Veterans Day November 11
Thanksgiving Fourth Thursday of November
Christmas Day December 25

INTERNATIONAL TRAVELERS

The following consulates and government liaison offices are hosted in Honolulu.
Australia (☎ 524-5050; 1000 Bishop St)
Germany (☎ 946-3819; 252 Paoa Pl)
Japan (☎ 543-3111; 1742 Nu'uanu Ave)
New Zealand (☎ 547-5117; Suite 414, 900 Richards St)

The USA continues to fine-tune its entry requirements and security guidelines post–September 11, so all foreign visitors should double-check visa guidelines. The **US State Department** (www.travel.state.gov) maintains the most comprehensive visa information and has application forms that can be downloaded.

The Visa Waiver Program allows citizens of certain countries to enter the USA for stays of 90 days or less without first obtaining a US visa. There are 27 countries currently participating: Andorra, Australia, Austria, Belgium, Brunei, Denmark, Finland, France, Germany, Iceland, Ireland, Italy, Japan, Liechtenstein, Luxembourg, Monaco, the Netherlands, New Zealand, Norway, Portugal, San Marino, Singapore, Slovenia, Spain, Sweden, Switzerland and the UK. Under this program you must have a return ticket (or onward ticket to any foreign destination) that is nonrefundable in the USA. You also need a machine-readable passport. Note that you will not be allowed to extend your stay beyond 90 days.

With the exception of Canadians and visitors who qualify for the Visa Waiver Program, foreign visitors to the USA need a visa. To apply, you need a passport that's valid for at least six months longer than your intended stay and a recent photo (50.8mm x 50.8mm). Documents of financial stability and/or guarantees from a US resident are sometimes required, particularly for those from developing countries. Visa applicants may be required to 'demonstrate binding obligations' that will ensure their return home. Because of this requirement, those planning to travel through other countries before arriving in the USA are better off applying for their US visa in their home country rather than on the road.

The validity period for a US visitor visa depends on your home country. The actual length of time you'll be allowed to stay in the USA is determined by US officials at the port of entry. If you want to stay longer, contact the **Citizenship & Immigration Service** (☎ 532-3721) to apply for an extension.

Upon arriving in the USA, all foreign visitors must register in the US-Visit program. This entails having their fingerprints scanned and a digital photo taken. For more information, see the **Department of Homeland Security** (www.dhs.gov) website.

INTERNET ACCESS

There are internet cafés in Maui's main tourist destinations; see the Information sections in the regional chapters of this guidebook.

If you have your own laptop, at most Maui hotels you can either hook into their dial-up or connect to wi-fi. If you bring a laptop from outside the USA, make sure you bring along a universal AC and plug adapter. Some hotels also offer online computers in their lobbies. When accommodations have provided some sort of internet access, this is noted with an internet icon (🖳) in this book.

Public libraries on Maui provide free internet access, but you need to purchase a temporary three-month nonresident library card ($10); for details, visit **Hawaii State Public Library System** (www.librarieshawaii.org).

For useful internet resources see p274 in the Planning Your Trip chapter.

LEGAL MATTERS

Anyone arrested in Hawaii has the right to have the representation of a lawyer, from the time of their arrest to their trial, and if a person cannot afford a lawyer, the state must provide one for free. You're presumed innocent unless or until you're found guilty in court. The **Hawaii State Bar Association** (☎ 537-9140, 800-808-4722) makes attorney referrals, but foreign visitors may want to call their consulate for advice.

It's illegal to have open containers of alcohol in motor vehicles, and drinking in public parks or on the beaches is also illegal. Drunk driving is a serious crime and can incur stiff fines, jail time and other penalties. In Hawaii, anyone caught driving with an blood alcohol level of 0.08% or greater is guilty of driving 'under the influence' and will have their driver's license taken away on the spot.

As in most places, the possession of marijuana and nonprescription narcotics is illegal in Hawaii. Tobacco smoking is prohibited in enclosed public places, including restaurants and hotel lobbies.

MAPS

The maps in this book are sufficient for most exploring. For the most comprehensive road atlas available, pick up a copy of the *Ready Mapbook of Maui County,* which covers virtually every road on Maui, Lana'i and Moloka'i, and is sold in Maui bookstores.

A good lightweight, foldout map is Nelles' *Maui, Molokai & Lanai.* The colorful Franko's *Maui, the Valley Isle* features water sports and is sold at dive shops; it is waterproof and rip-resistant.

The **United States Geological Survey** (☎ 888-275-8747; www.usgs.gov) publishes full-island and detailed sectional maps, though some were drawn decades ago. You're not likely to need these unless you're planning a big bike adventure or doing some serious backcountry hiking.

MONEY

As throughout the USA, the US dollar is the only currency used on Maui. The dollar is divided into 100 cents. Coins come in denominations of one cent (penny), five cents (nickel), 10 cents (dime), 25 cents (quarter) and the rare 50-cent piece (half dollar). Notes come in one-, five-, 10-, 20-, 50- and 100-dollar denominations.

All prices quoted in this book are in US dollars. See the Quick Reference inside the front cover for exchange rates and Planning Your Trip (p268) for information on costs.

ATMs, Cash & Checks

Major banks such as the **Bank of Hawaii** (www.boh.com) and **First Hawaiian Bank** (www.fhb.com) have ATM networks throughout Maui that give cash advances on major credit cards and allow cash withdrawals with affiliated ATM cards. In addition to traditional bank locations, you'll find ATMs at most grocery stores, mall-style shopping centers and convenience stores.

If you're carrying foreign currency, it can be exchanged for US dollars at the airport and larger banks around Maui. Out-of-state personal checks are not readily accepted on Maui.

Credit Cards

Major credit cards are widely accepted on Maui, including at car-rental agencies and most hotels, restaurants, gas stations, grocery stores and tour operators. However, many B&Bs and some condos – particularly those handled through rental agencies – do not accept credit cards.

Tipping

In restaurants, good waiters are tipped at least 15%, while dissatisfied customers make their ire known by leaving 10%. There has to be real cause for not tipping at all. Taxi drivers are typically tipped about 10% and hotel bellhops about $1 per bag.

Traveler's Checks

Traveler's checks provide protection from theft and loss. Keeping a record of the check numbers and those you have used is vital for replacing lost checks, so keep this information separate from the checks themselves. For refunds on lost or stolen travelers checks, call **American Express** (☎ 800-992-3404) or **Thomas Cook** (☎ 800-287-7362).

Foreign visitors carrying traveler's checks will find things easier if the checks are in US dollars. Most midrange and top-end restaurants, hotels and shops accept US dollar traveler's checks and treat them just like cash.

PHOTOGRAPHY

For a complete, short course on photographic ins and outs, and dos and don'ts, consult Lonely Planet's *Travel Photography*.

You can transfer digital images onto CDs at Kinko's (p103) in Kahului. Both print and slide film are readily available on Maui for approximately the same prices as elsewhere in the USA. Have your film developed promptly, as the high temperature and humidity accelerate the deterioration of exposed film. The Longs Drugs chain has good prices for film developing, including same-day processing.

Don't even think about taking snaps of military installations.

With the implementation of high-powered X-ray at airports, don't pack film into checked luggage or carry-on bags. Instead carry your film in a transparent baggie to show separately to airport security officials (known as a hand check). Remember to finish off the roll in your camera and take it out, too, or those photos may end up foggy.

POST

By world standards, the US Postal Service is reliable and inexpensive. You can get detailed 24-hour postal information by dialing toll-free ☎ 800-275-8777.

First-class mail between Maui and the mainland usually takes three to four days and costs 42¢ for letters up to 1oz (17¢ for each additional ounce) and 27¢ for standard-size postcards.

International airmail rates for postcards and letters up to 1oz are 72¢ to Canada or Mexico and 94¢ to other countries.

You can have mail sent to you c/o General Delivery at most big post offices on Maui. General-delivery mail is usually held for up to 30 days before it's returned to sender. Most hotels will also hold mail for incoming guests.

SHOPPING

Maui is a haven for craftspeople and other artists. The best way to ensure that what you buy is authentic is to shop at well-respected art galleries and artists' cooperatives. Maui Crafts Guild (p150) and the Lahaina Arts Society (p69) are great places to start.

Highly prized souvenirs are the bowls made of beautifully grained native Hawaiian hardwoods such as koa. Hawaiian bowls are not decorated or ornate, but are shaped to bring out the natural beauty of the wood. These, however, are very expensive. Hula musical instruments such as nose flutes and gourd rattles also are uniquely

Hawaiian and make interesting gifts at the affordable end of the spectrum.

Hawaii's island-style clothing is colorful, often with prints of tropical designs. The classiest aloha shirts are made of lightweight cotton or linen with subdued colors like those of reverse-fabric prints. And of course there are plenty of places selling T-shirts with cool, homegrown Maui designs.

Maui has lots of great food items to take home. Macadamia nuts, Maui coffee and *liliko'i* (passion fruit) preserves all make delicious and compact gift items. Unless you're really set on it, forget pineapples – they're a pain to lug around the airport and likely to be just as cheap at home.

Flowers such as orchids, anthuriums and proteas make good gifts if you're flying straight home. Proteas stay fresh for about 10 days and then can be dried. Foreign visitors should check with their airline in advance, however, as there are commonly restrictions against taking agricultural products across international borders.

TELEPHONE

Always dial '1' before toll-free (☎ 800, 888 etc) and domestic long-distance numbers. Some toll-free numbers may only work within the state or from the US mainland, while others work from Canada, too. But you'll only know by making the call.

AGRICULTURAL CHECKS

All luggage and carry-on bags leaving Hawaii for the US mainland are checked by an agricultural inspector using an X-ray machine. You cannot take out gardenia, jade vine or roses, even in lei, although most other fresh flowers and foliage are permitted. You can bring home pineapples and coconuts, but most other fresh fruits and vegetables are banned. Other things not allowed to enter mainland states include plants in soil, fresh coffee berries (roasted beans are OK), cactus and sugarcane.

However, seeds, fruits and plants that have been certified and labeled for export aren't a problem. For more information call the **Plant Protection and Quarantine Office** (☎ 861-8490).

Pay phones are readily found in shopping centers, beach parks and other public places. Calls from one point on an island to another point on that island are considered local and cost 50¢. Calls from one island to another are long-distance calls. Hotels often add a hefty service charge ($1 and more) for calls made from a room phone.

Private prepaid phone cards are available from convenience stores and pharmacies. Phone cards sold at post offices are generally better value and have no expiration. Faxes can be sent at the front desk of most hotels at reasonable rates.

Cell (Mobile) Phones

The US uses a variety of mobile-phone systems, 99% of which are incompatible with the GSM 900/1800 standard used throughout Europe and Asia. Check with your cellular service provider before departure about using your phone on Maui. Verizon has the most extensive cellular network on the Islands, but AT&T, Cingular and Sprint also have decent coverage. Cellular coverage is good on most of Maui, but spotty in remote areas like the road to Hana.

Long-Distance & International Calls

To make international calls direct from Hawaii, dial ☎ 011 + country code + area code + number (except to Canada, where you dial ☎ 1 + area code + number).

For international operator assistance, dial ☎ 0. The operator can provide specific rate information and tell you which time periods are the cheapest for calling.

If you're calling Hawaii from abroad, the international country code for the US is ☎ 1. All calls to Hawaii are then followed by the area code ☎ 808 and the seven-digit local number. Also dial the area code when making a call from one Hawaiian island to another.

TIME

Hawaii does not observe daylight saving time. It has about 11 hours of daylight in midwinter (December) and almost 13½ hours in midsummer (June). In midwinter

READ THIS BOOK, NOW FORGET IT!

We love travel guides, we really do. But we also know that there's no replacement for a spirit of discovery. The very best travel experiences, not just on Maui but anywhere, are the ones you create yourself. They are the unexpected people you meet, the wonderful restaurant you found while escaping the rain, the trails you follow that no one mentioned.

Even in small, heavily visited places like Maui, there are tons of 'undiscovered' places. Indeed we've sprinkled this book with detours to help inspire your own independent explorations. In other words, read this book, then forget it. Put it down. It's your trip.

the sun rises at about 7am and sets at about 6pm. In midsummer it rises before 6am and sets after 7pm.

And then there's 'Hawaiian time,' which is either a relaxed pace or a euphemism for being late.

When it's noon in Hawaii, it's 2pm in Los Angeles, 5pm in New York, 10pm in London, 7am the next day in Tokyo, 8am the next day in Melbourne, and 10am the next day in Auckland.

TOURIST INFORMATION

Maui County's tourist organizations have loads of visitor information on their websites and will mail out material to those not online. Useful organizations:

Destination Lana'i (☎ 565-7600, 800-947-4774; www.visitlanai.net)

Maui Visitors Bureau (☎ 244-3530, 800-525-6284; www.visitmaui.com; 1727 Wili Pa Loop, Wailuku) Also represents Lana'i and Moloka'i.

Moloka'i Visitors Association (☎ 553-3876, 800-800-6367; www.molokai-hawaii.com; Kamehameha V Hwy, Kaunakakai)

TOURS

A number of tour-bus companies operate half-day and full-day sightseeing tours on Maui, covering the most visited island destinations. **Roberts Hawaii** (☎ 866-898-2591; www.roberts-hawaii.com; tours $60-100), a giant among Hawaiian tour companies, typically offers the best prices and most variety. The most popular routes include day-long jaunts to Hana and a Haleakalā sunrise trip that takes in many of the Upcountry's sights. **Polynesian Adventure Tours** (☎ 877-4242, 800-622-3011; www.polyad.com; tours $70-100) is the other big player and offers similar tours.

You'll pay a bit more, but family-run **Ekahi Tours** (☎ 877-9775, 888-292-2422; www.ekahi

.com; tours $90-130) offers similar runs with more local flavor and less canned commentary. Best of all they take a deeper cultural slant on the places they visit, so you end up with more than just snapshots.

Helicopter tours (p35) cruise above inaccessible waterfalls and over the West Maui Mountains, Haleakalā, Hana and pretty much any other place that's a knockout from the air. There are also specialized adventure tours like whale-watching cruises and snorkeling trips to Lana'i. For details, consult the Activities sections under each town. All of these tours can be booked after arrival on Maui.

Elderhostel (☎ 800-454-5768; www.elderhostel .org) offers educational programs for those aged 55 or older. Many of these focus on Hawaii's people and culture, while others explore the natural environment. Fees are $800 to $3500 for one- to two-week programs, including accommodations, meals and classes, but excluding airfare.

See US Mainland (p286) for some operators offering package tours to Maui and Sea (p287) for cruises to the Hawaiian Islands.

TRAVELERS WITH DISABILITIES

Maui has decent infrastructure for travelers with disabilities, and most public places comply with *Americans with Disabilities Act* (ADA) regulations. Many of the major resort hotels have elevators, TTD-capable phones, wheelchair-accessible rooms and other features to smooth the day. Major car-rental companies will install hand controls and provide accessible transportation to the vehicle pick-up site with advance notification. Most public buses, including all of those operated by Roberts Hawaii, are wheelchair accessible. The visually impaired are allowed to bring guide dogs into Hawaii without quarantine, provided they meet the Department of Agriculture's minimum requirements.

If you have a disability parking placard issued by other states or countries for parking in designated accessible parking spaces, bring it with you – it's valid in Hawaii.

For specifics, contact the **Disability and Communication Access Board** (DCAB; ☎ 586-8121; www.hawaii.gov/health/dcab). From its website, you can download Travel Tips brochures with information on airlines, transportation, medical and other support services on each island.

For a list of services available to disabled passengers by airline, go to the **Allgohere Airline Directory** (www.everybody.co.uk/airindex.htm).

On the mainland USA, the **Society for the Advancement of Travel for the Handicapped** (☎ 212-447-7284; www.sath.org) publishes a quarterly magazine and has various information sheets on travel for the disabled.

VOLUNTEERING

Opportunities for volunteering abound on Maui, providing a memorable experience of Hawaii's people and environment that you'll never get by just passing through. Some require extended time commitments but lots ask for just a day.

The best central place to find out about volunteer opportunities is **Malama Hawaii** (www.malamahawaii.org), a network of community and nonprofit organizations. It posts a wide-ranging calendar that also includes fundraising concerts, educational events and cultural workshops. Volunteer by doing trail maintenance, restoring ancient fishponds, cleaning up wetlands and much more. Also see Environmental Issues in the Green Maui chapter (p45).

Volunteer at Ko'ie'ie Fishpond   GREG ELMS

The **Sierra Club, Maui Chapter** (www.hi.sierraclub.org/maui) is active on all sorts of fronts. Check out their weekend outings that eradicate invasive plants along Maui's trails.

The **Hawaiian Islands Humpback Whale National Marine Sanctuary** (www.hawaiihumpbackwhale.noaa.gov) has numerous opportunities for volunteers, from reef fish surveys (p34) to student internships.

The **National Park Service** (www.nps.gov/volunteer) coordinates volunteers at Haleakalā National Park (p165) but requires long-term commitments.

One of the most memorable volunteer opportunities is the five-day trip to the uninhabited island of Kaho'olawe (p226) run by **Protect Kaho'olawe 'Ohana** (www.kahoolawe.org).

WOMEN TRAVELERS

Maui presents few unique problems for women travelers and is generally more relaxed and comfortable than many mainland destinations. The one place where women – especially solo travelers – might feel uneasy is in local bars, but no more nor less than anywhere else in the world. If you're camping, opt for secure, well-used camping areas rather than isolated locales where you might be the only camper; this advice pertains to anyone.

WORK

US citizens can pursue work on Maui as they would in any other state – the problem is finding a decent job. Foreign visitors in the USA on tourist visas are not legally allowed to take up employment.

Finding serious 'professional' employment is difficult since Hawaii has a tight labor market. Casual work, on the other hand, can be much easier to come by, especially if you're young and perky. Waiting on tables at restaurants and working check-out counters in shops are positions with a lot of turnover, and hence openings, especially in Lahaina. Folks with language, scuba, fishing or guiding skills might investigate better-paying employment with resorts.

Also check the **Maui News** (www.mauinews.com) classified job ads and continue surfing at www.jobshawaii.com.

GETTING THERE & AWAY

It's all so simple: the vast majority of visitors to Maui arrive by air because Hawaii is a tiny dot in the middle of the vast Pacific Ocean. While there are an ever-increasing number of direct flights between the mainland and Kahului, many visitors come via Honolulu.

AIR

Hawaii is a very competitive market for US domestic and international airfares, which vary tremendously in price by season, demand, number of stopovers and ticket details. Since nothing determines fares more than demand, when things are slow, airlines lower their fares to fill empty seats. There's a lot of competition, and at any given time any one of the airlines could have the cheapest fare.

Airports

Because of the sheer distance, travelers arriving from Europe will often have to change planes on the US mainland. Major gateway airports include the following:

Atlanta International Airport (ATL; ☎ 800-897-1910; www.atlanta-airport.com)

Chicago O'Hare International Airport (ORD; ☎ 773-686-2200; www.ohare.com)

Denver International Airport (DEN; ☎ 303-342-2000; www.flydenver.com)

Los Angeles International Airport (LAX; ☎ 310-646-5252; www.los-angeles-lax.com)

New York JFK International Airport (JFK; ☎ 718-244-4444; www.panynj.gov)

San Francisco International Airport (SFO; ☎ 650-821-8211; www.flysfo.com)

Most travelers arriving on Maui will disembark at Kahului, which has the busiest airport in Hawaii outside Honolulu. North of Lahaina in West Maui, Kapalua Airport (also known as Kapalua/West Maui Airport) is Maui's second-busiest airport. It's strictly an interisland airport, connecting to other Hawaiian Islands. The tiny Hana Airport sees only a few flights a day, all by prop plane, including from Kahului ($50).

Kahului International Airport (OGG; ☎ 872-3830; www.state.hi.us/dot/airports/maui/ogg) There's a visitor information desk (☎ 872-3893; open 7:45am to 9:45pm) in the baggage-claim area. Nearby are courtesy phones for contacting accommodations and ground transportation, plus racks upon racks of free tourist magazines and brochures. Near the departure gates are newsstands, gift shops, ATMs, a restaurant and a cocktail lounge.

Kapalua Airport (JHM; ☎ 669-0623; www.state.hi.us/dot/airports/maui/jhm) The terminal of this airport is off Hwy 30, about midway between Kapalua and Ka'anapali, within easy reach of Lahaina.

Hana Airport (HNM; ☎ 248-8208; www.state.hi.us/dot/airports/maui/hnm) This airport is off the Hana Hwy, about 3 miles north of Hana in East Maui.

If you don't have a transpacific flight into Kahului then you'll be flying into O'ahu at **Honolulu International Airport** (HNL; ☎ 836-6413; www.honoluluairport.com) and taking an inter island flight from there. The terminals for interisland flight and transpacific arrivals are adjacent and connected with a free bus.

To reach Lana'i or Moloka'i by air, you'll have to fly via Honolulu or Kahului.

Lana'i Airport (LNY; ☎ 565-6757; www.state.hi.us/dot/airports/lanai)

Moloka'i Airport (MKK; ☎ 567-6140; www.state.hi.us/dot/airports/molokai)

Airlines

At press time, the following airlines land at Maui's Kahului Airport, with direct flights to Maui from the mainland:

Air Canada (AC; ☎ 888-247-2262; www.aircanada.com)

American Airlines (AA; ☎ 800-433-7300; www.aa.com)

Delta (DL; ☎ 800-221-1212; www.delta.com)

THINGS CHANGE...

The information in this chapter is particularly vulnerable to change. Check directly with the airline or a travel agent to make sure you understand how a fare (and ticket you may buy) works, and be aware of the security requirements for international travel. Shop carefully. The details given in this chapter should be regarded as pointers and are not a substitute for your own careful, up-to-date research.

Hawaiian Airlines (HA; ☎ 800-367-5320; www
.hawaiianair.com)
United Airlines (UA; ☎ 800-241-6522; www.ual.com)
US Airways (US; ☎ 800-428-4322; www.usairways
.com)

As well as the airlines listed above, numerous national and international airlines fly into Honolulu International Airport on O'ahu, including the following:
Air New Zealand (NZ; ☎ 800-262-1234; www.air
newzealand.com)
China Airlines (CI; ☎ 800-227-5118; www.china
-airlines.com)
Continental (CO; ☎ 800-523-3273; www.continental
.com)
Japan Airlines (JL; ☎ 800-525-3663; www.japanair
.com)
Korean Airlines (KE; ☎ 800-438-5000; www.koreanair
.com)
Northwest (NW; ☎ 800-225-2525; www.nwa.com)
Qantas Airways (QF; ☎ 800-227-4500; www.qantas
.com.au)

Tickets

With so many airlines flying into Hawaii competition is fierce and good deals are plentiful. The best deals are often found on the internet. Check both the airline websites and travel websites – the best price could be on either one. Start searching at **Travelocity** (www.travelocity.com), **Expedia** (www.expedia.com), **Orbitz** (www.orbitz.com) or **Kayak** (www.kayak.com). You could also try **Priceline** (www.priceline.com), but first get advice at **BiddingForTravel.com** (www.biddingfortravel.com).

Round-the-world (RTW) tickets allow you to fly around the world using an alliance of airlines; Circle Pacific tickets are similar, but itineraries focus on the Pacific region. Only consider them if you want to visit other parts of the world in addition to Hawaii. The two main alliances are **One World** (www.oneworld.com) and the **Star Alliance** (www.staralliance.com).

US MAINLAND

Competition among airlines flying to Hawaii from the major mainland cities is intense. Typically, the lowest round-trip fares from the US mainland to Hawaii are around US$850 from the east coast and US$400 from the west coast, though that certainly fluctuates throughout the year.

During peak demand times like Christmas and New Year's expect to pay a premium of about 50% over those prices.

Most mainland flights to Maui involve at least one stopover, but direct flights to Maui are possible from some cities, including San Francisco, Los Angeles, Seattle, Dallas, Phoenix, Chicago and Las Vegas.

For those with limited time, package tours can sometimes be the cheapest way to go. Basic ones cover airfare and accommodations, while deluxe packages include car rental and all sorts of activities. If you're going to Hawaii on a short getaway, packages may cost little more than what airfare alone would have cost. One of the main Hawaii-bound players, **Pleasant Holidays** (☎ 800-742-9244; www.pleasantholidays.com), has departures from various US mainland points.

And then there's the Air Tech Space-Available FlightPass, which is often the cheapest way to fly between the west coast and Maui. **Air Tech** (☎ 212-219-7000; www.airtech.com) offers super deals (from $170 one way), but you must be flexible with your travel time; it offers unsold seats at the last minute and doesn't guarantee a specific flight.

The nonstop flight time to Hawaii is about 5½ hours from the west coast. East-coast flights typically range from 11 to 14 hours, depending on stops.

WITHIN HAWAII

For years the two main interisland players, Hawaiian Airlines and Aloha Airlines, had a monopoly on interisland flights. That ended in 2006, when upstart go!, an affiliate of Mesa Air, entered the fray and Aloha subsequently went belly-up. Both surviving airlines offer frequent flights in full-bodied planes between the four main islands. Their advantage over the smaller carriers is frequency and dependability of service. Island Air provides service to the main islands as well as less-frequent connections to Moloka'i and Lana'i; it's the largest commuter airline and offers an extensive schedule, but it's infamous for late and cancelled flights. On any of these carriers, full fares are around $100, but discounts are common and web browsing pays off.

For Maui visitors, even more exciting is PWExpress, run by Pacific Wings. It flies prop planes between all of Maui County's airports (except Kapalua), as well as to and from Honolulu, and charges a flat rate of $50 for every seat on every flight. It's a convenient way to get from Kahului to Moloka'i where, for example, the ferry schedule is less than optimal. It's also a tad cheaper than the ferry. Another bonus: PWExpress prop planes fly so low to the ground they almost double as sightseeing planes.

Interisland airlines:

go! (☎ 888-435-9462; www.iflygo.com) Flies frequently from Honolulu to Maui, Kaua'i and the Big Island.

Hawaiian Airlines (☎ 800-367-5320, on O'ahu 838-1555; www.hawaiianair.com) Flies over 100 daily routes on 717s between Honolulu, Kaua'i, Maui and the Big Island.

Island Air (☎ 800-652-6541, on O'ahu 484-2222; www.islandair.com) Flies small 37-passenger planes between Honolulu, Moloka'i, Lana'i, Maui, Kaua'i and the Big Island.

Moloka'i Air Shuttle (☎ 567-6847, on O'ahu 545-4988) Flies prop planes between Honolulu and Moloka'i, with flights on demand.

PWExpress (☎ 888-866-5022; www.flypwx.com) Flies small prop planes between Maui, Moloka'i, Lana'i and Honolulu, as well as the Kahului–Hana route.

AUSTRALIA

Hawaiian Airlines flies nonstop between Sydney and Honolulu. Qantas flies to Honolulu from Sydney and Melbourne. Agents serving Australia include **Flight Centre** (☎ 1300-133-133; www.flightcentre.com.au) and **STA Travel** (☎ 1300-134-782; www.statravel.com.au).

CANADA

Air Canada offers direct flights to Maui from Vancouver and to Honolulu from Vancouver, Calgary, Edmonton and Toronto. Agents serving Canada include **Travel Cuts** (☎ 866-246-9762; www.travelcuts.com) and **Travelocity** (☎ 877-282-2925; www.travelocity.ca).

JAPAN

Japan Airlines flies to Honolulu from Tokyo, Osaka, Nagoya and Fukuoka. Continental and Northwest have several flights to Honolulu from Tokyo and Osaka. All Nippon Airways also flies to Honolulu, departing from Sapporo and Kumamoto. Agents serving Japan include **STA Travel** (☎ 03-5391-2922; www.statravel.co.jp).

NEW ZEALAND, MICRONESIA & SOUTH PACIFIC ISLANDS

Continental has nonstop flights from Guam to Honolulu, and Air New Zealand flies from Auckland. Agents serving New Zealand include **Flight Centre** (☎ 0800-24-35-44; www.flightcentre.co.nz) and **STA Travel** (☎ 0800-474-400; www.statravel.co.nz).

As for other South Pacific islands, Hawaiian Airlines flies to Honolulu from Tahiti and American Samoa. Air New Zealand offers return flights from Fiji to Honolulu via Auckland; it also flies to Honolulu from Tonga, the Cook Islands and Western Samoa.

SOUTHEAST ASIA

Northwest flies to Honolulu from Hong Kong, Bangkok, Manila, Seoul and Singapore. Korean Air, China Airlines, Philippine Airlines and others also offer numerous flights between Southeast Asian cities and Honolulu.

Bucket shops in Bangkok, Singapore and Hong Kong should be able to beat standard fares, perhaps by half price. Agents serving Southeast Asia include **STA Travel** (☎ 2148-9800; www.statravel.com.my), **Concorde Travel** (☎ 2526-3391; www.concorde-travel.com) and **Traveller Services** (☎ 2375-2222; www.taketraveller.com).

UK & CONTINENTAL EUROPE

In addition to the national carriers, American, United, Delta and Continental offer flights to Honolulu from various European cities. The most common route to Hawaii from Europe is west via New York, Chicago or Los Angeles. If you're interested in heading east with stops in Asia, consider getting a RTW ticket.

London is arguably the world's headquarters for bucket shops specializing in discount tickets. Two good, reliable agents for cheap tickets in London are **STA Travel** (☎ 0870-162-7551; www.statravel.co.uk) and **Trailfinders** (☎ 0845-058-5858; www.trailfinders.com).

SEA

The following cruise lines offer tours to Hawaii with stops on Maui:

Holland America Cruise Line (☎ 877-724-5425; www.hollandamerica.com) Typically departs from San Diego, Seattle or Vancouver.

Norwegian Cruise Line (☎ 800-327-7030; www.ncl.com) The only company that operates a cruise between the Hawaiian Islands that starts and ends in Hawaii. The seven-day interisland cruises make round-trips from Maui and Honolulu and visit the four main islands. Longer 10- and 11-day itineraries are possible.

Princess Cruises (☎ 800-568-3262; www.princess .com) Offers the most cruises; most depart from Los Angeles or Vancouver.

The **Hawaii Superferry** (www.hawaiisuper ferry.com), a four-story, state-of-the-art catamaran capable of carrying 866 passengers and 282 cars, had grand plans when it started runs in 2007, with the intention of making two return trips daily between Honolulu and Maui. Instead, however, it had problems getting off the ground because of rough seas, islander protests and unantici-pated maintenance issues that put it out of operation for lengthy periods of time (see the boxed text, p44). After getting snarled on legal issues surrounding the failure to com-plete all the requisite environmental reviews, the Superferry indefinitely suspended Ha-waii operations in March 2009. Two months later, it filed for bankruptcy. The boat is now back on the US mainland, docked next to a sister ship that was also intended for inter-island ferry service in Hawaii. Those hopes are now dim at best.

For information on the ferries from Maui to the other Maui County islands of Lana'i and Moloka'i, see Boat (p289).

GETTING AROUND

If you really want to explore Maui thor-oughly, and reach off-the-beaten-path sights, you'll need to have your own wheels. Public transportation is limited to the main towns and tourist resorts.

Be aware that most main roads are called highways whether they're busy four-lane thoroughfares or just quiet country roads. What's more, islanders refer to highways by name, and rarely by number. If you ask someone how to find Hwy 36, chances are you'll get a blank stare – ask for the Hana Hwy instead.

The best road map for getting around the island is the encyclopedic *Ready Map-book of Maui County,* but it's bulky. See also Tours (p283) in the Practicalities section of this chapter.

TO/FROM THE AIRPORTS

With either of the following Kahului Air-port transfer services you can make ad-vance reservations for your arrival to speed things along. Both services have courtesy phones in the baggage-claim area. Keep in mind you must reserve in advance for your *return* to the airport – and don't wait till the last minute.

Speedi Shuttle (☎ 661-6667, 800-977-2605; www .speedishuttle.com) is the largest airport-trans-fer service on Maui. One nice thing about Speedi is that they have converted to bio-diesel, using recycled vegetable oil to fuel their vehicles, so if you take them you'll be traveling green-friendly. Fares from Kahului Airport to Lahaina are $50 for one person and $59 for two people. From Ka-hului Airport the fare for one person is $54 to Ka'anapali, $74 to Kapalua, $35 to Kihei and $40 to Wailea. Add $7 to $10 more per additional person.

Executive Shuttle (☎ 669-2300, 800-833-2303) is cheaper and can be less backlogged. Like Speedi, their price depends on the destina-tion and the size of the group. For example, Kahului Airport to Lahaina costs $39 for one person and $45 for two people.

Kahului Airport's taxi dispatchers are near the exit of the baggage-claim area. Approximate fares from the airport: to Wai-luku $20; to Kihei $40; to Lahaina $75; to Ka'anapali $87; and to Kapalua $105.

Taxi fares from Kapalua Airport average $18 to Ka'anapali and $25 to $35 to most other places along the West Maui coast. Check with your hotel first, though, as many resorts in Ka'anapali offer free shut-tles to and from Kapalua Airport.

BICYCLE

Cyclists on Maui face a number of chal-lenges: narrow roads, an abundance of hills and mountains, and the same persistent winds that so delight windsurfers. Maui's stunning scenery certainly will entice hard-core cyclists, but casual riders hoping to use a bike as a primary source of transportation around the island may well find such condi-tions daunting.

Getting around by bicycle within a small area can be a reasonable option for the average rider, however. For example, the tourist enclave of Kihei is largely level and now has cycle lanes on two main drags, S Kihei Rd and the Pi'ilani Hwy.

The full-color *Maui County Bicycle Map* ($6), available from bicycle shops, shows all the roads on Maui that have cycle lanes and gives other nitty-gritty details. Consider it essential if you intend to do your exploring by pedal power. For information on bicycle rentals, see specific destinations around the island.

Bringing your own bike to Hawaii costs upwards of $100 on flights from the mainland; interisland flights charge an additional $25 or more. The bicycle can be checked at the airline counter, the same as any baggage, but you'll need to prepare the bike by wrapping the handlebars and pedals in foam or by fixing the handlebars to the side and removing the pedals.

In general, bicycles are required to follow the same state laws and rules of the road as cars.

BOAT

Passenger ferry services connect Maui with its sister islands of Lana'i and Moloka'i. Advance reservations are always a good idea, though they are not required.

The **Expeditions** (☎ 661-3756, 800-695-2624; www.go-lanai.com; adult/child one way $25/20) ferry is an unbeatable way to island hop between Maui and Lana'i. Spinner dolphins are a common sight with morning sails and whales are sometimes spotted during winter sails as well. Boats depart from both Ma'alaea and Lahaina. The more frequent Lahaina ferry leaves from in front of the Pioneer Inn at 6:45am, 9:15am, 12:45pm, 3:15pm and 5:45pm, arriving at Manele Boat Harbor in Lana'i, just a few minutes' walk from fabulous Hulope'e Beach. The return boat leaves Lana'i at 8am, 10:30am, 2pm, 4:30pm and 6:45pm. The Ma'alaea boat operates twice daily in each direction, leaving Ma'alaea Harbor at 7am and 3:30pm, and leaving Lana'i at 9am and 5:30pm. Sailing time to Lana'i is about an hour from both Lahaina and Ma'alaea. You can buy tickets online, by phone or on the boat.

Lahaina Cruise Company's **Molokai Princess** (☎ 662-3355, 866-440-6284; www.molokaiferry .com; adult/child 4-12 $40/20) operates between Lahaina Harbor and Moloka'i's Kaunakakai Wharf. Unlike the ferry to Lana'i, the Moloka'i ferry schedule is geared for transporting Moloka'i residents to jobs in Lahaina, which makes it less than ideal for day tripping. It just doesn't leave you with enough time to see anything other than Kaunakakai and, truth be told, there's simply not much to see in town. Departures from Lahaina are at 7:15am and 6pm. The boat leaves Kaunakakai at 5:30am and 4pm. The 90-minute crossing through the Pailolo Channel can get choppy. Buy tickets online, by phone or on the boat a half-hour before departure.

BUS

With the exception of O'ahu, Maui has Hawaii's most extensive public bus system. But don't get too excited – the buses can take you between the main towns, but they're not going to get you to many prime out-of-the-way places, such as Haleakalā National Park, Hana or Makena's Big Beach. And some of the buses, such as the one between Ma'alaea and Lahaina, make a direct beeline, passing trailheads and beaches without stopping.

Maui Bus (☎ 871-4838; www.mauicounty.gov /bus), the island's public bus system, operates several routes, each of them daily. The main routes run once hourly throughout the day and several have schedules that dovetail with one another for convenient connections.

The handiest buses for visitors are the Kahului–Lahaina, Kahului–Wailea, Kahului–Wailuku, Ma'alaea–Kihei, Lahaina–Ka'anapali and Ka'anapali–Napili routes.

Fares are just $1 per ride, regardless of the distance. There are no transfers, however, so if your journey requires two separate buses, you'll have to buy a new ticket when you board the second bus. Monthly passes ($45) are also available.

Maui Bus also operates a couple of loop routes around Wailuku and Kahului, serving two dozen stops, including all of the major shopping centers, the hospital and government offices. These buses are mainly geared for local shoppers, but are provided free to everyone – just hop on and see where it takes you!

All buses allow you to carry on only what fits under your seat or on your lap, so forget the surfboard.

In addition to the public buses, free resort shuttles take guests between hotels and restaurants in the Ka'anapali (p87) and Wailea (p136) areas.

CAR

The majority of visitors to Maui rent their own vehicles. The minimum age for driving in Hawaii is 18 years, though car-rental companies usually have higher age restrictions. If you're under 25 years, you should call the car-rental agencies in advance to check their policies regarding restrictions and surcharges.

Automobile Associations

The **American Automobile Association** (AAA; ☎ 800-736-2886; www.aaa-hawaii.com) has its only Hawaii office in Honolulu. It provides members with maps and other information. Members also get discounts on car rentals, some air tickets, some hotels and some sightseeing attractions, as well as **emergency**

DRIVING DISTANCES & DRIVE TIMES FROM KAHULUI

Average driving times and distances from Kahului are as follows. Naturally, allow more time during weekday morning and afternoon rush hours, and any time the surf is up on the North Shore if you're heading that way.

Destination	Distance (miles)	Time
Haleakalā Summit	36	1½hr
Hana	51	2hr
Ka'anapali	26	50min
Kapalua	32	1hr
Kihei	12	25min
La Pérouse Bay	21	50min
Lahaina	23	40min
Makawao	14	30min
'Ohe'o Gulch	61	2¾hr
Pa'ia	7	15min
Wailuku	3	15min

---

road service and towing (☎ 800-222-4357). AAA has reciprocal agreements with automobile associations in other countries, but be sure to bring your membership card from your country of origin.

Driver's License

An International Driving Permit, obtained before you leave home, is only necessary if your country of origin is a non-English-speaking one.

Fuel & Towing

When you take a country drive on Maui, you need to be conscious of your fuel gauge. There are no gas stations on several long stretches of road, including the road to Hana; the Kahekili Hwy between Wailuku and Kapalua; and the Haleakala Crater Rd to the national park.

Expect to pay about 75¢ more per US gallon than on the mainland. At the time of research, the average gas price on Maui was about $4 a gallon. Unless you have a lot of passengers, it's wise to insist on a smaller car at the car-rental booth. These days, they'll commonly try to 'bump you up' free to a larger car because of higher demand for smaller, fuel-efficient cars.

If you get into trouble with your car, towing is mighty expensive on Maui and therefore to be avoided at all costs. Figure the fees at about $75 to start, plus $7 per mile you are towed. How to avoid it? Make sure your car is in good shape before taking off into any remote areas, and be aware that some of these places may be 'off limits' according to your car-rental agreement. Always ask when booking if the company has any road restrictions for its vehicles.

Insurance

Liability insurance covers people and property that you might hit. For damage to the actual rental vehicle, a collision damage waiver (CDW) is available for about $15 a day. If you have collision coverage on your vehicle at home, it might cover damages to car rentals; inquire before departing. Additionally, some credit cards offer reimbursement coverage for collision damages if you rent the car with that credit card; again,

Evening on Front St, Lahaina   GREG ELMS

check before departing. Most credit-card coverage isn't valid for rentals of more than 15 days or for exotic models, Jeeps, vans and 4WD vehicles.

Rentals

Be sure to reserve your car in advance, especially if you're traveling during high season or arriving on a weekend. That said, with advance notice, you shouldn't have any problem getting a car on Maui.

Similar to air fares, car-rental rates vary significantly with demand. Rental rates spike if you pick the car up on a holiday such as Christmas or Thanksgiving. With advance reservations, the daily rate for a small car ranges from $30 to $50, while typical weekly rates are $150 to $250. Getting the best deal on a car rental is 10% timing, 10% science and 90% persistence (that's right, it takes 110%). Auto clubs and frequent-flier programs typically warrant a discount of 5% to 10%. Shop around between rental companies, and check their offers against online agencies (use the same ones as for airline tickets – see p286).

Rental rates generally include unlimited mileage, but confirm that when you book. If you drop off the car at a different location

from where you picked it up, there's usually an additional fee.

Having a major credit card greatly simplifies the hire process. Without one, some agents simply will not rent vehicles, while others require prepayment, a deposit of $200 per week, pay stubs, proof of return airfare and more.

Alamo, Avis, Budget, Dollar, Hertz and National all have booths at Kahului Airport. Alamo, Avis, Budget, Dollar and National also have offices on Honoapi'ilani Hwy (Hwy 30) in Ka'anapali and will pick you up at the nearby Kapalua Airport. Dollar is the only rental agency serving Hana Airport.

Use the toll-free numbers if booking outside Hawaii:

Alamo (☎ 871-6235, 800-462-5266; www.alamo.com)

Avis (☎ 871-7575, 800-331-1212; www.avis.com)

Budget (☎ 871-8811, 800-527-0700; www.budget.com)

Dollar (☎ 877-7227, 800-800-4000; www.dollarcar.com)

Hertz (☎ 877-5167, 800-654-3131; www.hertz.com)

National (☎ 871-8851, 800-227-7368; www.nationalcar.com)

In addition to the national chains, there are a couple of local car-rental agencies on the island that are worthy of consideration:

Bio-Beetle (☎ 873-6121, 877-873-6121, www.bio-beetle.com; 55 Amala St, Kahului; rental per day/week from $50/240) This company offers a green alternative to Maui's car-rental scene, with Volkswagen Jettas and Beetles that run on recycled vegetable oil. Plan your outings carefully, though, as you'll need to do all your refueling in Kahului.

Kihei Rent A Car (☎ 879-7257, 800-251-5288; www.kiheirentacar.com; 96 Kio Loop, Kihei; rental per day/week from $35/175) The cars are a bit older than at the major rental agencies but this family-owned operation rents to 21-year-olds, accepts cash deposits and includes free mileage.

Road Conditions & Hazards

Drunk drivers can be a hazard; so can livestock on the road in some rural areas. However, the main hazards are usually narrow, winding or steep roads that sometimes wash out after heavy rains. Sections of some roads, including the Road to Hana (p187) and the Kahekili Hwy (p95), are particularly susceptible to wash-outs. It's always best to inquire before setting out.

Stay alert for one-lane-bridge crossings: one direction of traffic usually has the right of way while the other must obey the posted yield sign. Downhill traffic must yield to uphill traffic where there is no sign.

Road Rules

As with the rest of the USA, driving is on the right-hand side of the road. If it's an unpaved or poorly paved road, people tend to hog the middle stripe until an oncoming car approaches.

Drivers at a red light can turn right after coming to a stop and yielding to oncoming traffic, unless there's a sign at the intersection prohibiting the turn. Island drivers often just wait for the next green light.

A popular bumper sticker here reads: 'Slow Down. This Ain't the Mainland.' Locals will tell you there are three golden rules for driving on the Islands: don't honk your horn, don't follow too closely, and let people pass whenever it's safe to do so. Any cool moves like this are acknowledged by waving the *shaka* (Hawaiian hand greeting) sign. Horn honking is considered rude unless required for safety, or for urging cattle off the road.

Hawaii requires the use of seat belts. Heed this, as the ticket is stiff. State law also strictly requires the use of child-safety seats for children aged four and under. Most car-hire companies lease child-safety seats for around $5 per day, but they don't always have them on hand; reserve one in advance if you can.

Speed limits are posted *and* enforced. If you're stopped for speeding, expect a ticket as the police rarely just give warnings.

HITCHHIKING

Hitchhiking, though technically illegal statewide, is not unusual. However, hitchhiking anywhere is not without risks, and Lonely Planet does not recommend it. Hitchers should size up each situation carefully before getting in cars, and women should be wary of hitching alone. People who do choose to hitchhike will be safer if they travel in pairs and let someone know where they are planning to go.

MOPED & MOTORCYCLE

You can legally drive both mopeds and motorcycles in Hawaii as long as you have a valid driver's license issued by your home country. The minimum age for renting a moped is 16; for a motorcycle it's 21.

There are no helmet laws in the state of Hawaii, but the rental agencies listed here provide free helmets, and cautious riders will use them. Also remember that the windward side of Maui generally requires hard-core foul-weather gear, since it rains early and often.

State law requires mopeds to be ridden by one person only and prohibits their use on sidewalks and freeways. Mopeds must always be driven in single file and may not be driven at speeds in excess of 30mph. Bizarrely, mopeds can be more expensive to rent than cars. Rental agencies:

Aloha Toy Store (☎ 662-0888; 640 Front St, Lahaina) Rents Vespa mopeds ($65 per day), Kawasaki classic 800 motorcycles ($120) and Harleys ($150).

Hula Hogs (☎ 875-7433, 877-464-7433; www.hula hogs.com; 1279 S Kihei Rd, Kihei; per day from $115) Also rents Harleys and decks you out in full, with saddlebags and rain gear included.

TAXI

You can't just flag a taxi down in the street. You need to call ahead for a scheduled pick-up. Pick-ups from remote locations (for instance, after a long through-hike) can sometimes be arranged in advance, though you may have to also pay in advance.

Fares are county-regulated. The metered rate is $3.50 per mile. Two larger companies with service throughout Maui are **Royal Sedan & Taxi Service** (☎ 874-6900) and **Sunshine Cabs of Maui** (☎ 879-2220).

BEHIND THE SCENES

GLENDA BENDURE

Glenda has been traveling throughout Hawaii for nearly three decades. She loves digging into each island, driving the roads, hiking the trails, snorkeling the waters and tasting everything there is to taste till the *poke* bowl is empty. But if you're a first-time visitor to Hawaii and ask her which island you should choose, she'll point to Maui every time. Together, she and Ned wrote the first five editions of Lonely Planet's *Hawaii,* and they've collaborated on several other Hawaiian Islands guides for Lonely Planet.

NED FRIARY

Ned first experienced Maui after a long teaching stint in the urban jungle of Osaka, Japan. So inspired by what he saw, Ned, with his travel mate Glenda, went on to write Lonely Planet's first guidebook on Hawaii. He's been exploring Maui ever since, covering the island from the depths of Molokini to the summit of Haleakala. Maui's raw natural beauty, creative energy and emphasis on the outdoors, the organic and the eco-friendly never fails to inspire. If Ned one day ends up being a Kula strawberry farmer, no one who knows him will be surprised.

LONELY PLANET AUTHORS

Why is our travel information the best in the world? It's simple: our authors are independent, dedicated travelers. They don't research using just the internet or phone, and they don't take freebies, so you can rely on their advice being well researched and impartial. They travel widely, to all the popular spots and off the beaten track. They personally visit thousands of hotels, restaurants, cafés, bars, galleries, palaces, museums and more – and they take great pride in getting all the details right and telling it like it is. Think you can do it? Find out how at www.lonelyplanet.com.

THIS BOOK

This third edition of *Maui* was written by Glenda Bendure and Ned Friary. Contributions were also made by Jake Howard and Emily K Wolman. The previous edition was written by Kristin Kimball. This guidebook was commissioned in Lonely Planet's Oakland, California, office and produced by the following:

Hawaii Product Development Manager & Commissioning Editor Emily K Wolman
Coordinating Editor Pete Cruttenden
Coordinating Cartographer Andrew Smith
Senior Editor Katie Lynch
Managing Cartographer Alison Lyall
Assisting Editor Stephanie Pearson
Assisting Cartographer Tadhgh Knaggs
Series Designer Gerilyn Attebery
Layout Designer Megan Cooney
Cover Designers & Image Researchers Yukiyoshi Kamimura, Marika Kozak, Nic Lehman, Michael Ruff, Kate Slattery
Indexer Ken DellaPenta
Project Manager Eoin Dunlevy
Language Content Coordinator Quentin Frayne

Thanks to Glenn Beanland, Keli'i Brown, Michaela Caughlan, Gennifer Ciavarra, Heather Dickson, Ryan Evans, Rana Freedman, Jennifer Garrett, Suki Gear, Aimée Goggins, Brice Gosnell, Bronwyn Hicks, Lauren Hunt, Lisa Knights, Marina Kosmatos, Naomi Parker, Paul Piaia, Raphael Richards, Frank Ruiz, Suzannah Shwer, Christina Tunnah, Vivek Waglé.

Internal photographs by Greg Elms for Lonely Planet Images except for: p7, Old Lahaina Luau; p8, Maui Ocean Center; p9 (top), Eric Lin; p9 (bottom), Karl Lehmann/Lonely Planet Images; p10, Ann Cecil/Lonely Planet Images; p12, Ned Friary; p13 (top) Simon Foale/Lonely Planet Images; p13, (bottom) Mitchell Silver; p14, Karl Lehmann/Lonely Planet Images; p15, Abbot Low Moffat III/freelance; p17 (top & bottom), Karl Lehmann/Lonely Planet Images; p29, Casey & Astrid Mahaney/Lonely Planet Images; p34, Ned Friary; p41, Sabrina Dalbesio/freelance; p43, Bio-Beetle ECO Rental Cars; p45 Ned Friary; p49, Sabrina Dalbesio/freelance; p51, Greg Vaughn/Alamy; p65, Kent Hwang; p69, Ned Friary; p71, Ned Friary; p73, Ann Cecil/Lonely Planet Images; p82, Ned Friary; p83 Douglas Bowser; p85, Abbot Low Moffat III/freelance; p97, Ned Friary; p107, Ned Friary; p108 (top), Tony Novak-Clifford; p110, Ned Friary; p115, Ned Friary; p118, Ned Friary; p126, Ned Friary; p131, Bill Brooks/Alamy; p158, Abbot Low Moffat III/freelance; p159, Ned Friary; p165, Wes Walker/Lonely Planet Images; p174, Karl Lehmann/Lonely Planet Images; p177, Ann Cecil/Lonely Planet Images; p179, Ned Friary; p183, Karl Lehmann/Lonely Planet Images; p184, Sabrina Dalbesio/freelance; p187, Douglas Peebles/Alamy; p193, Ned Friary; p195, Ned Friary; p201, Karl Lehmann/Lonely Planet Images; p202, Sabrina Dalbesio/freelance; p209, Ned Friary; p213, Tom Till/Alamy; p214, Ned Friary; p220, Karl Lehmann/Lonely Planet Images; p221, Ann Cecil/Lonely Planet Images; p224, Ann Cecil/Lonely Planet Images; p225 Karl Lehmann/Lonely Planet Images; p233, Peter Hendrie/Lonely Planet Images; p234, Karl Lehmann/Lonely Planet Images; p236, Lee Foster/Lonely Planet Images; p237, Ned Friary; p238, Lee Foster/Lonely Planet Images; p239, Karl Lehmann/Lonely Planet Images; p240, Ned Friary; p253, Abbot Low Moffat III/freelance; p254, Hawaiian Slack Key Guitar Productions; p258, Abbot Low Moffat III/freelance; p259, Lee Foster/Lonely Planet Images; p262, Ned Friary; p264, Kent Hwang; p268, Kent Hwang; p270 (#1), Karl Lehmann/Lonely Planet Images; p270 (#2), Old Lahaina Luau; p270 (#3), Ann Cecil/Lonely Planet Images; p270 (#4), Hawaiian Slack Key Guitar Productions; p271 (#2), Whalers Village; p271 (#3), Kent Hwang; p271 (#4), Ann Cecil/Lonely Planet Images.

All images are copyright of the photographer unless otherwise indicated. Many of the images in this guide are available for licensing from Lonely Planet Images: www.lonelyplanetimages.com.

THANKS from the Authors

A big *mahalo* to Allen Tom and Nancy Daschbach of the Hawaiian Islands Humpback Whale National Marine Sanctuary; Glynnis Nakai of the Kealia Pond National Wildlife Refuge; and Sandi Lehua Takashiro and Keith Shibuya of Haleakalā National Park. And a special thanks to those who took the time to be our Island Voices: Emily Carlson, Sandra Hueu, Malihini Keahi-Heath, Karen Camara, Nan Cabatbat, Ali'i Chang, Nancy Plenty, Kimokeo Kapahulehua and waterman extraordinaire Robby Naish. And finally, *mahalo nui loa* to Emily K Wolman for her brilliant guidance on this new book.

THANKS from Lonely Planet

Many thanks to the travelers who used the last edition and wrote to us with helpful hints, useful advice and interesting anecdotes: Jesse Alder, Danielle Blaine, Paul Konwiser, Steve Marsh, Nathan Naef, Samantha Smithe, Ken Stuart, David Torrey, Eric Zigas.

Send Us Your Feedback

We love to hear from travelers – your comments keep us on our toes and help make our books better. Our well-travelled team reads every word on what you loved or loathed about this book. Although we cannot reply individually to postal submissions, we always guarantee that your feedback goes straight to the appropriate authors, in time for the next edition. Each person who sends us information is thanked in the next edition – and the most useful submissions are rewarded with a free book.

To send us your updates – and find out about Lonely Planet events, newsletters and travel news – visit our award-winning website: **www.lonelyplanet.com/contact**.

Note: we may edit, reproduce and incorporate your comments in Lonely Planet products such as guidebooks, websites and digital products, so let us know if you don't want your comments reproduced or your name acknowledged. For a copy of our privacy policy, visit **www.lonelyplanet.com/privacy**.

THE LONELY PLANET STORY

Fresh from an epic journey across Europe, Asia and Australia in 1972, Tony and Maureen Wheeler sat at their kitchen table stapling together notes. The first Lonely Planet guidebook, *Across Asia on the Cheap,* was born.

Travelers snapped up the guides. Inspired by their success, the Wheelers began publishing books to Southeast Asia, India and beyond. Demand was prodigious, and the Wheelers expanded the business rapidly to keep up. Over the years, Lonely Planet extended its coverage to every country, and into the virtual world via www.lonelyplanet.com and the Thorn Tree message board.

As Lonely Planet became a globally loved brand, Tony and Maureen received several offers for the company. But it wasn't until 2007 that they found a partner whom they trusted to remain true to the company's principles of traveling widely, treading lightly and giving sustainably. In October of that year, BBC Worldwide acquired a 75% share in the company, pledging to uphold Lonely Planet's commitment to independent travel, trustworthy advice and editorial independence.

Today Lonely Planet has offices in Melbourne, London and Oakland, with over 500 staff members and 300 authors. Tony and Maureen are still actively involved with Lonely Planet. They're traveling more often than ever, and they're devoting their spare time to charitable projects. And the company is still driven by the philosophy of *Across Asia on the Cheap:* 'All you've got to do is decide to go and the hardest part is over. So go!'

INDEX

GREENDEX

GOING GREEN

It seems like everyone's going 'green' these days, but how can you know which businesses are actually eco-friendly and which are simply jumping on the sustainable bandwagon?

The following listings have all been selected by Lonely Planet authors because they demonstrate an active sustainable-tourism policy. Some are involved in conservation or environmental education, and many are owned and operated by local and indigenous operators, thereby maintaining and preserving Hawaiian identity and culture.

We want to keep developing our sustainable-tourism content. If you think we've omitted someone who should be listed here, or if you disagree with our choices, email us at talk2us@lonelyplanet.com.au. For more information about sustainable tourism and Lonely Planet, see www.lonelyplanet.com/responsibletravel.

MAP LEGEND

MAP LEGEND

ROUTES

Primary	One-Way Street
Secondary	Mile Marker
Tertiary	Walking Tour
Lane	Walking Trail
Unsealed Road	Walking Path
	Track

TRANSPORT

Ferry	Rail

HYDROGRAPHY

River, Creek	Reef
Intermittent River	Glacier
Swamp	Water

BOUNDARIES

State, Provincial	Regional, Suburb
Marine Park	Cliff

AREA FEATURES

Airport	Land
Beach	Market
Building	Park, Reserve
Forest	Sports

POPULATION

◎ CAPITAL (NATIONAL)	◉ CAPITAL (STATE)
● Large City	○ Medium City
○ Small City	○ Town, Village

SYMBOLS

Sights/Activities
- Beach
- Bodysurfing
- Buddhist
- Canoeing, Kayaking
- Christian
- Diving
- Golf
- Monument
- Museum, Gallery
- Point of Interest
- Pool
- Ruin
- Snorkeling
- Surfing, Surf Beach
- Trail Head
- Windsurfing
- Winery, Vineyard
- Zoo, Bird Sanctuary

Eating
- Eating

Drinking
- Drinking
- Café

Entertainment
- Entertainment

Shopping
- Shopping

Sleeping
- Sleeping
- Camping

Transport
- Airport, Airfield
- Bus Station
- Cycling, Bicycle Path
- General Transport
- Parking Area
- Petrol Station
- Taxi Rank

Information
- Bank, ATM
- Hospital, Medical
- Information
- Internet Facilities
- Police Station
- Post Office, GPO

Geographic
- Lighthouse
- Lookout
- ▲ Mountain, Volcano
- National Park
- Beach Park
- Picnic Area
- Shelter, Hut
- ÷ Spot Height
- Waterfall

Published by Lonely Planet Publications Pty Ltd

ABN 36 005 607 983

LONELY PLANET OFFICES

Australia
Head Office
Locked Bag 1, Footscray, Victoria 3011
☎ 03 8379 8000, fax 03 8379 8111
talk2us@lonelyplanet.com.au

USA
150 Linden St, Oakland, CA 94607
☎ 510 250 6400, toll free 800 275 8555
fax 510 893 8572
info@lonelyplanet.com

UK
2nd Fl, 186 City Rd
London EC1V 2NT
☎ 020 7106 2100, fax 020 7106 2101
go@lonelyplanet.co.uk

Printed by Fabulous Printers Pte Ltd
Printed in Singapore